Heart & Soul

Revealing the Craft of Songwriting

Printed and bound in Great Britain by MPG Books Ltd, Bodmin

Published by Sanctuary Publishing Limited, Sanctuary House, 45–53 Sinclair Road, London W14 0NS, United Kingdom

www.sanctuarypublishing.com

Cover: Dan Froude

Photos: Doug McKenzie

ISBN: 1-86074-641-1

Heart & Soul
Revealing the Craft of Songwriting

Chris Bradford
Foreword by Guy Chambers

In association with the British Academy of Composers & Songwriters

Sanctuary

CONTENTS

ACKNOWLEDGEMENTS

This book is dedicated to my mum and dad, for all the support they've provided throughout my music career.

Special thanks and love go to Sarah, who is the real music in my life.

Thanks to Chris Green, David Ferguson, Mark Fishlock, Patrick Rackow, Richard Taylor, Chris Harvey, Alan Heal, Iain MacGregor and Michael Wilson, who together have made this project possible.

Thanks to all the contributors for giving their time to this book, including Pete Kirtley and Tim Hawes (Jiant), Billy Steinberg, Mark Hill, Billy Bragg (and Mushi), Wayne Hector (and Jackie Davidson), Ali Tennant, Francis Eg White, Deke Arlon, Bill Padley and Jeremy Godfrey (Wise Buddah), Sharon Woolf, Steve Levine, Rob Davis (and Brian Reza), Don Black, Rick Nowels, Colin Emmanuel, Bill Bruford, Chris Difford, Richard Kerr, Allan Dann, Jonathan Little, Ivan Chandler, Jay Mistry, Brian Willey, Guy Fletcher, Brian and Eddie Holland, Lamont Dozier, The Darkness (and Phyl), David Stark, Kizzy Donaldson, Bryan Borcherds, Michelle Escoffery, David Stoll, Jake Shillingford, Mick Leeson, Barry Mason, Tony Moore, Frank Musker, Ruth Graham, Tricia Kilner-Smith, Matthew Bould, Samantha at Essential Secretary, James Sellar at the MMF and Ant Varney.

Thank you also to the teams at Sanctuary Publishing and the British Academy for their hard work, and to all those who have been involved in the making of *Heart & Soul*.

The Community Of Music Writers

By David Ferguson,
Chairman Of The British Academy Of
Composers & Songwriters

No two artists seem to write music in exactly the same way. Some improvise briefly with or without collaborators, and the finished piece appears as if from nowhere, while for others it takes months of solitary toil, locked away until the carefully crafted jewel sees the light of day. The question most frequently asked of composers and songwriters is, 'Where do you get your inspiration?', and there is no standard answer. Some of us write while surrounded by a warehouse of computer technology, whereas others need only a battered acoustic guitar or a piano. The starting point can be a lyric, a riff, a loop or even an abstract noise. There are no rules. This means that music writers are a very varied bunch of people. There is, after all, very little in common between the swaggering menace of Prodigy's 'Firestarter' or the measured introspection of David Gray's 'Babylon'. So what do songwriters have in common?

Well, it's a big bad world out there. It's also a very complicated world. The music industry is one of the most varied and diverse businesses it's possible to imagine, and by far the best way to try to understand it is to talk to those who are already working in it.

When I was starting out in a band, our management made us join the Performing Right Society. None of us had any idea what the PRS was or what it did. When my first PRS royalty statement turned up, it was a complete surprise. Now income from the PRS has become the centrepiece of my existence.

But it doesn't end there. It's only through having met with other music writers that I now know many of the wrinkles to the whole business of understanding my royalty statements. All the knowledge I have about the business of being a music writer comes from being a member of the Academy and its predecessor organisations. The collection societies do exactly what you might expect: they collect and distribute money. The Academy, however, is a very different beast. It is only through coming together that music writers can get their voices heard. And those voices need to be heard.

There are many threats to the whole business of being a songwriter. Governments can introduce legislation that can change the whole landscape in which music writing takes place. The policies of large multinational corporations can have devastating effects on the marketplace for music. The policies of collection societies can completely alter the way in which monies are distributed. Mergers and take-overs by record companies and broadcasters can have fundamental effects on songwriting. It is only through speaking with one voice that we can hope to have any influence over the outside world.

The Performing Right Society has 40,000 members, but less than ten per cent of these are earning a living from their royalties. The songwriting community is a small one, but it is probably the most important in the music universe. We are the creators of new music, and our work underpins musicians, singers, music publishers, record companies and everyone else who works in the music business. While we need to speak with one voice, we also come together because of our shared love of music and creativity. Whether we have a lifetime of writing behind us or are taking our first uncertain steps, it is this which unites us above everything else.

David Ferguson
May 2005

FOREWORD

By Guy Chambers,
Songwriter And Producer

For me, a great song makes the hairs on the back of my neck stand on end. It's as simple as that. It could be a full studio production or it could be someone simply singing *a cappella*. Yet the ingredients that evoke such a reaction can be difficult to pinpoint. As a producer, I have to analyse why certain pieces of music 'work' for a listener, both physically and emotionally. This can be tricky, since songwriting is a craft – an art – and a person's reaction to it is personal.

Yet there are now artificial intelligence computer programmes being used within the music industry to assess the 'hit' potential of a song. I personally don't think that this is a good direction to head in – not least because such a computer recently turned down one of my songs! I realise that A&R executives might argue that such a machine has a good strike rate, but it potentially creates a scenario in which music becomes homogenised. Furthermore, as you'll discover through reading *Heart & Soul*, songwriting doesn't follow any rules, and to impose a formula is a recipe for failure.

The hardest thing to achieve as a songwriter, especially when writing on your own, is objectivity. It was only when I began to collaborate with a writer better than myself that I started to learn and appreciate the craft of songwriting. So my advice to you as a songwriter would be to find a writing partner who is more experienced than yourself. In my case, the first person to fulfil that role was Karl Wallinger of the band World Party, who really fired my creativity. In your case, this book gives you unprecedented access to the skills and insights of a whole host of experienced songwriters, from Holland, Dozier and Holland to Rob Davis to myself – skills that have taken years to hone.

Lastly, an important piece of advice for anyone considering entering the music business: *never give up*. There will always be people (or, more ominously, computers!) who won't like the music you're creating or who don't understand it. That's fine, as there will be just as many – if not more – who will like it. Simply because one A&R person rejects your track doesn't mean that the song is bad and can't be a success. If you want to be a successful songwriter, you'll need to have 'a bus load of faith', as Lou Reed put it.

Heart & Soul amounts to a collaborative experience in itself. I hope it fires your creativity

Good luck!

Guy Chambers
May 2005

INTRODUCTION: HEART & SOUL

'The entire music business is an inverted pyramid. At the top, at the big bit of that pyramid, are bands, gigs, lighting crews, television shows, magazines and everything else. At the bottom of that pyramid, at its tip, is a song. Without the song, none of the pyramid would exist. So always remember that, when you're writing a song, you're the whole reason for the business being there, and it's important to get it right.'
— Bill Padley, songwriter/producer with Wise Buddah

The song is the heart and soul of the music business. Without the song, there simply would be no music business. There would be no music, no bands, no Top 100, no first dances at weddings, no loud parties, no soundtrack to our lives. The song is the linchpin of contemporary music.

In terms of being the sole source of a multi-billion-dollar industry, however, the craft of songwriting remains an extraordinary enigma. To consider that the business is still reliant on a process that is almost inexplicable and unguaranteed is staggering. Guy Fletcher, songwriter and former Chairman of the British Academy of Composers & Songwriters, clarifies the situation: 'Successful and enduring music is invented by individuals in a series of solitary creative acts which cannot be automated. As long as this is the case, composers and songwriters will hold all the trump cards.' It is this mysterious creative process that generates both the song and the value in that song.

'Mystery is at the heart of creativity.' — Julia Cameron, The Artist's Way

Songs are born out of a unique strain of inspiration that only certain people seem able to tap into on a regular basis. Even then, such runs of inspiration are sporadic and uncertain. Musician and songwriter Leonard Cohen once famously remarked, 'If I knew where the good songs came from, I'd go there more often.'

Yet songwriting need not be seen as some kind of black art. Everyone has the potential to become a songwriter. Music is all-encompassing, and the creation of music is about inventing, experimenting, taking risks, breaking rules, making mistakes and having fun. The motivational writer and author Earl Nightingale defined creativity as 'a natural extension of our enthusiasm', and songwriting is simply an extension in turn of this philosophy. If you want to be a songwriter, you can. You need only make the decision as to what kind of songwriter you wish to be. Are you happy modestly writing for your own pleasure? Do you simply desire to write a song for your partner or loved one? Do you aspire to earning a living from the craft? Or are all your sights set on being famous, and songwriting is the vehicle with which you hope to achieve it? Whatever your aspirations as a songwriter, as James Broughton once said, 'The only limits are, as always, those of vision.' This book can help you on your journey to being that songwriter.

THE SONGWRITER

'If I was articulate and could talk to people about how I really felt, I wouldn't need to put it in a song.'

– Aimee Mann, songwriter and artist

Songwriting is an intense form of expression, of using the twin vehicles of lyrics and music to say something that could not be articulated in words alone.

So strong is the creative and emotional bond between songwriter and song that it has been said that songwriting is like giving birth to a child. Lyricist Don Black explains: 'We songwriters often refer to our songs as "our children". As every parent knows, one child can do well, while the other can't seem to get started. However, both have to be cared for, protected, guided, nurtured and loved. The same is true of songs.' And, like children, songs will have a life of their own. Being a songwriter, therefore, involves learning the ability to let go.

'I used to think that myself and my songs were the same thing, but I don't believe that any more. There's myself and there's my song, which I hope is everybody's song.'

– Bob Dylan

Professional songwriting requires commitment of the highest level. Every successful composer or lyricist is adamant that their achievements were due in part to their unwavering passion, desire and commitment to the craft. US jazz/blues artist Ray Charles stated unequivocally his dedication to the music: 'I was born with music inside me. Music was one of my parts, like my ribs, my kidneys, my liver, my heart. Like my blood. It was a force already within me when I arrived on the scene. It was a necessity for me, like food or water.'

There is the long-standing joke that you should become a musician only if you have absolutely no other way of making a living. This is because the music business can be a business of rejection. For every artist or songwriter who achieves their dream, there are millions of others who are rejected, overlooked or passed over. Pete Kirtley, multi-million-selling songwriter of the fastest-selling single in history, 'Pure And Simple', sums up the reality of being a professional songwriter: 'My advice to anyone aspiring to be a professional songwriter is to climb the tallest building that you can find and jump off of it. There's a better chance of survival.'

While Kirtley's view might be accurate in a business sense, this is certainly not the case with respect to the creative side of being a songwriter. Songwriting should first and foremost be about enjoying yourself. Writing should be a pleasurable activity with commercial success merely a by-product of that, never its overwhelming focus.

This is worth remembering when the Holy Grail of a Number One record appears but a distant dream. Focus on the song. Concentrate on writing a great song and the rest will follow. Great songs attract attention, attention generates interest, interest leads to commitment and commitment results in success. But first and foremost, the song needs to be written.

Many people live and die with their music still unplayed. They never dare to try. This circumstance highlights another vital characteristic of the songwriter: an ability and willingness to take risks.

'Nothing encourages creativity like the chance to fall flat on one's face.'
– James D Finley

It's important to take a risk with songwriting. Don't be afraid to write a song. It can be very daunting to expose oneself in music; there is a powerful sense of revealing the innermost workings of one's heart and soul, of being naked. Opening up something as delicate as one's own song to public comment and criticism can be overwhelming to the point of paralysing. A songwriter must be able to take risks.

This combination of taking risks, being able to be expressive in words and music, being willing to let go, having a deep-rooted commitment to the craft and, above all, having a sense of enjoyment in all that you create characterises a good songwriter.

TEACHING THE UNTEACHABLE

'I don't really believe you can teach people to write songs. There are virtually no rules. In fact, to be successful, one usually needs to break whatever rules there are.'
– Sir Tim Rice

There is great debate over whether the craft of songwriting can be taught. Like Sir Tim, many people rightly contest, 'How can you teach something with no rules?' And that's certainly one aspect of the debate that's not up for discussion: songwriting has no concrete rules, only guidelines, and they change constantly.

> *'The fact is there are no rules, and there never were any rules, and there never will be any rules of musical composition except rules of thumb, and thumbs vary in length, like ears.'*
>
> *– George Bernard Shaw*

In my experience, however, the craft of songwriting *can* be taught. I've helped many aspiring songwriters who have never written a song in their lives to compose their first song. I've witnessed the progress of more seasoned writers hone their craft using their newly discovered knowledge and produce songs of a far greater quality than they had ever been able to achieve six months earlier. Yet this isn't to say that a songwriter can be taught to write a 'hit song'; as Don Black observed, 'You can teach people to write songs, but you cannot teach people taste and you cannot teach them flair.'

This is perhaps the crux of the argument. Someone can be taught to write a song, and maybe even a good song, but a great song? That's a factor solely reliant on the innate talent (or luck) of the writer.

Another important consideration is that a person doesn't necessarily need to be taught to write them in order to be able to write songs, unlike a pianist, who needs to be taught to play the piano before he or she can use it effectively. Such creative ability can come completely naturally. And even if that person was tutored by the greatest songwriter in the world, there's no guarantee that that student will be able to conjure up the next worldwide hit.

In fact, it could be argued that learning impedes the creative process. In a recent interview on BBC Radio 2, George Michael revealed that he shied away from music theory and, despite writing numerous hit records, still didn't know what the notes were on the strings of a guitar. His reasoning was that he had 'this innate feeling that the more knowledge I had, the less fumbling around I would be able to do and the less likely I was to come up with anything really original'.

There are scores of examples of hyper-successful songwriters and artists with limited musical knowledge; Eric Clapton, for instance, famously does not read music, while Elvis Presley admitted, 'I don't know anything about music. In my line, you don't have to.' Even Irving Berlin – arguably America's greatest songwriter – couldn't read harmony, composed completely by ear and only ever played in the key of F♯. These esteemed artists didn't need to know music theory to write songs. Great songwriting comes from the heart.

> *'Music is an outburst of the soul.' – Frederick Delius*

The Purpose Of Heart & Soul

'To encourage talent is to create it.' – Anonymous

Heart & Soul isn't intended to make you a genius songwriter or to guarantee you instant success, millions of dollars in royalties and a superstar lifestyle. What it will do, however, is provide you with the tools and the mindset with which to write great songs.

The first chapter, 'Soul', explores the creative aspects of songwriting, and the 'Song Craft' sections here will guide you through the rudiments of songwriting. These are supported by contributions from and interviews with some of most successful and gifted songwriters of recent generations.

The next chapter, 'Heart', uncovers the intricacies of the music business – a seemingly impregnable and threatening institution – and describes how to handle the business of being a songwriter. The information here reveals how the industry affects the songwriter (and vice versa) and contains the fundamental business knowledge a writer will need to have in order to survive in the industry, including contributions from many high-profile industry representatives offering their experience and expertise.

Chapter 3, 'Mind', looks back over the history of songwriting. One of the prime learning tools of the developing songwriter is knowledge of past writers, and this section introduces some of the most significant songwriters of the last 200 years. As part of the 50th-anniversary celebrations of the prestigious Ivor Novello Awards, there is also detailed coverage of the Awards themselves.

The final chapter, 'Body', provides all the necessary information that a songwriter should ever need, including details on songwriting competitions and showcases; recommended listening and reading material and websites to encourage further exploration; and the principal societies and organisations with which a songwriter will need to be in contact.

As songwriter, publisher and former Chairman of the Academy Guy Fletcher highlighted, 'Self-promotion is the key to your survival as a songwriter. You have to be a combination of writer, publisher, instrumentalist, recording artist, producer, computer operator, recording engineer and, above all, a confident salesperson. It is a bitter pill for many writers, but it is the real world, so grit your teeth and get out there and do it.'

By the conclusion of *Heart & Soul*, any aspiring songwriter should be fully equipped with the knowledge and expertise to tackle the challenging yet rewarding business of songwriting.

'Songwriting is like making love: either all or nothing.' – Isaac Stern

THE BRITISH ACADEMY OF COMPOSERS & SONGWRITERS

BY CHRIS GREEN
CHIEF EXECUTIVE OF THE ACADEMY

A SHORT HISTORY: THREE INTO ONE DOES GO

The British Academy of Composers & Songwriters was established on 1 January 1999 with the amalgamation of the Association of Professional Composers (APC), the British Academy of Songwriters, Composers and Authors (BASCA) and the Composers' Guild of Great Britain (CGGB). The new organisation was formally launched a few weeks later in London at a memorable event in the Arboretum at Coutts Bank in the Strand, attended by a host of celebrity composers and songwriters and senior representatives of the many music-industry organisations. After the premiere performance of a specially commissioned trumpet fanfare, written for the occasion by the distinguished film composer Ron Goodwin, there were speeches by the Academy President, Sir Tim Rice, and the government's Culture Secretary, Chris Smith. At last, the composer and songwriter community had a representative trade association that could speak with one voice on behalf of music writers of every genre.

But what had brought about this coming together of these three different and diverse musical voices? BASCA (originally the Songwriters' Guild) and the CGGB (mainly a home for classical writers) had both celebrated their golden jubilees earlier in the decade. The APC was a much younger organisation, originally a breakaway group from the Composers' Guild, which had been established by a couple of hundred or so senior composers, mainly writing for film and television, and committed to speaking up for and maintaining the standards of professional music writers. Members of the three 'guilds' had all got to know each other much better as a result of sharing offices in the West End of London, firstly in Hanway Street and subsequently in Brook Street. They had also all been represented by the newly established BMR (British Music Rights), an organisation set up jointly by themselves, the MCPS–PRS Alliance and the MPA (Music Publishers' Association) to defend and speak up for the writer/publisher copyright-owning community.

The three guilds soon realised that there was an increasing number of issues that were common to each of their causes and that it made much more sense to work together rather than separately. Despite receiving funding support from the PRS (Performing Right Society), the guilds were also individually very strapped for cash and saw the good sense in pooling their resources.

A remarkable and very welcome piece of serendipity had also provided an unexpected opportunity for the guilds to move forward together much faster than would otherwise have been the case. This was an approach by Kopinor, a Norwegian Collection Society that distributes monies collected from the photocopying of sheet music. Kopinor explained that it was administratively impossible to distribute the bulk of this income to individual composers and publishers, and offered to hand it over instead to the representative organisations of composers, songwriters and publishers, to be used by them to the general benefit of their members. It was from this source that the three guilds were able to fund a transitional body, the Alliance of Composer Organisations, which was set up with the prime purpose of exploring the possibility of amalgamation.

It was at this stage, in the autumn of 1996, that I was brought in as the consultant to manage the ensuing research, to come up with a firm proposal for the amalgamation of the guilds and to help to steer the proposal through the necessary consultations with the membership of all three organisations, without whose overwhelming support the amalgamation could simply not take place. After two long and hard years, with much soul searching amongst the membership and with all the usual territorial concerns eventually satisfied, all three guilds put the amalgamation proposal to the vote within their respective constituencies, and by September 1998 it had won overwhelming support, with only five dissenters out of some 3,000 (and three of them later admitted that they hadn't understood the question!). The new British Academy of Composers & Songwriters, with approaching 3,000 members, thus emerged as the largest and potentially most influential composer organisation in the world.

WHAT THE ACADEMY DOES

From its inception through to the present day, the main thrust of the work of the new Academy has been:

- To act as one voice for all composers and songwriters;

- To raise the profile and the value of all UK music writers within the music industry, with the decision makers in government and with the public at large;

- To protect and promote the value of copyright with collection societies, broadcasters and music publishers;

- To improve working and contracting conditions for writers in every genre;

- To provide a comprehensive range of benefits and support services for its members;

- To provide social and networking opportunities for its members;

- To provide information and learning opportunities for its members;

- To celebrate the wealth of British music-writing talent;

- To provide additional support for career beginners.

THE ACADEMY'S MEMBERSHIP AND GOVERNANCE

The Academy has almost 3,000 members writing across all genres of music. Of these about 1,800 are mainly songwriters, 600 are classical composers and nearly 300 write for film and television, with the remainder being jazz composers, new-media composers and writers of musicals or folk and traditional music.

The Academy has three main levels of membership catering for those who are at the beginning of their careers, the professional composer and songwriter and those individuals and organisations who support the work of the Academy while not necessarily being writers themselves.

To preserve the best traditions of the three original guilds and to ensure that the special interests of the main areas of music writing are properly represented, the Academy is divided into three electoral colleges, with the members of each college respectively electing Executive Committees, which function in the concert, media and pop areas of music. Each of these in turn elects three representatives to serve on the Academy's main Board, along with two External Directors with specialist corporate and legal expertise. The Academy also owns a subsidiary production company, responsible for its various commercial activities, and a charitable trust that operates in the educational field.

The Academy currently employs myself as Chief Executive and five other full-time members of staff who are responsible for the Academy's publications and website, administering the Academy's events programme, servicing the three Executive Committees and providing and maintaining a wide range of support services for the Academy's members.

ACADEMY FUNDING

The Academy is a comparatively lean and mean machine, with an annual turnover of some £750,000. While annual subscriptions make a significant contribution to the Academy's income, the largest source of finance is event sponsorship and ticket income, with welcome additional funding coming from grants, donations and income from advertising.

THE ACADEMY AS A CAMPAIGNING ORGANISATION

The Academy's most vital role is that of providing a single voice for all music writers in campaigning to protect and increase the value of copyright and to improve the working environment and opportunities available to composers and songwriters. To achieve this, the Academy's Chair, leading Board and Executive Committee members and Chief Executive meet regularly with politicians of all parties and senior civil servants in all those government departments that deal with music, including the Department for Culture, Media and Sport, the Department of Trade and Industry, the Department for Education and Skills, the Office of Fair Trading, the Patent Office and the Office of Communications (Ofcom).

The Academy regularly lobbies government ministers and MPs on new legislation and other issues affecting the music-writing community. Key action areas in recent times have been the Licensing and Communications Bills while they were passing through Parliament, the renewal of the BBC Charter and other matters to do with public-service broadcasting. The Academy recently played a key role in helping to resolve a dispute over the PRS tariff levels for classical music, which had been referred to the Copyright Tribunal. After many years of failed negotiations with the relevant parties concerned, the Academy has recently lodged an official complaint with the Office of Fair Trading.

As part of its general brief, the Academy holds regular liaison meetings with the Performing Right Society and the Music Publishers' Association, and it confers and co-operates with the Incorporated Society of Musicians (ISM), the

Society for Producers and Composers of Applied Music (PCAM) and, most notably, the Musicians' Union.

A great deal of the Academy's policy-development and lobbying activity is carried out in harness with other organisations. The most significant of these is British Music Rights, which represents and promotes the interests of all music-copyright owners, and here the Academy works alongside the Music Publishers' Association and the MCPS–PRS Alliance. British Music Rights is a centrepiece for the Academy's political lobbying and provides an invaluable resource.

Of equal significance is the research and lobbying work the Academy undertakes alongside other creators' trade associations and trades unions across the creative industries through the Creators' Rights Alliance, which the Academy played a key part in setting up in 2001. The CRA represents 17 major organisations and focuses especially on matters relating to film and television.

The Academy has also been a major player in the increasingly important lobbying undertaken through the Music Business Forum, which represents the music industry as a whole. Since it was set up in 2001, the MBF has provided government with a single music-industry voice on key issues where the community is united and has specialist sub-groups dealing with skills training, broadcasting and live music.

The final grouping within which the Academy is a key player is the recently established ACCORD Alliance for New Music. Representative of those organisations that focus primarily on new music in the classical genre, ACCORD aims to set up a number of initiatives intended to raise the profile of new music and to take it to a wider audience.

THE ACADEMY AND ITS MEMBER SERVICES

The Academy offers a wide range of services in support of its members, including:

- Seminars and workshops;

- Free legal and financial advice;

- Commissioning-rate guidelines for media and concert composers;

- A members' register;

- A collaboration service;

- A comprehensive website;

- Discounts on broadband access, hire of recording studios (from a substantial database) and high-tech music equipment, and travel and holiday accommodation.

Members also benefit from reduced-rate entry to Songsearch UK and up-to-date notification of a wide range of competitions in all genres of music.

The Academy publishes the high-quality bi-annual magazine *The Works*, which contains major cross-genre feature articles, coverage of key campaign issues and news of a wide range of activities and events. In addition, the Academy publishes the bi-monthly, eight-page newsletter *Fourfour*, which focuses on current issues and provides reports from the Academy's Concert, Media and Songwriter Executives plus an events timetable.

Amongst the most popular of the Academy's activities is its regular programme of seminars, workshops and masterclasses. These activities, which range from major events featuring well-established composers and songwriters through to small-scale business affairs and songwriting clinics, help members to learn about and share information on key aspects of the music industry and to be brought up to date on current issues. Each year, the Academy takes a number of these events outside London to provide support for those members who live further afield.

PROUDLY RECOGNISING A WEALTH OF TALENT

Many people who don't know much about the work of the Academy are familiar with the Academy's annual Ivor Novello Awards. Having celebrated their 50th anniversary in 2005, the 'Ivors' are internationally respected as the premier awards for music writers, reflecting the wealth of talent of British songwriters and composers and their contribution as the creative source of the British music industry. While the main thrust of the Ivors is songwriting, there are also two major awards for film and television work and a new award for achievement in the classical field. The Ivor Novello Awards are sponsored by the Performing Right Society.

The British Composer Awards is a new event (the first presentation having taken place in December 2003) at which concert composers receive recognition for work across a wide range of vocal, instrumental and new-media composition. The Awards are presented in association with BBC Radio 3 and are also sponsored by the Performing Right Society.

The Academy's Gold Badge Awards, meanwhile, go back over 30 years and provide for a unique annual cross-genre event at which artists, promoters, publishers, managers and others who have served the music-writing community with distinction are recognised by its leading members. These awards are sponsored by the MCPS (Mechanical-Copyright Protection Society).

LOOKING AHEAD

I have been privileged to serve the composer and songwriter community for eight years now, firstly as consultant to the amalgamation of the guilds project and then as the new Academy's Chief Executive. I have seen ideas and aspirations grow into reality. I have seen members come and go. I have shared with my Board and Executive Committee masters the sweet joy of a job well done, and we have equally wallowed together in frustration at failure. But the one overwhelming certainty I have is that the Academy is increasingly finding that strong and united voice needed to influence those who make decisions in higher places. The great strength of the Academy is the sense of solidarity that exists among our very varied composer and songwriter communities.

As is so often said, writing music can be a lonely activity. To many of our members, the most important thing we do is provide them with the opportunity to meet others, compare notes and establish friendships.

Looking ahead, who can predict exactly what the nature of the music industry will be in five years' time, let alone ten or twenty? Who can guess what new issues will arise, or when? This is why we need a strong and united composer organisation. This is why it's in your best interests – if you're a songwriter or composer – to join the Academy.

THE SONGWRITERS

The following songwriters and music-industry professionals have kindly contributed their time and wisdom to *Heart & Soul*. In recognition of the quality and expertise of their input, a brief background is provided for each contributor.

Deke Arlon has had a distinguished and varied career in music, TV and publishing, from performing in his own band – Deke Arlon And The Tremors – to cutting his teeth in the world of television (most notably by playing a lead role in the soap opera *Crossroads*) and going on to become one of the UK's most respected and successful music publishers. As a publisher, Deke has signed hit after hit, including Louis Armstrong's 'What A Wonderful World', Bobbie Gentry's 'Ode To Billy Joe', 'Everybody's Talking', Jimi Hendrix's 'Hey Joe' and 'Think' by Aretha Franklin. He has also signed theatrical successes like *Fiddler On The Roof*, *Blood, Sweat And Tears* and *Chicago* and writers including Gilbert O'Sullivan, James Taylor, Kenny Young and Nicky Chinn, and has worked with artists such as Sheena Easton, Elaine Page, Mike And The Mechanics and Ray Davis of The Kinks. As a publisher, Deke has received one BMI Award for over 3 million plays and four BMI Awards for over 1 million, and he once won Publisher of the Year three years running.

Don Black made his West End debut as a lyricist with composer John Barry on the musical *Billy*, starring Michael Crawford. Since then, his career has earned him countless awards, including an Oscar for his song 'Born Free', five Academy Award nominations, three Tony nominations and two Tonys (for the book and lyrics to *Sunset Boulevard*), a Golden Globe and five Ivor Novello Awards. Among Don's many successful songs are 'Ben', a Number One for Michael Jackson; 'To Sir With Love', a US Number One for Lulu; 'Take That Look Off Your Face' (Marti Webb); 'Love Changes Everything' (Michael Ball); and his first ever hit, Matt Monro's 'Walk Away'. Don has also written over 100 songs for films including *The Italian Job*, *Dances With Wolves*, *Out Of Africa* and a quintet of James Bond theme songs, including 'Diamonds Are Forever'. He has collaborated on four theatrical productions with Andrew Lloyd Webber: *Tell Me On A Sunday*, *Aspects Of Love*, *Sunset Boulevard* and *Bombay Dreams*. In 2004, together with Christopher Hampton, he completed the book and lyrics for a musical version of *Dracula*.

Bill Bruford, drummer and writer with the bands Yes, Bruford and King Crimson, pioneered the revolutionary use of electronics in developing the melodic side of percussion. In 1986, he formed the electro-acoustic jazz group Earthworks, whose first release was named the 'third-best jazz album of the year' by America's *USA Today*. Bill continued to tour with both King Crimson and Earthworks throughout the '90s, during which time he variously recorded and toured with Kazumi Watanabe, David Torn, The New Percussion Group Of Amsterdam, Jamaaladeen Tacuma, Akira Inoue, Al Di Meola, The Buddy Rich Orchestra, Tony Levin, Pete Lockett and his old firm, Yes. In 1990, the readers of *Modern Drummer* magazine voted him into the magazine's Hall of Fame.

Billy Bragg has made an indelible mark on the conscience of British music, being described by *The Times* newspaper as a 'national treasure'. Also hailed as a 'one-man Clash', Bragg's stark musical style and even starker vocals belie a keen sense of melody and passionate, deeply humane lyrics (eg 'The Milkman Of Human Kindness'). His credentials as a songwriter were confirmed when Kirsty MacColl released her Top Ten classic version of Bragg's 'A New England'. Bragg's third album, *Talking With The Taxman About Poetry* (1986), was also a Top Ten hit and spawned the hit single 'Levi Stubbs' Tears'. In 1991, Bragg issued the critically acclaimed Top Ten album *Don't Try This At Home*, featuring the hit single 'Sexuality'. In that same decade, he released two Woody Guthrie cover albums, *Mermaid Avenue Volume I* and *Volume II*, both of which were nominated for Grammy Awards. In 2003, Bragg's two decades of work were celebrated in a double-CD retrospective titled *Must I Paint You A Picture?*, revealing a songwriting capability of extraordinary depth and breadth, chronicling his transition from strident political dissenter to insightful social commentator to compassionate and touching balladeer and back again.

Ivan Chandler began his musical career as a pianist for Dusty Springfield, Lulu and Kiki Dee. In 1969, he became involved in the music-publishing industry, and in 1992 he was appointed as the music consultant to PACT (Producers Alliance for Cinema and Television), who subsequently published his book *The Music Copyright Guide For Television And Film Production*. Since 1995, Ivan has run Musicalities, one of the leading independent companies specialising in music-copyright clearance, music supervision and music publishing for the entertainment industry. Visit www.musicalities.co.uk for more details.

Allan Dann is Business Affairs Manager with the Peermusic Group of companies in the UK and co-writer (with John Underwood) of the leading beginners' guide to the business, entitled *How To Succeed In The Music Business* (see 'Recommended Reading For Songwriters' for further details).

The Darkness are a band that have grabbed rock 'n' roll by its shoulders and given it a swift snakeskin-booted kick right where it counts. With their acclaimed Atlantic Records debut, *Permission To Land*, the London-based quartet delivered an irresistible – and unapologetic – blend of anthemic hard rock and sheer showmanship, complete with virtuoso guitar solos, killer hooks and massive singalong choruses. *Permission To Land* was released in the UK in July 2003 and debuted at Number Two before quickly rising to Number One, marking the first debut album by a British artist to hit the top spot since Coldplay in 2000. The album was subsequently nominated for Britain's prestigious Mercury Music Prize, and in 2004 the band were honoured with an Ivor Novello Award as Songwriters of the Year.

Rob Davis is most famously known as the co-writer of Kylie Minogue's phenomenal single 'Can't Get You Out Of My Head' (2001), which went to Number One in over 20 countries and earned him an astonishing three Ivor Novello Awards. Originally the guitarist in '70s rock band Mud, Rob also co-produced the early Ibiza Number One anthem 'Jibaro' by Elektra before writing the huge 'Not Over Yet' for Grace. Since then he has written hits including Spiller's 'If This Ain't Love', the UK Number One 'I Need A Miracle' for Fragma, Sophie Ellis-Bextor's Number Two hit 'Get Over You', and 'Down Boy' for Holly Valance, which also reached Number Two. In massive demand as a writer and producer, Rob has worked with Eg White, Chris Braide, Wayne Hector, Gregg Alexander, Steve Mac, Paul Barry, Marcella Detroit and Lamont Dozier, among others. In 2004, Kylie Minogue's Davis-penned 'Come Into My World' won its writer a Grammy Award.

Chris Difford was the lyricist and guitarist of Squeeze, one of the most acclaimed and longest surviving new-wave bands of the '70s. The band's smart, sophisticated brand of pop featured in many classic songs, including 'Pulling Mussels (From The Shell)', 'Tempted' and 'Black Coffee In Bed'. Their third album, 1979's *Cool For Cats*, provided their major UK chart breakthrough, resulting in a pair of Number Two singles: 'Up The Junction' and the cult classic title track. Chris has also worked with artists such as Paul Young, Helen Shapiro, Billy Bremner, Elvis Costello and Jools Holland. In 2004, Sanctuary published a biography of his songs with Glenn Tilbrook, titled *Squeeze: Song By Song*.

Francis Eg White started his career in the band Yip Yip Coyote and then in Brother Beyond, who subsequently had several hits courtesy of Stock, Aitken and Waterman. In 1989, Eg signed to Warner–Chappell publishers (before moving to Universal Publishing in 2002), for whom he produced two albums as an artist in his own right and collaborated with a whole spectrum of artists including Will Young, Joss Stone, Natalie Imbruglia, Seal, Charlotte Church, Sophie Ellis-Bextor, Terri Walker, Amy Winehouse, Lucie Silvas and Liberty X. In 2003, Will Young recorded White's 'Leave Right Now', which went to Number One in the UK charts and earned Eg an Ivor Novello Award for Best Song, Musically and Lyrically.

Colin Emmanuel, a UK-based R&B producer and songwriter, started out as a programmer with pioneering British rappers Definition Of Sound before cutting a path as a remixer, often under the pseudonym C-Swing. He has built up an impressive array of credits, from Mary J Blige and D'Angelo to En Vogue and Beverley Knight. Colin has also shown his versatility outside the R&B arena, producing The Beta Band's *Hot Shots II* album and working with artists such as Craig David, J'Nay, The Sugababes and Skinnyman. However, it is his work with Jamelia that has brought true credibility to the British R&B scene; he co-produced and co-wrote tracks on her first two albums, including the singles 'Money' and 'Call Me'.

Michelle Escoffery, a former member of girl R&B trio Truce, scored hits as a professional songwriter first with Damage ('In Your Eyes', 'Storytella'), then with Hinda Hicks ('I Wanna Be Your Lady', 'Child') and Fierce ('Dayz Like That'). 'Dayz Like That' went on to be a Number One smash for the band Sugar Jones and was the biggest selling track of 2001 in Canada. In 2002, Michelle penned *PopStar* offshoots Liberty X's UK Number One single 'Just A Little', which won her an Ivor Novello Award for PRS Most Performed Work in 2003. Her other writing credits include songs for The Honeyz, Stevie Wonder, Andrea Bocelli, George Michael, Beverley Knight, Shola Ama and The Lighthouse Family. In 2005, Tina Turner recorded her song 'Complicated Disaster', which was the first single off Tina's multi-million-selling *Greatest Hits* album.

Ana Gracey is a songwriter, session singer and vocal coach. She is the Vocal Lecturer at the Academy Of Contemporary Music. For further information, visit www.ana-gracey.co.uk or www.thevocalathlete.com.

Mark Fishlock, a professional composer and songwriter for over 20 years, has written music for various media projects, including the filmed version of the English Shakespeare Company's *The Wars Of The Roses*, *Flesh And Blood* and Anneka Rice's *Adventure* series; commercials for Bic and the Carphone Warehouse; library tracks for Carlin and Off The Shelf; and music for the BBC's late, lamented soap *Eldorado*. In recent years he has written and produced around 900 songs for English-language productions aimed at the international market. Mark is a founder director of the British Academy of Composers & Songwriters and serves on the board of British Music Rights.

Guy Fletcher, a respected songwriter since the '60s, has won many awards, including an ASCAP Award and an Ivor Novello Award. His body of work includes songs and music for TV, commercials and the stage, while recordings of his songs by stars like Elvis Presley, Cliff Richard, Ray Charles, Frankie Valli and Joe Cocker have ensured Guy's place in British pop history. Guy was a founding director of British Music Rights and Chairman of the British Academy of Composers & Songwriters. He is currently Creative Director of Music Copyright Solutions Plc and a director of the PRS.

Tim Hawes and **Pete Kirtley** (Jiant Productions) joined forces in 1999 to focus on their talents as pop songwriter/producers. In the six years since then, they have written and produced tracks for artists including The Spice Girls, 5ive, Hear'Say, Mis-teeq, Steven Gately, Aaron Carter, Gareth Gates and The Cheeky Girls. They have notched up five Number Two singles, a Number One hit in Germany and two UK Number Ones, the first of which was the record-breaking single 'Pure And Simple' by the first TV *PopStar* winners, Hear'Say, which went on to sell 1.3 million copies. This not only earned Pete and Tim an Ivor Novello Award for Best Selling Single in 2001 but was also recognised as the UK's fastest selling debut single ever and gained them an historic placement in the *Guinness Book Of Records*.

Wayne Hector has written over 30 Number Ones around the globe so far, including 'All Or Nothing' for O-Town (USA), 'Feels Like Today' for Rascall Flatts (USA) and 'He Don't Love You' by Human Nature (Australia). He has also produced hits for Michael Bolton, Def Leppard, Kate Winslet and Charlotte Church. As executive producer on Westlife's first and second albums, Wayne wrote almost 30 of the boys' hits, including 'World Of Our Own' and 'Flying Without Wings', which was also a Number One for *American Idol* contestant Ruben Studdart. He enjoys working with some of the most accomplished songwriters and producers in the business, including Steve Mac, Steve Robson, Elliot Kennedy, Andy Goldmark, Gary Burr, Chris Lindsay and Chad Elliot.

Mark Hill began his career as half of Artful Dodger, the duo who bought UK two-step into the mainstream with their cross-over successes 'Re-Rewind' (1999) and 'Moving Too Fast' (2000). At the same time, Craig David signed a record deal and Mark co-wrote and produced his first album. Craig's first solo track, 'Fill Me In', earned Mark an ASCAP Award. Mark has since been awarded four Ivor Novello Awards, including a Dance Award for 'Re-Rewind', a Best Contemporary Song Award for 'Seven Days', 2001's Songwriter of the Year Award and an Ivor Novello Dance Award for 'Woman Trouble'. Meanwhile, he has also worked with Christina Milian, Tom Jones and Liberty X and remixed artists as diverse as Sisqo, BB Mack, Gabrielle,

Jennifer Lopez, Paul McCartney and Dido. In 2004, he completed work on Craig David's third album.

Holland, Dozier and Holland – Brian Holland, his brother Eddie and Lamont Dozier – comprised one of the most successful writing and production teams in popular-music history. They almost single-handedly fashioned the Motown sound of the mid-1960s, writing hits for Marvin Gaye ('Can I Get A Witness?', 'How Sweet It Is [To Be Loved By You]'), Martha And The Vandellas ('Heat Wave', 'Nowhere To Run') and Diana Ross And The Supremes ('Where Did Our Love Go?', 'Baby Love', 'Come See About Me', 'Stop! In The Name Of Love', 'Back In My Arms Again' – all US Number One hits). The team's place in history was further secured through writing songs for The Four Tops ('Baby I Need Your Loving', 'I Can't Help Myself' and their 1996 worldwide Number One smash 'Reach Out [I'll Be There])'. Between them, they have written over 52 Number One hits worldwide, and in 2004 they were bestowed with the prestigious Ivor Novello Special International Award.

Richard Kerr has written the music for such major hit songs as 'Mandy', 'Somewhere In The Night', 'Looks Like We Made It', 'I'll Never Love This Way Again', 'Shine On' and 'No Night So Long'. These six titles alone represent 11 BMI Special Awards, 2 Grammy nominations, 1 Grammy Award, more than 12 million airplays and the sale of approximately 40 million records. Richard's songs have been recorded by Barry Manilow, Frank Sinatra, Roy Orbison, John Denver, Kenny Rogers, Dionne Warwick and The Righteous Brothers, to name but a few. He has also recorded four solo albums and written title songs for motion pictures and television, mainly with Academy Award-winning lyricist Will Jennings. Most recently, Westlife took 'Mandy' to Number One in the UK, and the track was voted Record of the Year in 2003 by the UK public.

Mick Leeson, with his songwriting partner Peter Vale, has had songs recorded by Ray Charles, Maxi Priest, Alvin Stardust, The Commodores and many others. Their biggest hit was 'Would I Lie To You?', by Charles and Eddie, which won three Ivor Novello Awards and was Number One in 12 countries. Their US rock hit 'Take Me Home Tonight' by Eddie Money made the US Top Three and has enjoyed 2 million US radio plays. Mick also wrote the lyrics to the James Bond theme song 'For Your Eyes Only'. The pair's most recent success was 'If There's Any Justice', a UK Top Three hit for Lemar. Mick has been a Director of the PRS for the last ten years.

Steve Levine began as an engineer at CBS Studios, where he worked with many punk bands of the day, such as The Clash, The Jags and The Drones, as well as pop acts like Sailor. He then proceeded to write and produce his own tracks and those of other bands, including Culture Club, a collaborative project that went on to sell over 20 million records. Steve has continued to work with a wide spectrum of artists, including The Beach Boys, Ziggy Marley, Louise, Mystique and 911. He also produced the Honeyz album *Wonder No. 8*, featuring the hit singles 'Finally Found' and 'End Of The Line'. He has won many awards, including BPI Producer of the Year, *Music Week*'s Top Singles Producer and a Grammy for his work with Denice Williams.

Dr Jonathan Little is a writer and composer, co-founder and managing editor of the *Music Business Journal* and principal of the Academy of Contemporary Music in Guildford, UK.

Barry Mason is one of the world's leading songwriters whose many gold records include such international favourites as 'Delilah', 'Love Grows (Where My Rosemary Goes)', 'The Last Waltz', 'Here It Comes Again', 'Love Is All' and 'There Goes My First Love'. His songs have been performed by Tom Jones, Elvis Presley, David Essex, Engelbert Humperdinck, The Drifters, Rod Stewart, Barbra Streisand, Des O'Connor, Petula Clark and The Dave Clark Five. An ex-Royal Marine, he has received five Ivor Novello Awards and nine prestigious BMI and ASCAP Awards. He is Chairman of the Xenex Music Group and a long-serving council member of the British Academy of Composers & Songwriters.

Jay Mistry, former Royalty Tracker Manager for BMG, now owns the successful royalty-tracking company Musical Sleuth Ltd.

Tony Moore, a singer/songwriter, performer and promoter extraordinaire, was the driving force behind London's legendary Kashmir Klub. He now promotes an even more successful live acoustic club, the Bedford. His nights have featured stars including The Finn Brothers, Guy Chambers, Lucie Silvas, Dave Stewart and Sheryl Crow. Prior to his role as promoter, Tony made his name with the band Radio Java, writing the Number One Dutch radio hit 'Fool', followed by The Cutting Crew's worldwide Number One hit '(I Just) Died In Your Arms'. Since then, Tony has worked with many different artists, including Marie Claire D'Ubaldo (whose hits include Celine Dion's 'Falling Into You') and Lulu. In 2004, he was inducted into the Music Managers Forum Roll of Honour for 'outstanding contribution to the music industry'. Visit www.tony-moore.com and www.thebedford.co.uk for more details.

Frank Musker has written an extraordinary number of successful songs, including Air Supply's million-selling and BMI Award-winning 'Every Woman In The World'; 'Senza Una Donna', recorded by Zucchero, featuring Paul Young, which was a Top Five hit in 20 countries; the Ivor Novello Award-winning 'Too Much Love Will Kill You', featured on Queen's final album, *Made In Heaven*; and Stardust's worldwide Number One dance smash 'Music Sounds Better With You'. Frank has collaborated with some of the world's most important artists, including The Gypsy Kings, Carly Simon, John Denver, Randy Crawford, Sister Sledge, Dionne Warwick, Bette Midler, Cher, Lisa Stansfield, Robert Miles, Luciano Pavarotti, Eric Clapton, Macy Gray, Ronan Keating and Stevie Ray Vaughan. A truly international composer/lyricist and producer, he has more than 30 gold and platinum records to his credit so far and is responsible for record sales conservatively estimated at over 80 million to date.

Rick Nowels is a Grammy Award-winning songwriter/producer and a multi-instrumentalist (guitar, keyboards, bass) who incorporates contemporary sounds and rhythms within classic songwriting. Having worked with some of the most innovative programmers and musicians, he has had numerous successful records, both nationally and internationally, including smashes with Madonna, Dido, The New Radicals, *NSync, Belinda Carlisle, Jewel, Stevie Nicks and Santana. His hits include 'White Flag' (Dido), 'The Game Of Love' (Santana), 'The Power Of Goodbye' (Madonna), 'Falling Into You' (Celine Dion) and 'Heaven Is A Place On Earth' (Belinda Carlisle).

Wise Buddah's Bill Padley and Jem Godfrey's mission is to make great, radio-friendly pop records that cross the boundaries of both nationality and genre. Their Number One singles to date include production credits on 'Tide Is High (Get The Feeling)' (which they also co-wrote) and the 2 million-selling 'Whole Again' for Atomic Kitten, the latter of which also earned them two Ivor Novello nominations. Recent collaborations those with include Jud Mahoney (DreamWorks US), Play (Columbia US), Gareth Gates (BMG), Sarah Whatmore (BMG UK/19 Management) and Jennifer Ellison (East West UK). Their songwriting collaborators include Billy Steinberg, Pam Sheyne, Rob Davis, Eg White, Elliot Kennedy and Gary Barlow. Their background in radio gives them a rare affinity for balancing the demands of the medium with the musical and artistic requirements of the artist.

Patrick Rackow was called to the Bar in 1992, having previously worked as an investment manager for a leading investment bank. Since then he has worked both in-house and in private practice, advising a wide range of music clients. He is a consultant with Steeles (Law) LLP, a Director of the British Academy of Composers & Songwriters and a member of the Rights Committee of British Music Rights.

Pam Sheyne made her mark as the writer of Christina Aguilera's 'Genie In A Bottle', which stayed at the top of the US's *Billboard* Hot 100 for five weeks, making it the country's biggest selling single of the year. Since then, her songs have been hits in all major territories of the globe, with sales in excess of 18 million records. Artists such as Dream, Billie, Sheena Easton, Myra, Tina Arena, Jessica Simpson and the aforementioned Christina Aguilera have all recorded her songs and she has won an Ivor Novello Award. In 2003, she starred in the UK's *Fame Academy* TV show.

Jake Shillingford was founder of the cult orchestral alternative Britpop band My Life Story, who released three successful albums, six Top 40 singles and toured with the likes of Blur, Pulp and Oasis. In 2000, he formed ExileInside, an autonomous electronic-music project funded solely by its own fans, the Investor Angels. ExileInside have already released a debut album, *EI034*, as well as a live EP and have an ambitious plan to release an album a year for the next five years via their own recording studio and label, Exilophone Records. Visit ExileInside's official website at www.exileinside.co.uk for more details.

David Stark is Editor/Publisher of the songwriting and music-publishing tip sheet *SongLink International*, which has successfully provided leads to the industry since 1993. He also publishes *Cuesheet*, a similar publication for film and TV music professionals. Starting his career in 1974 with Dick James Music, David has been a press officer (Decca and MAM Records), editor (*Billboard/Music & Media's* 'Eurofile' directory), co-author (*Inspirations: Original Lyrics And The Stories Behind The Songs* [Sanctuary Publishing, 1999]) and research consultant for the Ivor Novello Awards. He is also co-founder of the Unisong International Song Contest.

Billy Steinberg is one of the most successful songwriters of the past two decades, co-writing (with Tom Kelly) five Number One singles in the *Billboard* Hot 100 chart, including 'Like A Virgin' (Madonna), 'True Colors' (Cyndi Lauper), 'Eternal Flame' (The Bangles), 'So Emotional' (Whitney Houston) and 'Alone' (Heart). In addition, he has written six other US Top Ten pop hits, including 'I'll Stand By You' (The Pretenders), 'I Touch Myself' (The Divinyls), 'How Do I Make You' (Linda Ronstadt), 'I Drove All Night' (Cyndi Lauper) and 'In Your Room' (The Bangles). He was presented with a Grammy Award for co-writing Celine Dion's 'Falling Into You', while Madonna's 'Like A Virgin' was honoured by *Rolling Stone* magazine and MTV as the Number Four song on their list of the '100 Greatest Pop Songs'.

David Stoll's concert music spans orchestral, choral and chamber works, including performances of his Cello Concerto, his Sonnet for string orchestra, his Octet 'The Path To The River' and his score for the Royal Shakespeare Company's production of *As You Like It*, while his Third String Quartet, 'Fools By Heavenly Compulsion', was released on CD in 2005. David acts as a

Consultant in Musical Creativity in Schools, is a former Chairman of the British Academy of Composers & Songwriters and is a Board Director of British Music Rights. In 2002, the Royal Academy of Music honoured him by electing him to an Associateship position for distinction in his profession.

Richard Taylor is a partner at the Simkins Partnership (www.simkins.com), a London firm of solicitors who focus on media industries, where he specialises in music law. He negotiates and advises on recording and music publishing, and on appearances, sponsorship, content production and delivery, service contracts, trademarks and copyright issues.

With Wayne Hector, **Ali Tennant** had two Top 40 hits as the 1992 swing group Rhythm And Bass before becoming the songwriting team Aliway and writing for Damage ('Love II Love', 'Forever') and Ant And Dec ('Falling', 'Crazy About You'), while in 1997 Ali released his debut solo album, *Crucial*. Ali has collaborated with – amongst others – Salaam Remi (The Fugees), Jeffrey Smith of The Family Stand (Des'ree, Paula Abdul), Bob Brockman (Mary J Blige, Sean 'Puffy' Combs), Dave Cox and David Steele (Fine Young Cannibals, Al Green) and Characters (Boys II Men). His current writing projects include Jamelia, VS, Billy Crawford, Samantha Mumba, Blue and Rod Temperton. In 2004, he co-wrote the UK Number One 'All This Time' for *Pop Idol* winner Michelle McManus.

Brian Willey has written songs together with such names as Cliff Adams, Frank Barber, Eric Cook, Peter Hart, Peter Knight, Johnny Pearson and Les Reed. His songs and themes have been used as radio and TV signature tunes and have been recorded by such historic artists as Eve Boswell, John Hanson and Elaine Paige. In 1970, Dorothy Squires sang a song co-written by Brian at the Gibraltar International Song Festival, since when it has become regarded as that country's second National Anthem! He is currently Deputy Chairman and Finance Chairman of the PRS Members' Fund and a Director of the British Academy of Composers & Songwriters.

Sharon Woolf first made a major impact as the vocalist on Shanks And Bigfoot's worldwide hit 'Sweet Like Chocolate' and Doolally's Top Ten single 'Straight From The Heart'. Since then, she has provided vocals for Fatboy Slim's album *Palookaville* and written a single released on his label, Southern Fried Records. She has also written two songs on the Mike And The Mechanics album *Rewired* (Virgin/EMI) and worked with Mathew Knowles' World Entertainment Company (Destiny's Child, Beyoncé, The O'Jays, etc), The Valley Girls and Michael Garvin on several Jennifer Lopez tracks. At the time of writing, Sharon was collaborating with Jay Sean, The Stereo MCs, Tin Tin Out and Liberty X.

SOUL

THE CRAFT OF SONGWRITING

Soul: The Craft Of Songwriting

Introduction

'The most important element of a song is the feeling. I like to hear a song that tugs at you straight away. It's about the soul and integrity of a song that makes you feel as if it was written for you.'

– Colin Emmanuel, producer/writer

The song is a very powerful form of expression. Here's why.

A song can alter or enhance the emotions. To truly express a moment of celebration – for example, that special occasion – demands a 'feelgood song', like Katrina And The Waves' 'Walking On Sunshine', while at the other extreme the impact of a song such as 'Drive' by The Cars, accompanying the images of the African famine of the 1980s, was so profound that it moved hundreds of thousands of people to tears and, more importantly, action.

A song can enhance or break down culture. Standards, like the Andy Williams track 'Can't Take My Eyes Off You', have become part of the fabric of our musical landscape, while The Sex Pistols' 'Anarchy In The UK' attempted to demolish the presumptions of culture.

A song can speak for society – such as Irving Berlin's 'God Bless America' – as well as speak for those without a voice in society (ie Woody Guthrie's 'I Ain't Got No Home').

A song can reflect or even change the course of history. Witness the biggest selling single of all time, Elton John's re-release of 'Candle In The Wind', in response to the death of Princess Diana, or the unifying strength of a patriotic song like Ivor Novello's 'Keep The Home Fires Burning' during World War I. In the words of Doron K Antrim, 'A good war song is more powerful than tanks or tons of TNT in helping to win a war…for a song gets under the skin of the man at home or afield and keeps his batteries charged.'

It's clear from the above that a song is a truly potent force, and therefore one to be highly respected. Martin Luther, the 16th-century German priest and scholar, stated that, 'Next to the Word of God, the noble art of music is the greatest treasure in the world.' Perhaps this is due to a song's unique ability to express the inexpressible, a power that renders so many people in awe of songs and songwriters.

> 'Love cannot express the idea of music, while music may give an idea of love.'
> – Louis-Hector Berlioz

WHAT IS A SONG?

In simple terms, a modern song today comprises five key elements:

1. Lyrics;
2. Music (melody and harmony);
3. Rhythm;
4. Arrangement (including production);
5. Performance (with emphasis on vocals).

The first three could be thought of as the bones of the song, while the remaining two are the flesh. Each of these elements will be covered in detail in this chapter, before we take a look at how their amalgamation results in a great song – or, equally, a bad song!

WHAT MAKES A GREAT SONG?

This is the songwriters' Holy Grail, the magic formula that produces a hit song every time.

> 'What makes a great song? If the hairs go up on the back of my neck, that's my gauge of a good song. It can be the most beautiful ballad with the most lush string arrangement, or it can be something very, very simple. Or it can be a dance tune which is right in your face. It's very difficult to know what the formula is. If I knew that, I'd be knocking them out left, right and centre.'
> – Mark Hill, producer/writer with Craig David

While there might not be such a formula, a great song is instantly recognisable. Great songs tend to have one or more of the following:

- A catchy lead melody line;
- Hooks, both instrumental and vocal;
- A strong chorus;
- A great groove;
- A lyrical subject that's personal yet universal in its appeal;
- A memorable title;
- A strong, distinctive vocal delivery;
- An effective structure;
- An interesting arrangement, clever production or unusual choice of instrumentation;
- A distinctive atmosphere or mood.

Then again, it might not have any of these!

THE MURPHY'S LAW OF SONGWRITING

'For every rule, there is an exception.'

This is an underlying truth that will forever taunt the songwriter. It's also the same law that makes the creation of songs so exciting and satisfying. After all, if songwriting was easy, there'd no fun in it, let alone any money! So, with this in mind, please be aware that, with any of the statements made in this book concerning the craft of songwriting, you have the option of responding to them in any of three ways:

1. Obey;
2. Ignore;
3. Contradict.

Although there are certain sequences, methods and techniques applicable to composing, there is never a single catch-all method of writing songs.

THE SECRET TO SONGWRITING

There are three simple philosophies when it comes to successful songwriting:

1. Enjoy the experience;

2. There are no right or wrong ways to write a song;
3. Work hard at the craft.

It's important to remember why you're writing a song in the first place. Songwriting should always be about satisfying your own personal happiness; you should enjoy the experience of creation. The results will be far more fulfilling and remarkable if you do. So keep this philosophy in mind any time you lose focus, or feel at a loss, or are depressed because your song has been rejected for the umpteenth time by a seemingly impregnable music industry.

The second philosophy dictates that there are no right or wrong ways to write a song. Many of my students, when they first start to write their own songs, presume too much with regard to the expectations of the teacher, their class peers and the general listening public. I find it crucial to establish an atmosphere of openness and to encourage experimentation in my classes. Otherwise, students are immediately limiting their creative abilities by adhering to unwarranted presumptions. Similarly, when you're working through this book, don't presume that it's targeted purely at pop writers, or that heavy-metal riffing doesn't apply; songwriting embraces all forms of contemporary music, and the techniques, theories and methods described herein are relevant to all genres. Furthermore, when it comes to your own songwriting, you have to trust your own intuition; if it feels right to have no chorus in your composition, simply don't have one. You should always obey your gut instinct.

Finally, the only way you'll improve as a songwriter is if you keep working at your craft. Just as with any other area of creative endeavour, if you study it hard enough and long enough, you'll eventually become good at it, so keep writing. Some songs will be good, some will be average, some will be awful and a few will be great. It amazes me that so many wannabe songwriters are put off early in their development because their first few songs weren't their 'Hey Jude' or 'American Pie'. After all, you wouldn't expect to pick up an easel and paintbrush for the first time and create a Picasso or a Van Gogh, so don't put yourself under the pressure of comparing your preliminary efforts against the classics. Take your time to develop, make mistakes and grow into writing great songs. Songwriter and artist Sheryl Crow once described in an interview her attitude to being a songwriter: 'To me, it's like being a professional athlete: the more you build your strength and the more you work those muscles, the stronger you become and the better athlete you become.'

Each subject area discussed in this chapter comprises three sections:

1. Song Craft
This element deals with the fundamentals of songwriting, from the generation of ideas to writing lyrics and to basic production

philosophy. The guidelines contained within these sections are exactly that: guidelines. For every 'rule' or suggested technique, an example of a successful song not utilising it can be found. These guidelines are to be obeyed, ignored or contradicted, depending on your gut instinct.

2. The Songwriter

These are found throughout each 'Song Craft' section and contain personal contributions, opinions and advice on the craft of songwriting from a number of top professional songwriters. These sections are designed to supplement the information contained within each 'Song Craft' section.

3. An Interview With...

As you might expect, these are interviews with successful songwriters. While supporting and expanding on the ideas discussed in each 'Song Craft' section, they aren't directly related to the surrounding chapters that they precede or follow; rather, they offer further insights and opinions into the craft.

By the end of this part of the book, you should possess the necessary knowledge to write your first song, or – if you're already an experienced writer – be capable of honing your songwriting skills to generate better songs. Ultimately, though, this creative progress will be down to how dedicated you are. In other words, whatever you put in, you'll get out. As Brian Holland says, 'If you don't feel it then nobody else is going to feel it. It's about putting in your heart and soul.'

Song Craft 1:

The Songwriter's Tools

'Any songwriter who cannot produce work of a certain quality on demand is as much use as a plumber who can't plumb or a carpenter who can't carp.'

– Frank Musker, songwriter

Like any true craftsman, a songwriter should be armed with a specific set of tools. These are:

1. Imagination;
2. Dictaphone;
3. Notebook;
4. Instrument;
5. Recording system.

Dealing with each in turn, the following section includes advice and direction on the choice and application of the songwriter's tools.

1. Imagination

This is the most essential tool of the songwriter: the ability to imagine lyrics, melody lines and chord patterns. There are scores of successful songwriters who can't sing, can't play an instrument or can't write lyrics, but all of them have the ability to imagine a song into existence. A songwriter needs to approach the craft with an openness of mind and an enthusiasm of spirit that stimulates his or her imagination.

2. Dictaphone

The importance of this piece of equipment can't be emphasised enough. Buy a decent Dictaphone on which to record all your ideas, lyrics, melodies, chord patterns, jams – anything that might grow into a song. Either a cassette or digital Dictaphone will do, but whichever you choose, make sure you have a logical system in place for storing your ideas. Make sure you label each cassette or download the MP3s regularly into properly organised folders on your computer.

Some musicians contest that, if they don't remember the idea that they had in the shopping mall or in the shower, it wasn't a good enough idea to start with. To a great extent, this is false thinking. As I'll explain in 'Song Craft 2: Inspiration', great ideas can be fleeting, and the majority never ever return, which could be a great loss. Paul McCartney famously thought up one of the all-time most popular songs, 'Yesterday', in a dream, and immediately made a note of it on waking. Imagine if he hadn't and instead had forgotten this classic tune! Meanwhile, singer/songwriter George Michael admitted in an interview on BBC Radio 2, 'I felt that, if I didn't remember it, it wouldn't be a hit, whereas I understand now that, with the passage of time, you can forget some of your best ideas because they don't necessarily clump you over the head straight away.'

This is the reason why, if you're a songwriter, you should always carry a Dictaphone or, at the very minimum, a pen and notebook with which to make note of any flashes of inspiration you might have.

3. NOTEBOOK

This is the workstation of the songwriter. Again, make sure yours is properly organised. Have one section in which to note down any lyrical or musical ideas, a second section in which ideas can be developed into complete songs and a third section dedicated to title ideas.

Also, make sure you buy yourself a pad or notebook that makes you want to write in it. Whether this is a pink and fluffy covered diary or a leather-bound, skull-encrusted tome, it doesn't matter, just as long as it inspires you and encourages you to create.

Always remember to carry a pen, too. There's nothing more frustrating than frantically searching for a pen as your idea fades or you're distracted by the outside world. Writing in blood is a colourful but draining experience!

4. INSTRUMENT

The three main songwriting instruments are the voice, the guitar and the piano. It's beneficial (but not essential) to have knowledge and working skills in all three, although being familiar with just one is adequate if you intend to collaborate with someone who has skills in one of the other instruments. Nor is there a need to be an auspicious talent at your chosen instrument; you simply need to be of a good enough standard to be able to realize any musical ideas you might have.

The Voice – This is the primary instrument for working with lead melody lines. It's the most flexible of all instruments and can generate the widest range of sounds. Every songwriter should develop their vocals to some degree; the ability to sing is invaluable when it comes to expressing song ideas of all kinds. Find a local singing teacher and invest in six months' worth of vocal tuition. Alternatively, there are many vocal-tuition books available, such as Roger Kain's *The Complete Vocal Workout* (SMT [Sanctuary Publishing], 2003).

The Guitar – This is the most popular instrument for writing pop songs. A relatively easy instrument to get to grips with, it offers a solid chordal foundation on which to develop songs and allows for experimentation of melodic ideas. The full sound and strong sense of rhythm that it provides means that it shouldn't take you long to get a song sounding pretty good. Again, six months' worth of personal tuition, or a tuition book like David Mead's *10 Minute Guitar Workout* (SMT [Sanctuary Publishing], 2004), is money well spent. The guitar's portability and associations of coolness are perhaps why it's favoured over the piano.

Mick Leeson says:
'*Songwriting embraces many things that can be learned, but on one level it's like a golf swing or scoring goals in football: partly technical, partly mystical. As with all creative endeavours, it's a balance between trying very hard and not trying too hard, both at the same time! Songwriting is actually not hard; we're surrounded by songs on the radio, on TV, in shops – you name it. To learn songwriting, you do what you would do to learn any new skill: analyse, deconstruct, copy, try to replicate your model.*'

Rick Nowels says:
'*I play guitar, keyboards and bass. I feel that I have a strength in vocal production and background vocal arranging, but I have various people who program beats for me. I always try to write over cool beats, and while beats are constantly evolving and changing, songwriting to me remains fairly constant. It's still about a strong, compelling melody and a great lyric. It's a populist art form. Anybody can do it. A 16-year-old kid can write a song that will change the world in his or her bedroom on a Casio. It takes time, repetition, practice and a lot of chasing ghosts in the fog.*'

The Piano – This is arguably the best songwriting tool, since it can realize both melody and harmony over the broadest range in a way that the guitar could never hope to equal. Songs sound complete when played on a piano. The instrument's main advantage, in terms of songwriting, is the opportunity it provides to experiment with melodic ideas over chord progressions. Again, learning the basics of the piano is an easy matter, and a few months' tuition or a decent tuition book will pay dividends. Furthermore, a knowledge of the keyboard is essential if you're planning on recording your songs with modern-day sequencing packages.

Nowadays, songs can often be composed 'bottom up' – ie starting with the rhythm first and creating a groove over which chords, melodies, vocals or rapping are laid down. It's therefore beneficial to acquire the rudiments of drum programming, a skill most definitely required in styles such as hip-hop and R&B.

With respect to collaboration, even if you don't play a particular instrument, it's useful to have a guitar or piano to hand so that writing sessions can be held at your own home without too much inconvenience. Often, it's the most impromptu of sessions that generates the best songs, so be prepared.

5. HOME RECORDING SYSTEM

This is now a standard part of the professional songwriters' kit and will be explored in greater detail later in this part. In today's music industry, the standard of quality for song demos is so high that a basic piano-and-vocal recording simply can't compete, and with home recording technology being so affordable and relatively easy to use there's no excuse for a songwriter being unable to record a semi-professional demo. As Bryan Borcherds of the Arbiter Group points out, 'Anyone who owns a computer can have a professional

Bob Dylan says:
'I just wanted a song to sing, and there came a point where I couldn't sing anything, so I had to write what I wanted to sing because nobody else was writing what I wanted. I couldn't find it anywhere. If I could, I probably would never have started writing.'

Ali Tennant says:
'Do you really have the full passion it takes? If you have any shadow of doubt, be an interior designer.'

Louis Armstrong said:
'Musicians don't retire; they stop when there's no more music in them.'

recording studio in their own home.' The minimum equipment that a songwriter needs is:

- A computer with a fast processor, ample memory resources and a CD burner;

- A high-quality soundcard;

- A decent-quality microphone and pre-amplifier;

- A MIDI keyboard;

- A software sequencing package, such as Cubase SX (PC and Mac) or Logic (Mac only).

A decent recording package will cost anything between £1,000 and £3,000 ($1,500–$5,500), although quality second-hand systems can often be found for half this price.

Many songwriters are frightened by the sheer technological knowhow that such a system will demand of its user, yet this shouldn't be a barrier to your development as a songwriter. Paul White, editor of the UK magazine *Sound On Sound*, has written a series of user-friendly, easy-to-understand guides on the art of music technology; his *Basic* series of books (SMT [Sanctuary Publishing], 2000) come highly recommended. Or, if you prefer a one-stop alternative, I suggest Paul's best-selling *Home Recording Made Easy* (SMT [Sanctuary Publishing], second edition, 2001).

George Harrison of The Beatles said:
'I think people who can truly live a life in music are telling the world, "You can have my love; you can have my smiles. Forget the bad parts – you don't need them. Just take the music, the goodness, because it's the very best, and it's the part I give.'

Jem Godfrey of Wise Buddah says:
'I wish I'd known at the start that songwriting isn't at all glamorous in any way, shape or form. What I do every day is, I get up, I get on the train and I go to the office, then I come home again. I'm as much of a commuter as the next person. It's just two blokes in a room, writing songs. Don't expect songwriting to be this rollercoaster ride of sensationalist marvellousness.'

The Mindset Of A Songwriter

Here's how you should begin to approach writing songs:

1. Begin to think and act like a professional songwriter;

2. Be prepared for inspiration to strike at any time;

3. Be capable of turning your ideas into songs.

Burt Bacharach says:
'We worked in a smoke-filled room: no view, a window that didn't open and a beat-up piano.'

Wayne Hector says:
'Songwriting is like any subject. Some kids are good at maths, some kids are good at biology, some kids are good at drama. Similarly, some people find it easy to do uptempos, some people can write rock, some people can write ballads. I sometimes find it difficult to do uptempos, but I can write ballads all week long.'

Ali Tennant says:
'As soon as your pen hits the pad, it must be doing something very positive and something that feels right to you.'

An Interview With Rick Nowels

When did you write your first song? What did it feel like?
When I was 13, in the seventh grade – a long time ago. I had a duo with my best friend, Scott, who was already a singer and guitarist when I met him. I thought it was completely cool that he could sing and play, and I wanted in. He showed me a few chords and we started working up songs like 'Mr Tambourine Man', 'Greenback Dollar', 'The Sound Of Silence' and other hits of the day. I realised pretty quickly that all these songs had pretty simple chord progressions and that it was really about a melody and a lyric, so I started creating my own songs. I wrote a lot of bits and pieces for the first six months, and then one day Scott came over to my house after school and we sat down and wrote our first serious song together. It was called 'Masquerade Of Life' and we finished it in about two hours. I remember going out into the kitchen and playing it for my parents. I felt really proud of it and got on a path that day that I am still on. I might add that my parents didn't quite give us the reception that I had hoped for.

What's your process for writing a song?
I once read an interview with Brian Wilson in which somebody asked him, 'Which comes first, the lyric or the melody?' and he answered, 'The chord progression!' In the simplest terms, that's generally how it is: it usually starts by strumming or playing a chord progression and making up a melody over it. From the age of 13 to 30, I mostly wrote by myself. I would usually have a title in my head and something to say before I started to write something. To me, the lyric, the message of the song, is everything. Over the years, I've written in every conceivable way: lyric first, melody first, backing track first – whatever's happening in the moment. But the bottom line is that a song has to be about something. It has to have a message.

You describe yourself as a 'producer/writer'. What does that mean?
It just means that I never had anybody else help me produce my songs when I was younger, so I did it myself. I'm sure everybody who writes a song knows how they want it to eventually sound as a record. The process is just learning how to make it sound like that.

Making a record is a bit like building a house. You have to have a solid foundation, which are the drums and bass. You need solid beams and walls, which are the keyboards and guitars. Once it's up and running, then you have to furnish it, which is all the little colours and special parts of the arrangement. Finally, the thing that separates a house from a home is who's living in it. The singer is the magical intangible something that means everything.

Why did you want to be a songwriter?
I was a kid in the late '60s, so it's not hard to understand why I would want to be in music. To me, songwriters were the messengers, philosophers and cultural leaders. Great songs had the power to touch people and affect society. Plus you could dance to them, make out to them or lie in your bed and dream to them.

How long did it take you to get your first song success?
Too long. I started writing at 13 and had my first hit at 30.

How did you survive prior to your success?
I painted houses. Sold advertising in my dad's newspaper. Worked as a composer/musical director at the Magic Theatre in San Francisco. Scored porno films for the Mitchell brothers. Wrote children's music for Harcourt Brace. Played lots of clubs.

How are you inspired to write?
As a lyricist, I get inspired by emotional situations. The song concept is usually a metaphor for this. Hopefully the song lyric will depict a certain aspect of the human condition on a larger canvas and maybe offer a bit of salvation somewhere, like a spiritual.

As far as being inspired goes, you have to trust that you're an inspired person and put in the time and get out of the way of your inspiration. There's a lot of banging away that you have to go through in the process.

Have you experienced writers' block? If so, how did you break it?
I had one period of writers' block at the ages of 27 and 28, after I quit my last group. I was depressed. My best friend had died. I knew I had to move out of San Francisco and start over. I knew I was going to leave my girlfriend. I was facing the possibility that it might all be going nowhere. I wasn't really thinking about writing songs for other artists. After I had my first success, I never had writers' block again. It help me to trust that what I did was OK.

How long does it take you to write a song?
I used to start a song and spend two or three weeks finishing it. Now I try to start and finish as much as possible in one day, with maybe a second day to complete it. As Allen Ginsberg said, 'First thought, best thought.'

How is piracy affecting you as a songwriter?
It's affected the entire music business, because there's less money for everybody.
A lot of people have lost their jobs. Record labels take less chances on artists,
signing safe artists who they can promote with product tie-ins. It's made the
entire record business more conservative. When I was young, I took my cultural
cues from the musicians I admired. What does this do to culture when young
people are fed safe artists who have no problem promoting huge corporations?

Where do you think songwriters will be in the future?
Melody and lyrics have certainly taken a back seat to rhythm, production and
attitude. Most songs don't require 24–32 bars of original, compelling melody
and lyric anymore; the art of classic songwriting doesn't seem to be passed down
through the generations. It's always been hard to be just a songwriter who isn't
a recording artist. Only the obsessed need apply.

**Describe the process behind writing your Ivor Novello Award-winning song
'White Flag'. What's the story behind it?**
I'd written songs with Dido during the production of her first album, *No Angel*,
on which I produced 'Here With Me', 'Hunter' and 'All You Want'. We wrote
five songs over a short period of time and then went straight into production
mode on 'Here With Me'. It was quite effortless for us to write together, really
pure pleasure. She's so musical and loves simple folk melodies, which I also love.
At that time, she was at the end of making her record, so unfortunately none of
our songs made *No Angel*.

A few years later, when she was writing what was to become the *Life For Rent*
album, we met in London for a week to write. She had a lot of [her brother]
Rollo's lyrics, which were really great. He has wonderful concepts and is a real
poet. He had a lyric for 'White Flag', and I believe the entire chorus lyric was
intact. We wrote the verse melody first, which came fairly effortlessly, and then
tried different ways of doing the chorus. Originally, we had a different chorus
melody, but we knew it wasn't great, so we worked hard and finally got the chorus
melody that you hear today. I remember Dido saying, 'This is my first single.'

**What one thing do you wish you'd known at the start of your career as a
songwriter?**
I wish I could have spent my band years in Los Angeles or New York. I had two
great bands who played every club in San Francisco and northern California,
but never made it out of that scene.

What advice would you give on collaborating?
Work with talented people. Let your subconscious do as much work as possible
before craft takes over.

What's the most important thing in a song for you?
Lyric, melody and groove, in that order.

How many songs do you write in a year?
I co-write about 30 songs a year.

How many songs do you reject?
I don't reject any song. Other people do. If I finish it, it gets my stamp of approval.

How do you keep track of all your ideas?
I have a huge pile of lyric books going back to my teen years. When I started collaborating with recording artists full-time, things changed. I don't want to put words in their mouth; I expect them to have their own poetry and language.

How do you come up with titles for your songs?
Life gives you titles.

What advice would you give an aspiring songwriter?
Number one: be prolific. Start and finish songs. Try to write every day.

Number two: study the great songwriters. Read the great poets. Learn to play their songs.

Number three: learn to sing, whether you have a good voice or not, and play with other musicians.

Number four: never accept mediocrity or complacency.

Number five: go for it hard while you're young.

Seek and ye shall find.

Song Craft 2: Inspiration

'Creativity is the ability to look into the darkness and not blink.'
– Steve Earle, songwriter and artist

According to the *Oxford Concise Dictionary*, 'inspiration' is defined as:

1 (a) a supposed creative force or influence on poets, artists, musicians, etc, stimulating the production of works of art.

   (b) a person, principle, faith, etc, stimulating artistic or moral fervour and creativity.

   (c) a similar divine influence supposed to have led to the writing of Scripture, etc.

2 a sudden brilliant, creative or timely idea.

3 a drawing in of breath; inhalation.

In songwriting, inspiration is all of these. Even the third definition applies when a great idea causes the originator to pause for breath! Inspiration is the starting point for all songs and can be the launching point for a single lyric, a simple melody or even a complete song. Sometimes the sheer magnitude or totality of an idea will lead a songwriter to question whether or not their inspiration is of a divine nature.

Wayne Hector says:
'I'm a very spiritual person, so I believe that all songs are given to us. Although songwriters do work at crafting their product, the moments of true inspiration come out of nowhere. Often I'll think, "Where the hell did that idea come from?", but I'll never be able to give an answer.'

Eg White says:
'At what point does the credit for songwriting stop being appropriate? The verse for "Friday's Child" was inspired by a Dolly Parton song, while the bridge comes off a Johnny Cash song. Everybody steals their inspiration.'

THE SOURCE OF INSPIRATION

Where ideas originate is an enigma. The songwriter Will Jennings confesses, 'I don't understand half of what I do. There's a dreaming that goes on. I go into an altered state and I know it when I get there.'

There is a keen belief that songs are somehow always out there, waiting to be picked up. John Lennon famously said he was merely a 'receiver', and his contemporary Keith Richards from The Rolling Stones was also adamant that 'You don't create songs. They're not all your creation. You just sort of pluck them out of the air if you're around and receptive.' And the singer/songstress Tori Amos is of a similar mind: 'The songs just hang out. They come in and move in. To me, the songs already exist. I'm just an interpreter for them.'

The skill for these writers lies in being receptive and open to these ethereal ideas. This instinctive awareness typifies many of the great songwriters. Some people, it appears, are naturally more aware than others, but such a talent is attainable by all. The key is to recognise inspiration when it hits and then to do something creative with it.

STIMULATING INSPIRATION

> 'The creative process is a process of surrender, not control.'
>
> – Julia Cameron, The Artist's Way

Being receptive to inspiration is firstly a matter of a shift in perception. Inspiration is something that can rarely be forced or controlled. The process needs to be given dedicated time in order to allow an idea to develop, but the initial inspiration doesn't respond to pressure; any demands for instant ideas are sure to founder. The best songs or ideas are often not the result of routine or structure but the happy coincidence of accidents, surprises and a willingness

Frank Musker says:
'The old adage of genius being 10 per cent inspiration and 90 per cent perspiration is a good one to remember when you're sitting in a state of panic, staring at a blank sheet of paper without a usable idea in your head. The truth of the matter is that a professional writer will write hundreds of songs in the span of a career, not all of which will be masterpieces, but if he or she consistently aims to make each tune as good as it can be, then they're opening themselves up to the possibility of miraculous accidents – those occasions where you listen to your finished song, scratch your head in genuine amazement and think, "How the hell did that happen?" Or, "Did I really write this?" When that happens, it's as close to a mystical experience as most people ever get in a lifetime – more like being a channel than a creator; more like catching a fish than building something. Suddenly you're in possession of this complete thing, which has a life and a destiny of its own, and all you have to do thereafter is sit back and collect the plaudits and royalty cheques.'

to let go and try something new. 'Sometimes you've got to let everything go, purge yourself,' explains singer Tina Turner. 'If you're unhappy with anything, whatever's bringing you down, get rid of it. You'll find that when you're free, your true creativity, your true self, comes out.'

So, stimulating inspiration is about having the courage to let go. This courage comes as a result of being able to trust yourself and your instincts. A very effective methodology to developing this ability to trust your creativity is taught in Julia Cameron's multi-million-selling book *The Artist's Way* and is covered briefly here in 'Song Craft 4: Creative Blocks And How To Break Them'.

In a nutshell, if an idea feels right, just let it come. Don't question prematurely the validity of your inspiration. When you're struck by an idea, simply go with the flow. As songwriter Barry Mason once prophesied, 'Stream-of-consciousness outpourings can contain the seeds of greatness.'

One method of stimulating such freeform creativity is to engage in an activity that's completely different from purposefully trying to create something. This could be anything distracting – walking, driving, going to the cinema or treating yourself to a weekend away. Songwriter and artist Neil Young once revealed that he had 'written some of [his] best songs driving on a long journey, scribbling lyrics on cigarette packs while steering'. It's exactly this form of 'soft' mental distraction that allows the brain to work in the background, generating fresh ideas for songs.

The basis of these ideas will have originated from your conscious and subconscious observations of the world around you. However, there are also a few simple techniques you can use to take advantage of the many potential inspirational sources you might encounter. Bill Padley and Jem Godfrey from Wise Buddah offer their advice on encouraging this skill below:

Wise Buddah On Inspiration
'Ideas for songs are everywhere and anywhere – films, television, books, magazines, advertisements, conversations, your own life, or even someone else's. A fantastic place for song titles is the

---

Don Black says:
'I've never been one of those writers who looks for inspiration, because I was brought up working in Denmark Street, the British Tin Pan Alley for publishers. There were great old-time songwriters there who wanted to make a living. They wanted their five-quid advance, and they wouldn't get it unless they delivered a song.'

Wayne Hector says:
'Corrective writing is a really good way to write. Get the idea of what you want to say down without questioning it, then look at the result and begin to chisel and knock away all the bad things.'

headlines in Agony Aunt sections or the Letters pages in *Vogue* or *Elle*. As a songwriter, you have to be on the lookout all the time. You need to develop a mindset that is constantly aware. For example, when reading a book, every time there's a phrase that leaps out at you, write it down. Subliminally, your brain should always be working on that level, as a songwriter. We were in a pub about a year ago and some bloke said, 'It just takes a leap of faith,' and we went, *Click! That's it!* Another time, one of our co-writers was walking down the street and she saw a girl with a T-shirt on that said, 'I must not chase the boys,' and she went, *Click! That's it!* It's that sort of creative vibe you need to be hunting for.'

For many successful songwriters, inspiration is simply an astute awareness. Buddy Holly and his co-writer, Jerry Allison, were inspired by John Wayne's catchphrase 'That'll be the day' from the movie *The Searchers*. Bob Gaudio – the songwriter for The Four Seasons – was prompted to write the band's comeback Number One hit 'Who Loves You Baby' after hearing Telly Savalas utter the phrase several times during an episode of *Kojak*. Meanwhile, the Nashville writer Tom T Hall was prompted to write his biggest hit, 'Old Dogs, Children And Watermelon Wine', when an elderly waiter in a Miami hotel lounge kept repeating the phrase while serving him.

This method of 'awareness' also works when stimulating musical ideas. As well as magazines and films, a songwriter can plunder the wealth of their musical heritage while listening to every form of music they can get their hands on. Whether you particularly like the style or not, other artists' music can be an endless source of melodic, rhythmic and harmonic inspiration. Old music stimulates new music. Genres cross-fertilise to create new styles of music. We all know that rock 'n' roll was born out of the blues; in similar vein, sometimes a songwriter has to play the role of a cunning thief when creating a new piece of music. German-American physicist and Nobel Prize winner Albert Einstein couldn't have been closer to the truth when he wrote, 'The secret of creativity is knowing how to hide your sources.'

Pete Kirtley says:
'You probably have an hour of really, really creative flow in a day and the rest is just the mechanics – the oily-rags working away, fine-tuning little bits.'

Dan Hawkins of The Darkness says:
'When I get to that zone, it doesn't matter how stressed I am. If I'm playing on a guitar, with the aim to write a song, I forget about absolutely everything.'

So, inspiration is primarily down to:

- Allowing yourself to be receptive;

- Being open and uncritical of any ideas that do come;

- Constantly feeding your conscious and subconscious mind with data from the world around you.

WORKING WITH INSPIRATION

Once you have an idea, there are many ways in which to develop it into a full song, and the following 'Song Craft' sections will explore these. If you're finding it difficult to stimulate any form of inspiration to begin with, take a look at 'Song Craft 4: Dealing With Creative Blocks', which contains a number of methods for dissolving such obstacles to your creativity. When you do experience that moment of inspiration, there are a number of useful tips that you should consider when working with your ideas in their early stages:

1. Always write down or record any idea you have. The good ones will surface and make themselves apparent.

2. Never throw any idea away. An old lyric or melody might fit a future composition or spark a different idea and create a hit.

3. Don't question what you write; just let it happen.

4. Don't put songs aside halfway through due to fear of criticism.

5. Don't rewrite too much in the early stages of inspiration, as this can stem the flow of creativity and tarnish the special quality of an idea.

6. Don't automatically put ideas aside just because someone who sees or hears them isn't as enthusiastic about them as you are.

7. Don't shelve a song if the first recording isn't as good as you'd hoped it might be. If the material is strong enough, record it again and get it right.

8. Don't drop an idea because you feel that ideas by other writers are better. Use it on another occasion.

9. Be true to yourself and your ideas. For instance, don't try to create with other people in mind.

10. Always go with your gut reaction.

Guy Chambers says:
'I constantly fool around with riffs – often when starting a song I'll begin with a riff written by another writer and then attempt to subvert it into being mine, either by changing the chords around or moving a note or two. It was a combination of Moby's music and 'Praise You' by Fat Boy Slim, for instance, that inspired me to write the principal piano riff for 'Feel'. Another approach of mine is to compose a song based on the feel of a hit record. There will be certain songs that give me a particular buzz and I'll try to re-create that same buzz in one of my own songs. When I worked with Robbie Williams, for instance, we'd talked about composing a track along the lines of 'Sympathy For The Devil'. This inspired us to write 'Let Me Entertain You'.

THE SONGWRITERS:

HOLLAND, DOZIER AND HOLLAND ON INSPIRATION

Eddie Holland:
I consider creating music in the same way an artist creates a painting. Both are an inspiration – almost like divine inspiration, because it comes from nowhere. It's like you're driven by a force that causes you to go to a piano and then creates a spark. It's some force that guides your fingers from one chord to another, when there's all kinds of other chords you could have gone to. If a person breaks up that cycle, if some distraction occurs, you lose it. And sometimes you never find it again, because for that moment you were on a high, unique ride. To me, it's divine intervention.

It's the same process when I'm writing lyrics. It is still amazes me. At the time of Motown, I had no experience as a lyricist; I was learning at the same time as working. It was almost unheard of at that time to create that many songs that were successful with a person who had no experience, but I was on that same ride with Lamont and Brian. Sometimes I would write a lyric and I wouldn't know where in hell it came from. I fed on the inspiration of Brian and Lamont's music. I would listen to it over and over again until I became transfixed, and then I'd start writing. I didn't know what I was writing; it was as if I was in a subconscious state, channelling the same energies as those which had created the music.

The thing is, you can't force creativity, and of course Motown's demanding that I clock in from nine to five went completely against this. They felt that it disciplined the creative people, but there's no such thing when you're at the whim of a creative force beyond your control. Just because you have a person doing nine to five doesn't mean they're going to come up with a damned thing. Then one day one of Motown's office men threatened that if I didn't punch their clock then they'd find somebody else to write for Holland and Dozier. I said, 'Go ahead, but you won't find anybody like me!' That wasn't because I thought I was the best, or that somebody else couldn't do my job; I just didn't think they could work with Brian and Lamont as well as I did, because I gave something else to the pot, something beyond the writing of a lyric.

I stayed on that same spiritual high that Lamont and Brian were on when they wrote the music, working that feeling any time of day or night. I might go to sleep at one o'clock in the morning, then wake up three hours later and get back to writing lyrics. I knew that writing lyrics for this type of music took a certain type of tenacity; I just didn't believe that the average lyricist would do that, because I sensed that Brian and Lamont's music went beyond simply rhyming words and writing quickly. Like I said, it was a spiritual experience.

Lamont Dozier:
Ideas could come from anywhere, particularly for titles. 'Sugar Pie Honey Bunch', for instance – I got that from my grandfather, who got that from the South, where they used those sort of catchphrases. My grandmother had a beauty shop, and when all the women came in my grandfather would be working in the front garden, and he would flirt with them: 'How you doing, Ms Carey Sugar Pie Honey Bunch?' And when it came time to use some of these catchphrases, they came back just when we need something to say. That's what happened with this song.

Eddie Holland:
Lamont and Brian are like any other creative people. You don't just push a button and there it is. Lamont could be doing things at home or walking along the street and ideas would hit him, just like any other creative person. Brian would be the same way; it could hit him at any time. So at Motown we tried to create a relaxing, social environment. There was a room there that became our office, where we would meet and sit, sometimes laughing and joking, sometimes talking about other songs, sometimes just doing nothing. Then we'd fool around. Brian and Lamont would go over to the piano, and maybe an idea would come, but maybe it wouldn't. When an idea did come – say, for instance, if Brian was at the piano and something sparked him – then all of a sudden Lamont would be sparked too by what he heard Brian playing, and Lamont would jump in – almost scooting Brian off the piano – and begin to bang out an extension of what Brian was doing. Other times, the situation was reversed. Then they would play what they'd come up with without me, and I'd write the lyrics to their music.

When I was there, I'd listen to the ideas, and that would be my time to say, 'Well, I need this type of a structure to do the lyric. Can you extend those bars?' Furthermore, as I had a feel for singing, I could say, 'You need something more here, not only to write but to sing,' and I'd look for a certain dynamic movement. Mostly, I was there to enhance the structure, as far as the lyric was concerned.

Brian Holland:
When we say our songwriting was done this way or that way, often we just shot from the hip. Whatever felt good, that's what we did.

AN INTERVIEW WITH MICHELLE ESCOFFERY

What was your first experience of writing a song?
I was introduced to songwriting by my sister, Sandra. When I was about seven, I'd started singing with my sisters, who were already in a group, singing in churches and doing shows. By the time I was 11, I was singing and performing full-time, travelling and touring. We signed a deal with Atlantic Records in America when I was 16 and recorded the album while I was doing my A levels – absolute madness. That's when I started flexing my muscles in songwriting, writing two songs with my sister for our first album. She was the main songwriter for the group. Then one night she locked me in a room with her and said, 'You're not leaving until you help me write some songs.' I was in there from eight until two in the morning, and we wrote two songs. At first my mind was blank; I had no idea what I was going to write about. Then, once I got into it and we started bouncing off each other, it was a real buzz. When we'd finished, I thought, 'Wow! I've just created something.' The buzz stuck, because I'm still doing it.

When did you realise you were a songwriter?
I was always more comfortable with poetry. I used to write little raps, but I never thought I'd be a songwriter. The poetry ignited an interest for writing my own songs, but it was never in my head that I should try to be a songwriter. Then one of the very first songs that I wrote after that session with my sister was actually released, and I thought that maybe I did have a talent for songwriting and decided to give it a more serious go. In 1996, about five years after I wrote those two songs with my sister, I wrote Hinda Hicks's first single, titled 'I Want To Be Your Lady'. The moment I heard it on the radio was the moment I thought, 'I'm a songwriter.'

How did that make you feel?
It was amazing, hearing it on the radio and seeing the video on TV. It was even nicer to know that people liked the track. For me, that's where the satisfaction comes from, when people relate to something that you've written. If you can write something that can touch somebody in some way, it's all worth it.

At the time of the Hinda Hicks track, you were also in the girl group Truce. Did the performing get in the way of your songwriting?
At that time I was writing for Truce, Damage and an artist called Celicia, amongst others. It was very much an in-house situation at Big Life, the label I was signed to. Following the Hinda Hicks success, interest started to come from other publishers. The whole songwriting side became bigger than all my other musical aspects, and that's when I started to feel the pressure of being in a group and trying to be loyal to them but at the same time exploring my writing.

In 1998 I discovered that my desire to be a writer was stronger than that of being an artist. I found writing a lot more satisfying. Creating was more consistent, and it felt more natural to me than performing. It was also a potentially more long-term career than performing. People can be very fickle; one day they love you and the next day someone else comes along and you're on the shelf. As a songwriter, you can benefit from writing for all the latest 'in' artists.

As a 'top-line writer', how do you approach writing a song?
I normally start with the melody, and then the words will come with the melody. I write purely vocally. I have very good pitch, although it's not perfect. Then I build on top of the melody, singing the root and the rough melody before adding harmony and counter-melodies, trying to create chords with my voice. Then I take those ideas to another writer with instrumental skills and they put music to my top-line melody. I tend to have very clear ideas of structure. From being a singer, I've absorbed song structures naturally; I understand what's supposed to go where and when. I never question it.

Lyrically, my style of writing is very narrative. I try to tell stories in my songs. I always put myself in the place of that person and think, 'What would they be going through? What would be happening now if...*this* happened?'

Where do you think your songwriting ideas come from?
For me, it's novels – I read a lot – and through talking to a lot of people. It's one of the reasons why I travel so much. Good songwriting is about grasping ideas from people's experiences, putting that moment into a song and trying to convey that message or situation to everyone else. Sometimes you meet people and they touch you in such a way that you have to write about it, or there'll be a significant moment or comment that you don't actually pick up on until much later on. Then you write a song and think, 'Oh! *That's* what it's about.' To be honest, I haven't written much that's personal. Mostly, it's secondary experience.

What style of songs do you write?
Ballads come naturally to me. In the early stages of my career, I found it extremely hard to write uptempo songs, so I'd always veer towards ballads. I

did that for a couple of years. But as I became more involved in the industry and my experience of writing deepened, I began to write more uptempo material, more out of necessity than ability; the industry demands uptempo tracks to be released as singles. So I had to start honing my skills to write faster songs.

What do you enjoy most about songwriting?

I think what creates the excitement in writing is that you start off with a small idea and eventually it becomes this massive production. Your idea grows from something so small, recorded onto a little Dictaphone, to being this finished piece of music on a CD. For me, that's the buzz.

How do you find working with other writers or producers on your song ideas?

I'm quite liberal. I try not to be very precious when it comes to people adding music to what I've written. As long as it maintains the essence of the song and stirs the same feeling that I felt when I wrote originally it, I'm happy. If the music is completely different, or doesn't sound right, it usually has to change. If, on the other hand, melodically something needs to change slightly so that it fits with the music, I have no problem with that, either.

What do you look for in a collaborator?

I look for creativity and musicality. I prefer to work off chords and harmonies, so I need something organic to bounce off. Consequently, I find it more difficult to work with writers who are loop-orientated.

Whoever I work with also needs to be laid back. I work extremely well with people who are committed to music rather than to making money. I find that, when a musician or a producer is passionate about music, it creates something excellent, something outstanding. When the focus is more on money, the results tend to be formulaic.

Finally, any collaborator needs to be open to suggestions. They can't be too precious about their music. If someone is uptight and precious, someone who isn't willing to change any parts of their music, you get a stalemate, and that's just a waste of time for everyone. So songwriters have to be quite open-minded and explorative.

What skills have you learned by collaborating with other people that have helped with your songwriting?

Steve Robson taught me to let go, to allow for whatever comes out and, regardless of what it sounds like, just to go with it. He made me think on an entirely different level and go for notes that I would never have thought of.

Johnny Douglas taught me always to push for something better, and that it's OK to do that. He's the sort of person who, if you write something for him, will listen to it and maybe consider it all right, but that the idea could be better, and he'll ask you to come up with a better one. He helped me to stretch and stretch and stretch. To excel.

Do you ever doubt your ability to write good songs?
All the time. Sometimes I listen to a song that I thought was great and think it's awful second time around. I'm always trying to reach that next level. Sometimes I inhibit myself; I'll hear an idea and think, 'I could never write something like that,' or 'That's just too complicated,' or 'That's just the wrong genre.'

Over the last two years, I've let go of that obstructive way of thinking, and now I accept a good song as a good song, regardless of what genre it's in. I now steer myself into different genres, rather than sticking rigidly to R&B or pop. I listen to a wider range of music, take their different influences and inject them into what I do.

How was the Ivor Novello Award-winning song 'Just A Little' written?
That was written with George and John Hammond Hagan, who I write with a lot. It was just a normal day; we chatted away for a good portion of the day and finally said, 'Let's write something.' George started this beat, then put the guitar lick on it and I said, 'I like that.' I wrote the verse first very quickly, but he wasn't sure about it. Still, he put a bass line on it and the song became funky. From there, the idea in my head was that of an older person looking at a younger person and seeing how much sexuality they exude and yet aren't even aware of it. It's like, 'Damn, you're so sexy and you don't even realise what you've got. If you just worked it a little bit more, you'd have it all.'

We all had a great feeling about the song by the time the demo was finished. Then the track got out amongst the industry and soon there was this buzz going on around it. David Massey wanted it for Anastacia, and then Malcolm Dunbar wanted it for Liberty X. David put it on hold for Anastacia, who was in this dilemma of what she was going to do next, whereas Liberty X were ready to release it as their single. I was pregnant at the time, and it was all too much drama for me, so it was agreed that Liberty X would record the song if I could produce the vocals. This was because the song had a certain energy and needed to be performed with that energy in order to work. Having written the song, I knew what it needed to sound like, and I didn't trust anyone else to do it. So the girls came to my house five days after I had my baby, we rehearsed, and five days after that I went into the studio with baby in tow and we recorded it.

You appear to getting more and more 'cuts'. Are you writing more songs?
My publishers would say that, over the past two years, my hit rate has gone up, but in fact they've gone up because I've slowed down; I'm not writing as many songs as I used to. Before, I would write five or six songs a week and just keep pushing them out, whereas now I might write only two or three but they're

better songs because I've spent more time crafting them. Quality outshines quantity all the time.

How important is the vocal to the success of a song?
It's everything. Ultimately, it's the singer's performance that gets a song across. The vocals are what people are going to hear, and they'll relate to the intensity of the singer's emotion. The vocal line tells the story, and that's what creates and stirs a person's feelings towards a song.

How do you approach a vocal recording of one of your songs?
Before I record with an artist, I like to spend a little bit of time with them, just to understand them and their voice – where their voice can go and what I can do with it. I try to get into their head. After that, it's about making them comfortable so that they can let go enough to perform that song with the right intensity. Finally, it's their individual tone, projection and unique vocal quality that gets the song's point across.

I was classically trained, so I know all about breath control, the Alexander technique, etc. As a result, I've always been aware of breath control and how that carries you, as a singer. I'm also aware that many of today's singers don't know how to use their voice properly; they rarely know anything about breath control. Sometimes, just sharing two or three techniques can make all the difference in the world when an artist is trying to sing.

What three core techniques do you work on to improve a vocal performance of a song?
Diction, breath control and projection.

Diction is being able to hear the words that a singer is singing. Often, when someone sings, you don't actually hear a word, so it's important to make sure that their words are coming out properly, that they're enunciating, so that the listener can appreciate what the song's about. I just tell artists to smile so that they don't think about this aspect too much. When you smile and sing, the whole line comes out better.

Breath control is all about using your breath more effectively. For instance, if you're going to sing in falsetto, you have to use more breath than if you're singing in your chest voice. One of my favourite exercises is where you breathe in, put your arms up above you head and hiss out slowly, bringing your arms down at the same time. After a while, this allows you to control your breath, rather than pushing it all out at once.

Projection is about throwing your voice. Many people are very introvert when they sing; they don't sing out, sing forward. This is often to do with their posture. If you simply raise your chin a little bit and aim to hit past the mic, this will immediately make your performance much more confident, a lot stronger.

From this point, the vocal performance is all about creating tones and textures within a song.

Can you make a living as a songwriter?

Yes, a good living, but in the current environment it's more of challenge. The business isn't as creative as it used to be. Many tracks that are being released sound the same. The process is very generic and formulaic. Once you learn a certain formula that's successful, you can keep using that to sustain a relatively long career.

Has the fact that you're a woman made your career as a songwriter easier or more difficult?

Initially it was challenging, because I wasn't taken seriously. In fact, I had two barriers to deal with: as a female, I was expected to write airy-fairy songs, and as a black female I was expected to write just R&B or reggae. When certain writing opportunities come my way, I know it's because I'm black. However, that attitude is starting to change now as I keep surprising people with my results. Now, they don't have a particular place to put me; it's more a case of, 'If you want a good song, call Michelle,' which is the best position to be in.

What advice would you give an aspiring songwriter?

Always strive to be excellent and strive to be better. Sometimes you can listen to your own material and think that it's great, but don't settle; play it to other people and get them to point out weaker elements. You also have to be able to be your own critic and truly listen to your own work, honestly asking yourself, 'Is it as good as what I'm hearing on the radio? Is this better than what I'm hearing on the radio?' Be honest with yourself and your music. Obviously, you need to believe in yourself, but at the same time you have to know whether or not you can do better. If you start from that point, you can't lose.

After that, you have to stand up for what you think is right and good. If you truly believe that your song is great, stick by that. Eventually, the cream will rise to the top.

Have you had to make sacrifices to get where you are now as a songwriter?

Yes, but it's all relative. If you want to be good, you're going to have to make certain sacrifices. If you want to be a good drummer, for instance, you're going to have to practise. You might not get to go out as much as everyone else, but in the end you'll be a great drummer. Similarly, if you want to be a good songwriter, you've got to put in the practice. I don't see it as a major sacrifice, so I don't feel like I've missed out on anything.

Any time I've felt like giving up, I've got through it with my passion for music. I don't know if there's anything else in this world that can replace that feeling when you've done something good and creative and you just feel great about the whole process.

What do you get out of being a songwriter?
I get to express myself on a daily basis, which is good medicine for anyone.

Song Craft 3:
Melody Or Lyrics First?

This is the eternal question asked of every songwriter, and there are as many answers as there are songwriters...

'I hardly ever have the words first. A piece of a melody or a figure of some kind will be enough to get me going, and sometimes I'll be right there where you can see the end of it. Sometimes I won't, and I'll change it and go someplace different from where I thought I would.'

– Randy Newman

'On "The Wind Cries Mary", the words came first, and then the music was so easy to put there. The whole thing just melted together.'

– Jimi Hendrix

'We had the tune first every time. [Andrew Lloyd Webber would] play it for me and I'd pick it up. If I couldn't pick it up quickly, obviously it wasn't a very good tune. I'd tape it on a recorder...or if not, I'd have it in my skull.'

– Sir Tim Rice

'Music is much easier than lyrics, because lyrics are craft and music is an emotional response to a situation or a particular feeling, so I handle the lyrics first. It's important that I get as much of the lyric done as possible because, once the music is done, that's it for me. I'm trapped in that form.'

– Stephen Schwartz

'The tune inspires. It must come first!'

– Yip Harburg

There's simply no universally agreed-upon answer to this age-old question. The only real option is the one lyricist Don Black gives: 'Every time, it's different.'

Like all creative processes, writing a song is very personal. What works for one person might not work for someone else. The words can come out all in one go, or you might get just a title. Alternatively, you might have a melody going around in your head for ages but with no words. Perhaps you have a great drum beat but nothing else. You might even create an inspiring chord progression before the words or tune fall into place. If you're extremely lucky, the song writes itself, almost complete, and you have your own 'Yesterday'!

The crucial point is that you have a start, an idea, a seed for a song.

STARTING WITH THE LYRIC

This is often the preferred method of launching into the songwriting process. Whether you start with the title or a few key lines, the lyric can suggest the mood of the music by virtue of its subject matter. Here's an example:

> Late-night shopping in the old town mall,
> I meet a girl whose hair shines as golden as the Boston fall.
> Isn't she pretty? Isn't she something to behold?
> How I hope I'm still there when we both are old.
> I'm rising in love, rising in love with her first sight.

This lyrical extract is about love at first sight and is stylistically suggestive of either a ballad or a light pop song. The attitude of the lyric is positive, so the tone of music can reflect this. The person singing it is intended to be male, so this will guide the level of the vocal line. The rhythm of the lyrics is also helpful in evoking a melody, since words are more conducive to singing tunes than are indefinite humming or nonsensical lyrics. Therefore, starting with the lyrics is

Frank Musker says:
'Question number one at any social gathering where the subject of what you do for a living is raised: "What comes first, the music or the lyrics?" Stock answer number one – and thank you, Sammy Cahn – "The phone call." It generally gets a laugh and neatly avoids having to go into lengthy dissertations on the creative process which may be sincere enough but generally tend to make people's eyes glaze over. This apparently facetious answer does, however, make a fundamental point, which is that songwriting is a craft, something you learn from endless repetitions of a process to the point where it becomes second nature to you.'

Wayne Hector says:
'For me, the words and the melody usually come at the same time. They're more like ad-libbing sessions that I'll then shape afterwards. This was how it worked for "Flying Without Wings".'

an extremely progressive way of writing, as so much of a song's makeup is already in place.

STARTING WITH THE MELODY

Known as 'top-line' or 'top-down' writing, this method of composition begins solely with the melody line, with the lyrics and/or harmony being added later. Constructing a song this way frees the melody from the constraints that a chord sequence might impose on a songwriter. However, this approach is considered to be more difficult as it is so free-form, giving the writer nothing to latch onto, musically, although it can produce more original and memorable lead lines. Furthermore, if the melody is effective without reference to a harmonic base, it will sound even better once the chords have been added.

STARTING WITH THE HARMONY

This is a very common approach to songwriting and is certainly easier for people who are more proficient at their instrument than they are with words. Like lyrics, chords sequences can be very inspiring, suggesting a mood or an emotion and implying a melodic direction for the song. However, the disadvantage is that the melody can be controlled by the harmony to its detriment. The creative result may be a linear or horizontal tune that's quite monotonous because it sits within a very narrow range of notes.

Also, the changes in a chord progression can influence the length of the melodic phrases. Sometimes this can sound great, but it can have a tendency to box them in artificially or cut them up into bite-sized, disjointed pieces, resulting in a song that doesn't flow naturally.

None of this is meant to imply that composing from the harmony up is seriously flawed, but it's important to be aware of its potentially restrictive influence and to avoid creating dull lead lines that slavishly follow the harmonic progression.

Jiant (Pete Kirtley and Tim Hawes) say:
'It should be made clear from the start that, while there are sequences to writing a song, there is no formula for a hit. If there was, we'd be writing guaranteed hits every day. Jiant write by finding a groove that we both like and then jamming out ideas between the keyboards and the guitar. Once we find a nice feel that inspires us, we come up with a chorus between us. We tend to leave the song at this point, having created a basic backing track, and bring in the artist, who hopefully will then get excited or inspired by our ideas and finish off the song. The key benefits of this method of co-writing are that, firstly, the chorus – which is the most important part of a pop song – is assured, and secondly, it encourages commitment from the artist to the song.'

STARTING WITH THE RHYTHM

This is where a song is composed 'bottom-up' – ie from a drum loop, programmed drum pattern or live drum groove. It's a method of writing typical of genres in which the principal component of the music is the rhythm, such as dance, drum 'n' bass and hip-hop.

Working from a rhythmic base point is superb for creating a rhythmic lead-melody line. A common accusation levelled at much singer/songwriter material is that it lacks rhythmic interest and holds no groove in itself, and this approach to writing avoids this trap. Once a bass line has been played in, the song will start to take shape and various harmonic directions will become clear.

OTHER STRATEGIES FOR KICKSTARTING A SONG

If the methods outlined above don't work, here are four other techniques that can be employed to get the ball rolling:

Compose on a different instrument. Choose one of the methods above that you don't usually favour, or try an alternative or unusual instrument. By breaking the familiar patterns encouraged by your customary instrument, you'll be open to different chords and progressions and will be stimulated by the different sounds created by your new instrument. Then, once you've been inspired, you can either return to your preferred instrument to develop the idea further or continue composing with the new instrument.

Borrow from another song. This is an interesting technique for creating songs. Choose a song that you either like or admire and then choose one of the four options outlined above. If you're working on your own, analyse the song's structure and then, while keeping the same tempo, length and form, eliminate the

Don Black says:
'I know people like anecdotes with every song, but there are no anecdotes for "Born Free" or "Diamonds Are Forever". I simply got up in the morning, had a shower, sat down and wrote "Born Free". It happened to be a good day.'

Brian Holland says:
'The piano was the catalyst for all our Motown hits, the main instrument that we used to write our songs on. We would get together and start hashing out any ideas we had. Lamont [Dozier] and I came out with the melodies and Edward [Holland] came in later with the lyrics.'

chords, melody and words and come up with a new harmony, lyric and lead line. If you're collaborating, either take the original lyrics and write a new melody or listen to the melody and write a different set of lyrics. Then take your finished piece and give it to your collaborator and ask them to come up with a new piece of music or set of lyrics, but without revealing the original source of inspiration.

Write within self-imposed limits. This is a good method for developing the skills that are covered in this book. Decide on a specific key, tempo and style, and then set yourself the challenge of composing a song that's perhaps only two minutes long. Alternatively, write a piece that has an unusual time signature, an odd number of bars for the chorus or a key change.

Write a pastiche. This is a common method of writing in the pop industry when working to a brief. The aim is to write a song in the style of a particular singer or band. For instance, try to write a song that sounds like Britney Spears' 'Baby One More Time'. (Be very careful not to plagiarise using this technique!)

TIME TO CRAFT

Once an idea has taken shape, the primary stumbling block for most songwriters is what to do with it next. How does that single lyric, catchy melody or funky groove grow into a fully formed adult song? This is where the true skill of a songwriter comes in. For country-and-western artist Hank Williams, it's a process guided by external forces: 'I pick up the pen and God moves it.'

Bill Bruford says:
'I started writing alongside the team of Jon Anderson and Chris Squire, with whom I'd formed the multi-million-selling band Yes. Jon was my first big influence. His attitude was that the songwriter was really the main man, and instrumentalists were subsidiary to that role. It's the classical conception of the composer's wishes being communicated to the functionaries through a conductor, with the composer always remaining the key to it all. Jon would say, "It's OK playing those drums, Bill, but the real deal here is the music that I'm about to write and, even more important, the words I'm about to sing." Having said that, his method of songwriting then largely consisted of playing something highly questionable, with absurd lyrics, while defying anybody else in the room to do better, at which point the guitar player would probably suggest an alternative chord or sequence, and then somebody might propose a different lyric. By sheer abrasiveness, the so-called composition that had started life as a dismal, ugly thing began to turn into something that sounded pretty good, largely through the skill of the functionaries in the room: the musicians.'

For George Michael, it's a matter of experimentation: 'I go round and round the backing track and go with stream-of-conscious gibberish until something gets me. Within that, I'll start to grab melodies and lyrics, and I'll find that things I've been thinking about will coagulate into a song. There's never any point in a song where I sit and think, "What should this be about?"'

Fleetwood Mac's Lindsey Buckingham says that, in his experience, 'You may start off with a certain intent and start putting strokes on the canvas, but because it's intuitive the colours will lead you in a direction you didn't expect to go. Or you may have a preconception of what the song is going to be, melodically and otherwise, and end up in a totally different place. And that's probably more the norm than the exception.'

Brian Wilson, meanwhile, has a different approach to the songwriting process: 'When I've thought out a theme, I go to the piano and play "feels", which are rhythm patterns and fragments of ideas. Then the song starts to blossom and become a real thing.'

For the lyricist Hal David, who built his songs bit by bit with Burt Bacharach, 'Most of the time the idea comes to me with a title, but often it occurs in two lines. I see things in hunks, like an eight-bar phrase, rather than specific sentences. With Burt and me, the question asked most repeatedly was, "What do you think of this? What do you think of that?" Either my lyric would set him off to write a melody or vice versa.'

With Sir Paul McCartney, there is no resolute songwriting routine: 'Every time is different, and I like to keep it that way. I don't have any set formula, so each time I'm pulling it out of the air.'

For most songwriters, a great deal of crafting, experimentation and editing has to take place before a song can start to take shape. The initial idea can sometimes be the easiest and quickest part of the whole songwriting process. It's as much a matter of hard work as it is that initial burst of creativity; that old axiom of genius being 10 per cent inspiration and 90 per cent perspiration holds true for songwriting.

Rarely will a song arrive fully formed and complete; such songs are the exception rather than the rule, although they're typically the ones that prove to be the best! In those cases, the trick is to keep the song as true to the original vibe as possible.

With songs that don't arrive in such an immaculately conceived state and need to be worked into a song, the method of crafting is again very much a matter of individual preference, a very personal art.

For every songwriter, there will be a different approach to crafting an idea into a song. Completed songs are the direct result of the personality of the songwriter, his or her particular methods of working combining with the creative pull that a song naturally exerts.

As I mentioned earlier, the 'Song Craft' sections in this book cover various songwriting techniques with regard to writing lyrics, creating melodies and crafting songs. It's therefore important that you choose only those methods and creative processes that appeal to you and your personal mode of working.

'He Has Your Eyes And His Mother's Nose'

The offspring of a songwriter, or a songwriting team, often bears their distinctive characteristics, forever marked by its creators' methods, choices and personal preferences. Consequently, songs become identifiable with certain artists and writers. The favoured techniques of such artists as Elvis Costello, Neil Finn and Paul Simon leave perceptible audio 'watermarks' that distinguish their songs from those of other artists. This individuality implicit in their songs generates that songwriter's particular appeal and, if all goes well, results in their commercial and personal success.

It is because of such personality traits inherent in a song's development that many songwriters preach the principle of being honest to yourself when songwriting. Indeed, this attitude invariably produces the best results because, rather than imitating another's success and consequently sounding false, a writer's song will be unique, true to them and relevant to others.

A Final Point

It's important for a songwriter to consider the amount of time he or she spends on a song's concentrated development. As Tim Hawes, songwriter with Jiant, observes, 'There are only X amount of creative hours in the day. I don't think you can push yourself hour after hour; at some point, you've got to step back and be objective.' The duration of this peak period of creativity will be personal to each songwriter, but there's a general agreement of about three hours. As Sir Paul McCartney points out, 'You start to fray at the edges after that.'

THE SONGWRITERS:

WISE BUDDAH

We always start with a title, because we find it easier and quicker to write a finished song when we have a firm direction and conclusion. For example, let's say that your song is going to be called 'My Dog Is Dead'. In the first verse, you have to describe that you've got a dog and that something tragic happened to it. So really you've already written your first verse and your bridge; you already know where you're going with the song. On the other hand, if you start your first verse without a title and just say, 'I have a dog,' you have no idea what's going to happen to that dog by the time you get to the chorus, by which time you could be in all kinds of trouble: the dog could run off and marry a giraffe or do anything. But if you start with the title, you have your first verse written. Furthermore, by that point you've formulated a conclusion; obviously the dog is dead, but there's a whole set of adventures for the dog to have achieved before it carks it.

So we start with the title. We don't have a strict modus operandi after that point; we'll write the chorus or a verse or whatever feels right next. However, we do like to make a point of writing songs, as opposed to making records – in other words, songs based on a piano and/or a guitar, as opposed to focusing on the production and sounds and thinking, 'How great is this hi-hat pattern?' A song should be able to be played on a guitar or a piano and sung by someone. The production is the icing on the cake. From there, we'll suggest ideas to each other: 'How about this, with this rhythm? And then these chords could go here. And if you try that, I'll do this…' It's the same with the lyrics and the production.'

A MONOLOGUE WITH BILLY BRAGG:

MUST I PAINT YOU A PICTURE?

TALENT BORROWS, GENIUS STEALS

Like most kids, I wrote poems at school, but, unlike my classmates, I didn't stop. When I was 12 or 13, I was asked to read out on local radio a poem I'd written. That recognition gave me a lot of confidence, and I think I realised then that I must have had some sort of aptitude for this. I'd failed all my O Levels, apart from English Language – the poets' O Level – in which I got grade A.

At the time, songs were the art form that emotionally moved me. I enjoy all sorts of music, but the music that appeals to me most is that which offers a different perspective on life, whether that's a relationship or a socio-political situation. So I found myself in my early teens, listening earnestly to a strange mixture of singer/songwriters, particularly Simon And Garfunkel and black American pop music like Motown and Stax. It was an interesting mixture, the folk narrative of singer/songwriters and the socially conscious attitude of the black music of the Civil Rights movement. They taught me that songwriting was the best means of expressing myself. So, as a songwriter, I specifically began to write songs that were aimed to challenge people's view of the world.

I didn't come from a political background. There was no politics in my life when I was growing up. I sometimes wonder where it came from. Perhaps politics chose me. The only thing I can think of is that every day my father brought home the *Daily Mirror*, which I read voraciously from cover to cover. That was back in the late '60s, when it was still quite a campaigning newspaper, and it prepared me for Bob Dylan.

It was early Dylan that I was drawn to, particularly the album *The Times They Are A-Changin'*. A school friend swapped me his father's copy of the album for my copy of The Jackson Five's *Greatest Hits*, and this exchange sums up what happened to me as a songwriter, as eventually I found myself drawn more towards the political side of things, rather than the 'ABC, 123' route. Dylan's album had come out eight or nine years before I got hold of a copy, so

I was hearing it a little out of context, but the starkness of it and the immediacy of the lyrics spoke to me.

I was the only person I knew who'd heard Bob Dylan, and consequently I identified with him in a very personal way and took it upon myself to play him to other people. That music that you discover yourself means so much more to you than something that's rammed down your throat every day by TV adverts.

I could see how Dylan wrote his songs as a craftsman; it was an easily understandable form. But I could never work out how to write a Jackson Five song like 'I Want You Back'; that was such a complex song. Conversely, I could work out how to write something like The Miracles' 'The Tracks Of My Tears' because it was a very simple song. Holland, Dozier and Holland and those other songwriters were coming out of jazz and, although they were writing what sounded like simple songs, they were using very complicated techniques inside them. It was more difficult for me as a songwriter to identify with that, whereas the straightforward form of what the singer/songwriter does – which is much more firmly rooted in folk music – was a lot more accessible, especially if, like me, you wanted to write your own songs.

I'd been learning to write songs by analysing how my favourite songs were constructed and then trying to write songs like those. I was writing for about five years before I learned to play the guitar. From the age of about 12 to 16, I was filling up exercise books with songs, just keeping them in my head. Then the kid next door taught me how to play guitar, which enabled me to sing my songs to a musical accompaniment. This in turn allowed me to write more songs like those by Jackson Browne or Smokey Robinson, and then eventually those by people I really admired, like Elvis Costello.

Eventually, at just about the time of punk, I came up with some songs that weren't easily identifiable as Rolling Stones or Rod Stewart soundalikes. They were 'Billy Bragg' songs, in that I'd taken all those influences and put something new into the equation, so that they weren't 100 per cent original but they had enough originality to stand out from the other songs I'd been writing.

The idea in developing your own style is that you manifest your influences by resynthesising them into something that's new and touches people who perhaps haven't heard those phrases before. As Morrissey later told me, 'Talent borrows, genius steals.'

WALK IT LIKE YOU TALK IT

As a songwriter, I've written more about relationships than I've written about politics. However, because so many people do write about relationships, the fact that I've written about and continue to write about politics – which isn't particularly fashionable – means that people think of me as a political songwriter. I don't mind that, but I do object to being dismissed as a political songwriter. Anyone who's been to a Billy Bragg gig or bought one of my albums will know that it isn't just a load of polemical hectoring; there's a lot of humour and humanity as well in what I do, because I'm trying to reflect the world as I see it. Sometimes that's the world in my bedroom, sometimes the world in my life and sometimes the world out there.

It's like TV. During an entire evening's TV, there'll be soaps, documentaries, news, a footie programme. Songwriting should be like that. You shouldn't just write one particular song; you should try to engage with people by using different forms of music and coming out with different ideas.

I like to think that the reason I write a song is because I've got something to say that I don't see reflected in the mainstream discussion or media, and that I have an interesting way of saying it. Now, that interesting way of saying it may be:

> How can you lie there and think of England
> When you don't even know who's in the team?

In this, I'm trying to say something about relationships, on where the people in those two relationships connect. In my song 'Take Down The Union Jack', I'm talking about identity, what it means to be an Anglo-Saxon in england.co.uk. To ask a question like that in a song, or the lyric above, is to bring those kind of questions to bear in a more engaging way than perhaps writing an straightforward intellectual speech would be.

And why am I writing about those things? Because they're situations I've found myself in. I've found myself in that strange situation, somewhere between sex and football, and found myself wondering, with all these England flags around without ideology any more, if I should be writing about Englishness. When I first started writing about Englishness, it wasn't very popular among my audience because people on the left generally don't want to talk about those issues. From my position, I'm trying to point to where I think the fire is: 'Look! There's something happening here about the English and British identity, whether we like it or not.' I could easily keep writing songs about how horrible Margaret Thatcher was, but time has moved on, and now this issue of contested identity is back on the agenda and I find myself compelled write about that.

But can such songs make a difference? I wouldn't do it if I felt they couldn't. But it's not a difference in the sense that they can change the world. That's not the job of a singer/songwriter; that's a much more complex situation to try to work in. But I know from my own personal experience that your perspective of the world can be changed by listening to music.

The first political thing I ever did was to go on a 'Rock Against Racism' march to see The Clash in 1978 at Victoria Park in Hackney. When we got to the park, there were loads of bands, one of which was The Tom Robinson Band. When Tom sang out, 'Sing if you're glad to be gay,' all these guys around us started snogging each other. I was only 19 or 20, from Barking – a working-class suburb of London – and I'd never seen an 'out' gay man before. My initial feeling was, 'Why are they doing this at a anti-racist gig? This is about black people, not about gays.' But it didn't take long for the penny to drop and to realise that the fascists were afraid of anybody who was in any way different. It wasn't just about black people; it was about anybody who challenged their narrow world view, and I promised to be as different as I could and always challenge them. So I came away from that gig with my world view changed, and a whole new perspective on politics opened up to me by reading the newspaper, watching the TV and going to school. So, yes, I know from personal experience that it's possible to bring about change through songwriting.

Of course, such a change doesn't happen at every gig, but it's possible in certain circumstances, particularly for young people in their early teens to late 20s who have that enthusiasm for wanting to make the world a better place. They're choosing popular culture as a way of expressing their identity. By connecting with them early on, in the way that I connected with The Clash, it's possible to set someone out on a road that leads to certain world-changing conclusions.

I'm currently involved in trying to reform the House of Lords. If that happens in the way I'd like, it will be partly due to the fact that I was a Clash fan in 1977. I'm not saying that, if it wasn't for The Clash, there wouldn't be a reform of the House of Lords, but what I'm doing traces back to there. That's as worthwhile as writing 'The Tracks Of My Tears'.

I believe that, if you're going to write political songs, you have to come up with the actions to match the songs. For instance, as part of the album *The Internationale*, I went to Nicaragua and subsequently recorded 'Nicaraguita'. The gigs I did for the Nicaragua Solidarity Campaign were part of my effort to match my actions with the lyrics that I was writing about, because if you're going to write these songs, you can't just write them in isolation or you're just exploiting these people's misery. You've got to walk it like you talk it.

The songwriters I respect – people like Phil Ochs and bands like The Redskins – try very hard to do this, but it's very difficult in popular music because not only do you have the marketing aspect to it but you're always swimming against the tide of fashion. This was just as true in the 1980s, at the height of all the activity that we took part in, which all seems incredibly political compared to where we are now. At that time, all the older journalists were sitting around saying, 'Well, this is nothing like 1968,' and that's fair enough, as it *wasn't* as intense as that, but equally a very important aspect of political songwriting is that you can't write political songs in a vacuum. There has to be an argument going on in society so that you can reflect it. The Civil Rights movement in the USA didn't happen because Bob Dylan wrote 'The Times They Are A-Changin''; it was the other way around. Dylan was reflecting what he saw on the streets.

Now, when people say to me today that bands aren't political anymore, I say, 'How could they be?' It's much more difficult now to see the ideological nuances that were so clear in the 1980s, when there were two political parties that were diametrically opposed to each other. We don't presently have such a situation.

FOUR AND TWENTY WAYS

My father had been in India during the World War II, and when I was a kid he used to read me Rudyard Kipling poems, many of which were about being in the Indian Army. One of them contains the line 'There are four and twenty ways of constructing tribal lays/And every single one of them is right,' and that notion stayed with me. There is no one right way to create a song; there are hundreds of ways to put a song together.

People often ask me, 'Do you write the music first or do you write the words first?' but it just doesn't work like that. Sometimes it all goes *bang!* on a piece of paper and you've got it; another time you're carrying around a tune or a lick in your head for a couple of years before you find a lyric that does it justice; and another time you've got two lines of a lyric that are really good while the rest of the song just doesn't quite fit.

With regard to lyrics, it is very true that words matter, so much so that when I was working on the Woody Guthrie project, where I only had to come up with the tunes to Woody's lyrics, I found it quite simple. I suddenly realised that, for me, writing the music is all about feel; there's nothing technical there at all. I feel it, I pick up the guitar and I can do it while watching the footie. I've written tunes, semi-consciously playing chords, while concentrating on the TV. I'm very fortunate like that. I don't read music, but I can play by ear. I can just pick up, recognise and follow tunes, which is a great skill to have. But the lyrics I sweat blood over.

At the moment, I have three or four tunes for which I have the choruses, I know what the lyrics should be about and I know which way they should go, but I can't settle on them. I'm supposed to be playing them this weekend for the 20th anniversary of the miners' strike and I'm thinking, 'Oh shit! I've got to finish this.' This kind of situation is much more difficult, because when you're writing a political song you really have to get the sense right. When you're writing a love song, you can use a little more poetic licence. I've never wanted to write those incredibly earnest love songs; I've always wanted to reflect the human failings in a relationship, the things that we never quite live up to.

I have a song called 'Life Of The Lions' that begins, 'I hate the arsehole I become every time I'm with you.' Here, what you want the listener to do is think, 'Oh, yeah. I recognise that. I know that feeling, although I've never articulated that to anybody.' The best way to do that is to articulate a feeling that touches a lot of people – not by finding the lowest common denominator but by holding a mirror up to yourself and being as honest as you can about yourself and your failing. If you can express those failings in self-deprecating terms, that makes the listener more receptive to what you've got to say.

Even some of my political songs are ironic, like 'Waiting For The Great Leap Forwards', particularly the way I sing it now. The problem with a topical song is that sometimes you have to change the lyrics. In some ways, that song was me trying to come to terms with mixing pop and politics. There were huge struggles going on in Britain and the world in the 1980s, and I was writing songs to try to reflect that. I wanted to make sure people realised that it's a much more difficult thing to change the world. It's the audience's responsibility to change the world, not the music's.

Song Craft 4:
Creative Blocks And
How To Break Them

'The old adage of genius being 10 per cent inspiration and 90 per cent perspiration is a good one to remember when you're staring at a blank sheet of paper without a usable idea in your head.'

– Frank Musker

The Three Laws Of Creative Blocks

1.   All writers experience creative blocks.

2.   Blocks have nothing to do with your talent or songwriting ability.

3.   A creative block is a subjective phenomenon that has no basis in the real world.

A creative block is that sense of impasse or feeling that all your ideas have dried up. It can manifest itself in a number of ways, from that rising, choking panic that freezes your writing abilities to that cloying, thick mud that seems to clog up your brain, slowing your thinking down to the pace of a snail. A creative block can even occur in the middle of a song. Whatever form it takes, a creative block can be a disturbing thing for a creative person to encounter. However, if it does strike, remember the Three Laws.

Creative blocks often stem directly from your own unfeasible expectations, or your perceived expectations of others, towards your work. It all boils down to a desire to be in control of a process that's far more complex and intangible than you'd like it to be. The piano man, Billy Joel, explains his own experiences: 'The thing you don't have control of is writing. You have to pull it out of yourself. You pace the room with something like the dry heaves, having no control over the muse, horrified that it won't come. All that's out there with you is the piano, this big black beast with 88 teeth.'

Writers' block can even result from the opposite symptom: too much writing. Songwriter Wayne Hector explains: 'Writers' block sometimes can be attributed to the fact that you're doing so much writing that you can't tell the difference between what's good and what's bad anymore. You lose your perspective.'

In the following section, Wise Buddah offer their wisdom on the creative block:

> **Wise Buddah On Writers' Block**
>
> People find it difficult to believe that we can just go to work at ten in the morning, write a song with a bunch of strangers and then go home at five, but it is actually really easy. The ideas don't stop coming. We never get writers' block, because we're disciplined. We try not to allow ourselves to meander. We don't allow ourselves to go down avenues without knowing exactly what's at the other end.
>
> Writers' block comes only when you try to patch up that wounded animal of a song. You have an idea that you're not convinced about, yet you try to convince yourself that it could actually be good if only you spent another few hours on it, whereas what you really should do to avoid the writers' block is to discard that idea and move on.
>
> Because of this, we're not at all precious about the songs that we write. We're completely comfortable and honest about the fact that some them aren't going to be as good as others. That's just part of the process.
>
> Writer's block happens only when you're fixating on one thing and have run out of ideas for it. At that point, work on another idea. Do something entirely different. Change your focus a little. Writer's block is not a terminal disease!

BREAKING THE BLOCK

If writers' block isn't a terminal disease, what are the cures for this pathological inconvenience?

1.   **Time.** First, give yourself time to create. Give yourself freedom to let the ideas come. Give yourself space for inspiration to strike. Pressurising yourself to have an idea

NOW isn't going to encourage the muse! Songwriter and artist Ali Tennant explains his method of negotiating blocks: 'When a block creeps up, I really listen to myself and pull back from songwriting for maybe a day or two, and then go back to it. I don't try to force it; the minute you do that, it just leads to more block, so step back from it, like an artist from his easel.'

2. **Take a break.** If you're truly stuck, try a change of scenery. Go for a walk, visit the gym, catch a movie or even take a trip away for the weekend. 'Remedying a block is about stepping back, forgetting music completely and doing other activities,' says Wayne Hector. 'Then, when you feel that writing bug coming back, you can start again, and you're excited to be there.'

3. **Work on a different idea.** Don't limit yourself by freezing completely just because one song is causing you problems. Instead, put it to one side and work on another project. Often that simple shift of perspective sparks solutions for your problem idea. It's a technique that works for songwriter Rob Davis: 'If I get writers' block, or an idea isn't working, I go for something new, or take the rest of the day off and come back fresh to it the next day.'

4   **Clustering.** This is a good trick for getting the creative juices flowing again and involves simply writing down a central thought or idea (ie 'sunset'), circling it and writing down every thought triggered by it, joining them up with lines. (It's a technique that's also known as 'brainstorming' and using a 'spider diagram'.) Each word or phrase can then be the centre of its own cluster, and in this way you can create a substantial number of ideas and images from which to develop songs.

5. **Quantity versus quality.** This method is a matter of opinion. Some professional writers believe that quality should always be the focus of song creation, and yet this way of thinking can cause a block for writers as they kill each idea before it's had a chance to grow, since it's measured against an impossibly high benchmark. Look at it this way: an athlete doesn't run a marathon without first training at shorter distances. It's more important in the initial stages of creation, therefore, to put

down as many ideas as possible. Once you've done this, you can take the time to work on the quality afterwards. It's a technique that Wayne Hector endorses: 'Corrective writing is a really good way to write. Get the idea of what you want to say down without questioning it, then look at the result and begin to chisel and knock away all the bad things.' It's therefore my belief that talent is sometimes a question of quantity; as Jules Renard wrote, 'Talent doesn't write one page; it writes 300.' So don't feel pressured to write a hit song every time. Just write for the sake of writing. Trust in yourself that the ideas will come out and they will – some good, some bad. The more you write, though, the better chance you have of composing a masterpiece.

6. **Banish the censor.** We all recognise that little voice in our head that questions everything we do or create. We've all experienced that nagging spectre of doubt that quashes our ideas before they've even touched the page or sprung from our lips. It's often so unignorable that it drowns out our real voice and we fail to recognise who is truly speaking. This 'censor' is the root of all creative blocks, and it's so deeply embedded in our psyche and self-confidence that it's one of the most difficult and most creatively rewarding blocks to remove. To deal with it effectively, however, would require a whole other book, although there are a few techniques you can try out immediately. These deal with the core fear that the censor feeds on: the fear of writing.

The principal fear for most writers is that what they write will be bad. This sets up an immediate presumption, which becomes a self-fulfilling prophecy because the writer visualised a bad piece of writing, which confirms their initial presumption, and so on, degenerating into a negative-feedback loop. The first technique for remedying this situation, therefore, is simply to start thinking positively. Believe that you'll write a good song. Secondly, learn to 'free write'. One method is to choose a topic – for instance, love at first sight – and then to write freely on the topic for five minutes without stopping, thinking or questioning what you're writing. Look back over it once you're done, and if anything stands out, write that in your ideas notebook, but don't chide yourself if any or all of it didn't turn out particularly well. Instead, try another topic until something does catch your eye.

A similar method is to turn off your computer monitor and type blindly. This is a wonderful way of banishing the fear of writing. After all, if you can't see it, how can it hurt you?

7.   **Be honest with yourself.** The philosophy of writing for yourself rather than someone else has been raised time and again by professional songwriters, so don't try to please others by creating what you think they want you to create. After all, they often don't know themselves. You'll get better results if you're honest with yourself and write what your heart tells you. (Incidentally, country-and-western writer Tom Hall objected that his blocks come 'when producers, publishers, agents and managers are on my back'.)

8.   **Have fun with songwriting.** Don't take the process of writing a song too seriously. An attitude of grave determination can be just as damaging as a fear of writing. Enjoy the creative process. Enthusiasm is a potent tonic to inspiration. As the Kate Bush once said, 'The real buzz is in the songwriting.'

THE ARTIST'S WAY

As mentioned in point six above, the topic of the 'censor' deserves a whole book to itself – and, in fact, such a book exists. Novelist, playwright, songwriter and poet Julia Cameron's book *The Artist's Way* is a seminal book on the subject of creativity. A truly inspirational and provocative volume, it offers 'a course in discovering and recovering your creative self'. Its approach and style is quite spiritual and alternative, so it might not appeal to everyone. However, the results of following the course can be profound and the ensuing flood of creativity can be almost overwhelming.

If you're experiencing seemingly insurmountable creative blocks or you simply wish to tap into your hidden reserves of creative energy, you'd be well served by dipping into this book. Reading it requires significant commitment, but the majority of readers benefit from the experience.

DE-BLOCKING EXERCISES

If you're in the unhappy situation of being blocked and you need some ideas to kickstart yourself, try these de-blocking exercises:

Cluster – Write down anything that comes into your head in relation to words such as 'gold', 'sunset' and 'California'. Spend two minutes on each.

Memory Lane – Choose one item that holds a significant memory, is inspiring to you or creates strong emotional reaction. Free-write for five minutes, using the item as inspiration.

Instant Lyrics – Free-write the first four lines of lyrics that come into your head using the following subjects as starting points. Give yourself one minute for each.

- Free-write on the title 'Don't Let Go'.
- Free-write on the lyrical topic of days of the week.
- Free-write using all the following words in the lyric: 'blue', 'drink', 'fold'.

FIVE KEY SONGWRITING PHILOSOPHIES

1. Creative blocks are all in the mind.
2. Believe that you can write a great song.
3. Banish the censor.
4. Write for yourself.
5. Enjoy the experience.

Mitch Murray says:
'Every songwriter suffers from the occasional dry or stale period, but the bespoke tunesmith is usually able to weather the storm and rebound with another string of successful songs. The inspiration of writing for different artists keeps him fresh and motivated. When a singer/songwriter or group writer dries up, however, you've often lost both the act and the songwriter forever. One of the reasons why Cliff Richard – who doesn't write songs – has remained consistently successful is because he's free to choose the very best material from whatever source.'

Brian Holland says:
'Writers' block, whether it's with a lyric, a painting or a melody, occurs when you're trying to force that "divine inspiration". It becomes an issue as you're forcing the force.'

THE SONGWRITER:

WAYNE HECTOR

In my experience, many songwriters consider a day without writing a song to be a failure. One of the unwritten rules that Steve Mac and I agreed early on – and I think this is why we've had considerable success together – is that all we had to do together as writers was come up with one great song a week. If we could come up with 52 great songs in a year, we'd be winners.

The problem for many songwriters is that they press themselves to write a song. They rush the process and consequently don't focus on what they're saying or writing. They might come up with 400 songs by the end of the year, but 399 of them aren't that good or well-crafted.

If you're going to write a song, aim to write a great song. If you fall a little short, that's all right; shoot for the moon and, if you miss, you might hit a star instead.

I spent a long time writing mediocre songs and putting considerable pressure on myself for no reason at all. Creative people all have a habit of doing that: we shoot ourselves every time we get something a little wrong. Part of being a professional songwriter is being able to realise that the creative process isn't something that you can force; it will either come or it won't. If the ideas don't

Lamont Dozier says:
'Everybody talks about writers' block, but I find that that's a cop-out. Writers' block is a non-issue; it is purely an issue you have with yourself, inside your own head. If you keep writing, you are going to break the block. There is no such thing as a block. If you stay with it long enough, something will come out. You might not like it, but something will come out.

'In this situation, it's truly a matter of 'let go and let God'. Sometimes less is more. When you back off a situation and let loose of the bond, you'll let that force or intervention come in of its own accord. You should let inspiration come down to you, rather than always reaching so hard for it. The muses are always there; you just have to know when to give, when to play and when to fold.

'If somebody was taping us with a camera when we were working, they'd say, "These people are crazy," because they'd see us playing around with musical ideas and then all of a sudden we'd simply start playing cards or something, because nothing great was coming and we didn't want to force it. I might then wander back to the piano, and suddenly a spark would come.'

come to you on a particular day, relax. If you start to think, 'What's wrong?', that leads to cramping up mentally, which leads to even more self-doubt, and so you end up in a vicious circle with writers' block. You have to be prepared that sometimes you'll write great songs and sometimes you won't. Even when you're at the top of the game, every writer knows that they'll have peaks and troughs in their creativity. They might compose ten hit songs one week and then none for another for ten years. That's just how it goes.

Wise Buddah (Bill Padley and Jem Godfrey) say:
'We're quite brutal when we write. We're very focused on getting things done. If it takes us more than two or three hours to write a song, there's something wrong with the song.

'We're not afraid to spend half an hour on an idea, then decide it's rubbish and move on. Instead of trying to rescue a wounded animal of a song, we put it down and get working on another idea. It's important for people to realise the importance of this attitude, because we've seen people spend too much time working on an idea that's actually not very good to start with, yet they'll still attempt to make it better. If you ask 100 songwriters who have written massively successful songs how long it took them to write those songs, the answer would come back, "No time at all." The best songs always seem to be the ones that happen most naturally and quickly.

'We're not doing nuclear biology here. Professional songwriting is a job. We'll have an artist or band for one day, and that's it: the song has to be finished, at the end of the day. So, if we're working on an idea and it's not working, we move on. We don't have the luxury to take three or four days to write a song.'

An Interview With Pam Sheyne

By Ruth Graham

What did you get up to before becoming a songwriter, and how did you feel about your previous jobs?
I started singing and playing guitar at the age of seven. When I moved to the UK, in 1980, I worked in various cover bands, then as a session singer. A big turning point for me was singing backing vocals for the Pet Shop Boys' world tour in 1991. After that, I started concentrating on my songwriting and got my first publishing deal in 1992.

How do you define a great song? At what stage do you know that you've written something that has 'hit' written all over it?
A great song is one that simply cannot be ignored. It subconsciously gets into your system and won't leave you alone, whether that's because of a strong melody or a memorable lyric. It undoubtedly moves you. However, I've written songs that I thought would have been hits and they're weren't, so songwriters aren't always the best judges of their own work.

How did your songwriting eventually take off? What was your first break?
My first publisher – who has subsequently become my manager and my husband – had total belief in me from the start. He taught me the importance of networking and has encouraged me to think globally as a songwriter, which has resulted in many writing trips abroad. I know my career wouldn't be the same without him there to kick my butt.

So after all that butt-kicking, what was your first cut?
My first cut was Sheena Easton's 'All I Ask Of You', co-written with Chris Eaton.

Generally, do you find the words or music come first? Or both together? And do you prefer to write alone or with other people?
I usually get a title first, though sometimes a melody will take the lead and I'll fit the words to that. I love co-writing, too, the process of bouncing ideas

back and forth and discussing all the directions you could take a song, lyrically.

You've enjoyed great success, but what do you honestly think the chances are for aspiring songwriters just starting out these days?

It's difficult for today's songwriters to get their songs cut, especially if they have no previous track record. That has a lot to do with the nature of the business; there's music, and then there's business – two very different things. There are fewer artists and record companies taking on outside songs; record companies tend to have their favourite producers, and they sign production deals with them to make sure that they work with many or all of their artists. This is where I think the business has shot itself in the foot. Some production teams are under so much pressure to deliver their work so quickly that we start to hear substandard material coming through. I think that could change if we all looked at the bigger picture and realised that the song should always be king.

The music business is all about contacts, and any aspiring songwriter should go to all the songwriter clubs, like Tony Moore's Bedford Club; Tony's a great believer in encouraging new talent. Also, *SongLink International* magazine (www.songlink.com), run by David Stark, has a load of information for songwriters and has definitely been a big help in my career, especially when I first started out.

Are you ever compared with the American writer Diane Warren? And would you ever have had the chutzpah to sell your songs like she did? (She admits to driving past Lionel Richie's house with a megaphone and shouting, 'I have a song for you!' until he came out.)

No, not really, though I think Diane is a great writer. I guess if I ever get desperate enough for a cut in the future, I might do something crazy. I tend to leave that bit for my manager and publisher; that's their job.

What song are you proudest of to date?

Obviously, Christina Aguilera's 'Genie In A Bottle' was a really proud moment and my most successful song so far, but one the songs of which I'm proudest I wrote with Cece Winans and Adam Anders. Cece has been a favourite of mine for years, and to have the opportunity not only to write with her but to hear her beautiful voice on one of my songs was a dream come true.

On average, how much time do you spend away, working on all these great hits, over the course of a year?

It's different each year. We might be in the US for three to four months.

Are you able to shut off when you're not officially working?

Music is both a blessing and a curse. I have trouble sleeping sometimes, especially when I've been in the studio all day, hearing the same song over and over again. It can drive you crazy. It normally takes me three or four days to shut down when I'm not working.

How do you split a song when there are several of you working on it? Are there ever any arguments?
Usually, if you're in a room with, say, two other people, you split it three ways. It's a different scenario when I work to a track and write the melody and lyrics on my own. Yes, naturally there have been arguments over splits in the past, but very few, and they've always been resolved.

Do you have any career regrets?
Not really. Everything I've done to date has been a learning curve and has hopefully made me better at my craft. I just love being a songwriter.

SONG CRAFT 5: SONG STRUCTURE

'I'm always trying to push the boundaries of form, but I don't analyse it when I'm writing.'
– Tori Amos

As I mentioned earlier, songwriting isn't about rigidly following rules, and the only way to improve at it is actually to do it. However, it's still important not to try to run before you can walk. An aspiring songwriter needs to understand the key elements that comprise a song and their respective functions before experimenting on their own.

It's the same as if you wanted to build a high-performance sports car. Without any instructions, you'd need to dismantle a fully functioning sports car to see how it worked, and what parts did what, and what elements made the car so fast before then building your own car based on those criteria.

Songwriting should be approached in a similar fashion: first of all, you need to deconstruct a great song and analyse what makes it great. Then you can construct your own song based on those values. Once you have a theory of what makes a great song and have purposefully put it into practice a few times, this understanding will become part of your subconscious and you'll start to apply the techniques you've learned without thinking about them. As Jem Godfrey of Wise Buddah says, 'Awareness comes from experience.'

THE BUILDING BLOCKS

The form of a song is made up of several sections, principally:

1. The intro;
2. The verse;
3. The chorus;
4. The bridge (or middle-eight);
5. The pre-chorus;
6. The instrumental break;
7. The outro.

1. THE INTRO

The intro usually establishes the tempo, key, style and mood of the song, although there are of course exceptions (ie the intro to Frankie Goes To Hollywood's 'Two Tribes'). Its key function is to grab the attention of the listener.

The length and style of the intro will depend a great deal on the target audience. If the song is aimed at a radio audience, for instance, the intro will usually be brief, catchy and immediate, while if it's written for a dance-club environment or a chillout album it will be longer and more progressive, building the listeners' expectations. If the song is destined to be an album track, the intro won't be as restricted by the commercial considerations of radio as a single cut would be, and so more aesthetic values can be adopted.

A song can start with any of a whole range of intros, including the following:

- Guitar intro ('[I Can't Get No] Satisfaction, The Rolling Stones);
- Vocal intro ('Hound Dog', Elvis Presley);
- Horn intro ('Crazy In Love', Beyoncé);
- Drum intro ('Superstition', Stevie Wonder);
- String intro ('Come On Eileen', Dexys Midnight Runners);
- Spoken intro ('Mambo No. 5', Lou Bega);
- Synthesiser intro ('Born Slippy', Underworld);
- Unusual instrument ('Get Ur Freak On', Missy Elliot);
- Sound effect (school bell on 'Baggy Trousers', Madness).

Whatever the intended audience and opening instrument, the intro needs to be distinctive. Ideally, a listener should be able to recognise the song within the first five or so seconds. All of the songs listed above fulfil this criterion.

2. THE VERSE

The verse is the principal section for conveying the song's subject matter, or 'story'. The lyrics contained here prepare the listener for the chorus. Generally, the melody will stay the same from verse to verse (with perhaps small variations to allow for emotional expression), allowing the listener to concentrate on any lyrical developments.

The common mistake for an inexperienced songwriter to make is to treat the verse as simply a way of getting to the chorus, and consequently not spending enough time crafting the melody or lyric of the verse. In the words of Björn Ulvaeus of ABBA, 'Don't think a good chorus is enough to disguise a bad verse.'

3. THE CHORUS

The chorus is generally the 'hook' of a song, expressing the song's fundamental meaning in one succinct and memorable statement. It often contains the song's title, and its lyrics and melody generally remain the same with each iteration. Occasionally, the chorus might alter lyrically as the song's story progresses, or in order to allow for a turnaround at the end.

Another common fault of inexperienced songwriters is to write a verse and call it a chorus. Typically, songs written this way sound like a series of verses strung together. The chorus must be strong, it must stand out and, above all, it must be memorable.

The repetition of the chorus is the key to establishing a hook (a single melody, rhythm or lyric that grabs the listeners' attention), and it's best to keep it as uncomplicated and memorable as possible. It's also preferable to reach the chorus as early as the song allows. As the industry adage goes, 'Don't bore us; get to the chorus!'

4. THE BRIDGE (OR MIDDLE-EIGHT)

The bridge provides a change of gear, re-invigorating the listeners' attention by introducing a fresh melody and new lyrical direction or perspective. It should therefore sound as different as possible from the other sections without sounding obviously out of place. The lyric should provide an alternative point of view on the song's subject or else summarise the song in another way. Both lyrically and melodically, the bridge should be another high point of the song.

While it can prove beneficial in a song, having a bridge is entirely optional. As Paul Weller explains about his own songwriting technique, 'In some ways I write in an old-fashioned way, because I always have middle-eights in my songs and not many people do anymore. It's usually just verse and chorus.'

The bridge is also known as a 'middle-eight' because, traditionally, it was eight bars long and came somewhere in the middle of the song. Generally, the

Guy Chambers says:
'I often leave the middle-eight until the end because generally you won't know how much of a bridge a particular song will need or what the middle-eight needs to accomplish until all the verses and choruses are in place. Sometimes a bridge needs to be really short and punchy; other times the bridge can be much longer and really transform a song. A good bridge should make the last chorus sound somehow different, because by the time you get to the middle-eight section a listener will have heard the chorus at least twice, possibly three times. As a songwriter, you need to twist the song so that it sounds fresh to the listeners' ears – and the bridge is the tool with which to twist the last chorus. That's one of its main purposes.'

middle-eight appears only once in a song, and these days, while it doesn't have to be eight bars long, it is still relatively short (usually between 4 and 16 bars in length).

The hardest thing about a bridge is writing a good one. 'It's quite an art to write a good bridge, because it lifts you into another area,' explains film composer John Barry. 'It's got to be a variant on what you've done before, but you have to come up with some surprise so that, when you get back to that last familiar strain, it's almost like falling into something.'

5. THE PRE-CHORUS

The pre-chorus is used extensively in contemporary music to generate further interest in a song and to augment the dynamics. It's also known as the 'pre-hook' and is also very often referred to as the 'bridge', just to confuse matters. Whatever you prefer to call it, its effect should be to lead up to the chorus by building melodic and lyrical tension. In the pre-chorus, the melody usually stays the same, if repeated, although the lyrical matter might change, if appropriate.

Examples of effective application of the pre-chorus can be found in Michael Jackson's 'Billie Jean', 'She Will Be Loved' by Maroon 5 and The Bee Gees' 'Staying Alive'.

6. THE INSTRUMENTAL BREAK

The instrumental break, or 'solo section', provides a contrast to the vocal sections. Used less frequently today than on older records, it can be exploited to develop a song's dynamics, to express the emotional height of a song in a way the vocal might not be able to, or to provide breathing space before a new vocal section kicks in. It can occur over the harmony of the verse, chorus or bridge, or it might even have its own chord progression.

Justin Hawkins of The Darkness expresses his thoughts on the classic guitar solo associated with rock music: 'With a guitar solo, you can take a song somewhere completely different than could ever be reached with a vocal line. The guitar solo definitely makes a real difference to the way The Darkness arrange their songs. We take great care that the solos are in the right place and that they're played for the right amount of time.'

7. THE OUTRO

The Outro is often overlooked by songwriters, yet this section is as important as all the previous elements, because this is the last part of a song that the listener hears, so it's important to leave them with a good impression.

In pop music, the outro is traditionally a repetition of the chorus, slowly faded out, the idea being that the chorus is hammered home into the memory of the listener. It's an effective method, but there's so much more that can be done with the outro. For instance, it can serve as a hook in itself, sometimes being even longer than the rest of the song. The classic instrumental outro is Lynyrd Skynyrd's epic guitar solo ending their song 'Free Bird', while the all-time great singalong outro is the 'na na na' chant closing The Beatles' 'Hey Jude'. With these classics in mind, it's clear that you shouldn't neglect the outro's potential to enhance a song.

HORSES FOR COURSES

'I think of my new songs as pop songs, as they are arranged to the standard pop format: verse, chorus, verse, chorus, solo, bad solo.'

– Kurt Cobain

As a songwriter, you'll encounter different methods of identifying the various sections of a song. One popular system is to label the sections alphabetically. For the purposes of this book, a verse is indicated by the letter A, a chorus by B, a bridge by C, a pre-chorus by D and an instrumental by the letter E.

Songs can be arranged in an infinite variety of ways, but there are five common commercial arrangements:

1. A A A
2. A A C A
3. A B A B A B (variation: A B A B C B)
4. A D B A D B
5. A A B A B B

1. A A A

This is the simplest and oldest structure for popular songs. Traditionally, it's used for ballads since it's a great vehicle for 'story songs', where the lyric has priority and doesn't require the repetition of a chorus section to augment it. The slower tempo implicit in the ballad style allows for duplication of the melody without fear of monotony. The title of the song will often appear in the first or last line of each verse, with the vocal hook generally being the last line. Examples of the A A A form include Jim Webb's 'By The Time I Get To Phoenix' and 'I Will Survive', sung by Gloria Gaynor.

2. A A C A

This was once one of the most popular arrangements due to its concise and flowing form. It allowed for greater expression than A A A format thanks to the inclusion of a bridge section. The form favours slow to mid-tempo ballads due to its length and is exhibited in the songs 'Raindrops Keep Falling On My Head' (Burt Bacharach and Hal David), 'Yesterday' (John Lennon and Paul McCartney) and 'Song For The Asking' (Paul Simon).

3. A B A B A B

This is the most widespread structure in contemporary music, particularly in the fields of rock and pop, due to the dominant repetition of the chorus, establishing a strong hook. Songs written in this form will often open with a chorus or half chorus in order to have the greatest impact possible. The downside of this form, however, is that it can rapidly become monotonous, so it's often adapted to include a bridge – ie A B A B C B – to offer a melodic and lyrical contrast. Bob Dylan's 'Knocking On Heaven's Door' is an archetypal A B A B A B song, while Maroon 5's 'This Love' offers an example of this format with a bridge inserted, which forms the traditional blueprint for power ballads. As Justin Hawkins from The Darkness explains, 'The reason why everyone [writes songs] like that is because it's the best way, so don't be afraid of using a traditional arrangement. Don't try to be clever for the sake of it.'

4. A D B A D B

This form offers the excitement of three different melodic sections and so avoids the potential monotony of the A B A B A B arrangement. Used well, this structure can be the most effective of all. The Bee Gees' 'Staying Alive' and George Michael's 'Faith' are just two successful examples of songs written in this form.

5. A A B A B B

Not as common as its predecessors, this arrangement relies on a strong verse lyric to carry the song until its first chorus. The form suits more uptempo songs since the chorus will be reached quicker than in a ballad. Allowing for the instrumental interlude, Van Morrison's 'Brown-Eyed Girl' is a good example of this structure.

CHOOSING THE CORRECT FORM

'Structure is really important. Some I've really had to work at; others have come really quickly. Keep the whole thing interesting – that's what it all comes down to.'
– *Paul Weller*

The choice of form is an important consideration for four reasons:

1. A particular structure will help to express certain songs more effectively than other forms. A deeply lyrical song, for instance, might be better served by a more consistent arrangement (A A A) or a form that emphasises the verse (A A B A B B).

2. Some forms are more suited to a particular style or genre of music. Pop and rock songs, for example, favour the A B A B A B format.

3. A song might have a dynamic development that overrides its fundamental structure. U2's 'With Or Without You' is commonly cited as an example of a song that builds to a climax and then ebbs away without formal reference to a structure.

4. A song might be written with live performance in mind. Such songs will be influenced by the emotion of the crowd rather than an imposed format. Many of Bruce Springsteen's early songs, such as 'Rosalita' and 'Jungleland', have complex structures and feature several dynamic moments that reflect their evolution on the stage rather than in the studio.

While a song's arrangement might develop naturally as part of the creative process, just as Tori Amos indicated at the start of this 'Song Craft' section, it's important to reconsider the song's initial structure in case there are alternatives that are better suited to the song's final effect.

Inexperienced songwriters tend to limit their creativity through the habit of using just one or two preferred formats, which can result in the creation of songs in unsuitable structures; what would work brilliantly at three minutes, for instance, is overlong and tedious at five minutes. In this case, not only is the writer faced with a rewrite of the song but they also have to handle a

Lamont Dozier says:
'The definitive sound of Holland, Dozier and Holland comes from the fact that we take our listeners on a musical journey. With our songs, you actually hear a beginning, a middle and an end. From the beginning of a courtship to a dramatic finish, from the inception to the birth, from the cradle to the grave, our songs are a journey.'

restructuring. This can be quite a hard habit to write yourself out of.

The key consideration is to make structural decisions based on a firm knowledge of the options and factors that might influence them, including:

Tempo
A slow song might suit a shorter form, while an uptempo track might need a number of sections to help sustain the musical interest.

Lyric
The mood and subject matter will perhaps dictate the tempo and, therefore, the form. ABBA's 'Dancing Queen', for example, creates an impression of a slow, intimate ballad, while Louis Armstrong's 'We Have All The Time In The World' would be inappropriate for a fast dance song.

Another lyrical consideration is the number of words used. A simple lyric works well in the dance genre, as demonstrated in DJ Otzi's version of 'Hey Baby', but a wordy lyric might prove difficult to sing over a high-tempo dance track, producing incomprehensible results.

Style
The particular genre of a song will greatly affect its final arrangement. There are certain traditional forms for each genre, and the expectations of each generally need to be met. As a rough guideline:

- Pop music gets to the chorus immediately, is fast moving, rarely includes a solo section and has several repetitions of the chorus (eg B A B A B B).

- Country/ballad songs tend to be narrative, having greater emphasis on the verse, taking longer to reach chorus (if there is one) and being more drawn-out (eg A A B A C B).

- Hip-hop tracks often open with hard-hitting intros followed by long verses of rapping and insistent chorus sections, and rarely feature a bridge (eg B A A B A A B A A B).

- Dance music favours builds and ebbs, the emphasis being on the rhythm and instrumentals, while verses are almost superfluous and the chorus serves as the high point (eg E A D B E A D B E)

- Rock/metal anthems emphasise the song's guitar riff and contain one or more solo sections, the structure traditionally being a basic verse–chorus arrangement (eg E A B A B E B B)

- Chillout songs favour long intros and slow builds, and are traditionally instrumental and longer, less defined structures that echo the classical genre.

Ultimately, however, the correct form is that which feels right to the songwriter. If a song written in a simple verse–chorus form works, don't try to be clever with more intricate forms as it will lose its uncomplicated appeal. If a song demands more complex or unconventional structures, follow your muse and it could result in your opus, like Led Zeppelin's 'Stairway To Heaven' or the mini-operas of Meat Loaf's 'Bat Out Of Hell' or Queen's 'Bohemian Rhapsody'.

Once you've experimented with each of the different forms, they'll become second nature to you and you won't need to analyse each structure to know which one is best for your particular song. Furthermore, if you get into a musical rut at any point, applying your knowledge of the different structures is often a valuable method for finding innovative solutions to help you finish a song that has lost its creative momentum.

LISTENING ANALYSIS EXERCISE

In order to develop your comprehension of song structure and an understanding of which arrangements are more successful for certain types of song, make a concerted effort to listen to a variety of hit songs and see if you can work out their form using the alphabetical system of identifying the different sections listed above.

THE SONGWRITER:

MICK LEESON

A pop song isn't a solid three-minute lump; it's a series of building blocks joined together – hopefully seamlessly. I might be oversimplifying here, but there are two basic song structures.

The first one is verse/bridge/chorus – 'She Loves You' – or simply verse/chorus, like 'Hang On Sloopy' or 'California Girls'. This may or may not add a middle-eight, eg 'Please Please Me'.

The second structure is chorus/chorus/middle-eight – 'I Cannot Help Myself', 'Roll Over Beethoven'. Here, the song doesn't resolve to a chorus but gets its title and hook into a hybrid verse/chorus that can be repeated melodically but varied lyrically, so structure two will usually start with the hook and repeat it much quicker than structure one.

Arguably, the quicker you get to the hook or chorus, the better, and structure two generally gives you more, quicker. But structure one doesn't always hang around, either. Look at 'Please Please Me'; by one minute and three seconds, we've had verse/bridge/chorus twice and we're into the middle-eight (ie 'I don't want to start complaining'). Many hit songs don't get to the chorus until 50 seconds in or later.

The hybrid 'chorus'-as-verse song (structure two) can cram the hook in even more. In 'I Cannot Help Myself', the title doesn't happen in every 'chorus' (although the backing vocalist sings the line when the lead doesn't sing it), but the 'chorus' is repeated six times in a row (once as half instrumental) before the middle-eight comes in at one minute 40 seconds. And after that we get the 'chorus' three more times, making a total of nine times in the song.

Generally we want to hear the hook as early and as many times as possible. Bill Withers, for instance, doesn't mess around; in 'Ain't No Sunshine', the first 'chorus' is over at 29 seconds. He repeats it, then breaks into 'I know, I know, I know...' and then repeats the 'chorus' again and the song is over.

Sometimes a verse/bridge/chorus song will start with the chorus rather than keep the listener waiting the 40 or 50 seconds it would take to get there. Your hook, title or whatever the song revolves around, musically or lyrically, should be a piece of magic that you want the listener to hear as often, or as optimally, as possible. Structure is therefore the medium by which you maximise your song idea.

Wise Words From Wise Buddah

1. Avoid 'narrowcasting'.

Many aspiring professional songwriters make the mistake of 'narrowcasting'. Some writers compose songs that, when listened to all in a row, sound like their solo album, because they're all of a particular genre/style. If you're going to be a professional songwriter, you have to write songs that will appeal to different artists. If all the songs sound of a similar style and genre and you can't get one of those tracks recorded by an artist, then the rest of your songs will have no chance, either. You can't become blinkered and shoot at one target all the time. Write an R&B song one day, then do a rock song the next, then a ballad, and you'll make your songwriting better by pushing yourself.

2. Keep your songwriting simple.

Don't have thousands of sections. Keep the songwriting devices very simple. A trait of inexperience in songwriting is to write three songs in one. If you have three great ideas, write three great songs.

3. Focus your songwriting.

At the same time as not narrowcasting, focus each song that you write. We went through a phase of just writing songs, and all you end up with then is a CD full of songs. It's really important to target a song at an artist or a genre. We do a lot of writing with artists, which is much easier than just writing songs, because if you're writing with an artist then there's a point to the song, a goal. If the artist is involved, we know who the song is destined for, as opposed to just writing a song and then going, 'Oh, we've just written a song. Now, who can that be for?'

4. Always, always, always keep a Dictaphone.

Take a Dictaphone with you everywhere you go. Don't assume that you'll remember that great melody you sang ten minutes ago. You won't. When you're writing a song, run the Dictaphone, because somebody will sing something and you'll all go, 'What was that that you did?' We've lost a couple of really good songs because we weren't recording.

5. Network.

Ultimately, it's about who you know. If you befriend a person who knows a publisher, for example, and that person loves your track, you've already sidestepped 2,500 other submissions for that same project when he or she passes it on to their publisher with their personal recommendation. You need to meet people who know the right people in the industry because, to be honest, if you posted a track to a major label unsolicited, the chances of it getting listened to are remote.

SONG CRAFT 6: THE LYRIC

'I'm a true believer that it's not what you say, it's how you say it. And I damn sure know how to say it!'

– Shaggy

The purpose of the lyric is to communicate the meaning of the song.

For some people, the skill of lyric writing comes naturally; lyricist Hal David, for instance, reveals that, 'When I hear music, I hear words, just as I assume the composer hears music when he listens to lyrics.' For others, it's a matter of devoting the necessary time to the craft.

Many songwriters struggle with writing lyrics; their words seem banal or inaccurate in their expression, or they have difficulty in putting down words that generate the appropriate impact. This can be due to the unattainable expectations that a songwriter sets him or herself. Really, lyric writing is a completely separate skill to composition and therefore requires a great deal of attention and crafting. As a consequence, some musicians shy away from lyrics, concentrating on their musical strengths or de-emphasising the lyrics' importance in the song.

'When I write a song, the lyrics are the least important thing. I can go through two or three different subjects in a song and the title can mean absolutely nothing at all.'

– Kurt Cobain

However, the lyric can be the most significant element in a song, and for three reasons. Firstly, a song with a good lyric will stand proud from all the other songs vying for attention. Publishers, in particular, are sensitive to the quality of the lyric. Deke Arlon, CEO of Sanctuary Music Publishing, states, 'For me, the most important element of the song, and the biggest influence for me as a publisher in selecting songs, will always be the lyrics.'

Secondly, a good lyric can be extremely helpful during the composition process. The lyric can evoke the mood and direction of the song, and the rhythm of the words can even suggest a possible melody. Songwriter Stephen Schwartz says, 'I always get down as much of the lyric idea as possible first. I think music is much easier than lyrics, because lyrics are craft and music is an emotional response to a situation or a particular feeling. It's therefore important that I get as much of the lyric done as possible, because once the music is done, that's it for me. I'm trapped in that form.'

Thirdly, lyric writing is one skill within the craft of songwriting that can be improved upon quickly and with striking effect. There are a number of straightforward techniques that can be easily applied in order to focus and craft a lyric. Before exploring these techniques, however, a common misconception about lyrics needs to be cleared up.

ARE LYRICS POETRY?

'Poetry is music in words, and music is poetry in sound'
– Thomas Fuller, 17th-century British scholar, preacher and author

This question compares two very different modes of expression and is therefore difficult to qualify. While some lyrics – for instance, those to Bob Dylan's 'All Along The Watchtower' – do have poetic qualities, such as metaphor, imagery and phrasing, they are inextricably tied to the music. Their effect and meaning are reflected and affected by their musical context. As a further example, the lyrics to 10cc's 'I'm Not In Love' are clear in their meaning, but the poignant and longing quality of the music undermines the singer's denials, making them sound more like excuses than statements of fact.

True poetry is intended to convey its meaning and emotion purely through the context of the words. It's often too complex to be set to music and has much less tolerance for clichés and common, everyday images. Conversely, a banal phrase such as 'get on up', when delivered by a singer of the calibre of James Brown, can sound fresh and full of meaning.

The key to this debate is the concept that poetry is written to stand alone

Wise Buddah (Bill Padley and Jem Godfrey) say:
'We get the actual writing of the lyrics over with pretty damn quick because, if a songwriter deliberates for hours on end about whether it should be "and" or "the" or "or" in a lyric, they're actually missing the point of pop music. We're not trying to write songs that will go down in history as pieces of art; we're writing pop songs. There's nothing bad about pop songs. We're simply writing good pop that will sound great on the radio.

'It's important to bear in mind the target audience for your song. When Bill was a presenter on radio, for instance, there was no point in him going on the radio at seven o'clock in the morning for a breakfast show and having no idea who he was talking to. He might say all the wrong things and not reach the right person in the right way. So, our advice to any writer is always to have an understanding of who your target audience is. There's not a 100 percent rule to this, but the song should match the audience of the artist you're writing for. There's no point in getting too clever if the artist's previous songs weren't lyrically complex. You wouldn't necessarily put Sting lyrics into a record for Steps, for example, because this would just sound out of place.'

and be complete in its effect, while lyrics invariably need music if their true and full meaning is to be expressed. The legendary songwriter Stephen Sondheim puts this more eloquently: 'One difference between poetry and lyrics is that lyrics fade into the background. They fade on the page and live on the stage when set to music.'

TEN GUIDELINES FOR WRITING LYRICS

'My lyrics are only obscure to the extent that they're not taken directly from the dictionary of writing songs. They're not slavish to the lyrical rulebook, so you'll never catch me singing, "Oh baby, baby, yeah." My only priority is to use lines and words in a way that hasn't been heard before.'

– Morrissey

Lyric writing can be very personal, and as I established at the beginning of this book, there are no rules, only guidelines. The following guidelines reflect the elements that characterise respected songs and so are useful in helping a songwriter to craft their lyrics into the best possible form. However, since every lyric is different, these guidelines should be individually tailored to the lyric in question.

1. WRITE PERSONALLY ABOUT A UNIVERSAL IDEA

The best lyrics describe something that everyone has experienced in his or her life but doesn't know quite how to express. They offer a fresh perspective on a common idea, situation or emotion. Occasionally, they might express a brand-new concept, although this is now relatively rare, since most topics have already been covered.

Jiant (Pete Kirtley and Tim Hawes) say:
'The scope of the songwriter/production team now tends to be limited to the realms of pop, country and R&B, and in the UK musical taste has dictated the predominance of pop. These pop acts are generally aimed at younger (and younger!) audiences. Consequently, market tastes have an impact on the songs that are written. On a lyrical level, such songs aren't going to be particularly creative or emotionally deep. The younger listener doesn't wish or need to delve into areas of darkness, of light and of shade and all the different emotions that complex lyrics may express. With typical guitar bands, where the listening audience is more mature, there's always room to be more expressive. When you're an artist like Bowie, for instance, you can delve deeper. It's a different approach to writing pure pop songs. In pop writing, you have to work to very strict "briefs" – short descriptions of what the track is expected to sound like – so it's more about creating a vibe with the words than ploughing new lyrical territory.'

'The whole love topic has been torn to pieces. Everyone has done it. As a songwriter, you have to re-invent the wheel every time.'

– Ali Tennant

The key to a great lyric is the concept of making the universal personal, offering a unique take on a universal experience. However introspective or clever the lyrics become, people need to be able to relate to them. The best lyrics express either a clear attitude (eg Aretha Franklin's 'Respect'), a particular experience (The Temptations' 'My Girl') or a single emotion (Katrina And The Waves' 'Walking On Sunshine').

2. USE A MEMORABLE TITLE

A strong title ensures that the general public and the music industry will remember your song. It should capture the attention of the listener. If you had a choice between two songs, one called 'I Love You' and another titled 'Let's Get It On', which would you rather hear first?

The title should summarise the essence of the lyric and, ideally, be identifiable after one hearing, so that the listeners know what to ask for when they go to the record shop to buy it.

Many professional songwriters, such as Rob Davis and the Wise Buddah team, start by creating a title, since it's helpful in providing a focus for the composition process. This demonstrates just how significant it should be to your writing. At the very least, the title needs to suggest the subject (eg 'Baby, Please Don't Go') or convey the mood of the song (eg '[I Can't Get No] Satisfaction').

Intriguing titles are an excellent way of attracting a listener's attention – for instance, 'You're So Vain', 'Me And Mrs Jones', 'Mama Told Me Not To Come', 'The Future's So Bright (I Gotta Wear Shades)'. Titles featuring unusual word combinations are also effective – for instance, 'Karma Chameleon', 'Strawberry Fields Forever' and 'Champagne Supernova'.

Another common technique in creating a title is to use everyday phrases, such as 'Knock On Wood', 'I Heard It Through The Grapevine', 'Don't Get Mad, Get Even' and 'Another One Bites The Dust'. To make the idioms more interesting, some writers twist them, and here 'Stop! In The Name Of Love', '(Love Is) Thicker Than Water' and 'Unbreak My Heart' are all good examples.

Remember, a title cannot be copyrighted. One effective technique for generating a title, therefore, is to take an already successful song and twist its title, just as some writers have done with everyday idioms. It's probably best not to copy a title outright, however, since this can lead to confusing the listener and the possible misdirection of your royalties by collection societies.

3. Keep It Simple

One of the most common factors of successful songs is that they focus on a single idea and build the song around that. The writers of such songs haven't muddied the waters with references to other emotions, experiences or ideas. A classic fault of many aspiring songwriters is that they throw too many ideas into one song. This, as well as adopting too abstract an approach to a lyric or an inconsistency in emotion or attitude, simply confuses the listener.

In good lyric writing, the aim is to...

- say only what you need to say;

- say clearly what you mean.

Songs need to be accessible if a listener is to be able to relate to them, so keep to a single attitude, experience or emotion and focus on that.

The plot of a well-crafted lyric can be summarised in one short sentence – for example, a man sees a beautiful woman in a red dress and asks her to dance, only to realise that she's actually his partner (Chris de Burgh's 'Lady In Red') – or a single emotion – for example, longing ('Ain't No Sunshine' by Bill Withers).

4. Focus The Lyric

To achieve this simplicity and clarity, it's necessary to focus the song's lyrics. The best way to achieve this is to ask yourself a series of questions in relation to the lyric. To begin with, carefully consider the following:

- Who is singing the song? Are they male or female? Is it you or someone else?

- Is the song being thought internally or expressed out loud?

- Who is the song being sung to? A lover? The general public? God? A friend?

- What does the singer want to accomplish through the song? Do they wish to express an emotion? Criticise? Arouse? Educate? Tell a story?

- What's the point of view and the tone of the singer? Are they angry? Happy? Sad? Grateful? Indifferent?

- When is the story of the song taking place? Morning, evening or night? Will this enhance the emotional impact of the song or evoke a mood?

- Where is the story taking place? In a bar, a bedroom, a street or a completely abstract situation? Is this important to the song?

Such questions will help you to focus the song, as your answers will establish the tone, attitude and appropriate language for the piece. This will in turn provide a solid foundation on which to build the lyric.

The important issue is that, once you've decided on these elements, you stick to them (unless of course the change is obvious or predictable or necessary, eg the shift into a middle-eight section). This will avoid the possibility of confusing the listener.

This consistency and clarity is very important when considering the point of view of the song. Be very clear about who exactly is saying or doing what within the song. When it comes to using a pronoun, make it clear who it's substituting, keep it relatively close to the subject and avoid using too many of them.

First person ('I' or 'we')
This is the most popular view, as the writer is often writing from experience, and it appeals to singers, allowing them to identify with the song's subject and with their audience. Examples of songs written in the first person include 'Angels' by Robbie Williams and Dionne Warwick's 'I Say A Little Prayer'.

Second person ('you')
With this view, the lyric is addressed to another person. It's useful

---

Don Black says:
'With movie theme songs, you have to sum up the film in three minutes. The film producers want a title at all costs, because it's three minutes of advertising every time someone plays it. With Bond films, the lyrics should be seductive, provocative and have a whiff of the boudoir about them. They should be slightly over-written, in your face, delicious and sinful. "Diamonds Are Forever" is palpable; you can taste the lure of the forbidden coming at you.'

John Lennon said:
'I remember, in the early meetings with Dylan, he was always saying to me, "Listen to the words, man!" And I said, "I can't be bothered. I listen to the sound of it, the sound of the overall thing." Then I reversed that and started being a words man. I naturally play with words anyway, so I made a conscious effort to be wordy, à la Dylan.'

for expressing positive sentiments, such as 'You're amazing', or for putting some distance between the singer and the subject, as in 'What do you do when you fall in love with someone who doesn't love you?'

Third person: 'he', 'she' or 'they'
This mode offers an excellent way of distancing the writer or singer from subject matter that might be too personal or inappropriate, or to tell a story from more than one person's perspective – for instance, 'There She Goes' by The La's or 'He Ain't Heavy (He's My Brother)' by The Hollies.

Generally, a songwriter sticks to a singular point of view in a song to avoid confusion. It's a very skilled songsmith who can jump between points of view effectively and smoothly. Sting manages it in his song 'Fields Of Gold', switching between the second person in the verse to the third person in the chorus and to the first person in the bridge, holding the song together with strong, clear imagery.

5. HAVE A STRONG OPENING LINE

First impressions count, so the first line is crucial. When a publisher, producer or listener hears that opening line, they could be deciding whether or not to keep listening or turn it off. The music might grab them, but is the song going to tell them anything interesting or relevant? This is why it's important to avoid uninspiring clichés, such as 'I'm just sitting here.' The first line sets the tone for the whole song and should encourage a listener to hear more. Prince's 'Kiss',

Ali Tennant says:
'Recently I spent a whole week writing with Rod Temperton in his house. It was an amazing experience and I soaked up his knowledge like a sponge. I would try to probe his mind about how he wrote "Thriller", and he would simply say, "Ali, it just came to be." He said he knew the melody he had come up with felt solid, so he worked on it for a couple of weeks, but he still didn't have the full lyric. He played me the actual early demo of the song. The melody sounded exactly the same, but Michael [Jackson] was just singing silly words over it. When the demo came to the chorus, I was expecting to hear "Thriller", but Michael sang, "Starlight, starlight love." It totally threw me. Rod and Michael had then spent another couple of weeks searching for the exact right lyric to what eventually became "Thriller".'

Michelle Escoffery says:
'In order to make a song authentic, it is the songwriter's job to tune into the heads and hearts of the listeners and to share something of himself or herself or a third-party experience, giving life to words on paper. Self-knowledge is therefore a key attribute.'

Alanis Morissette's 'Ironic' and Don McLean's 'American Pie' are all fine examples of songs featuring a strong opening line.

6. USE REPETITION EFFECTIVELY

Repetition is one of the primary techniques for making a song stick in a listener's head. Repeating important words and key lines – often the title – satisfies a person's desire for familiarity and ensures that the song will be remembered. This is obviously an important commercial consideration.

There are several methods of lyrical repetition to consider:

- **Repetition of sections** – For example, the multiple recurrence of the chorus, as in The Beach Boys' 'Good Vibrations', Queen's 'We Will Rock You' and 'Sing It Back' by Moloko.

- **Repetition of key lines or phrases** – For example, the reiteration of the title in Eminem's song 'My Name Is' or the phrase 'Don't know much about...' in Sam Cooke's 'Wonderful World (Don't Know Much)'.

- **Alliteration** – This is the repetition of accented consonant sounds in successive or neighbouring words. Using alliteration creates phonic patterns by linking words you want to emphasise – for example, 'I left the lights on for my lover.' It can easily be taken to absurd extremes, however, so it's best to keep this technique subtle, as in 'The Sound Of Silence' or 'Same Old Lang Syne' (viz 'She would have liked to say she loved the man, but she didn't like to lie').

- **Assonance** – This occurs when the stressed vowels in a word

Wayne Hector says:
'In anybody's life, a conversation between two people is a point of contact. People share a considerable deal in those moments. My songs are a conversation between myself and the listener. When I'm writing, I want to talk to whoever is out there, and I'm asking a rhetorical question: "Have you been through this too?" That's why I'm always listening out for phrases in people's conversations in everyday life. Somebody might say, "We've got a little world of our own, you and me," and I'll think, "That's a good title. That's an interesting way of expressing love." I'm the sort of person who will look at people on the street and wonder what their lives are like and what they do. I attempt to capture snippets of life in my songs. My songs are therefore usually about myself or about somebody I know who has gone through a particular experience – though I don't actually tell them that I've spilt their business to a couple of million people!'

agree but the preceding consonants don't – for example, 'They name the game' or 'They won't be going home.' Applied effectively, this technique lends cohesion and a subtle emphasis to a lyric.

- **Parallelism** – This is a method of presenting similar or contrasting ideas in a similar grammatical construction (also known as 'list lyrics'), again imparting cohesion and polish to a lyric. A perfect example of parallelism can be found in the verses of The Police's 'Every Breath You Take'.

7. APPLY RHYME EFFECTIVELY

It is a fallacy that all lyrics have to rhyme. There are examples of numerous hit songs that don't follow this policy, such John Denver's 'Annie's Song' and 'I Got Rhythm' by George and Ira Gershwin. However, strong, predictable rhymes are beneficial in triggering the memory, creating a sense of unity, fulfilment and adding impact to a statement or an emotion. This is why nursery rhymes are so memorable, years on from childhood.

The constant challenge in contemporary songwriting is to find the best rhymes possible while still retaining the natural flow of speech. Songwriter Paul Simon, for instance, is a master of the conversational style of lyric, as demonstrated in Simon And Garfunkel's 'The Sound Of Silence'.

There are many forms of rhyme, including:

- **Perfect rhymes** – This is where the sounds are exactly the same, eg 'day'/'play', 'snow'/'glow', 'moon'/'June'.

Mick Leeson says:
'People often say that today's songwriters can't write lyrics like Cole Porter. Maybe not, but that misses the point. How many hits of the last 30 years have had lyrics like Cole Porter's? That's right: none. So what would be the point of replicating Cole, apart from guaranteed failure? Today's hits reflect today's times, just like Cole's genius reflected his times.'

Rick Nowels says:
'To me, the lyric is everything. The message is of utmost importance. The artists that last are the artists who have something to say, a philosophy, a code to live life by, the poetic life view, a new way of thinking.'

Hal David says:
'When I hear music, I hear words, just as I assume the composer hears music when he listens to lyrics.'

- **Imperfect or false rhyme** – This is approximate rhyme and is used a great deal in contemporary music today. Examples of imperfect rhymes are 'time'/'mine', 'around'/'down' and 'world'/'girl'.

- **Open rhyme** – This is rhyme that ends softly – ie words that don't end in hard consonants, such as 'fly'/'try' and 'free'/'be'. These are excellent rhymes to use alongside sustained notes in a vocal line.

- **Closed rhyme** – This is rhyme comprising words that end in a hard consonant. Words ending in B, P, D, T, Q and K sounds force the singer to close their mouth, so such rhymes are impossible to sustain. Words ending in M, N, L and R sounds can be sustained without problem. Words ending in V, F, Z and S sounds, meanwhile, are sustainable but not very pleasant. This factor is important when considering the singability of your lyrics.

- **Internal rhyme** – This is rhyme occurring within a line, such as 'We all hope to fall by the end.' The best inner rhymes give lyrics rhythmic grace, smoothness and a professional touch.

To make rhyme work as a memory technique, there is a need for consistency. It's therefore important to set up an appropriate rhyming scheme. It's also best to maintain the same pattern across verses and, in order to avoid monotony, to employ another pattern in the chorus, and yet another for the bridge.

On a four-line lyric, there are a number of possible options for the end rhyme:

a

a

a

a

Ali Tennant says:
'Writing lyrics for R&B is another language – a street, urban language. It's that hip-hop language they use in rap. It's very much the way you're putting the subject matter across. You have to be current.'

Frank Musker says:
'I would make a plea to lyric writers everywhere to remember that words are music. Lyrics convey meaning, not only literally but sonically. That's not to say that you must write good-sounding gibberish, but that a truly accomplished lyricist will find the perfect middle way between lyrics that read well and look good on the page and lyrics that sound like a perfect fit with the music – what the ancient Greeks called prosody. Listen to the glorious, meandering words of 'Like A Rolling Stone' and how powerfully and passionately they fit the music, and then read them off the page and you'll know why Dylan is still considered a genius. There are very few real geniuses among us, but the principles of the craft apply to everyone and the punters instinctively know it when they hear it, even if they can't tell you why.'

This rhyme scheme can become monotonous, but is useful in hammering a point home.

---

a
a
b
b

This is a more balanced approach as it offer a change in the second half.

---

a
b
a
b

This is the most common form of rhyming pattern

---

a
b
c
b

This form is useful as it provides space in which the lyric can be developed and relief from potential over-rhyming.

Eddie Holland says:
'The tracks Brian and Lamont cut provided a basic foundation of feelings that I could build my lyrics on. In general, they would give me an almost completed track. If there was a title, I would finish it. Usually there was a two- or three-line tag or hook in the song, and I would take that and use it as a guide. I didn't have to, but my belief was that, since they were the producers, I tried to give them what they were looking for, lyrically, within the given framework.

'Most of the titles I would use had some meaning. I would try to use titles that I felt had an appeal, from an emotional point of view. A lot of the titles were things that were said to me that I had direct personal experiences in dealing with, so they would actually be titles that ladies would say to me, sometimes out of anger. If you're a creative person, it just sticks to you. As soon as you hear it, it catches you right away. I could be in an argument or on the phone, and the other person would say certain things and I would say, "Hold on for a minute," and I'd go and get a pencil and write it down...because being a creative person – especially knowing your responsibility is writing the lyric – you have to think it and feel it and live it all the time. It's a natural thing. I think all songwriters are like that. They hear something, they jot it down. If they don't jot it down then, they take mental notes and it sticks. I've had titles in my head for 25 years. They just stick; they just stand out.'

a
b
a
a

This is a more unexpected pattern

There are many other variations, but given that the function of rhyme is to help the listener remember the song, rhymes in any consistent scheme should work. The key considerations when applying rhyme are:

1. Does the rhyme fit with the music?
2. Does the rhyme sound comfortable and unforced? Remember, it's preferable to maintain the natural flow of language.
3. Do the positions of the rhymes enhance the mood and meaning of the song?
4. Does the rhyme emphasise the right words, or does it land on an inconsequential word?
5. Is the rhyme naturally phrased or has it been twisted to fit the particular rhyme scheme? The latter is known as *inversion* and, in general, should be avoided, as it sounds old-fashioned in the context of a song.

Being proficient in the art of rhyming is a vital skill of the professional songwriter. Some inexperienced writers will find that they've said what they want to in the first two lines but are swayed by the need to complete a rhyme scheme and consequently finish the verse weakly. It's important that you spend the necessary time on crafting the lyric in order to avoid such a pitfall. This is why it's useful to have a good songwriting rhyming dictionary to hand for when you get stuck. Ultimately, though, as with all elements of songwriting, you must go with what emotionally feels right for you.

8. KEEP IT SPECIFIC

'I try to say what's commonly said, without saying it the way it's commonly said. I don't just want to say, "I love you"; I want to tell the woman how much I love her and make a comparison to something.'

– Shep Crawford, songwriter/producer

A song is a very compact form of creative expression, so it's important to make every word count. This can be done very easily by...

1. Removing any unnecessary words (eg 'very', 'just') and meaningless terms (eg 'smiling happily').

2. Where appropriate, choosing specific descriptions ('She walked like a tigress') over general ones ('She walked like an animal').

3. Selecting concrete ideas ('You don't send me flowers anymore') over abstract ones ('You don't love me anymore'). By applying this process, an emotion can be shown rather than told. The result is a song that's meaningful, powerful and contains an emotional punch.

9. EMPLOY APPROPRIATE LANGUAGE

As established in point seven with regard to rhymes, it's important to ensure that the words are singable – ie that long notes land on comfortable, open-vowel sounds. Also, you should ensure that the words flow into one another smoothly and don't force an impossible tongue-twister through being over-complicated or awkward, or from having too many words for the number of notes allocated. This is why it's useful to sing or at least talk through lyrics out loud.

It's also important to use words that are consistent with the genre in which you're writing. For instance, if you're writing pop music, keep the tone light. If you're writing rap, use the appropriate slang and adopt the correct attitude. 'Writing lyrics for R&B is another language – a street, urban language,' notes songwriter and artist Ali Tennant. 'It's that hip-hop language they use in rap. It's very much the way you're putting the subject matter across. You have to be current.'

You need to be particularly careful when using slang expressions. They can be great sources for new rhymes, as well as for making your song immediate and relevant, but the drawback is that in 20 years' time the song might sound dated, as with the '70s word 'groovy' in Paul Simon's '59th Street Bridge Song'.

A further consideration in working with language is to employ appropriate poetic devices. These include:

Similes – These are comparisons using the words 'as' or 'like'. The simile is a standard lyrical device, so it's advisable to try fresh comparisons, such as the line 'Like a cat in a bag, waiting to drown' in The Verve's song 'The Drugs Don't Work'.

Metaphors – These are comparisons between two dissimilar things without the use of 'as' or 'like'. Paul Simon's 'I Am A Rock' is a fine example of this powerful lyrical device.

Personification – This device attributes human characteristics to inanimate objects, as demonstrated in the line 'the stars look down' in Coldplay's 'Yellow' and the title to Bruce Springsteen's 'Hungry Heart'.

Hyperbole – This is an obvious exaggeration employed to drive a point home, such The Beatles' song 'Eight Days A Week'.

Allegory – This is a device that allows a writer to treat an abstract idea with concrete imagery, as in Stevie Wonder and Paul McCartney's 'Ebony And Ivory', where the keys of a piano are an allegory for racial harmony.

Characterisation – This is the creation and representation of convincing characters. The art here is in imparting information about the character through their actions or images rather than simply by stating their character. In The Beatles' song 'Eleanor Rigby', for instance, rather than merely saying that Eleanor Rigby is lonely, the song provides the listener with an representative image, where Eleanor 'picks up rice in the church where a wedding has been'.

Used intelligently, these techniques can make a lyric truly stand out and sound fresh, but they shouldn't distract from the overall flow and meaning of the lyric.

10. BE HONEST

'I come in straight with honesty. I make the lyrics honest.' – Ali Tennant

Writing from the heart always produces better, more believable and more relevant songs, so write about situations and emotions that you understand or of which you have direct experience. There's no substitute for the true expression of feelings or beliefs. In order to move and convince others, you must first be moved and convinced.

Guy Chambers says:
'The first line in a song is very important. Just like in a book, it has to grab the attention of the listener.'

Summary Of The Ten Guidelines

1. Write personally about a universal idea.
2. Use a memorable title.
3. Keep it simple.
4. Focus the lyric.
5. Have a strong opening line.
6. Use repetition effectively.
7. Apply rhyme effectively.
8. Keep it specific.
9. Employ appropriate language.
10. Be honest.

THE SONGWRITER:

DON BLACK

MORE TO WRITING THAN MEETS THE EYE

Bill Kenwright wants my life.

The Everton Chairman and one of the leading London theatre producers, Bill considers that of a 'songwriter' to be the perfect life. He knows what I do. I live in Holland Park, London, and if I'm writing a song, I go to the park and sit down and look at the peacocks and write.

It's misleading, though, to give the impression that it's all one big holiday. 2004 was the year of my trilogy – the musicals *Bombay Dreams*, *Dracula* and *Brighton Rock* – and it was the busiest time of my life. There's so much thinking time and crafting involved in writing a lyric.

My world of songwriting is perhaps different to other writers' because I straddle two worlds, theatre and contemporary pop, and they require very different skills from a lyricist.

When writing for Broadway and the West End, the lyric has to be ever so carefully crafted. It has to rhyme. Each line has to further the story. Each word has to illuminate character. The lyric is all about digging deep into the story. These are different skills to writing a contemporary pop song with Steve Mac, for instance, and saying, 'Steve, let's write a song for whoever, and let's come up with a title.' I can be a lot more fluid with pop and make creative choices simply on the fact that an idea fits or sounds right. In theatre, I may come up with a great line, but the next question is, 'How do we get that in?', because every line has to further the plot in some way. It can't simply sound good.

This is not to say that writing contemporary music is easier. In fact, it's perhaps harder than writing for the theatre, because, as Alan J Lerner used to say, there is no scenario. In theatre there is always a character to write to. When I was writing *Sunset Boulevard*, for example, from the beginning I was dealing with a faded film star who hadn't made a movie for years, and when she comes on stage, she has to sing about how she came to be. As the writer, I know where she comes from, know what her song has got to be about, and this helps enormously, lyrically. I write her character into each song. In comparison, when I sit down to write with Steve Mac for a day, he may have half a tune and I may have two or three titles but no other direction than that. The song can go anywhere, be about anything. The advantage with theatre, therefore, is very much the illumination of character.

In preparing to write with John Barry for *Brighton Rock*, a famous Graham Greene novel about a 17-year-old psychopath and murderer, I just immersed myself in the story. I read the book ten times. I saw the movie. Then I was into it and would have ideas – a title, maybe two or three lines – on what the boy, Pinkie, should be singing about. John would then come back with a tune. For example, Pinkie is a bastard, cold and horrible, but there had to be some reason why he has turned out like that, so I had an idea for a song that would explain where Pinkie was coming from, which turned out to be 'Some Things Never Leave You'. That way, he could talk about his life and what happened to him as a kid.

I'd never written about a 17-year-old psychopath before, but this is what I love about the theatre. In *Bombay Dreams* I was writing songs for a eunuch, and in *Dracula* I was writing about the undead. Theatre writing is always so different and varied.

Theatre writing is also different to contemporary writing in that there isn't as much sitting in the same room as the composer, bouncing ideas off each other. Musical lyric writing is too specific for the kind of immediacy required in contemporary writing. That's not to say that the writing is rigid; it's never a case of, 'Here's my tune; put words to it; see you at the opening!', but the lyric does need to be crafted thoroughly, since there's far more emphasis laid upon the words in theatre. In a musical, you obviously still require a marvellous melody, but when the audience is actually sitting in a theatre for the first time, they're hanging on every word that the character is singing, because they're following a story. Consequently, the lyric has to be concise. It cannot meander. It has to be instant.

Most people don't appreciate lyric writing in the theatre, because they don't understand what lyric writing is supposed to do in stage shows and what makes a lyric particularly good in such a context. In reviews for any musical, critics often dismiss the lyrics, summing them up in a word – 'banal' or 'serviceable' – but never going into depth about them because they miss the function of a lyric on a stage. A theatre lyric is supposed to illuminate character, further the plot, simultaneously say something fresh and be concise yet eloquent. That is a great deal to demand of a single lyric.

I presumably fulfilled that demand with *Sunset Boulevard*, my lyrics for which were recognised with a Tony Award. That play is such a great story, and people could empathise with the main character. It's about someone who is over the hill – something we all dread – and as such it was a lyric writer's gift to write about it, because there's a tremendous amount one can write about disappointment. Big themes like disappointment, loss, love – they're meat and potatoes to the lyric writer.

Great lyrics are ultimately about looking for the truth. They say something that hasn't been put in the same way ever before. This could be an old-fashioned thought, but a great lyric elicits that 'Oh, that's me' reaction in the listener. Cole Porter's 'Every time we say goodbye, I die a little', for example, is so true and so beautifully put that it stands the test of time. In the song 'Ben', which I wrote for Michael Jackson, Michael loved the bridge, because it says it all in so few words: 'I used to say "I" and "me". Now it's "us"; now it's "we".'

Great lyrics are snippets of eavesdropping on life. They give intensity to everyday feelings. As a lyricist, I'm always aware of words or phrases that say something fresh about the human condition. That's the secret of being a good lyricist. If I was in a restaurant and I heard someone at the next table saying to a loved one, 'You've lost that loving feeling,' I would write it down. My mind is always on red alert. I could be watching a play, reading a book or enjoying a movie when someone says something and I think, 'There's a song in that idea, and I have never heard a song like that.' I have a constant, if not necessarily conscious, awareness.

Bill Kenwright might want my life, but there's a lot more to it that sitting in Holland Park and looking at peacocks!

THE PUBLISHER:

DEKE ARLON

The excitement of music publishing lies in finding a great song – ie songwriter. To that end, you spend your time listening to endless material – the mundane, the clichéd, the downright bad, the good – but always seeking out the one that makes your heart stop, that instinct tells you is special.

Of course, within the commercial world of the music business, there are diverse tastes and opinions and the term 'great' will be carelessly bandied around and attached to many a recording, and frequently within their genre these *can* be great, although generally their appeal and shelf life are limited.

If I had to define a great song, I'd say that it's a musical expression of a great story or emotion that reaches out to you, that touches you and remains with you, sometimes for the rest of your life. It is emotive, potent, appealing. The music stirs you; the lyrics speak to you. It is timeless.

As a publisher, I know full well that a great song needs a complementary balance of a well-constructed melody and lyrics. Of course, I love and appreciate the music, but I have to admit that, in the final analysis, it is the lyrics that seduce me, that nail the song for me. Great songs are emotive – you meet and fall in love to them; they highlight your life. I would also guarantee that it's the words and not the melody that define the moment.

A great lyricist has the ability to condense and focus his thoughts, and to express them in the best possible way within a three- or four-minute musical structure. He says things you only wish you'd said. He paints immediate, accessible pictures with words; he speaks the mundane with an original voice.

Ninety per cent of songs are love songs – that's a lot of 'I love you'. It took an inspired lyricist, Lionel Richie, to write, 'You're once, twice, three times a lady.' What a way to say, 'I love you.'

In the 1960s and '70s, I was fortunate to represent many wonderful songwriters – James Taylor, Gilbert O'Sullivan, Chip Taylor, Fred Neil, etc, and my first American writer, Kenny Young, who wrote 'Under The Boardwalk', 'Captain Of Your Ship' and many others. He also wrote a song that contained the following lyric:

> She was born out of love to a coalman's wife
> When the lake was just a pond
> And the wood was crackling in the fireplace
> And her mother's labour was done.

A simple enough country lyric, but what lifts it above the ordinary is the line 'When the lake was just a pond.' He could have said, 'A long, long time ago,' and possibly that was in the original draft, but how much more evocative, how much greater, is the sense of time passing in the image of the pond swelling over the years into a lake? It is that extra imagination that defines the talent divide between the A team and the B team of songwriters.

I've always had a way with words. In the late '60s, while working as an actor, I met and fell in love with Jill, my wife. Jill was an acclaimed actress but also a lecturer of speech and drama, and she introduced me to the world of poetry and fed my enthusiasm for lyrics. School had never excited me and I'd left at the earliest opportunity, but this void was soon filled, and when I became a young music publisher searching for hits, the knowledge I'd gained was invaluable.

I've worked with many songwriters and, in showing them what's wrong with their work, I can also tell them what they need to do to put it right and to whom they should refer for inspiration, such as the great poets like Dylan Thomas or the masters of the contemporary song lyric like Paul Simon, Bob Dylan, Hal David, Don Black or Tim Rice, Ray Davies, Morrissey and of course Lennon and McCartney.

Even so, with all that knowledge and experience gleaned from working for years with some of the most talented writers, I still couldn't write a great lyric myself, and more and more I am in awe of those who can. Songwriting seems so easy; it's such a short art form, everyone thinks they can do it. That's the beauty of a great song – the execution seems effortless – and yet how difficult it is to create that perfect marriage of words and melody! Take a song like 'Do You Know The Way To San Jose?' There we have a word per note, and still the song flows. It has technical brilliance, flair and simplicity.

An aspiring songwriter can have all the lessons in the world, but will that mean he can walk away and write a better song? Yes.

Will he walk away and write a good song? Possibly.

But will he walk away and, with all that knowledge, write a great lyric? I doubt it.

The difference between a good song and a great song is immense and often utterly indefinable. I believe it is only the truly inspired, those born with a special talent, who can write great lyrics.

AN INTERVIEW WITH FRANCIS EG WHITE

How does a typical songwriting day proceed for you?
Having kids means my writing day is practically a 'Nashville day' – 11pm until 6pm. No writer really wants to do pop music before 11, so usually I'll be finishing up sessions in the morning. Consequently, it's a very short day and is terribly pressured. The good news is that this means I get an unbelievable amount done for the amount of time; I get more songs written and there's more focus to them. I'm certainly more productive now than I've ever been before.

Do you prefer writing on your own or with another writer?
I find the very best songs I write are often done on my own, but I can only write those from a particular place. These really special ones come from somewhere unconscious, and they come rapidly and of their own volition. They usually arrive pretty intact. Writing on my own, though, I can't knock out as many tunes – not even half as many, bearing in mind that two people in a room should automatically double the output, at least. Also, if a writer is working on their own and there are no ideas coming, it can get a bit depressing.

Working with people, there's a demand to get something written. I believe that productivity has a lot to do with working with other people, because there's somebody else there expecting something good from you. It pushes you to create.

How important is the lyric to you?
I wasn't a lyricist until my late 20s. For me, it was all about groove and instrumentation. I came from the perspective of a player of musical instruments: piano, flute, violin, double bass, guitar, bass. Of course, I knew there was a singer and that they had the capacity to ruin the track or make it better, but that was basically as far as it went. Only later in my late 20s did I discover and understand the full power of the lyric. As I get older and older, the lyric becomes more and more overpoweringly important for me because it informs the emotion of the song.

If I know what the song is about or what I'm aiming for, I have the central lines from which to work the song. I have a guide pulling me through the song.

Is there a typical Eg White style of song?

I would hope not. I know there are certain trademarks in other people's work, but I hope I haven't got a 'sound' because, if I find myself doing the same thing over and over again, I'll be asking myself the question, 'Didn't I do that rather better last week?' Why would I want to be doing the same thing either a tiny bit worse or a tiny bit better? It's a crime to be working through the same idea each time.

Have you ever had writers' block? If so, how did you cope with it?

Yes, but I wouldn't say it was writers' block; I'd say it was simply a lack of a good idea. It never felt like it was an absolute and I've never experienced it when writing with other people.

I've witnessed listeners' block in A&R men – A&R who have lost the capacity to relate to music emotionally because they've got into such a muddle about what they're relating to, what the focus and function of music is. Every so often – once or twice a year – I'll get into that state, so I'll put on a record that I absolutely love, a killer song like 'Dancing Queen' or 'All The Young Dudes'. If I feel nothing, if I can't find the capacity to feel joy and goodness in a record like that, then I realise that I can't make music in that state of mind and will take a break from writing music. But that's rare.

What makes a good pop song?

If a song idea has very strong feelings, be they happy or be they suicidal, or if it makes the listener need to dance, then it's destined to be a good song.

How important is the vocal to a song?

The vocal is really important. It sets the tone for so many elements of the song. I've had songs on which I've sung and thought that the song was appalling. Then I've got a session singer in and suddenly the song is a golden, shining jewel – and that was the result of the singer.

What one lesson have you learned during your years as a songwriter?

One important point I have learned is that you can't really change the fundamental emotional feeling of a song. You can change its style and you can change its speed, and obvious, simple physical things like that, but you can't make a song that's ironic sound earnest or vice versa.

Do you recognise a hit song when it's written?

When I was in Brother Beyond, we'd written some songs that became minor hits. I remember one gig where we played our previous single. The crowd had all heard it numerous times before on the radio and they went 70 per cent mad, and that was great. But then we played a Stock, Aitken and Waterman tune that they hadn't heard before, which would subsequently go on to be a big hit, and they went 90 per cent mad from a first live listening. That's what happens when you look a hit in the face.

How did you feel when you had your first Number One hit song?

I remember when a friend of mine, Louis Elliot – a very good songwriter who had been in Kinky Machine – had his first proper hit. I asked him, 'How does it feel?', and he replied, 'It's a relief.' That's how it felt for me, too: it was a relief. Not a huge euphoria, just a quiet, good feeling of relief.

You have to understand that I'd been so close to success so many times before. I remember there was one point, while I was signed to Warner–Chappell, that I'd written and recorded a fantastic record with a girl called Emiliana Torrini, signed to One Little Indian; another album with a girl, Nicole Russo, who was signed to Telstar; and at the same time I was working with Jade Anderson, who had been signed by Columbia in the United States for a huge deal. I was thinking I was made, having been instrumental in the making of these three albums. They'd all been signed and given priority. It was so far away from the realms of possibility that all three would go down the pan, but for various reasons, they did.

Just prior to [Will Young's] 'Leave Right Now', I'd witnessed another record of mine go wrong: 'Surrender', by Javine. It was the first record I'd had out for a year and a half. It was very exciting, but to be honest the track was a bit poor, sonically. A very well-respected production company was called in and they made the verse miles better, but in so doing the extreme dynamic lift that had happened in the chorus was completely killed. When it came out, it went straight in at Number 15 and then it went straight back out again. The track had masses of airplay, but sales-wise it was genuinely a failure.

My feeling at the time was, how easily it can go wrong in this business. I had all the same feelings about Will's record. The record company had even expected it to fail, since they had printed only 60,000, which is a medium-sized printing. When it was released, the only people playing it were Magic FM, but I think it became a hit through Will's TV appearances. His personality sold it. He brought a humanity to the track. On the day it came out, two-thirds of the copies were sold and it went straight in at Number One. But to me, it was just a tiny change of fortune that sent it the other way. I would never have guessed that the difference between success and failure could be so small.

Song Craft 7: The Melody

'There are only 12 notes. You must treat them carefully.' – Paul Hindemith

From Beethoven to Linkin Park, Cole Porter to Eminem, Willie Nelson to Coldplay, every songwriter uses the same 12 notes – 12 simple ingredients that have amounted to a whole history of music and emotion. Perhaps more than any other aspect of songwriting, then, melody writing is the most powerful and most mysterious skill.

Great melodies have a certain magic about them that is indefinable in technical terms. A focused, well-written melody is effortless and timeless, but written down in musical notation there's nothing to distinguish between a good and a poor melody. The difference is only apparent when each is played. We can all recognise a poor melody; it meanders without purpose, is vapid, unmemorable and lacks distinction, whereas songs like 'Hey Jude', 'Raindrops Keep Falling On My Head' and 'Sailing' – to name only a few – simply sound and feel right.

On the whole, a great melody in popular music tends to:

1. Be catchy and singable;
2. Be easy to remember;
3. Blend well with the harmony;
4. Have a strong or agreeable rhythmic quality;
5. Work well with the words that accompany it;
6. Be a mix of the innovative and familiar.

Melodies, more than any other aspect of songwriting, are the result of pure inspiration. Ideas for great melodies tend to pop into songwriters' heads. Even so, an appreciation of how to develop these melodic ideas, to shape them and to link them with the right chords will help a songwriter to write and craft stronger, more memorable melodies.

WHERE TO BEGIN?

'In order to compose, all you need to do is remember a tune that nobody else has thought of.'

– Robert Schumann

The starting point for any melody is its initial concept or motif. In classical music, melodic ideas are built up over time and different themes are intertwined and overlaid to create a complex melodic texture. Contemporary music generally deals in shorter melodic ideas that are repeated and contrasted without much emphasis on thematic development beyond attaining the main chorus or hook.

There are several factors to consider when composing a melody:

CONTOUR

This is the rise and fall of a melody. It's worth contemplating the aesthetic quality of a melody to ensure that there's a natural flow. Jumping erratically between notes can make a melody sound jerky, and as a consequence such a tune won't be particularly easy to sing or pleasant to listen to. The artist Sade has composed numerous examples of melodies demonstrating smooth contour. Ultimately, though, it will be the style of music being composed that will dictate the overall contour of the tune.

In a connected point, the range of the melody should be considered. Melodies can be either of a linear or vertical quality, or somewhere in between.

LINEAR

Linear melodies lie within a very narrow range of notes. This can be due to the enforced habits of a songwriter or singer, uninspired writing or sometimes the consequence of a singer's restricted vocal range. The key consideration with respect to linear composition is that the melody runs the risk of losing the listener's interest very quickly as the tune become over-predictable, static or uninspiring. However, used skilfully, a narrow melodic range can work very effectively, as in the verse of Carlos Jobim's 'One Note Samba' or Paul McCartney's 'Let 'Em In'. Similarly, Mark Knopfler, Bob Dylan and Bruce Springsteen all compose melodies within a very narrow scale, due to their limited vocal ranges, yet have made a virtue of this very limitation.

Bob Dylan's 'Subterranean Homesick Blues' is a great example of a linear melody line being applied successfully within a song. Dylan uses only a few notes to create a driving melodic tension that emphasises the lyrics and pushes the core message of the song to the fore.

Other songs that have very successfully used a limited range, or held on one note, include 'I Am The Walrus' (The Beatles), 'We Didn't Start The Fire' (Billy Joel) and 'It's The End Of The World As We Know It' (REM).

VERTICAL

The opposite of the linear style is the vertical style of writing, where there are large jumps in the scale. It's often female singers – artists such as Kate Bush, Alanis Morissette and Tori Amos – who possess the vocal ability to push seriously the limits of vertical melodies, and in the right context such leaps can prove very effective and memorable. Judy Garland's 'Somewhere Over The Rainbow' is a classic example of this, featuring a melody that jumps a whole octave within the first two notes of the song, while Will Jennings and Richard Kerr's 'I Know I'll Love This Way Again' successfully leaps between octaves in the first six notes.

RHYTHM AND PROSODY

It's important to keep in mind that melody has rhythm as well as pitch. The rhythm of a melody needs to fit with the words. A strong accent or a held note in a tune should ideally coincide with a significant word in the lyrics. Otherwise, you could end up with the melodic high point of a song climaxing on some inconsequential word like 'and' or 'just'.

In some styles of music, the rhythm is paramount and can even supersede the pitch of the melody in significance. Such is the case in the genres of rap and hip-hop, as well as in some of Michael Jackson's songs that very definitely emphasise the rhythm over the actual harmonic quality of the notes – for example, 'Beat It' or 'Wanna Be Startin' Somethin''.

The issue of rhythm is actually part of the broader consideration of *prosody*. The dictionary definition of prosody is 'the respective stress and intonation patterns of the spoken word', and in music this translates to the proper and seamless blending of words and music. There are no actual rules to prosody; it is more a matter of artistic judgement. Some things to consider, however, are:

- Do all the elements fit together to deliver effectively the message you want to put across?

- Do accents in the melody coincide with the naturally accented syllables of the corresponding words?

- Is the melody effective and easy to sing with the lyrics?

For example, if the melody drops into a minor scale as you're trying to communicate a sense of happiness through the lyrics, this may comes across to the listener as odd, confusing or even ludicrous. However, your intention may be to communicate that the happiness implied in the lyrics is forced, reflecting this in the contradiction between music and lyric.

The important point with regard to all of these factors – contour, linear and vertical writing, rhythm and prosody – is that, as a songwriter, you're aware of them and are conscious of their effects and consequences when composing a melodic line.

MELODY FROM HARMONY

Most melodic ideas are written instinctively or come from playing around on a guitar or piano. However, having an understanding of some fundamental principles of harmonising a melody will help you greatly when it comes to constructing your own ideas and stretching your creative boundaries.

Melodies can be based on the chords over which they're played. With an awareness of how particular notes relate to certain harmonies (or chords), it's possible to build melodies note by note. Furthermore, if a melodic phrase doesn't sound particularly inspiring, a fresh direction can be derived from the chords and harmonies.

Note: A basic understanding of music theory is required for the following section. If you don't possess such knowledge, I advise you to read a recommended music-theory book. Information on these can be found in the section titled 'Body: Essential Information For Songwriters'.

First of all, it's important to classify the usefulness of the various notes in a scale, starting with the most important:

1.   **Notes that rest inside the chord**
       These are notes that are either the first, third or fifth degree of the scale from which the chord is derived (eg in the chord of C, this would be C, E and G, respectively). They blend perfectly with such a 'triad' (a basic chord comprising three notes), so a melody using these notes would sound very

comfortable. However, by solely using the first, third and fifth notes there's a chance that such a melody would quickly become rather bland, so other notes need to be considered.

If the chord is more complex – for instance, if a major seventh was added (eg B in the chord of C) – then the additional notes would also sit well with the chord, but not so perfectly. The general rule is, the more complex the chord, the weaker the effect.

2.   **Notes that rest outside the chord**
These are other notes of the scale beside the principal first, third and fifth – ie the second, fourth, sixth and seventh degrees of the scale, which, in the key of C major over a C chord, would be D, F, A and B respectively.

These notes can be more expressive and can create tension when set against the chord because they sound like they want to move to one of the principal, 'resting' notes. Each of the notes from outside the chord introduces a unique quality of tension depending on the desired effect, the flow of the melody and how long the melody remains on the note; the longer a note that rests outside the chord is held, the greater the sonic tension.

This is the key to effective melody writing. Music expresses the range and complexity of human emotion through the 'tension and release' mechanism of melody. Tension, asymmetry and dissonance are all techniques that help to convey a song's emotion.

3.   **Notes that rest against the chord**
The extremes of emotion can be expressed through notes that rest against the chord – in other words, the notes that aren't part of the scale from which the chord is derived. In a C major chord, these are D♭, E♭, F♯, A♭ and B♭.

Notes that rest against the chord create the greatest dissonance in conventional Western music. They can be extreme, such as the flattened fifth (F♯ in C major), or more musically appealing, as with the flattened third and seventh notes (E♭ and B♭, respectively, over a C chord). Blues music in particular consistently applies the flattened third and seventh to generate the genre's characteristic woeful, soulful feel. In most other styles of music, such notes against the chord are used as passing notes to make a melody more interesting, jazzy or sophisticated, and in the right context they can be very emotive. Like any technique, though, if they're over-used, their effect can become predictable and unconvincing.

The key point to remember is that most melodies are written instinctively or are the result of an idea having been experimented with until it sounds right. Most songwriters wouldn't consciously be thinking, 'Inside, outside or against?' while composing a melody line.

However, being able to understand what you're actually creating, and why it sounds the way it does, can help you to craft better songs. Say, for instance, that you've written a melody that works pretty well but its second section is weak. If you understand the principles listed above, you might be able to push the melody into different areas or use notes you'd not previously considered.

DEVELOPING MELODY

'Don't delude yourself. Ask yourself honestly: is [the melody] actually good enough? Many writers tend to meander on a melody. It's crucial that you analyse your melody and ensure that it has a strong enough hook for a listener to sing it back.'
– Jem Godfrey, Wise Buddah

The real challenge for the contemporary writer is to take the initial idea and expand upon it so that it develops into an effective song section (eg chorus, verse or bridge) and, thereafter, to build different sections into one complete and indivisible song.

Presuming that you've come up with a decent melodic idea, there are certain techniques that can be applied to develop it into a melodic section. These are:

1. Repetition
2. Variation
3. Contrast
4. Transposing

John Lennon said:
'All music is a rehash. There are only a few notes, just variations on a theme.'

Dave Barry says:
'I hate rap music, which to me sounds like a bunch of angry men shouting, possibly because the person who was supposed to provide them with a melody never showed up.'

131

Repetition

The first principle of melodic development is simply to repeat the idea. Repetition is a key technique for helping a listener to remember a song. After all, if the idea is a good one, why not repeat it? This is the basis of many standard rock and blues tracks, such as 'Hound Dog' and 'Shake, Rattle And Roll'. The simple pop melody below, for example, can easily be developed using repetition:

However, this technique can become boring, ineffective or even annoying if over-used. A song requires enough variety to withstand repeated listening, so the initial piece of melody needs to be developed beyond simple repetition.

Variation

Many forms of music use a 'call and response' style of melodic development. The blues, religious service music, folk, gospel and dance are all based on alternating between different melodic ideas.

With variation, the second phrase is only slightly different from the original melody, but this difference is enough to keep the melody from becoming too predictable. With variation, the two phrases start similarly but the second one lifts away from the original melody.

Contrast

Contrast takes the concept of variation one step further by following the original phrase with a different but compatible melody. In the following example, the original melody idea is now contrasted with a second idea in the same key:

Many pop and dance records use these three methods exclusively to build a track – for example, 'We Are Family' by Sister Sledge. The challenge is to write an alternate melody that complements the first but is distinct enough to stand out from it.

Transposing

This is another technique for developing a melody, and while it's not suitable in all applications, it can be very effective. Here, a melodic phrase is raised or lowered (ie transposed) by the same interval by which the chord sequence is shifted. In other words, if a melody over a C chord is subsequently sung over a G chord, the whole melody is sung the same but a fifth higher throughout. This is also known as a 'sequential repetition' and is a favoured technique of Brian Wilson, as demonstrated in the choruses of 'California Girls' and 'Good Vibrations'.

These are the basic techniques for developing a melodic idea. Obviously, there are more complex patterns than those discussed here, but it's best to keep things simple when you're learning your craft. Once you're comfortable with the methods listed above, you can become more instinctive in your writing techniques and write longer, more complex melodic patterns.

DEVELOPING A MELODY INTO A SONG

The hardest task for many an aspiring songwriter is that of building these melody sections into complete songs. It's often very easy to make the mistake of wandering too far from the original melody without enough repetition to maintain the interest of the listener, resulting in a melody that seems to drift without purpose, or else to tag on a melody line that contrasts too radically from the original idea and thus make the two concepts sounds like they come from two separate songs. Alternatively, the melody line doesn't develop enough and the song comes across as flat, resulting in the classic problem of a song without a chorus.

This ability to judge the right amount of contrast between sections is perhaps the most difficult and crucial aspect of effective melodic songwriting and will come only with experience. In the meantime, there are a number of basic techniques that can be applied to help develop sections into effective songs.

The same methods that were used to build an idea into a melodic section can also be applied here:

1. Repetition of sections (particularly the chorus);
2. Variation of verses, in terms of developing the melodic or lyrical content;
3. Melodic contrast between the different sections.

With regard to this last point, there are four primary ways of highlighting contrast between sections (ie verse, chorus, pre-chorus, bridge):

1. **Change the level of the melodic line.** This can be achieved by either raising or lowering the overall pitch of the section. Often, the melody reaches up for the chorus.

2. **Change the phrase length**. If the verses are long, write chorus sections that are short, and vice versa.

3. **Change the rhythmic pattern**. Change from a simple pattern to a more complex, syncopated rhythm, or alter the speed of

the melody from slow to fast or vice versa.

4.   **Define each section.** Use a break, stop, instrumental or short build to indicate a change. These elements help to prepare and lead a listener to the next section.

As a practical example, let's apply these techniques to the example ideas shown earlier. By a process of repetition, variation and contrast, the three key sections can now be built into a complete song:

The first section (itself a result of repetition) is contrasted by a second idea, which is then contrasted by a third section (itself developed via variation). In order to avoid wandering too far from the original melody, the song returns to the first section, but this is followed by the third section. As highlighted at the start of this chapter, a great melody comprises a mix of the innovative and familiar, and in this case the listener will be surprised by the change in order but will recognise the third melody.

With such a simple example, by this stage continued repetition cannot be sustained, so a fourth section – the bridge – is introduced. This section...

- changes the melodic line by raising the pitch slightly;

- changes the phrase length by doubling the length of the chords;

- defines the section with a stop, prior to returning to the third section.

The song is then rounded off with an instrumental, an unexpected return to the first section and a resolution of the second section.

From those four short melodic sections, a neat pop song of three minutes has been composed. This is the art of much of today's commercial melody writing; it's a matter of composing relatively short, catchy phrases and balancing them by using repetition, variation and contrast.

Guy Chambers says:
'My melodies tend to come immediately, as soon as I have either a riff or a chord sequence. I don't know where they come from, but they're definitely driven by the harmony. I'm not like Burt Bacharach, who can think of a melody first and then put the harmonies to it. That's why I'm always fiddling around on the piano or guitar, looking for riffs or chord sequences. It's an obsession of mine. It always will be.'

Bill Bruford says:
'Whatever happens with your writing, you're going to make mistakes, and some pretty big ones, but that's fine as a learning process. Selected technical errors for the amateur include writing things outside the range of the instrument, incorrect transposition, writing things that are unsuitable for the instrument or barely playable, forgetting to allow breathing spaces and confusing humans with computers. I once lifted a demon 16th-note repetitive bass line wholesale from my sequencer for a human bass player with The Buddy Rich Orchestra for a session at the Power Station in New York. The take started well until, after a couple of minutes into it, I looked up to see an unhappy bass player waving his wrist in the air with acute cramp! I'd given him a part with a big stretch in one hand position for about five minutes – OK for a sequencer but essentially unplayable by a human.'

TEN TIPS FOR MELODY WRITING

'When you capture a melody, it's like capturing a fish.'

– Damon Gough, aka Badly Drawn Boy

1. The importance of simplicity in the construction of melodies cannot be stressed enough. In most classic songs, the melodies sound effortlessly simple.

2. Keep writing and experimenting with the techniques described in this chapter. The ability to judge what works and what doesn't work when writing a melody will come with experience.

3. Speak the lyrics without trying to sing them. All speech contains its own innate melody. Listen to where the words naturally fall and rise, then exaggerate those movements into a melody, making the high notes higher and the low notes lower.

    Also, listen to the rhythm of speech. When a person speaks, some words are emphasised or appear to be held longer. Exaggerate those speech rhythms into your long and short notes. This will generate a natural lock between the words and the melody.

4. Wise Buddah suggest an interesting experiment: 'If you think your melodies are all brilliant and don't need any improvement, try writing a song with one chord in it. Compose a backing track with only one chord, then attempt to come up with a great melody over the top of that one chord. It's a very difficult exercise to succeed at but very beneficial.'

5. Try delaying a melody line. This is a technique oft used by singer/songwriter Nick Drake, most of whose melody lines are quite simple but tend to start on the third beat of a bar, which is quite unusual and gives his melodies a haunting quality. Play around with the timing of melodies.

6. Writing to an unusual harmony can help to bring about fresh melodic ideas, so try an odd chord progression or an extension of a chord that you wouldn't normally use.

7. Learn how to play a successful song that you admire and work out why you like the melody so much. There might be a certain dynamic between the notes and the chord or a particular interval you can adapt for your own compositions.

8. Write a straight melody and then alter the mood by changing the pitch or adjusting the rhythm.

9. Changing keys is sometimes a very effective way of getting 'fresh ears' on a melody. It also allows a singer to hit notes that they might find impossible to reach in a higher key.

10. Learn to self-edit your melodies. Be honest with yourself. As Bill Padley of Wise Buddah observes, 'You need to work the melody police in your head at all times. If the tune isn't good, bring them in and arrest yourself for not writing a good enough melody, and then write a better one!'

Ten Tips From Tennant
By Ali Tennant

Through my experiences as a songwriter, I've come to learn many important lessons. Here are ten that I've found useful:

1. *Make certain that you're putting the song first. Concentrate on exactly what your job is. Many writers nowadays are attempting the production as well as the writing, as well as the singing. You can't be a jack of all trades; you'll become the master of none.*

2. *Unfortunately, A&R people don't recognise a song's potential unless it sounds like it's coming out of a radio. So, as a top-line writer, it's important that you work with people that can take it to that stage, or that you have people on tap that can bring it to that level of production.*

3. *Get in with the right people and make certain that you're working to your full potential. You have to delegate your time effectively. It's important that you research a writing project to know where it's going and who is involved with it, with regard to knowing who to work with and who not to work with in this business.*

4. *If you can, find yourself a manager. They can knock on doors and do all the groundwork for you. Then you just walk straight in and can concentrate on the job of writing.*

5. *The basis of songwriting is feel. How does it feel when you're singing that lyric? How does it feel when you're singing that melody? If it isn't right, stop. It's as simple as that. If it feels right, you go with it and you can be guaranteed somebody else will feel it.*

6. *I rarely get writer's block, and I guess I'm lucky. My mind is always working some way or other. When a block does creep up, though, I really listen to myself and pull back from songwriting, for maybe a day or two, and then go back to it. I don't try and force it. The minute you try to force it, it just leads to more block, so step back from it, like an artist from his easel.*

7. *If you're a singer as well as a songwriter, it's important to sing with moderation on the demos that you're pitching to other artists. When myself and Wayne Hector worked together on demos, we sang the song like it was our own. You can't do that, because you then put too much of your personality into a song. You really need to make the song non-threatening enough for the artist to go, 'I can do that. I can add to that. I can put myself into that.' So don't overdo it and over-sell the song, because it'll just end up on the shelf, collecting dust.*

8. *Songwriting and singing is very much like acting: you have to put yourself in that role to write well.*

9. *When collaborating, be open and willing to learn – it's as simple as that. You have to be willing to learn, even from somebody who is less experienced than yourself, because you don't know what angle they're coming from and they could teach you something. I've been in situations just like that and, because I was open, I went away from that situation having added to my songwriting repertoire.*

10. *Surround yourself with people who are positive and people who are successful, and aspire to have the drive that they do, so it keeps you from doubting yourself. We doubt ourselves all the time in this business. I guess I've been lucky and blessed. I know a lot of people go through a feeling of giving up. It's frightening. Many of my friends who started in the industry at the same time as me, or even before I did, are still pushing, still struggling. I think how easily I could have been in that position. It's not that I am more talented than they are; it's just a matter of the right door being opened at the right time by the right person. So I count my blessings.*

THE SONGWRITER:

MARK FISHLOCK

SING SOMETHING SIMPLE

One of my favourite quotes is by the Spanish artist Pablo Picasso, who said, 'It took me four years to paint like Raphael but a lifetime to paint like a child.' Looking at the beautifully simple and free-flowing line drawings Picasso produced when he was in his 80s, you can see what he was getting at. There's a wonderful confidence and certainty of line in the art of young children, an instinctive quality that's lost through self-consciousness and learning. Yet most adults who claim they can't draw made fabulous pictures when they were kids.

Another quote by Picasso sums this up: 'Every child is an artist. The problem is how to remain an artist once he grows up.' The art of songwriting can be similar. There was a fresh exuberance to some of the songs I wrote as a teenager that was lost in my later material, after I'd learned more about the mechanics of composing.

But what is a simple tune? When does simple become bland? The Police's 'Every Breath You Take' is a perfect example of simplicity at its most brilliant. The chord sequence has been used a million times, the lyric and melody contain a high degree of repetition, and on the face of it there's no reason why the song should sound as fresh and original as it does.

I used to think that doing something that had never been done before constituted originality. In songwriting terms – particularly when I was in a prog-rock band – this meant writing outlandish leaps, melodic lines against unusual chords and generally working to the principle that something was worth keeping only if it hadn't been done before. More often than not, there was a very good reason why it hadn't been done before: it was rubbish.

It's one of the great mysteries of music that, with such limited raw material – 12 notes, a handful of chords and, as lyricist Barry Mason says, a comparatively small dictionary of usable words – it's possible to write anything original, yet people still do. Answers on a postcard…

The Beatles are fantastic role models, when it comes to songwriting. In their songs, what might start as a conventional progression is often upset by a moment of unexpected quirkiness – suddenly going into a minor key, for example. The middle-eight in 'Every Breath You Take' serves this function, and when the song returns to the A–F#m–D–E form the familiarity makes it even more effective. Like the little blemish that makes imperfection sexy, small things can give a song its unique signature.

Letting go of this conscious, often paranoid quest for originality was a big moment in my songwriting development and was brought about by the specific demands of writing a large number of children's songs. These days I ask myself where the melody wants to go, and where once I would block the way I now let it go there with my best wishes.

To my surprise, this new approach did not result in predictable and derivative tunes. Instead there was a natural flow, a 'rightness', to the melody that was also fresh and original. It didn't solve the mystery of what makes a good tune, but it stopped me driving myself crazy trying to find one.

Song Craft 8: The Harmony

A working knowledge of harmony is very important for a songwriter, as very often the distinctive appeal of a song relies on the composer's imaginative use of chords. As the songwriter Bill Padley explains, 'Nowadays it's too easy for people to pick up a sequencer and say, "I am now a musician." I'm not suggesting you should learn to read music up to Grade 8, but if you've had a grounding in how chords fit together and what sounds right and what doesn't sound right, you're off to a good start.'

Harmonisation could be considered as playing a similar role in music as that of colour in painting. Where melody and lyric create the basic black-and-white sketch, the particular choice of chords brings out the 'colour', or the emotion, in a song. It's a theory with which songwriter Michelle Escoffery agrees: 'By having a wide understanding of music, this enables a songwriter to marry melody and lyric with various genres and evoke the relevant emotions and create the scene, context and framework for each song.'

Chords are created when three or more notes are played simultaneously. Their individual quality depends upon their complexity (ie the number of notes they contain and the intervals between the notes) and their relationship to other chords in a musical sequence. They are the building blocks of harmony, which in turn forms a song's musical foundation upon which all the other elements rest.

Naturally, there are many songs that don't rely on harmony. Many songs in contemporary genres, such as dance, prefer to focus instead on vocal melodic lines, rhythmic tracks, bass lines and instrumental riffs. However, the majority of songs do require harmony, and a songwriter should acquire a working knowledge of what it is and how to use it.

Within the context of this book, the theory and technicalities of harmony won't be considered. It's recommended that this knowledge is gained either from learning a polyphonic instrument (ie one that can play more than one note at a time), such as the piano or guitar, or from a music-theory book. What *will* be considered, however, is the effect and relationships of harmony and how a songwriter might apply these to his or her work.

THE EFFECTS OF CHORDS

Different chords tend to express different emotions or attitudes, which is why certain genres of music attract particular groupings of chords and the application of certain harmonies. Rock, pop, country and folk styles, for example, tend to adopt the simpler major or minor triads, while jazz, funk and crossover styles attract more complex chords, such as augmented, diminished and sixth chords.

The following section describes the typical emotions or attitudes expressed by the most popular chords and chord patterns. Obviously, the manner in which they're performed and the instrument on which they're played will greatly influence the overall effect, but these guidelines should prove useful when applying them during the initial stages of songwriting. I recommended that you experiment with these chords on either a guitar or piano while reading this book in order to truly comprehend their sound and accompanying effect on the listener. Once you have a thorough understanding of each chord's emotive potential, this should help in your selection and application of harmony when songwriting.

Major Triad

This type of chord is generally considered to be bright, strong and happy-sounding (compared to the minor). However, it is capable of expressing a broad range of emotions, depending on how such chords are performed or voiced, from angry ('Smells Like Teen Spirit') to buoyant ('Twist And Shout') to melancholic nostalgia ('Sweet Home Chicago'). This is why – aside from their simplicity of construction – major chords prove to be the most common in contemporary music, from the blues to rock to pop.

Guy Chambers says:
'Piano and guitar are completely different songwriting tools. The guitar lends itself to playing more obvious chord sequences and is somewhat restrictive because of this, whereas with the piano it tends to be much easier to go to unusual keys and thus opens a writer up to many more riffs. You can obviously write riffs on a guitar, but in the cases where someone is writing on an acoustic guitar, it's very easy to fall into playing the standard G–D–Em–C progressions. Not that there's anything wrong with being obvious, but I tend to like creating harmony that's slightly different or unusual.'

Justin Hawkins of The Darkness says:
"I quite often write on keyboards nowadays. Because I am not that a good player, I sometimes stumble across chords that I would never have thought of using. So on this new album we have ended up with these wonderful piano parts that nobody else can play."

David Stoll says:
There are two main reasons why a knowledge of harmony can help your work. The first is that, as a general rule, inspiration is bounded by the limits of your capabilities. And so, though the technical expertise will not necessarily bring in the inspiration, it will expand your options as to how to use it. The second reason is that harmonic understanding can help you when you know that something is wrong but cannot quite put your finger on what. A bit of informed analysis can save you hours of trial and error.

Minor Triad

This type of chord is more fixed in its nature, producing a sound that can be described as 'sad' and featuring prominently in songs like Bill Withers' 'Ain't No Sunshine' and REM's 'Losing My Religion'. D minor is infamous for being heralded as 'the saddest chord' in the spoof rockumentary movie *This Is Spiñal Tap*. When combined with major chords in a song, the majority of human emotions and attitudes can be generated. However, by adding other notes to these basic triads, alternative, more subtle emotions can be suggested.

Dominant Seventh

The addition of the flattened seventh gives a chord a harder, bluesy quality. Seventh chords can be used to toughen up a chord sequence, as in Crowded House's 'Better Be Home Soon'; to create harmonic tension, as in 'Hey Jude'; or to prepare the listener for a key change, as in the intro to David Bowie's 'Let's Dance'.

Major Seventh

This chord tends to have a more romantic, jazzier, softer feel than the dominant seventh and so is more suited to expressing gentle, intimate emotions within a song. This type of chord is often found in ballads, soul, pop and MOR music, where the slower tempo allows it to have the most effect on a listener. 'Wild World' by Labi Siffre uses a major-seventh chord to great effect in the verse section, as does Andy Williams' classic 'Can't Take My Eyes Off You'. Many Latin-influenced songs also use the major seventh, despite generally having faster tempos.

Minor Seventh

This type of chord is very useful where the 'saddening' effect of a minor chord needs to be diminished slightly. A minor seventh acts as a diluted version of the minor chord, and so tends to combine well with major chords or major sevenths to create a smoother, more harmonious transition. The effect can be easily demonstrated by comparing the following chord progression...

| C | Dm | Em | F |

...with the more fluid...

| Cmaj7 | Dm7 | Em7 | Fmaj7 |

Minor/Major Seventh

This unusual harmony is regularly used as a passing chord, as demonstrated wonderfully in 'Something' by George Harrison.

Suspended Chords

These types of chord don't have an interval of a third in their construction, and so technically are neither major nor minor chords. Consequently, they always yearn to resolve to either the major or (less commonly) the minor, and their resultant sound quality is more tense. The suspended fourth, for instance, is perfect for building excitement when leading up to a transition between sections, such as verse to chorus, while the suspended second has more space and ambiguity and so tends to suggest a light, airy feel that is spacious and 'hung', producing an effect that's great for more atmospheric or acoustic songs.

Suspended chords also combine very well with each other. Try playing the following repeated sequence...

| Asus2 | A | Asus4 | A |

...and then lead this off into a D chord, as if you were going into a chorus.

Fifth Chords

This type of chord forms the basis for the classic power chord on the guitar. Like suspended chords, it doesn't contain a third, and it is this tonal neutrality that makes it suitable for hard-rock music, as it sounds 'hard' and both minor or major scales can be played over it, as there's less chance of notes clashing. The fifth chord can toughen up a harmonic progression and tends to combine well with full major or minor chords in arrangements for different instruments. When their two notes are doubled or tripled, fifth chords lend themselves well to moody, aggressive acoustic songs, as demonstrated in many of Noel Gallagher's compositions.

Sixth Chords

Major-sixth chords tend to lend a slightly jazzy or Latin quality to a song, while the minor sixth adds dissonance to a chord and intensifies its minor nature. This dissonant quality means that such chords are rarely used in contemporary music, although The Beatles made great use of them at the ends of many of their songs, such as 'She Loves You'.

Obviously, there many other types of chords in existence, and the more intervals they contain, the more complex they sound and the subtler their resulting 'colour'. Some, such as 13th chords, are too complex for any practical use in contemporary songwriting because their tone colours are too indistinct. The dominant-seventh, sharpened-ninth chord, however, is useful in funk and heavy rock and was made famous by Jimi Hendrix in such tracks as 'Purple Haze' and 'Crosstown Traffic', while the minor-ninth chord is great for intensifying the standard minor triad and is used in soul and MOR tracks, such as Eric Clapton's 'Badge'. Meanwhile, the added-ninth chord is great for creating tension, as demonstrated in Andy Summers' guitar part in The Police's 'Message In A Bottle'.

As a songwriter, the best thing to do to familiarise yourself with the various types of chord is to experiment with them. Play about with possible voicings of each chord to discover what works best for you. This is how a songwriter develops his or her unique style or sound.

The most important thing to remember, when composing harmony for a song, is that extended chords should be used carefully. One well-placed seventh or ninth chord that adds a touch of harmonic colour at a key moment in a song is better than a whole heap of fancy 11th or 13th chords that confuse the harmonic content.

CHORD PROGRESSIONS

'If you use more than five chords in a song, you should be arrested.'

– Sheryl Crow

The real skill in harmonisation lies not simply in knowing which chords to choose but in understanding the correct order in which those chords should be placed in relation to the melody and emotion of the song. The relationship between chords influences their overall sound, emotion and meaning, and it's this factor more than anything else that will ultimately determine the effectiveness of the harmony within the context of the entire song.

To understand how chords work together, they must be viewed in the context of a scale. The majority of songs can be harmonised completely using diatonic chords (ie chords comprising notes taken from within the scale). In the key of C major, these would be:

C Dm Em F G Am Bdim

I   II   III IV V VI   VII

Chords I, IV and V are considered to be *primary chords*, since they're the only major chords derived from the scale, they always sound good together and they're the most flexible in conveying the broadest range of moods and emotions, depending on how they're played. Primary chords are the foundation stones of hundreds of thousands of songs, such as 'Twist And Shout', 'Brimful Of Asha' and many traditional 12-bar blues songs.

Chords II, III, VI and VII are classed as *secondary chords*. These chords are minor in tonality and therefore sound sadder and darker than their major counterparts. As such, they are ideal for providing harmonic and emotional contrast within a song without departing from the root key. This 'push and pull' between light and dark can be heard in songs like Bob Seger's 'Against The Wind'.

When you're deciding which of these diatonic chords to use, it's also important to consider their respective functions within harmonic progressions. These can be divided into three main categories that remain the same, whatever the key or harmonic context: the tonic, the dominant and the subdominant.

As a songwriter, it's beneficial to remember the propensities of these chords because there's generally a strong inclination for music to want to move from being 'at rest' (ie the tonic chord) to 'moving along' (the subdominant) to 'needing to resolve' (the dominant) and back again. For example, with a basic chord progression in the key of E...

| E | A | F#m | B | E | etc

...the first chord is I (ie the tonic) and is the home sound – it is 'at rest'. The next two chords are IV and II and are subdominant in function, so have a feeling of 'moving along'. The B chord is the dominant (V) and therefore provides the need to resolve – which it does, back to E.

However, if a song demands greater emotional contrast or a less standard approach, chords from outside the scale can be used. These are known as *chromatic chords*, and in the key of C they include the chords D, E and Fm. Such chords are created by turning the chords of II and III into major chords and the chord of IV into a minor. They're considered to be 'slightly outside', as each has only one note that falls outside the scale. These chords have the effect of pulling the harmony away from the key and are useful for creating tension without throwing the listener completely from the 'home sound', or 'root', of the song. Their effect can be heard in the chorus of 'All You Need Is Love' by The Beatles as the song moves to the chords of A7 and B7.

Try playing the following two progressions and notice the difference:

| C | Dm | F | G | C | Em | F | G |

| C | D | F | G | C | E | F | G |

If an even greater contrast is required, try using chords containing more than one note from outside the scale. While not going as far as to alter the key of a song completely, these chords – deemed 'further outside' – comprise the flattened major versions of III, VI and VII. In the key of C, then, these are E♭, A♭ and B♭. When introduced effectively into a harmonic progression, these chords can lead a song in a fresh and unexpected direction. They're often used in pop and rock music due to their bluesy quality, while their hard-edged sound can be heard in numerous rock songs, including The Rolling Stones' 'Brown Sugar', Jimi Hendrix's 'Hey Joe' and the bridge section of Bryan Adams' 'Summer Of '69'.

From this foundation of primary, secondary, slightly outside and further outside chords, the natural tendencies of the diatonic chords and the emotive effect of a chord's various extensions (as covered in the previous section), a songwriter has all the tools required with which to build a song's harmonic structure.

BUILDING A SONG

Most songs are constructed from relatively short harmonic progressions comprising three or four chords, which are then repeated to form a song section. Each phrase, or 'turnaround', can be a single part ready to be matched with another verse, bridge or chorus progression, or it can function as the basis for a complete song, as in the cycled I–IV–V progression of 'La Bamba'.

It's also possible for a song to have just one chord, although such songs are rare and extremely challenging to write (Bob Marley managed it successfully with 'Exodus'). More common are two-chord songs, such as 'Get Up (I Feel Like Being A) Sex Machine' by James Brown and Bruce Springsteen's 'Born In The USA'. The challenge is to avoid monotony in the harmony, and there are a number of techniques that can be used to maintain interest, including:

- Ensuring that the lyric and melody are particularly strong, since the simplicity of a two-chord song will emphasise these elements;

- Using different voicings and inversions of the chords to keep them sounding fresh;

- Altering the lengths of the chord changes – for instance, if the chord changes every two bars in the verse, change it once every bar in the chorus;

- Using the bass to imply a chord change from that stated by the principal harmonic instrument (eg an E played under a chord of G will imply Em);

- Varying the tempo or time signature.

It can be very beneficial to experiment in writing two-chord songs. Firstly, it will stretch your abilities in lyric and melody writing, developing your skills in sustaining interest over a very basic harmonic background. Secondly, it will hone your instinct for listening and judging when a song is becoming boring or needs to finish. Thirdly, you'll start to become aware of the immense difference in expressive quality and attitude that a simple chord change can make. The movement from chord I to chord II (ie C to Dm in the key of C), for instance, is profound, since every note changes, and it's a very popular movement in reggae, whereas the switch from I to VI (ie C to Am in the key of C) incorporates only a single note change but creates one of the strongest shift in moods, from a major to a minor chord.

It's worth experimenting with all possible chord changes so you get to hear the expressive qualities of each, from the easy feel of I–IV (eg C to F) to the strong sense of key in a I–V movement (eg C to G) to the traditionally hard-edged blues shift experienced in the shift from I to flattened III (eg C to E♭) to the poignant change from I to the minor IV (eg C to Fm).

The most common turnaround occurs in the three-chord song. This has its roots in the traditional 12-bar blues, which itself leads onto the rock 'n' roll of the 1950s and beyond. Everything from Chuck Berry's 'Johnny B Goode' to The Clash's 'Should I Stay Or Should I Go?' to Pulp's 'Common People' have used the standard I–IV–V form.

From this foundation, many successful songs have been derived simply by adapting the order or by replacing I, IV or V with another chord from the harmonised scale (Radiohead, for instance, replaced chord V with II for their song 'High And Dry' [II–IV–I]) or even from outside the scale, such as in U2's 'Desire' (I–♭VII–IV).

The next logical step is to advance to the four-chord progression. This is considered to be the most stable songwriting form, since the four chords involved lend themselves well to the common 4/4 time signature, whereas three-chord songs have to repeat one of the chords if they are to achieve the same degree of musical symmetry.

The most popular four-chord turnarounds start on the I chord and end on the V chord, as this progression gives a strong sense of key and upward drive. The chorus to The Troggs' 'Love Is All Around' is a great example of the I–II–IV–V movement, while Marvin Gaye's 'Let's Get It On' utilises the I–III–IV–V progression and Ben E King's 'Stand By Me' exemplifies the all-time classic turnaround of I–VI–IV–V.

The disadvantage of such neatness and symmetry is that it can lead to predictability and monotony, so a songwriter should work hard at crafting a melody and lyric that sustains the interest of the listener throughout the song or else combine different sequences in order to avoid this potential pitfall.

Beyond these options, the variations of chord progressions and harmonic choices are as boundless as the songwriter's imagination. Ultimately, it will be a matter of what sounds good and what chords can be pitched with your written melody. Nirvana's classic sequence of I–IV–♭III–♭VI) in their song 'Smells Like Teen Spirit' demonstrates exactly what can be achieved by pushing the envelope of convention while remaining true to the benefits of simplicity. The song contains a very dislocated harmonic progression by jumping between one key and another, but it's the simple symmetry of the chords that holds it together. Similarly, the highly unusual yet natural-sounding movement from II to VIIm will forever be associated with The Doors' 'Light My Fire'. The harmonic choices that a songwriter makes will indelibly stamp his or her personality onto the songs that he or she writes.

HARMONISING A MELODY LINE

As a songwriter, you'll be faced both with the task of writing a melody to a set harmonic progression and the equally challenging mission of harmonising a pre-written melody, and it would be beneficial if you could approach either with the same consummate skill.

In order to harmonise a melody effectively, you'll need to have a thorough understanding of intervals, chords and their inversions, scales and something called the 'cycle of fifths' (see 'The Language Of Songwriting' at the end of this book), but you'll also need to develop your aural skills so you can tell what harmony sounds best for any given melody line. Since each melody can often be harmonised in a variety of ways, the ultimate choice of harmony is best left to the ingenuity of the writer. However, by applying the techniques described in 'Song Craft 7' on generating melody from harmony, combined with an understanding of the functions and effects of different chords and their relationships with one another, certain obvious choices for harmonisation will surface.

As I explained earlier, each chord type will evoke a different emotional response in the listener. The almost infinite number of harmonic permutations, therefore, allow for increasingly complex arrangements. Even so, it's often the more simple progressions that prove the most effective. The majority of British and American pop songs can be harmonised using just three chords: I, IV and V. With this in mind, it's best to start simply and work up from there.

If you're someone to whom harmonising doesn't come naturally, here are five areas to look at that will help with the process:

1.   **The key of the melody**. This will dictate the scale from which the primary and secondary chords will be generated, as well as those chords slightly and further outside the scale.

2.   **The overall tone of the song.** This will influence the appropriate application of minor or major chords.

3.   **The direction and emotion of the melody.** This will affect the type of chord chosen. A lifting, positive melody will encourage a happy, strong chord.

4.   **The song's lyrics.** This too will influence the quality of the chord. If the lyrics are particularly sad, an extension of a minor chord might be appropriate.

5.   **The style of the music.** This will definitely affect the type of chords chosen. Jazz, for example, will favour more complex extensions, while a pop song will be best served by basic major and minor chords.

David Stoll On...
...Harmonic Flow

This comes from controlling the tensions and releases which appear when you move away from and back towards the tonic, or perhaps, a temporary home key (say in the middle-eight).

I am going to expand that now and tell you that – for similar reasons – harmonic tension and release are also achieved by moving from more complex to simpler chords. (The acoustic reason is that, for the ear, once a tonic is established, the home chord is in fact the simplest chord and other chords – even common major cords – are complex relative to that tonic.) Enrich a chord with added notes or accidentals, or both, and the more you move away from the basic major chord, the more resolution is felt when you return to it. Without going into details, this is a way of explaining why the last chord of a song in the minor is often played in its major version.

A good song will have a flow of tensions and releases that's just right for that song. Just as effecting a rhyme on a main beat adds to its force, so resolving a harmonic tension in that same place will add yet more. The longer you delay that release – by moving though other chordal areas – the more powerful will be the effect of the return home. The biggest release will usually come at the end of a verse and can be spoiled by being anticipated earlier. One way of creating a false conclusion is by following a dominant with a submediant (V7–VI) – for example, G7–Am – and interrupting the expected close. Then you may repeat the phrase, but this time ending with the tonic.

As a general rule, moving towards the flat side of a key, the world of its subdominant, is a move into more restful areas. The opposite direction – going towards the sharp, dominant side – is to move out strongly into fresh fields. We all know what repeating a final chorus a note higher will do. The reason for the brightness is that, not only does the move up in pitch bring in a lift but we've moved into the dominant of the dominant – a very confident shift.

Another way of using harmonic dynamism is by increasing or decreasing the pace of change of harmonies. The more often the harmonies shift, the more the tension increases. So, for example, sitting on one chord for two bars, changing for one bar and then having two different chords in the next bar will add to the feeling of build.

Of course, other factors – such as rhythm, dynamics, texture, instrumentation, voice range, etc – will also affect the song's flow, as will the way in which the melody moves up and down in pitch, but the harmony is a strong way to affect the listener's mood beneath the surface, as it were.

And don't forget that it's possible to use these tools in reverse. For instance, if you want a feeling of incompletion at the end of a section or a song, leave the harmony hanging on a dominant or even a secondary dominant.

...Convincing Harmonic Flow

Generally, a chord moves most comfortably to another one which shares one or more of its notes. There is a very smooth move from I–VI – for example, C to Am – because two of the notes, C and E, are common to both chords. I-III is similarly smooth; in C major again, E and G are common to C and Em. Not quite so smooth, though easy enough, is the move from I to IV, where only one note is common – in C major, the C itself (the chords are C-E-G and F-A-C). This allows us to make some rather neat shifts into fairly unrelated keys. (Incidentally, notice how V–I involves a change of two of the notes, keeping only the dominant note itself common. This is another factor in making the chord of I seem a final achievement, this time for reasons of harmonic flow.)

...Harmony On Piano And Guitar

The guitar has an advantage in showing you directly (with barred chords) chordal relationships that are the same whichever key you're in. You can play chords in their different inversions (based on the unbarred E shapes, A shapes and C major shapes, in the normal tuning), but it's difficult to choose which notes in a chord are doubled; that's usually set for you by the strings which double (ie repeat) some of the notes at another register (ie up or down an octave). And which notes are doubled is an important element in imparting a chord's flavour.

The piano has the advantage of showing you the relationship between notes as one chord moves to another. You can affect which notes are doubled and – usually more easily than on a guitar – and also sort out the bass line. Both piano and guitar are supremely sophisticated harmonic tools. I'd recommend trying out your songs on both as you're writing them, if possible. It's true that one might well work better than the other for a rhythmic accompaniment that anticipates the final production, but by exploring the chord progressions on both, the harmonic world of the song will be opened up for you in new and useful ways. This could give you useful ideas for correction and improvement, if necessary.

...Bass Lines

Using inversions can improve a song dramatically. Our first instinct is often to use the bass note of a chord as the bass note of the song whenever that chord is played. However, great harmonic dynamism may be added by occasionally changing the bass note to another note in the chord. This also allows you to make a better line of the bass part itself. So, as a very simple example, in the progression C–C–F–C, try using an E as the bass note for the repeat of the C chord.

By judicious use of inversions and passing notes (ie linking the main harmonic support note to the next with notes in between – in the example just given, insert a D on a non-main beat between the first C and the E), the bass line starts to take on a life of its own. For various reasons, it's better not to use the fifth of a chord as the bass note (G as the bass of C, for instance) except in passing – for example, when going down the scale of C underneath a C major chord. One exception to this is when preparing a strong cadence, when having a dominant note under a tonic chord, followed by the same dominant note under its own chord, leads powerfully to the tonic in root position, with the tonic as the bass note – for instance, a chord of C over the note G, then G7 over the note G, then a final chord of C. It's when a chord has its root note in the bass that it sounds most stable.

Sometimes a repeated or held bass note underneath several different chords may be very effective. This is what's known as a pedal point.

...Harmonising A Melody

Most tunes have obvious harmonies. In a way, the melodies give a surface to their harmonic progression. In general, the notes on the main beats are notes within the chord that supports them, and other notes link between those defining notes, often by step-wise movement. So, when you're stuck trying to find a chord for a note, if it feels like a main beat note that's not standing outside its chord, you have a choice of six chords to try out. The most common three are the chords within the key which have that note as their bottom, middle or top note: for the note C, and in a song in C major, these chords are C, Am or F. The less likely chords to fit under the note C in a song in C major are Cm, Ab and Fm. Having found the right chord for that note, the next one should relate not only to the next notes in the melody but also to the previous chord to form a meaningful sequence.

Incidentally, a sustained note in the melody accompanied by shifting chords can sound very effective.

After taking these points into account, a songwriter's primary considerations are exactly which notes to harmonise and which chords to choose.

When applying harmonies to pre-existing melodies, the rhythm of the accompaniment will usually turn out to be much simpler than the rhythm of the melody, principally because the melody often moves faster than the harmony. Yet again, the choice of which notes in a melody should be harmony notes and which should be passing melodic notes will depend on the songwriter's own aural sense of direction. However, here are some guidelines that can be applied:

- Notes that fall on the beat tend to be treated as harmony notes;

- This is also true of 'leaping' notes (ie those that indicate a change of harmonic direction);

- By playing the original melody through, a songwriter can get a 'feel' for the natural harmonic rhythms. Any repetitions and similarities in the melody will help to suggest the harmonic structure. It's not enough simply to harmonise bar 1, then bar 2, etc, changing the chord each bar; a songwriter needs to listen to where a movement is most appropriate.

Once the harmony notes have been identified, these should inform the basis of the chord choice. Generally speaking, the note to be harmonised will be present in the accompanying chord, or else be an extension of it, and you'll also need to take a look at the melody notes that immediately follow on from it to ensure that they also fit with the chord. Then each chord needs to be linked with the next one in order to give a sense of progression – moving forward in some places and resting at 'goal' points, such as the ends of phrases. This is where knowledge of the tonic, dominant and subdominant chord functions becomes important.

Using The Police's 'Every Breath You Take' as an example to harmonise, the melody of the first line ends on G on the first beat of the bar. The harmony required therefore should have a G in it, which gives you the following basic options: G, Gm, Em, E♭, C and Cm. Chords that use G as an extension (ie A7), suspended chords, augmented chords or diminished chords could also be considered, but in the context of a pop song these might be too unstable for the first chord of a bar. The main decision, therefore, needs to be whether this chord is major or minor. In this case, the most natural-sounding chord is that of G, because the leading phrase outlines the same chord, with its repetition of the B note (ie B C B A G).

Continuing the harmonising process, the vocal melody line is echoed three times (with slight rhythmic and melodic differences each time), so there's no reason why the harmony couldn't stay on a chord of G. However, this would sound uninspiring, as there would be no sense of movement in the song. Instead, to create the requisite harmonic interest, the harmony can move to two of the other chord choices – the Em and then the C – while the melody repeats before 'leaping' to the note A, suggesting the next chord of D major. This progression could then continue throughout the whole song.

If a songwriter is skilled on their instrument, this procedure should come quite naturally, but for anyone new to the concept of harmonising a melody, here are ten basic steps that can be followed.

TEN STEPS TO HARMONISING A MELODY

1.   Listen to the melody.

2.   Decide on the key – major or minor?

3.   Write out the natural points of change.

4.   Analyse the melody for passing, 'leaping' and harmony notes.

5.   Work out the basic triads that these notes suggest.

6.   Analyse the phrase structure of the melody to find where there are repetitions or natural cadences (ie points of rest or resolution).

7.   Consider using chord I near the beginning (preferably on a strong beat), as this helps to establish the key.

8.   Consider all possible chord choices for each main harmony note as your choice will determine the unique texture of the harmonisation.

9.   Play melody and bass line together to make sure that this combination works and that there are no inappropriate clashes.

10.   Carefully select and voice all chords. Most music benefits from having the chords flowing into one another, which can be achieved through the use of numerous different voicings and inversions.

An Interview With Richard Kerr

How do you go about writing a song?
For me, there's no greater feeling than having written a song that you love.

If I have the heart of an idea there in my head and my hands when I'm sitting at the keyboard, literally any noises and distractions can be going on around me and I can't hear them. There could be a brass band playing down the street and I wouldn't hear it. Good music obliterates everything else for me.

Nearly all my songs are collaborations with a lyricist. That's my favourite way of writing, with me sitting at the keyboard and the lyricist in the room, just bouncing ideas off one another, musically or lyrically. Then I can muck around on the piano until suddenly I find myself or my collaborator saying, 'Oh, I love that!' I find myself searching for chord progressions that fit a picture that has come into my mind. It may be a situation or a story, whether it's a love lost or love gained, or simply the situation of the world. Ninety-nine times out of 100, though, my collaborator will ignore the lyrical story implicit in my melody and go their own way!

How did Barry Manilow's 'Mandy' come to be written?
I wrote the song with Scott English. We'd wandered next door to his neighbour's house, just off Curzon Street, to play her upright piano and we wrote the song there in an afternoon. There may have been a few lines that might have needed some tweaking later, but basically the whole song was down in the afternoon. I didn't ask Scott about the lyrics to 'Mandy'; I pictured this woman in my own way when I wrote the melody. At that time, though, the song was called 'Brandy'.

If anything, Scott believed in the song more than I did. I always believed it to be a good song, but he believed in it so much that he recorded it himself and had a hit with 'Brandy' in the UK. His version was also released in the States and got to about Number 85 for a week and then went out again.

The song was then picked up by Clive Davis, head of CBS and later Arista Records, as a possible vehicle for his new singer, Barry Manilow. Clive decided to change the original title because he'd just had a Number One on CBS with 'Brandy, You Are A Fine Girl' by Looking Glass. So the title was changed from 'Brandy' to 'Mandy' without anybody asking myself or Scott. I was really upset until it entered the *Billboard* Hot 100 at Number 65. And this was for a new artist who had never had a hit before! In January 1975, it was Number One. Today, the song has been recognised by BMI for over 4 million airplays in the USA alone. So no, I'm not so upset today!

Do you think it's easier to write ballads?
I've certainly had more success with ballads. I'm passionate about melody and am definitely an emotional guy, and that helps with writing ballads. I never started off writing purely ballads, though, but success found me falling into a pattern of writing more ballads.

Why do you not write lyrics?
I've tried so many times over the years, but I'm always too long-winded. I can never boil down an idea to three or four minutes. I've written lyrics on my own songs on my own albums in years gone by, but I've been blessed to have written with some of the best lyricists in the world and could never compete, or want to compete, on their level.

With Will Jennings, I loved where his mind came from on such songs as 'Somewhere In The Night', 'Looks Like We Made It' and 'I'll Never Love This Way Again'. We can all say, 'I love you', but it's the *way* you say it that counts. We were so simpatico in the way we viewed life that it didn't really matter if the melody came first or the lyric came first. It wasn't only a very successful collaboration but writing at its height of pleasure.

What do you consider makes a good lyricist?
Someone who can inject soulfulness and honesty into their words and make you feel that you're actually there and involved in the song. If you're simply sitting down to write a song for the sake of it, which is a hard thing to do these days, the ability to inject humanity and passion into it is a key to the song's success.

Furthermore, a lyricist needs to be adaptable. For instance, if you've been offered a particular subject to write for – whether it be for a piece of television, a film or an artist – which is not your normal style, then you need to be flexible enough to adapt to a new direction.

Have you ever suffered from writers' block?
Yes, but I think it's part and parcel of the creative process. You can't have great ideas all the time. You need to understand as a writer when to leave an idea alone and when to pursue it.

If I have a deadline and I'm actually working on a project, I just keep on working at it. Obviously, I have to take breaks and wander off somewhere for a while and clear my mind. Over the years I think I gradually gained the experience of knowing what to do, when to give it a rest and when to keep trying. I'm very capable of procrastination if there's no deadline.

How do you approaching the splitting of a song when collaborating? And what advice would you give?

Fifty-fifty. No question about that. Whatever the situation.

Here's an example. There was one song that was a hit for Natalie Cole that I'd written about 90 per cent of the lyric for and just couldn't finish. The melody for the whole song had been finished months previously, but no matter what I tried to do, I couldn't get the lyric the way I wanted it, so I presented it to a lyricist and told him to ignore the whole lyric if he wanted to, start afresh, but he liked what I'd done, lyrically. He came back, having finished it overnight. It was just a couple of lines, but there was never any question that it wasn't 50/50 in my head, because I couldn't finish the song on my own. There was never going to be any 70/30 split because he'd written only two or three lines.

If you have a lot of people involved in the writing or the production of the demo and they're all wanting a piece of the action, then you'd better have something written down on paper from the outset to prevent any comeback or problems after a record has been made or the songs have been completed.

What made you want to become a full-time songwriter?

I was buying the wines for Fortnum & Mason in Piccadilly at the same time as my songs were being published, and I had a recording deal offered to me by Deram, of Decca Records. They put Les Perrin in charge of promoting me; he was the publicist for the Stones and David Bowie. The angle Les took on me was as 'ex-public-school boy and Fortnum & Mason wine seller becomes pop star', because that was very interesting then, even if it sounds really tame today.

Fortnum & Mason hated the association with the pop industry and gave me an ultimatum: 'If we see our name in print again associated with your music, you're out.' I was terrified because I'd never dreamed, even at that stage, that I could ever make a living in the pop-music world, so I begged Les to make sure that Fortnum & Mason's name wasn't associated with me. When the first single came out, though, the PR train was already rolling. Fortnum's fired me. In a way it was a blessing in disguise because it pushed me away from dreaming about the great love of my life and actually living it.

What advice would you give an aspiring songwriter of today?

I'm probably the last person you should ask! Don't do as I did, but do as I suggest: collaborate, network as much as you can and meet as many artists, producers, managers, etc – no matter how up-and-coming – as possible.

In this country, there's such a stigma attached by people and the media to an artist if they record someone else's song. Why? It staggers me. Sinatra never wrote a song in his life, to my knowledge. Aretha Franklin, Gladys Knight, all the artists Holland/Dozier/Holland wrote for – nobody thought less of them because they didn't write their own songs. Such an attitude – along with piracy – has made it harder to be purely a songwriter.

Essentially, if you really believe you have something special to say, stick with it. As Dionne Warwick said after a 13-year comeback with 'I'll Never Love This Way Again', 'If you love what you do, you just keep on keeping on until you can keep on no longer.'

SONG CRAFT 9:
KEYS AND KEY CHANGES

'I hear the sounds and the places the music goes and then I look for the appropriate vocabulary to express it.'

– Nitin Sawhney

The 'key' of a piece of music is its tonal centre. Landing on the key chord or note gives a sense that the harmony is at 'home' or at 'rest'. Movement away from this home position within the same key provides a sense of distance, evoking various emotional associations. A change of key can be seen as the equivalent of visiting a foreign country: it could be nearby and similar in nature to the original key or far away and very different.

Choice of key is an important consideration when composing a song. Particular keys are associated with certain emotions, moods and 'feels'. Also, if a songwriter always writes in one key, a simple change to an unusual key can often inspire fresh melodic ideas. Furthermore, a different key will allow a singer or top-line writer to reach new notes and therefore stretch and vary the range of the lead melody line. As Mark Knopfler of Dire Straits puts it, 'Different keys suggest different moods. I can't always get any height on my voice, so I tend to choose keys that might not suit the song but happen to suit my non-existent range. Sometimes you pick the wrong key when you're recording. "Why Worry" was recorded in E, and you can hear it's the wrong key; I'm straining to sing it, and I think on our last tour we changed it to D.'

Major keys or scales are generally considered more positive than their minor counterparts. Dan Hawkins, guitarist and songwriter in The Darkness, explains how important choice of key is in determining a song's impact and his band's distinctive sound: 'We use the minor chords regularly. It's probably the most important thing we do. We need something that sounds emotive. "Love On The Rocks" is nearly all in a minor key. A big mistake with bands who are starting out is not to recognise the importance of key when songwriting. I'll literally go through every key there is to find the right one for Justin's voice so that, when we hit the chorus, his voice can really take off. Our Christmas song changed key probably about three or four times before we found the right place for it. Inexperienced musicians and songwriters tend to play their songs in the wrong key, but it's essential to get it right for the best vocal performance.'

WHY MODULATE?

The term *modulation* refers to a key change in a piece of music. In classical music, key changes are used to impose a structure on long pieces and to express different meanings and movements. In contemporary music, modulation is less crucial but can still be desirable to introduce interest and contrast within a song. 'Band On The Run' by Wings, for instance, has three key changes.

While all major keys have identical internal structures (ie the scale notes of each major key share exactly the same relationship, in terms of tones and semitones), there is a subjective sense of movement when a key change is introduced. Each move creates an individual impression of distance from the original key. Changing from the key of C major to B♭ minor, for instance, creates a more profound impression than that from C major to the key of G major, which shares more notes with C than B♭ minor.

In short, key changes can be used to...

- **Provide interest.** Numerous pop songs change key at the end, during repetitions of the chorus, in order to maintain a listener's attention and to increase the level of excitement.

- **Offer contrast.** Classic power ballads often change key when entering the bridge section in order to enhance the music's emotional content.

- **Express meaning.** There are many songs that use a key change to inject new meaning into a song. Such a shift might support the lyrical content or completely undermine it. A reverse use of key – for instance, a change to a major key under sad lyrics – might imply a different message than the literal one. Alternatively, a key change might enhance the lyrics' meaning; in Dionne Warwick's 'Walk On By', for instance, the key change between the verse and chorus – from A minor to F – expresses the lift in the song's mood at that point.

- **Enhance the emotive quality of the singer.** It's important to find the key that's best suited to a singer's voice, but it's often useful to consider recording or writing a song in a key slightly too high for the singer, so as to force more passion into his or her voice. (This was a trick that Holland, Dozier and Holland often used with Marvin Gaye and Levi Stubbs.) Different keys might therefore elicit different vocal performances from the singer.

CHANGING KEY

When it comes to modulating from the original tonality, there are 'near'-sounding keys and 'far'-sounding keys. The nearest keys are those whose scales (and, therefore, chords) share the most notes with the original. A key that's considered near will have three or more common chords, and it's this similarity of structure that makes it easier to change between keys. For instance, the relative-minor key (ie the key that shares the same key signature but is minor in nature) is considered a near key, and in the key of C the relative minor is A minor. The closest keys for a major chord are, in order: IV, V, VI, II and III of the original key. In C major, these are F, G, Am, Dm and Em.

There are several methods that can be employed to bring about a change of key:

- **The semitone shift**. This is very common in popular music and is often used to avoid monotony during repeated choruses at the end of a song. Essentially, such a change refreshes the familiar. The technique is usually achieved abruptly, but it can sound very harsh or inelegant since the chords of the original key and the target key share no common notes. The target key is therefore considered to be a 'far' key. The change can sometimes be disguised by the speed of change or by the arrangement. The Police's 'Don't Stand So Close To Me' contains a fine example of a well-executed semitone shift between verse and chorus.

- **Via the V chord**. This is the simplest way of changing key. If, for example, the change was from the key of C to G, then the V chord of the new key (G) would be D. To move between keys, a progression would simply replace chord II (Dm) in the original key with a chord of D or – for a stronger change – use the dominant seventh (G7) and play into the new key.

- **Using a common chord**. This method works by approaching a chord shared by both keys from the home key and then moving from this 'common chord' to a chord that occurs only in the new key. For example, changing from the key of C to B♭ via chord III of the new key would happen like this:

163

| C | G | F | Dm | E♭ | F | B♭ |

- **Through an intermediary key.** This is effected by modulating briefly through a near key to reach a far key. For instance, in order to reach the key of C♯ from C, a progression could move to A major via the IIImaj chord. Here's what this would look like:

| C | Em | E | A | G♯7 | C♯ |

- **Via the diminished-seventh chord.** This odd chord finds its role as an important bridge between keys because each note in the chord can be a leading note for a new key. For example, the chord Gdim7 is comprised of G (the seventh of A♭), B♭/A♯ (the seventh of B), D♭/C♯ (the seventh of D) and F♭/E (the seventh of F).

When applied effectively, a key change can greatly enhance a song. The resulting change of tone is a very musically assertive movement and is great for lifting a song into a chorus, as exemplified by The Police's 'So Lonely'. Finding the right key change and the best way to reach it, however, is often a combination of careful planning and trial and error.

THE SONGWRITER:

DAVID STOLL

The main sections of a song, be they verse or chorus, will generally be in the tonic key. In a full-scale song, there is then the opportunity for an extended stay in a new harmonic region in a subsidiary section, such as a bridge or middle-eight. It's usually fairly easy to change to a new key at this major structural moment: two adjacent chords that would sound quite wrong together in the middle of a verse will often sound fine as the last chord of one section and the first chord of the new section.

Even so, the whole song will ideally have a proper harmonic flow, so that the new key area of a central section is part of a complete structure which leads the ear from beginning to end. The key of the middle section is not arbitrary. This is why, although you can often jump straight into a subsidiary section, you often need to take more care to work back to the tonic when you want to return to a main section. If in trouble, you can try to work back towards the dominant of the original key, which will of course lead to a return to the tonic.

An Interview With Billy Steinberg

How did you get started as a songwriter?

In 1968 I was 18 years old and a freshman at Bard College, in upstate New York. It was there that I discovered that songwriting was my first love and destiny. I majored in Literature because I wrote poetry. At that time, the Music Department was solely for 'serious' students training to become classical composers or musicians. I would perform my songs for whoever was willing to listen. I sang them in dormitory rooms and outdoors under maple trees. My grandmother, Selma Freedman, bought me a beautiful Gibson acoustic guitar that I thoroughly thrashed. I still own it and treasure it because I wrote my first songs on it.

While at Bard, on a visit to New York City, I had one of my first music-business appointments at the offices of Jerry Leiber and Mike Stoller. I remember walking under the framed sheet music of their hit songs in the hallways. I played some of my songs for them and I remember receiving some encouraging words.

In 1968, Bard College was a great place to be. Dylan and The Band were nearby in Woodstock. Once, when I was hitchhiking, I got a ride from Richard Manuel in a big old stationwagon. Allen Ginsberg used to come to Bard and chant poetry and play harmonium in the gym. Donald Fagen and Walter Becker, of Steely Dan, were students at Bard. Carter CC Collins – Tim Buckley's percussionist – used to hang around the campus. Terence Boylan was a Bard student and an amazing songwriter. I remember fretting that I would never sing or play as well as he could.

In 1971, my beautiful hippie dream life shattered. I began having severe anxiety attacks. After my third year, I quit college, returned to my parents' home in Palm Springs, California, and started seeing a psychoanalyst. For a couple of years, the pain of my existence was only tolerable because I could write songs from it and about it.

What were your inspirations?

My passion for music started in Fresno, California, in the 1950s. I started collecting singles – 45s – when I was seven years old. The first records I owned included 'All I Have To Do Is Dream' by The Everly Brothers, 'Poor Little Fool' by Ricky Nelson, 'Little Star' by The Elegants and 'To Know Him Is To Love Him' by The Teddy Bears. Owning these records and hearing these songs had a profound, almost mystical impact on me as a child. I would sit in my bedroom and listen to them over and over again. It puzzled me that my friends weren't moved by music in the same way that I was.

My first career ambition was to be a baseball player. For some reason, that seemed feasible. It didn't even occur to me that a person could aspire to be a singer, musician or songwriter.

In 1958, our family moved from Fresno to Palm Springs. My record collection grew to include R&B hits like Jackie Wilson's 'That's Why', Hank Ballard's 'Finger-Poppin' Time', The Drifters' 'There Goes My Baby' and Doris Troy's 'Just One Look'. I was 13 years old in January of 1964, when The Beatles changed everything. I will never forget the electrifying jolt of hearing the singles 'I Want To Hold Your Hand', 'Please Please Me' and 'She Loves You' for the first time. Inspired, I helped form a rock band called The Fables. I was the lead singer. We didn't write any of our own material; our repertoire included The Beatles' 'You Can't Do That', The Kinks' 'You Really Got Me', The Animals' 'We Gotta Get Out Of This Place', The Rolling Stones' 'The Last Time' and The Beau Brummels' 'Just A Little'. The Fables performed at high-school dances and at private parties. Sometimes we would bring girlfriends along as go-go dancers.

Around this same time, I became aware of the melodic masterpieces written by Burt Bacharach and Hal David. At the Youth Center, we would slow-dance to 'Walk On By' or 'Wishin' And Hopin''. Roy Orbison's songs – 'In Dreams', 'Oh Pretty Woman' – had an enormous impact on me. His voice and emotional style of writing were amazing.

Ray Charles was the first artist I saw perform in concert. My mind was blown by Ray, his band – The Raelettes – and the audience. Children and adults were dancing in the aisles and clapping their hands.

In 1966, I started to listen to Bob Dylan. *Bringing It All Back Home* was the first Dylan album I owned. Earlier, I'd been aware of songs like 'Blowin' In The Wind' and 'The Times They Are A-Changin'', but I'd never heard Bob's versions or owned his records. 'She Belongs To Me', 'Subterranean Homesick Blues' and 'Love Minus Zero'/'No Limit' changed my life. I'd known The Byrds' hit cover of 'Mr Tambourine Man', but it was cool to hear Bob sing it, to hear all the verses left off The Byrds' single and to compare the recordings. By the time 'Like A Rolling Stone' – still my all-time favourite song – from the *Highway 61 Revisited* LP hit the airwaves, I was a Dylan disciple. The poetry in songs like 'Visions Of Johanna', 'I Want You' and 'Memphis Blues Again', from *Blonde On Blonde*, changed my way of thinking about songs. By that time I was writing poetry and playing the acoustic guitar. After hearing Dylan, I started trying to turn my poems into songs.

Also, in the mid-1960s I learned to love the blues. Muddy Waters' *Real Folk*

Blues, with songs like 'Same Thing', 'Mannish Boy' and 'Walkin' Blues', was a revelation. I wore out LPs by Fred McDowell, Big Mama Thornton, Jimmy Reed, Bo Diddley and Howlin' Wolf. I sang in a blues band with my pals, Bill Dennis and Richard Ray. We called the band Dirt.

Motown and Stax were monumental labels with great songs and recording artists. Songwriters Holland, Dozier and Holland and Smokey Robinson have been major influences on me. Voices like Smokey's, along with soulmen like Otis Redding, Al Green, Marvin Gaye and Stevie Wonder, were powerful inspirations. Other heroes during my formative years include Chuck Berry, James Brown, Hank Williams, Van Morrison, Jimi Hendrix, Laura Nyro and Marc Bolan.

When did your songwriting career begin to take off?
In 1973, I started feeling better and went to work in my father's vineyards in the Coachella Valley desert in southern California. I'd write lyrics in my red Ford pickup truck. In the late 1970s, I became very excited about new-wave music; Elvis Costello, Blondie, Tom Petty And The Heartbreakers, The Police, The Cars, Talking Heads and The Knack were all creating invigorating power pop. They influenced me to write rock songs, and I found myself able to write better songs than anything I'd previously written.

My new songs were intensely personal, often about my psychological travails or about my mother or father. In order to demo this material, I called on my good friend Mark Safan, who lived in greater Los Angeles and was writing great songs of his own. He came to Palm Springs, where I recorded in a friend's garage studio. Mark brought along singer/songwriter Wendy Waldman and electric guitarist Craig Hull. In addition, I recruited bassist Bob Carlisle and drummer Efren Espinosa from the Inland Empire [the San Bernardino/Riverside area]. I was elated with the results. Soon thereafter, Craig, Bob, Efren and I agreed to form a band. I named the band Billy Thermal after the small town of Thermal in the Coachella Valley where our grape-growing company was based. I wrote the band's songs and was the lead singer.

Billy Thermal started to play in small clubs in LA. Robin Gee became our manager and Peter Paterno – at Manatt, Phelps – became my music attorney. We played at the Bla Bla Café, Madame Wong's, the Troubadour and other places.

One night in early 1980, producer Richard Perry saw us perform. He'd started his own label, Planet Records, and signed us to a recording contract.

At about the same time, Wendy Waldman was singing backup for Linda Ronstadt. Wendy and Craig Hull played one of my songs, 'How Do I Make You', for Linda and she cut it. That was my first cover and the first money I ever made as a songwriter. I was 30 years old. 'How Do I Make You' was a Top Ten hit in the US. I started my own publishing company, Billy Steinberg Music, and joined ASCAP. The first time I ever heard 'How Do I Make You' on the radio, I was at work in the vineyard and the song played on one of the farm workers' transistor radios. It was unforgettably exciting and surreal.

The Billy Thermal LP was never released by Planet, but Pat Benatar recorded two of the songs: 'I'm Gonna Follow You' and 'Precious Time'. My childhood hero, Rick Nelson, recorded one titled 'Don't Look At Me'.

Then Billy Thermal broke up and I came to the conclusion that perhaps I was destined to be a songwriter, not a singer or a performer. In retrospect, it should have been obvious because I had stagefright and a limited singing voice. Most professional songwriters I know started out wanting to sing their own material. At first it was disappointing to think that that dream wouldn't come true for me, but eventually I came to realise that I was extremely fortunate to be able to forge a career as a songwriter.

How did you meet your writing partner, Tom Kelly? And how did your songwriting relationship develop?
In the summer of 1981, I met Tom at a party in the Pacific Palisades home of record producer Keith Olsen. I was still enough of a hick that I brought my acoustic guitar to Keith's party, hoping to play some of my songs. I asked Tom if he would like to collaborate. He said he would.

Tom is from Indiana. In many respects, he and I are opposites. I'm nervous; he's calm. I play tennis; he plays golf. I'm afraid to fly; he's not, etc. But we discovered that we had one thing in common: we loved the same music. As kids, we owned the same records and liked the same songs. Tom and I definitely knew we were meant to write together when we discovered that we both loved the obscure 1950s song 'Susie Darlin'' by Robin Luke. In addition, we both love The Everly Brothers, John Lennon, Laura Nyro, Roy Orbison, Al Green, Smokey Robinson and Prince. I'm more of a Dylan fan. Tom is more of a Beach Boys fan.

When I met Tom, I didn't consider myself more lyricist than music writer. Until that time, I hadn't separated the two in my songwriting process; I was accustomed to starting with a lyric or poem and writing a song to it on the acoustic guitar. As soon as I heard Tom play the piano and guitar, though, I realised he was a far better musician than I was. He could offer more interesting chords and prettier melodies. He was happy to learn that I excelled at writing lyrics. And I got lucky because Tom adapted well to my preferred method of starting with a song lyric and then writing music to it.

Between 1981 and 1991, Tom and I wrote approximately 150 songs together. Our biggest hits include 'Like A Virgin' (Madonna), 'True Colors' (Cyndi Lauper, Phil Collins), 'Eternal Flame' (The Bangles), 'In Your Room' (The Bangles), 'I Drove All Night' (Cyndi Lauper, Roy Orbison, Celine Dion), 'So Emotional' (Whitney Houston), 'Alone' (Heart), 'I Touch Myself' (The Divinyls) and 'I'll Stand By You' (The Pretenders).

Tom and I recorded an album for Epic Records under the name i-TEN, titled *Taking A Cold Look*. It was released in 1983 and features an early version of 'Alone'.

How did 'Like A Virgin' come about?

Writing 'Like A Virgin' was a big breakthrough for Tom and me. Until that time, we'd written mostly rock or pop/rock songs. In 1983, while working in the vineyard, I wrote most of the lyrics for the song. As soon as I wrote it, I knew I had something very quirky and special. I like playing with words, and I realised that the word *virgin* would be edgy and provocative.

Like many of my lyrics, it was very personal, describing the joy I was experiencing in a new relationship after the breakup of a difficult one. The first verse runs:

> I made it through the wilderness
> Somehow I made it through
> I didn't know how lost I was
> Until I found you
> I was beat, incomplete
> I'd been had, I was sad and blue
> But you made me feel
> Yeah, you made me feel shiny and new

When Tom and I got together to write, he read those words and started trying to write a sensitive ballad to them. It was okay until he hit the chorus:

> Like a virgin, touched for the very first time
> Like a virgin, when your heart beats next to mine

No matter how he sang those words, they sounded ridiculous. Tom tried to set the lyric aside, but I wouldn't let him because I knew it was a potential hit song. Out of sheer frustration, Tom started playing the bass line for 'Like A Virgin' and singing the words in falsetto. In its first seconds, it was a channelling of Smokey Robinson's voice and a tip of the songwriting hat to both Holland, Dozier and Holland's 'I Can't Help Myself' and Michael Jackson's 'Billie Jean'. I started shouting, 'That's it! That's it!' Tom stopped playing and said, 'What? Really?' Tom was used to belting out a song like Lou Gramm of Foreigner. He felt uncomfortable with the idea of using his falsetto, but I convinced him that it was cool. He sang the demo and I added some background vocals, including the 'Hey!' in the chorus.

Once the demo was finished, our early attempts to get the song recorded were unsuccessful. I remember one A&R person telling me that the song was 'catchy', but that 'no one will ever sing that lyric'. But, luckily for us, Madonna was starting her career. Warner Brothers A&R man Michael Ostin came to visit Tom and me in our studio at Tom's house in the San Fernando Valley. When we played him 'Like A Virgin', he said it would be perfect for Madonna.

In my enthusiasm, if I'm not mistaken, I suggested that in the video she could perform the song wearing a wedding dress. I have no idea whether or not Michael ever related this idea to her.

Michael advised us that Madonna loved the song and would record it with producer Nile Rodgers. During this period, Tom and I never met Madonna, nor did we hear the song until it was ready to be released as a single. When we first heard it, we liked her vocal and the production and we were flattered that she'd stayed true to the demo. Madonna copied every nuance and ad lib that Tom sang as our demo faded with the lines:

> Like a virgin
> Ooh, like a virgin
> Feels so good inside
> When your heart beats
> And you hold me
> And you love me
> Oh, oh...

On 14 September 1984, Madonna performed the song at the MTV Video Awards wearing a wedding dress. This was before the song was released to radio. The camera followed her as she writhed around the stage, offering the world what looked to me to be some unflattering shots of the then babyfat, voluptuous Madonna. Happily, nothing would derail Madonna or 'Like A Virgin'; it became the title track and first single from her second album. It shot to Number One in the US pop charts and stayed there for six weeks.

Did you ever meet Madonna?
In 1989, Tom and I received invitations to Freddy DeMann's 50th birthday party. Freddy managed Madonna. It was to be a black-tie affair at DeMann's Beverly Hills mansion. After all the success of 'Like A Virgin', I was chomping at the bit to finally meet Madonna. I arrived at the party with Tom and had a lot of expectations.

I was hoping to be personally thanked for contributing to her breakthrough song. I was hoping that Tom and I might be asked to co-write with her. I was hoping that she might think I was irresistible and want to have sex with me. Tom and I were standing on an outdoor terrace, talking to Stephen Bray, who collaborated with Madonna on some of her early dance hits, like 'Into The Groove'. Madonna, with Warren Beatty in tow, came walking toward us. It felt like the perfect opportunity to be introduced.

Stephen said, 'Madonna, this is Billy Steinberg and Tom Kelly, who wrote

"Like A Virgin".' Warren Beatty started to laugh, thinking it was a joke because Madonna would have surely already known the writers of her signature song. I gave her my biggest smile and said, 'Madonna, I've wanted to meet you for so long.' She said, 'Well, now you did,' grabbed Warren and walked away. I was devastated. Tom started to laugh. I can't remember what Stephen's reaction was. I think it's funny now. Sometimes the funniest things take some time to appreciate. And I've never met Madonna since.

'Like A Virgin' is still a high-profile song. It's on Madonna's ever-popular *Immaculate Collection*. In the 1992 film *Reservoir Dogs*, the characters discuss the meaning of the lyrics in the opening scene. In 2001, a riotous performance of the song was featured in the film *Moulin Rouge*. In 2004, in the movie *Bridget Jones: The Edge Of Reason*, 'Like A Virgin' is sung by the main character.

So what made you so successful as a songwriter?

That is an interesting question. I have key personality factors: perseverance, willingness to collaborate, resilience in the face of frequent rejection and belief in my own work and my ability to promote it. As well as these traits, I think a psychological factor played a big part in turning me into a songwriter.

By nature, I avoid confrontation. I am uncomfortable with anger or expressions of disappointment. I always try to maintain a placid surface, often at the expense of my inner self. I've been this way all my life. And one of the results is that I've transferred these powerful, repressed feelings and yearnings into my songs.

When I originally started writing, I had no control over what came spilling out of my unconscious mind. My early poems and songs are filled with imagery, but they're hard to decipher. As I gained experience, I learned to filter these wordplays through my conscious mind.

It's as if there are two writers at work: the unconscious, who is passionate, raw and symbolic, and the conscious, who is aware of song structure and of the need to be intelligible.

SONG CRAFT 10:
RHYTHM AND GROOVE

'In a rhythm-heavy world, the beat is becoming ever more important to the success of a song.'
– Bill Bruford, drummer/writer with King Crimson, Yes and Earthworks

Like a classic melody, a great groove has an indefinable yet magical quality. Tracks like Stevie Wonder's 'Superstition', Simon And Garfunkel's 'Cecilia' and Marvin Gaye's 'Sexual Healing' all open with the groove firmly in place and are immediately recognisable by their individual rhythmic signatures. The listener is already hooked by the song before a single note has been played. As Bill Bruford says, 'Get the groove right and the song is halfway there.'

A song's groove is essentially its basic rhythmic feel, and it can be more important than any other element in a song. Pop music's long-established connection with dancing has encouraged its beat to remain explicit.

The groove can even be the major hook in a song. From 1950s rock 'n' roll to 1960s R&B and Motown to 1970s funk and disco to 1980s pop and rock to 1990s dance and house, much pop music has focused on the rhythm. Despite the legacy of Tin Pan Alley defining a song as solely lyrics, melody and harmony, groove has always been a crucial fourth element of the popular song. It is essential, therefore, for a songwriter today to understand what gives a song 'groove'.

As a songwriter, you should never underestimate the power of a good groove. A groove can lift a track that was sounding inexplicably flat; it can hold a song together that was otherwise falling apart; it can even provide an excellent songwriting tool and be used to generate fresh ideas. Here's George Michael's approach to obtaining a groove: 'I go round and round the backing track and go with stream-of-conscious gibberish until something gets me.'

THE ELEMENTS OF RHYTHM

Rhythm is the foundation to a great groove. In order to understand what generates a groove, therefore, it's necessary to examine its rhythmic elements.

There are six key elements that together create the rhythm of a track:

1. Pulse
2. Tempo
3. Time signature
4. Rhythmic subdivision
5. Syncopation
6. Texture

1. Pulse

This is the regular, recurring beat in a piece of music, the feel that makes a listener tap their feet. In dance music, this is most often the '1, 2, 3, 4' of the bass drum, otherwise known as a 'four to the floor' beat.

2. Tempo

This is the speed of the pulse and is measured beats per minute (bpm). The higher the bpm, the greater a track's level of excitement. In very broad terms, slow ballads and soft pop are under 90bpm; pop, rock, R&B, soul and MOR are 90–130bpm; and dance, drum 'n' bass and techno are over 130bpm. It's important to ensure that each song is at its optimum tempo. Often the tempo at which the track was written is slower than would be most effective during performance, and it can be surprising how a slight increase in speed can improve a song dramatically.

3. Time Signature

A song's time signature is a reference to how its beats are grouped into musical bars. The most standard time signature in popular music is 4/4 (otherwise known as *common time*), and here the first 4 refers to the number of beats in a bar while the second 4 refers to their length, as a fraction. In short, a time signature of 4/4 indicates that there are four beats to a bar, each a quarter note in duration. Generally in songs written in 4/4, there's a slight emphasis on the first beat in each bar – ie '1, 2, 3, 4 | 1, 2, 3, 4 | 1, 2, 3, 4, etc.

Colin Emmanuel says
'In the rap and R&B worlds, the beat is paramount. Rhythm has always been an important part of black culture and music, but the groove has become ever more prominent as hip-hop continues to merge deeper with R&B. The beat is intrinsically part of the song itself, just as much as melody, lyric and harmony. Creating a definitive groove, therefore, is one of the keys skills of an R&B songwriter.

'Creating beats, though, takes a lot of talent, research, study and practice. It's not simply a case of being able to sit down and knock up a good beat. The beat has to be a groove that you feel from the heart, that comes from the soul. If Puff Daddy samples a record, for instance, you can guarantee that he's understood the background behind it and how important it is within that culture; it's not simply a case of 'Oh well, that's a nice rhythm. I'll use that one.' R&B has to be heartfelt on all levels: the performance, the actual song and the groove behind it. The beat should infuse all these elements. In fact, if it's a great R&B song, you should be able to listen to it simply a cappella and the song should still groove to you.'

Many other time signatures exist, but none are as successful as 4/4 since they don't adhere to the regular 'dance' feel that contemporary society demands. Even so, they are still used in popular music; 3/4, or waltz metre (1, 2, 3 | 1 2, 3, etc – ie three quarter notes per bar) occurs in the hit songs 'Moon River' and 'What's New, Pussycat?', while 6/8 (six eighth notes per par) crops up in Paul Simon's 'America' and Jeff Buckley's 'Hallelujah'.

One useful songwriting trick for adding freshness to an arrangement is to change time signatures, as in Elvis Presley's 'Suspicious Minds' – which goes from 4/4 to 12/8 at the bridge section and then shifts back again to 4/4 – or REM's 'Shiny Happy People', which switches between 6/8 and 4/4. There are a few tracks that have succeeded with highly unusual time signatures, such as Soundgarden's 'Fell On Black Days', which is in 6/4, and Pink Floyd's 'Money', which is in 7/4. However, these are rare exceptions.

4. Rhythmic Subdivision
This is the manner in which each musical bar in a song is split up with its beats, and it can be a determining factor for a song's style. As a general guide...

- The straight quarter-note beat indicates a dance feel, as in Daft Punk's 'One More Time';

- An eighth-note feel is indicative of Rock and MOR, as in Survivor's 'The Eye Of The Tiger';

- A triplet (three-note) groove is representative of the blues, as in Chuck Berry's 'No Particular Place To Go';

- A triplet groove that is 'swung' is associated most often with R&B and hip-hop, as in Brandy's 'Talk About Our Love';

- A 16th-note feel is characteristic of R&B, soul, funk and reggae, as in James Brown's 'Get Up (I Feel Like Being A) Sex Machine'.

5. Syncopation
Once the rhythmic subdivision has been established, the next most important feature to define a groove's style is how it's syncopated. The term *syncopation* refers to the accenting of the weaker inner beats of a groove – ie the off beats – and it's a feature that can create the unique rhythmic drive of a song. Off-beat syncopation is a characteristic of reggae, for instance, while the straight four-to-the-floor feel of dance music is often augmented by numerous additional syncopated patterns on other percussive instruments.

6. Texture

Each rhythm also requires its own unique texture, which can range from the sparse to the moderate to the full. A rhythm's texture is derived from the application of various percussive instruments, drum sounds and rhythmic patterns. Certain styles of music will demand particular choices of instrumentation and characteristic patterns, and it will be these choices, combined with the personal taste of the composer and/or producer, that will determine the uniqueness of the groove.

All of these six elements, when blended effectively, can result in a song's groove. However, the process behind writing a great groove is as mysterious as the factors that combine to form a great melody. Every potential song has an infinite choice of beats that will work with it, but it's the songwriter or drummer's job to find the exact right rhythm that perfectly synchronises with the lyric, melody and harmony so that the track grooves. As Ant Varney from the band Lease Of Life explains on his website www.drummingant.com, 'A good band with a bad drummer is a bad band, so when confronted with having to lay down a drumbeat on a track, I try to use a variety of different grooves and beats to find the one that will best fit. I think about the mood of the song, what the songwriter is trying to achieve. I also put myself in the shoes of the listener and think about what they would like to hear or dance to.'

THE DEFINITION OF BASS

Once a groove has been laid down, the part that provides the vital link between the rhythm, harmony and melody is the bass line. It's important to appreciate the significance that this part (which is typically provided by a bass guitar or synth) plays in both a rhythmic and a harmonic sense, as this will enable you to compose the most effective and appropriate bass lines for a song.

The bass line has two key functions in popular music:

1. To define the rhythmic activity;
2. To establish movement within the harmony.

On a rhythmic front, the bass line usually closely mirrors, or reacts to, the drum pattern. The kick (or bass) drum generally produces the most influential beat here, while any other key accents and off beats are played by the other percussive pieces – snare, toms, etc. In terms of writing a bass part, therefore, it's helpful first to establish what beats the kick drum is playing and then to have the bass line match some or all of these rhythms. This will help to maintain continuity, emphasise any rhythmic hook and enhance the groove.

With regard to harmony, the bass tends to provide the foundation for the main chord progression via the use of the root, third, fifth and octave notes. 'Passing notes' or 'non-chord tones' can then be played to add smoothness to the line and generate a sense of movement within the harmony. These passing notes can be chromatic or diatonic, and they often fall on the syncopated, weaker beats.

Alternatively, a song can be built entirely upon a bass riff. In such cases, the rhythmic and melodic pattern stays the same for whole sections, or even the entire song, and can often be the song's most distinguishing feature, as is the case in Queen's 'Another One Bites The Dust' and Michael Jackson's 'Billie Jean'.

In general, by applying an understanding of melody along with a firm consideration to the elements of rhythm, the bass line can also become a key factor in the success of a song.

The Rise Of The Machines

When drum machines and loop-based software music programs were first introduced, they were heralded as the beginning of the end for drummers. In fact, they had quite the opposite effect, pushing the boundaries of drumming to new frontiers, encouraging drummers to experiment with new techniques and technology and even generating new musical genres like techno and drum 'n' bass.

For the songwriter, they are both a blessing and a curse. A drum machine or loop-based sampler is a fantastic songwriting tool that can help a songwriter to establish a groove or beat quickly and with the minimum of fuss. Playing a pre-programmed beat can also be an enormous help for inspiring ideas for new songs. The technology is also excellent for creating certain forms of music, such as dance and drum 'n' bass, as well as for generating new musical hybrids; Mark Hill developed the genre of two-step by essentially fusing a house beat with an R&B rhythm.

The disadvantages of using loop-based technology and drum machines are that the results can be expressionless, sound mechanised, have little sense of dynamics in terms of tempo and velocity, and resemble the work of any other songwriter and producer working with the same gear. This method of song creation has also led to the phenomenon of the 'locked tempo' song – ie a song with a rigid, mathematically defined pulse – whereas before the advent of the drum machine songs drifted subtly, yet appropriately, according to the feel of the performance.

There is a great danger of becoming over-reliant on the technology. As songwriter Rob Davis makes affirms, 'You can write any old crap very easily, but the really good songs are much tougher to achieve. You can make a track and the groove sound great, but you can't always contrive a really good song like that.'

Wayne Hector agrees: 'The computer has made everything a little bit easier and a little bit harder. The creative process has suffered because you don't have to know that much nowadays in order to be able to put together a track, whereas back in The Beatles' day artists took a great amount of pride in learning their craft. Songwriting isn't the same craft it once was. There are lots of people who make great records with the bare minimum of knowledge, but we do miss out on the well-constructed, superbly crafted songs.'

It's essential, therefore, that care is taken when using drum machines, sequencers and loop-based technology. There's no getting away from using them, however, as they now form the basis of almost every contemporary rap, dance and pop song.

A ROUGH GUIDE TO DRUM PROGRAMMING

Nowadays, there are ample audio sample CDs available featuring percussion and drum loops. The best ones for laying down a track quickly and obtaining a natural feel are those containing long loops or those that are laid out as if they were songs, with standard verse and chorus sections. These are sometimes harder to find than the standard sample CDs, which usually feature short loops, but they're worth tracking down. There are also software programs and samplers that include libraries of rhythm loops and allow for creative adaptation, examples of which include Steinberg's Groove Agent, Native Instruments' Battery and one recommended by songwriter Rob Davis named Stylus. 'Stylus is wonderful for throwing up ideas for a great groove,' says Rob, 'and whatever bpm you want, you can ReCycle it [ie use a program of that name to chop up and alter the lengths of samples as you would MIDI data] so you can do an R&B groove, if need be, or a 130bpm dance beat. That's inspiring, because you can fling out ideas and mess around with chords.'

When buying a sample CD or a software package including samples, however, it's important to check that you can use the samples within your own songs without paying any additional fee, since not all samples are copyright-free.

Once you have the appropriate software and equipment, here are ten tips to help you to program a decent drum track:

1. Sound is everything. Simply using the right drum sounds can be enough to bring a track's groove to life.

2. Keep it simple. When it comes to effective grooves, as with most elements of songwriting, less is definitely more.

3. Copy real drum patterns from records that you like. This is a very good way of establishing a successful groove – borrow and adapt successful rhythms to your own purposes.

4. Avoid using preset rhythms. Rather than pressing Start on the drum machine or keyboard, attempt to write your own patterns.

5. Choose drum sounds that sound good with each other. It's very important that the sounds in the rhythm blend together if the groove is to gel.

6. Use quantisation (the automatic snapping of beats to the nearest subdivision in a bar) sparingly. It's better to keep a natural feel in most forms of music. If the beats on a track are really out of time, the software sequencers Cubase and Logic offer functions known as Iterative Quantise and Naturalize – respectively – to remedy matters without making things sound too mechanical.

7. Apply a variety of rhythms within a song, using plenty of small variations to keep the listener interested. A track that is unchanging can quickly become monotonous and dull.

8. Vary the sounds between song sections, such as by switching between a closed hi-hat and open hi-hat or between a cross-stick and full snare hit. This will help to vary the intensity of the drum track.

9. Add a touch of reverb to the overall rhythm track to make the drums sound more 'live'.

10. Experiment. Work on blending genres and sounds to come up with a unique groove that will capture the listeners' attention.

Creating a backing track is as much about observing the traditions of the genre as it is about the skill of the programmer. By using the appropriate sounds and key characteristics of a particular genre, you'll be halfway there to creating an appropriate groove for your song.

The best way to approach programming the right rhythm for a song is to establish its genre and then to study the patterns of typical songs of that style. For those occasions when you don't have access to reference audio material, I've included below a rough guide to the main stylistic characteristics of ten of the most popular genres. If you require further detail or wish to study the aspects of drum programming in greater depth, you might want to think about enrolling on a drumming or production course at a music college, such as those run by the Academy of Contemporary Music (ACM, Guildford, UK, www.acm.ac.uk), or study a book dedicated to drum programming, such as Mark Roberts' *Rhythm Programming* (SMT [Sanctuary Publishing], 2004).

MODERN R&B

Tempo:	80–135bpm.
Sound:	Generally a combination of live loops and MIDI-triggered sounds form a central rhythmic structure around which instrumentation and vocals weave.
Groove:	Tight, repetitive and accurate, but a human feel is often gained from the use of live loops. This style employs a diverse range of grooves, from heavily swung triplets to straight eighth notes.
Snare:	Dry and sharp-sounding, with top-end crack.
Bass Drum:	Always very bottom-heavy.
Hi-hat:	Thin and electronic but sounds very live.
Toms:	Distinct lack of toms and very few fills.
Cymbals:	Generally tight and short.
Percussion:	Shakers often used to give rasping rhythmic edge.

ROCK

Tempo:	Too broad a genre to specify.
Sound:	Traditionally a very live feel, drawing influences from all genres.
Groove:	Follows rather than dictates the structure of the song, so develops around the melody line.
Snare:	Can be deep and ambient or tight and thin.
Bass Drum:	Traditionally fat and full-bodied, recently the bass drum has gained a top-end slap.
Hi-hat:	Can range from open and trashy to tight and crisp, but can't be too mechanical.
Toms:	Create rhythmic and sonic interest through the use of a wide variety of sounds.
Cymbals:	Highlight accents and punctuate start and end points of sections. Rides are generally cutting and heavy, enhanced with the use of the bell.
Percussion:	No guidelines here. Anything that works, really!

DANCE

Tempo:	130–200bpm.
Sound:	Electronic, intensely hypnotic, often augmented with live percussion.

Groove: Four-to-the-floor rhythms with up-beat hi-hats while other instruments play around this figure. Overall feel is repetitive and hypnotic with unchanging velocities.

Snare: Traditionally comes from the Roland TR909 drum machine.

Bass Drum: Can vary from small and punchy to overdriven and slightly distorted. Invariably electronic.

Hi-hat: With top-end edge or slightly distorted for intensity.

Toms: Either non-existent or added to provide a 'tribal' flavour.

Cymbals: Kept tight and short to maintain the flow of the groove.

Percussion: Latin, African or ethnic influences may be used, depending on the particular style of dance music.

HIP-HOP (BREAKBEAT)

Tempo: 90–130bpm.

Overall Sound: Acoustic, lo-fi, combined with hypnotic loops.

Groove: Hi-hat is driven, constant, unaccented, playing with snare on beats two and four, plus ghost-note 16ths.

Snare: Usually an acoustic sample, either full or thin in sound.

Bass Drum: Also an acoustic sample, sometimes layered with electronic samples to provide a clean bottom end.

Hi-hat: Acoustic samples or electronic.

Toms: Used to highlight the groove or part of a loop but are uncommon in hip-hop.

Cymbals: Not over-applied in order to maintain space in groove. When used, though, their sound is often detuned.

Percussion: Conga and tabla sometimes used to provide atmosphere or set up groove.

HIP-HOP (SWUNG)

Tempo: 85–100bpm.

Sound: Thick, heavily dampened and very bottom-heavy.

Groove: Based on dotted-16th-note feel, sparse and uncluttered.

Snare: Can range in sound from a dull, detuned thud to a high-end crack.

Bass Drum: Always heavy with lots of bottom end.

Hi-hat: Tends to be either a deep, thick, crusty low-end sample or a very tight, high and thin sound.

Toms: Tight and punchy. Can be electronic or acoustic and are used to augment the groove.

Cymbals: Sparsely used.

Percussion: Sometimes applied to provide atmosphere.

DRUM 'N' BASS

Tempo:	160–180bpm.
Sound:	A really broken style with unexpected twists
Groove:	Tends to be extremely complex with a light jazzy feel.
Snare:	Ranges from acoustic samples to thin, bead-like, hard electronic rock hits. Whatever the sound, the main beat is at a consistent dynamic, light and even, augmented by many ghost notes.
Bass Drum:	Either punchy or boomy, but traditionally crusty acoustic samples or hard electronic kicks.
Hi-hat:	Tends to be thin, consistent and driving
Toms:	Can only be thin, small and uncluttered, due to tempo.
Cymbals:	Have a very 'live' feel, with strong definition. Ride often carries a consistent flow with stronger accents to break up layered, intense feel.

GARAGE

Tempo:	120–130bpm.
Sound:	All electronic, due to style's disco origins.
Groove:	Computer-based and very driving, up-front and simple.
Snare:	Dry and sharp with top-end crack on beats two and four, although sometimes replaced or augmented by handclaps.
Bass Drum:	As in dance music, provides a four-to-the-floor pulse using a bottom-heavy electronic sound.
Hi-hat:	Tends to be thin and electronic.
Toms:	Not commonly used.
Cymbals:	Kept tight and short to maintain the momentum.
Percussion:	Sometimes applied to add colour by weaving in and out of the groove.

POP

Tempo:	90–120bpm.
Sound:	Combination of live and electronic, with main groove generally being programmed.
Groove:	Pop grooves generally draw on other popular genres, like dance, R&B or rock, so that they appeal to the broadest audience possible.
Snare:	Either a live sample or electronic. Can vary greatly from big to a high-pitched crack.
Bass Drum:	Usually a tight kick sample, sometimes supplemented to fit in with the characteristics of the song.
Hi-hat:	Thin and electronic, but sounds very 'live'.
Toms:	Generally electronic. Used occasionally to lead into new sections.

| Cymbals: | Again, applied as accents in a song but kept tight and short to keep the groove. |
| Percussion: | Bongos often used to supplement the groove, with other percussion added to increase excitement. Shakers and tambourines are pre-requisites in ballads and slow pop grooves. |

FUNK

Tempo:	60–170bpm.
Sound:	Similar to rock, in that it has a very live sound.
Groove:	Tight, repetitive and simple, with different instruments working around the drum pattern.
Snare:	Can vary widely from acoustic to electronic in sound.
Bass Drum:	Heavily dampened, preferably a warm and punchy sound.
Hi-hat:	Tends to be crisp and tight or else mellow and dark. Open and closed sounds should blend.
Toms:	Used as fills to keep rhythmic flow.
Cymbals:	Tend to be thin and high-pitched, with rides more mellow than the rock style and bell often used as an accent feature.
Percussion:	No guidelines here. Go with whatever works!

Bill Bruford says

'Drummers tend naturally to hear music from the bottom up, often paying attention to the lyric as a final afterthought, and as a writer I still sometimes start by working from the rhythm up. I might find something on the drum set that gets me going, and my imagination immediately begins to deploy other instruments in what I imagine to be an effective way around that idea. I haven't considered a top-line melody at this point, although there might be a shape forming in my mind. The rhythm then goes into a sequencer (blender?) and I add a basic bass line or a chord or two. It doesn't matter much what it is at this stage because my writing method is one of replacement; I'll put in any idea to start with, even if it's a nursery rhyme, and replace those parts that are either uninspiring or clichéd or both. Like a sculptor with a bunch of clay, I start to mould it, hack away at it and replace bits via a process of elimination until I'm left with the parts I like. And, like a sculpture, it might take a while for the piece to reveal its essence – 'Oh, it's a bolero; perfect for Julio Iglesias', or 'Oh, it's a factory rotting in a post-industrial wasteland; perfect for King Crimson' – at which point the going should get easier.

Often the material ends up in an odd time signature so I understand that mass popularity might not be around the next corner! I've just found it a little easier to inhabit odd time signatures than the conventional 4/4. To me, a time signature is as catchy as a melody is to a traditional songwriter. If there's a little kink in the rhythm somewhere – the beat going backwards, or some slippage, or a push – then I can respond to that. I feel enervated, excited, inspired to find the right chords to get the idea off the ground. The melody will come last, in most cases.'

LATIN

Tempo:	60–200bpm.
Sound:	Traditionally a percussion-based rhythm
Groove:	Heartbeat is the *clavé*, a repeating 'two-three' or 'three-two' pattern.
Snare:	Generally mellow and velocity-sensitive, either taking the backbeat or interacting with the ride cymbal.
Bass Drum:	Often non-defined, the bass here is quiet and ambient, has a rolling feel or is a pounding, relentless, hard-edged beat.
Hi-hat:	Again a rolling, accented feel, or else the rhythmic anchor on beats two and four. Clavé is played here on Afro-Cuban grooves.
Toms:	Give great depth to the rhythm and are used to replicate conga lines.
Cymbals:	Applied to highlight and punctuate phrases.
Percussion:	Bongos, congas, timbale, cow bells and claves give a Brazilian and Afro-Cuban feel.

AN INTERVIEW WITH MARK HILL

How did you get involved in music?

In my third year at university, my friend Neil Kerr and I took out various loans, amounting to £20,000, and set up a recording studio in Southampton's Ocean Village. We began by working with student bands. Our first session with a local band lasted seven days. We literally had to lock the band out of our studio and do all the programming from instruction manuals. Luckily the band came out with a reasonable demo or we would have probably given up there and then! It was trial and error – to be honest, more error than trial. We had no gameplan with the studio. In fact, we had no idea from the word 'go'. We actually prided ourselves on having no idea about what we were doing or where we were going.

We worked with mostly guitar-based bands, doing 15-hour days for £10 an hour, just to pay off the rent. Sometimes we would go for weeks without any work. We were literally starving and had bailiffs knocking the doors down. However, I used the time when there were no bands in the studio to write and record my own music.

How did Artful Dodger and its breakthrough sound come about?

Through the studio, I'd met up with a local DJ by the name of Pete Devereux. Pete had come to the studio to record a house track, but after spending some time recording his music and not getting great results I suggested we should develop the music together, and thus Artful Dodger was born.

We would generally start with beats and samples, work up a groove and then progress to the bass line, slowly building up the music from there and remixing *a cappella* vocals to create the top line. It was all about the vibe at this stage.

The Artful Dodger sound was a fluke. I created two-step totally by accident; I just wanted to make 'What You Gonna Do' a bit more funky, so I swung the rhythm a touch and made the groove more breakbeat, less four-to-the-floor – essentially fusing house with R&B. That's when the track really came to life. Craig David – whom we had first met when he had come into the studio to record a song for the Saints football team as part of the 'Kick Racism out of Football' campaign – really loved the track, and he adlibbed some vocals over the top, thus creating the first original-sounding Artful Dodger track.

From then on, myself and Craig struck up a friendship, and I realised that he was considerably better than some kid from Southampton who could knock out a couple of phrases to a track, so I listened to a few vocals he had written over some R&B instrumentals. It was early stuff, but I could hear the potential and I started working with him. That's when I sat down with a piano and a guitar and actually wrote real songs.

How was 'Re-Rewind' written?
That was just the two of us. We were in the studio one day, messing about with beats, samples and the decks, and we came up with the idea of a half-time breakbeat chorus for 'Re-Rewind'. The big bass line came simply from messing about on the keyboard. We set the beat down and Craig MC'd a bunch of vocals over the track. 'Rewind' was the phrase that we picked up on. It was really catchy. Unfortunately we lost the whole session when the hard drive on the computer totally corrupted. Luckily we had a cassette recording, but nothing else. It took us 24 hours solid in the studio to run up the track again. We didn't sleep; we were just getting so into it.

The verse was actually from another track that we'd written called 'Last Night', one of the tracks on his first album. Craig sang over the top of it and it sounded great, so we thought, 'Oh, shit.' Obviously we were using it in another track, so we started coming up with alternative melodies and lyrics, but nothing worked as well as that original idea, so we decided to bootleg our own song!

How do you approach writing with Craig David?
The first track Craig and I wrote was actually 'Cocoa Butter', which was the most dreadful, clichéd R&B. My production was a concoction of everything bad about American R&B at the time, and the lyrics were appalling.

The first time we actually thought we had something special was with a cover of a Human League track. The sound of Craig's vocals were fantastic. That was when the vibe clicked and we started writing and coming up with different ideas.

Many of Craig's songs would begin with the guitar or a sample, like on 'Walking Away'. Obviously that's a U2 sample, but Craig had never heard it. I'd caught the first eight bars of the U2 track on the radio and thought that it sounded really cool and wondered what it would sound like with a beat underneath it. It was never really intended for Craig, but he walked in, in his school uniform, and immediately came up with that smash chorus. It was so instant. We got it down there and then, with the guitar riff, onto a Dictaphone. I then built up the track, developing the verses and the choruses to make it more song-based in structure. Craig – like on many of our tracks – then took it away and sat at home with his headphones on, pen and paper in hand, and came up with different ideas. He would bring them back into the studio and we would listen to them and extract the best bits to develop.

With the track 'Seven Days', Craig had already written most of it on his own, in that he had come up with a melody over the top of someone else's instrumental. At the same time, I was playing around with a beat sampled from a song by the artist A Plus – but later programmed – and was mixing it with this Spanish-influenced guitar riff. Craig then sang the whole of his melody over the top and it sounded perfect.

Even though all the early Craig songs started like this, with a programmed beat and relying on the production, later we consciously worked hard to write songs that worked with just a guitar or just a piano. These tracks had to be great songs on their own, with the production coming afterwards.

The best material we've done has fused my rock, soul and dance influences in the backing tracks with Craig's R&B slant on singing and writing lyrics. This is what makes our material unique, more British.

How did you feel when success came knocking on your door?
We went through some horrible, horrible experiences trying to make the Artful Dodger work, with bailiffs at the door, bad managers and unscrupulous deals. It had been a struggle even to make our crap equipment sound great. But when we finally did produce a track that sounded special, we thought, 'We've actually got something here!' Those moments made all the grief worthwhile. Much of the time, it was like Del Boy: 'This time next year, we'll be millionaires.'

I'd actually put a date on achieving success and said, 'If I haven't made it by this time, it's not going to happen.' I think success came a year late, but it finally came with the release of Craig's debut album, *Born To Do It*, on Wildstar Records.

Obviously once Craig got signed to Wildstar Records, it took the music we were doing for love to the next level. All of a sudden, music also became business, with all the problems that are attached with that. It was a whirlwind ride from the time of 'Re-Rewind'. I've still not come to terms with it.

What lessons have you learned from being in the music business?
The biggest lesson I learned was not to let bad experiences spoil your focus. You have to struggle through all the hard times – the bailiffs, the bad managers and the dodgy deals. I can't honestly say I have regrets or that I'd never do those deals in hindsight, because if I hadn't signed with those companies, who knows if anything might have happened? I'd like to think that our talent and ambition would have shone through, but if you see the incredible number of talented people out there that really struggle, you think, 'Perhaps I did get taken for a ride and lost money I was entitled to, but at the end of the day those companies were passionate about more than just ripping me off. They were passionate about the music, too. They put it out and it became a massive hit, and look where I am now.'

What advice would you give aspiring songwriters?

Don't be knocked back by bitterness, because you're never alone. Pretty much everybody I speak to in the industry has some story of being ripped off. All my peers – all those who set up at the same time as me – they all went through hell in one way or the other. It's just that kind of business; it has *always* been that kind of business. But for every musical crook out there, there are as many fantastic and genuine people, so don't lose faith.

Secondly, you can't rely on anyone else to fight your corner and get work for you. You need to hustle and get out there yourself. Phone people up, knock the industry's doors down and believe in yourself while you do this.

Thirdly, remember that it doesn't take a record company to make a record a success. As long as you have people around you who are willing to put in the effort, you can achieve your dream.

In the early stages of Artful Dodger, we were really enjoying pressing up our own white labels. Because none of us were signed, none of us had any idea. We'd actually started out with bootlegs, which aren't strictly legal, but we'd press 1,000 of them anyway and Neil and I would stick them in his little Renault 5. We were skint at this time, surviving on McDonald's. We'd drive down to Brighton and up to Nottingham and Leeds and Cardiff in his Renault, full of vinyl, and give them to the DJ shops for sale or return. We were then actually too skint to pay for the petrol to go back and pick up the money when they were sold, which is hilarious in retrospect.

Later, when the Saints football team got through to the FA Cup final, we put together an unofficial football song for them. Again, we didn't have any distribution or any record company interested, but we managed to get the single into the Top 15 of the charts this time through sheer force of will. We literally had boxes arriving in our hallway and then went out in our cars to Asda and the like, dropping them off!

The established record companies can be great – when they work well, they work really well – but when you're trying to do something on an underground level, it's like wading through mud. Thankfully, you don't need a label to put out records; high-quality recording technology is so cheap. You can create fully produced songs on a laptop computer or a simple recording system. We proved that with Craig's first album; most of it was done on a £2,000 mixing desk and it went on to sell 7 to 8 million albums. You don't need to spend hundreds of thousands of pounds to make an album.

So, the biggest lesson I've learned is that you don't necessarily have to strive for the Holy Grail of a record deal. People are selling a good number of records and making all the profit themselves simply by using a website* and going out and playing in front of people.

---

* If you're interested in selling your own product, and you can get the money to set it up, companies such as www.recordstore.co.uk will help you to sell your CDs and other merchandise online. www.recordstore.co.uk will build you an online site from which to sell your CDs, DVDs etc and also provides a digital download service, enabling your fans to buy downloads and actual CDs at the same time.

SONG CRAFT 11: THE VOCAL

'To me, a record comes down to a singer and a song. Other elements must be subordinate.'

– Jerry Wexler, producer

In many popular styles of music, the lead vocalist carries the greatest responsibility for the success or failure of a song. Aside from any considerations of image, live performance ability or self-publicity, the singer's primary function is to interpret the 'story' of the lyric and to express the emotional content of the song.

'A truly great singer will infuse your creation with emotional power and make it live and breathe.'

– Frank Musker

The importance of the vocal in relation to the song can't be over-emphasised. When hearing a song, it's the emotion and vibe of the vocal performance to which the listener relates. The singer can be a very strong identifier and can even be considered one of the hooks in a song when he or she has a highly distinctive voice, like Tina Turner or Elvis Costello. For Bill Bruford, drummer/songwriter with King Crimson and Yes, 'The sound of the voice is as important as the words, if not more so. The singer Jon Anderson in Yes, for example, was much reviled for his nonsense lyrics, but that never bothered me in the slightest because his phrasing and the arc of the melody sounded great.'

It's also the singer's unique interpretation of a song that can lift it from being average to spectacular. Pete Kirtley from Jiant Productions explains: 'A good singer can interpret what you've done. They don't necessarily add anything, but they somehow bring a song to life, whereas a bad singer can ruin a good song. It makes me think about going back over old songs that people have said no to, but where we always thought, "That was a good song; you were wrong about this," and getting a new singer to work on them.' With this understanding, it's clear that a vocal can truly make or break a song.

SINGING THE SONG

The voice is the most flexible and characterful of any instrument. In fact, it's probably the most powerful and useful tool a songwriter can possess.

> 'I don't play an instrument at all. I'm a singer and I have a certain way of singing a melody that makes my ideas feel more like a record. My voice is the instrument. People are always surprised that I don't play, but a voice is just as relevant as a guitar or piano. It can play all the same notes, and probably a couple more.'
>
> – Wayne Hector

As a songwriter, it is extremely beneficial to develop your vocal abilities. Whether this is through six months of personal tuition, attending a music college or studying a vocal book, the time spent will be rewarded 100-fold in terms of your ability to come up with fresh melodic ideas, lay down demos for songs and improve the quality of your songwriting as a whole.

> 'The key factor in putting down a good vocal is the confidence as opposed to the actual technical ability.'
>
> – Colin Emmanuel, producer/writer

Confidence is central to anyone's ability to sing. A basic foundation of the techniques of singing will also be beneficial, yet at the same time there's no pre-requisite quality for being a virtuoso singer like Mariah Carey or Freddie Mercury. There are countless successful singers who have admitted that they don't possess particularly good or technically proficient voices. In terms of the conventional definition of being a 'good singer', Billy Bragg, Mick Jagger, Lou Reed and Macy Gray, to name but a few, all stand outside of such a classification, yet each one of their voices is immediately recognisable and enhances every song to which they lend their talents.

Whether or not you decide to develop your own vocal talents, there are a few simple things to remember that will remarkably improve a vocal performance when recording or performing:

1. Sing with confidence;
2. Sing clearly;
3. Live the song;
4. Find the correct key;
5. Prepare, practise and plan;
6. Create the right atmosphere.

1. SING WITH CONFIDENCE

As Colin Emmanuel notes, confidence is the primary factor in any good vocal take. You wrote the song so you should know exactly the message you want to express. Believe in your ability to do this, sound confident and the song itself will sound confident, honest and true.

2. SING CLEARLY

If the listener has to struggle to make sense of a song's words on first hearing, a great deal of the lyric's impact is lost. It's therefore important that you make every effort to be coherent so that a listener can connect with the song's message. Of course, incoherence could be a characteristic of your vocal style as an artist, but it's better to adopt a lucid approach. To ensure that the words come across clearly, talk the lyric through before you sing it. Note where you'll need to take breaths, but don't take one in the middle of a beautiful melody line; look for where the breathing falls naturally while not interrupting the lyric. Then try to taste the words, feel them and explore their sounds to help you sing with passion and colour.

If you're performing a rap, be aware of the importance of 'clarity, diction, timing and good stories', as Colin Emmanuel puts it. Ensure that all of these elements are in place before recording the track.

3. LIVE THE SONG

It's important that you approach the vocal seriously and with conviction. The singer's primary function is to interpret the song, and the most effective method of doing this is to truly understand and absorb what you're about to sing. 'Songwriting and singing is very much like acting,' observes singer/songwriter Ali Tennant. 'You have to put yourself in that role.' So study the lyrics and make sure you truly understand their overall meaning and where the emotional highlights occur.

Next, learn the lead melody line. Be certain that the lyrical phrases match the musical phrases and that you're breathing in the most natural places.

Once you've memorised the song, try performing it in front of a mirror and assess whether your body language and facial expressions reflect the song's emotional content. Then, before doing a committed take of the vocal, spend some time listening to a rough version and consider if all the vocal nuances and articulations are appropriate and timed correctly with the emotional and musical elements of the song. If you can understand exactly what's being said and how it needs to be said, the song will be expressed in the strongest possible light.

4. FIND THE CORRECT KEY

As I mentioned back in 'Song Craft 9', the choice of key is highly influential on the quality of the vocal performance, so experiment with different keys until you find the best one for your voice, then practise the song in that key. A last-minute key change can throw a vocal off badly, as your voice won't sound perfectly 'in'.

5. PREPARE, PRACTISE, PLAN

The ideal way to record a vocal is to get it as near perfect in the first few takes as possible. There's a natural spontaneity about the interpretation and a freshness in the voice that quickly dissipates as the day wears on. To make the most of the moment, therefore, it's crucial to prepare yourself in advance of the recording session. This means warming up your voice beforehand with simple vocal and physical exercises; knowing the song intimately, having practised it as described in the previous point; and planning the session so that you're performing during your peak performance period (ie the time of day at which you sing best). If you're planning on recording more than one song in one day, try spreading the vocals over the entire session.

6. CREATE THE RIGHT ATMOSPHERE

As producer Steve Levine observes, 'Getting a good vocal performance is mostly down to the vibe. Studios, for instance, can put singers off. I tend to get better performances when an artist is recording in a home environment, because they're more relaxed.'

It's important, therefore, that you're comfortable when recording your vocals. If the studio atmosphere is unpleasant in any way, the session won't progress well. A good atmosphere and environment will enable you to express yourself confidently and without restriction. Creating the right atmosphere in a studio can be very tricky, but the best thing to do is to make it as familiar and inspiring as possible, whether this means lighting up some candles, hanging a picture or even wearing the clothes you usually perform in – anything is appropriate if it helps to generate the right performing environment.

A key factor in providing the right atmosphere is working with the right producer (if you're not producing the session yourself, of course). It's important that you find someone whose work you admire and who genuinely understands your music and is committed to it. The producer's objective position is often the best for suggesting improvements in a vocal performance, so there needs to be total trust between you and the producer if you're to get the optimum result.

The Session Singer

'Deliver as strong a vocal performance as you can. If you can't deliver a good vocal, find someone who can and make sure that it's clear and that every word can be heard.'

– Colin Emmanuel

As a songwriter, you might simply not be capable or willing to sing your own song, or you might decide that a particular song is more suitable when sung by someone of the opposite sex. Whatever your reason for opting to employ the services of a session singer, it's extremely beneficial to have a choice of quality performers at your fingertips. The session singer is an important piece of the recording puzzle. 'You have to invest in a session singer,' affirms producer/writer Mark Hill. 'It makes such a difference to selling your song.'

The ideal places to discover session singers are local gig venues, where it's possible to assess a singer's capabilities and musical preferences prior to engaging their services. Other possible sources include recording studios, music colleges, recommendations from singing tutors, musician societies such as the UK's Musicians' Union, and session organisations such as Session Connection or Hobson's Session Agency in the UK.

Before you engage a session singer's services, however, take note of the following guidelines:

- Make sure you establish the working arrangement clearly from the start.

- Ask to hear samples of any previous demos that he or she has recorded.

- Establish what fee you can afford and that which they expect. In the UK, the Musicians' Union provides standard session-rate levels.

- Clarify exactly how long the session will last and what will happen if the session goes on any longer than this.

- Draw up, or acquire, a performer's release agreement that outlines the name of the performer and the session fee paid and clarifies the performer's role in the recording so as to prevent any unsubstantiated claims to copyright. These forms are available from music organisations such as the MMF (Music Managers Forum) and the MPG (Music Producers Guild) or can be drawn up by a music lawyer.

Similarly, when preparing for a recording session, there are a number of simple considerations that will help to ensure that your time is spent most effectively:

- Send the session singer an advance copy of the lyrics (clearly typed) and a clear, audible demo comprising one version with no vocal and another with a guide vocal. Even if you're not particularly great at singing, investing in some note-correction software such as Auto-Tune will greatly increase your chances of being able to produce adequate guide vocals. The songwriter Rob Davis uses this method. 'I'm good at harmonies and telling people what to sing, but I haven't got a good voice,' he confesses. 'When Auto-Tune came around, it was a gift for me because I could stick my voice on a song, tune it all up, play it to a singer and say, "Copy that."'

- Establish the time of day at which the singer is most comfortable performing and arrange the session to take place then.

Ana Gracey On...
...Getting The Best Out Of A Session Singer
It's best to work on the track section by section for speed's sake, completing one section with harmonies, etc, before moving on to the next. Keep everything that's sung, editing or comping after the singer has left – assuming that you have a few usable takes. Once the whole thing is finished, you might want the vocalist to sing the song through in its entirety with a couple of different approaches and/or ad libs, which can really bring things to life.

...Choosing A Session Singer
If you're writing for a specific artist, you need to research their sound musically and find a singer who can recreate their vibe vocally. So when you call an agency, tell them that you're looking for a 'Delta Goodrun meets Vanessa Carlton' vibe or a Tina Turner sound. It make things so much easier.

...Improving Your Voice
'There are a couple of very simple concepts that can dramatically improve vocal performance in singers of all abilities.

Firstly, posture greatly effects vocal efficiency. Just a minor adjustment to a person's physicality can re-align the muscles and organs involved in singing: the lungs, the diaphragm and the muscles of the back, neck and abdomen. The Alexander technique gives the performer a fantastic template for ensuring good posture:

1. *Keep the head forward and up. Don't throw your head back or stick your chin out when you sing. Balance a book on your head, if need be, to ensure the correct alignment of the head and neck.*

2. *The back should be lengthened and widened. Don't slouch forwards or force your shoulders back, thus arching the spine. Stand with your back against a wall as a guide.*

- Don't plan to record more than three songs in a single session. A singer's capabilities rapidly dissipate after an hour or so. Even experienced vocalists arc usually at their best for only three hours a day.

- Make sure there's somewhere private that the session singer can warm up or practise.

- Print up multiple copies of the lyrics, including all repeated lines, verses and choruses. Use a clear font that's legible in low light and number the lines and sections. Then attach the lyric sheet to the boom of a mic stand and cast a soft light on them. This will make the lyrics easy to read without the vocalist having to move his or her head and will cause fewer problems, acoustically.

3. *Keep your knees soft; try not to lock them back.*

4. *Keep your feet flat on the floor, hips' width apart. A nice wide, open stance helps with your alignment and gives you confidence.*

Secondly, anchoring is a technique by which a singer can access hard-to-reach areas of their range or, indeed, more intense voice qualities. Singers need to get used to the fact that their whole body is their instrument and are willing to try more physical methods of training their voices. In anchoring, the muscles of the back provide a framework – rather like a crab's shell – that stabilises the whole vocal mechanism to bring about added power and intensity. Here's how it works:

1. *In your correct standing posture, rotate your arms away from your body and clench your fists.*

2. *Pull downwards from just under your shoulder blades. You should have a strong sense of widening across your back.*

3. *See if you can maintain this feeling with your arms in a neutral position. Breathe deeply and slowly.*

4. *It might help you to imagine squeezing oranges under your arms to access this method.*

Use anchoring whenever you reach a challenging vocal passage or need to increase vocal intensity safely.
Finally, and perhaps most importantly, relax! It's important to be energised, but not tense. Warm up physically as well as vocally; ease out your neck, shoulders, spine and ribcage (yoga techniques are very helpful here) and massage the face and muscles of the jaw. Make sure your breath is low so that your belly gently fills on an in-breath and empties on an out-breath. Ensure that your shoulders and chest don't rise as you inhale, causing you to take a shallow breath which compromises tone and power when singing.

- Prepare the studio in advance. Discuss what kind of environment the singer prefers and make an effort to accommodate his or her needs, whether this includes a glass of water or a particular tea, a preference for a warm or cool environment or bright lighting rather than candles. The more comfortable you can make the singer, the better their performance will be.

- If at all possible, try to have a selection of different microphones at the ready. A microphone that makes one singer's voice sound great can make another's sound bassy or tinny. Also, have a pop shield set up to soften the effect of certain consonant sounds (Bs and Ps), sibilance and breath control.

- Make sure that the monitor mix in the headphones is well-balanced and comfortable. A monitor mix can dramatically affect a singer's pitch and timing, so due care and attention here is essential.

All this preparation might seem exacting, but it's worthwhile, as Frank Musker attests: 'The biggest buzz you can get from being a songwriter is to hear your song being interpreted by a real singer.'

THE PRODUCER:

STEVE LEVINE

THE VOCAL

One part of a recording on which the producer works hardest is the vocal track. In many respect, his role is similar to that of a film director's, whose primary responsibility is to elicit the best performance possible from the lead actor, since the success or failure of a film often relies upon this lead role. Similarly, a song's success will be based upon the effectiveness of its lead vocal performance. Like a film director, therefore, the producer has to treat the artist as if he or she is an actor and bring out that unique performance that will transform a good song into a great song.

Getting a good vocal performance is mostly down to an indefinable phenomenon known as the 'vibe'. Studios, for instance, often have a vibe that can put singers off. I tend to get better performances when they're recording in a home environment, where artists tend to be more relaxed. This is certainly one of the upsides of recording at home rather than at an expensive studio.

It's also important to consider that some of the best vocal performances aren't necessarily 100 per cent in tune. As a producer, I'm all for accuracy and making sure that there are no mistakes, but there's a fine line between getting a great performance and going too far and ruining a song by smoothing out all the problems. The tiny imperfections are exactly the things that get people excited. Taking my previous analogy a little further, the film equivalent is the difference between George Lucas's first and last *Star Wars* movie. The first film was wonderful but flawed in many ways, while the second prequel [his latest at the time this book went to press] was technically perfect but somehow came across as soulless. Likewise, super-produced records can be immaculate in every detail but can actually leave the listener cold. The emotion is all squeezed out. In comparison, recordings that are quite raw and poorly recorded by today's standards, such as the early recordings at the Motown studio [themselves the serendipitous result of a faulty mixing desk], have a real vibe to them that is a direct result of their imperfections.

Here's another example. Many of Boy George's vocal performances aren't completely in tune when compared to the Auto-Tuned boy bands of today, but they're very moving performances. The vocal on the master version of 'Do You Really Want To Hurt Me?' is a live vocal done in one take to a backing track. There are no drop-ins [ie pre-recorded sections spliced into the main recording] on it at all; it's a complete performance. The beginning is separate, but the main bulk of the song is a complete take.

That's not to say that the omnipresence of Auto-Tune and similar software is a negative development in music; one of the positive aspects of Auto-Tune is that a great performance marred by only one or two notes can now be corrected without losing the performance. Recently in my studio, a singer hit a wrong note whilst adlibbing, but it was a great moment that she caught so I simply corrected the pitch of the resolving note and we kept the take. Before, I would have had to punch in [ie drop in] on that take and lose the whole vibe of the melody that she'd captured, because it was one of those one-off ideas that she wouldn't have been able to replicate even if she'd tried 1,000 times.

Over the last year or so there has been an intriguing development amongst up-and-coming singers who have grown up in a world of quantising and Auto-Tune: they're starting to sing like Auto-Tune. Singers are picking up the way that Auto-Tune works. On several occasions I've recorded artists and come up with a track that sounds Auto-Tuned, but in fact the artists were actually copying the records they'd heard on the radio and mimicking Auto-Tune's characteristic rapid pickup.

The telltale signs of a vocal line that's been Auto-Tuned are quick, almost imperceptible vocal pitch corrections. Just as drummers took on board the possibilities of a drum machine into their performance, so it seems vocalists are now also impersonating machines. Some singers are even copying the very syncopated vocal style of tracks that have had their vocal cut and pasted to fit the instrumental groove of the song, such as is produced when a singer performs a particularly laid-back vocal track and the producer then has to spend three hours editing it to make it tight with the rest of the track.

In order to record a successful vocal, it's also important for the producer to capture the right 'feel' or 'groove' for the vocal. The vocal line should either reflect or dictate the rhythm of the track, depending on the style of the music. If you don't have those two elements in synch, they'll fight against each. In the case of reggae, for instance, both elements should be intrinsically locked. You should be able to solo the vocal for a while and still pick up the essential rhythmic vibe of the track. On a ballad, the vocal won't necessarily have a groove, but it will have a cadence or a metre that makes the song flow. This is something that great singers achieve naturally.

One way of helping less experienced vocalists achieve better results is choosing the right microphone. I've noticed that certain microphones enhance certain sonic frequencies, so that various singers sound better through different mics. Choosing the right mic for the job will enhance the artist's overall performance, because on listening back to their voice they immediately think, 'Oh, I sound really good!' They equate the hyped microphone version with their own voice and consequently give a better performance. With this in mind, experiment with several different microphones and decide which gives the best result.

This is a particularly useful tip for a producer in today's manufactured pop world. With the current spate of boy/girl pop bands, the concept of image is taking a higher priority than ever before over the song and the musical talent behind it. Such bands are really the Asda of pop music. What they're purveying sells, but people aren't going to be listening to it in five years' time, whereas the classy, elegant pop of The Beach Boys is still being listened to 40 years on.

HARMONIES

The key problem with many boy/girl bands is that they're put together for their looks; the balance of the vocal harmony is the last thing that the record company considers. Compare that to The Beach Boys, who each had very distinctive vocal sounds but, when they sang together as a unit, their voices blended. This is true of many of the Motown acts, too.

Getting that magic vocal blend, though, is a weird combination of the right tones – it's very much a matter of the sum of the parts being greater than the whole. If you listen to Westlife, for instance, you can't identify the individual voices greatly. The result is bland.

Very often siblings in a band have a positive and a negative within their collective singing – one will have a smooth voice and the other will be husky, almost like a mirror of each other – but the composite sound is fantastic. This might be because they've grown up together, singing in the bath from age three or four, and they've learned to listen to each other's voices and adapt. Whatever the reason, as a listener and a producer, the result is an immediate vibe.

Also crucial to the success of the vocal arrangement is the way the harmonies are balanced – not necessarily balanced equally, but in a way that the main melody comes across, wherever it lies within the stack of harmonies. I learned this from Bruce Johnston of The Beach Boys. With The Honeyz, for instance, I had a problem with Naima's voice because, although she's got a great, sexy little voice, I had to be very careful how I used it against Celena and Heavenly's voice. Heavenly has a very husky, deep voice, and that blended well with Celena's, but Naima's was difficult to blend and got lost in the mix. In the end, Naima sang the octave of the melody and her voice immediately blended well within the overall mix.

As a producer, getting a good vocal blend in pop can be hard, because the act may contain the greatest singers in the world but they may not blend effectively together. It can be a struggle to get that magic sound. But when a producer does get that sound, and they have a good song with a strong melody to go with it, they're dealing with the right ingredients for a hit record.

AN INTERVIEW WITH SHARON WOOLF

When did you decide to become a songwriter?
I've always written songs, my whole life. I was writing in a studio setting from an early age. It felt natural to me, and I knew that I always wanted to write songs, no matter what happened. As I grew more experienced, I realised that, in order to have longevity in the music industry, you have to be able to write songs – that is an absolute fact – so I decided to put all my energy into writing.

How important has your live work when it comes to songwriting?
Playing in a club is hard, especially if you're playing original songs. I think that playing in clubs and pubs is actually far harder than getting out on stage with a few thousand people who know every word to your song, who actually love it and have specifically come to see you. The live experience I had at an early stage of my music career gave me the ability to handle audiences and to feel comfortable with myself on stage. More importantly, it gave me a feel of how to formulate songs, because I could see how audiences reacted to certain songs and arrangements. The experience of writing songs in a studio from an early age and then performing them live gave me a basic level of musicianship that has been vital to draw upon as a songwriter.

How did you survive, financially, prior to signing your publishing deal?
In the early days, I had a regular job while being a session musician on the side. Then I got to a certain point and thought, 'It's now or never.' I jumped ship in a kamikaze way and went full-time. That's a scary thing to do. I had bills and a mortgage, just like anybody else. It was especially worrying in the first six months, because the phone didn't ring. Then I started to get more sessions and was fortunate enough to be part of a couple of hits: 'Straight From The Heart' (Doolally) and 'Sweet Like Chocolate' (Shanks And Bigfoot). It all kicked off after that. I did PAs for a year and a half – two or three a night at one point – and that was my lifesaver. It meant that, when I first started songwriting full-time, I had money to live off.

How do you write songs?
More often than not I hear a chord(s) or even a groove and automatically hear a melody. Then I hear words or word sounds. I might start singing random words

or sounds, but then somehow the consonants and vowels fall into place, or else I'll bring out my list of ideas that I've been collecting and maybe one of those will sound right for that song. This is usually the case if I'm either collaborating or writing a song at home on my own, either to a previously recorded backing track or, occasionally, from scratch.

What's important to you when writing a song?

Firstly, it's important to make the beginning of the song really strong. A&R people work quite quickly, for want of a better word, and your song needs to hit them between the eyes.

Secondly, when you're writing a song, you need to cut out any weak points. I imagine that I'm the A&R person listening to my track for the first time, then tweak the song until I can't hear any weak points.

What do you aspire to when writing lyrics?

It's really important to me that a song has a strong concept and that each line flows and, wherever possible, brings something new to the table. I also look at whether the song sings nicely. Certain vowels or consonants put together don't sing sweetly. As a singer, I can feel that. The words should roll off the tongue easily.

Does being a singer help you to write better songs?

Definitely. It helps me when I'm working with an artist on a song because, having been there myself, I can understand the artist's point of view, which means I can help them in the studio.

Technically, my singing ability allows me to record a high standard of demo. I can sing in different styles, track up my own backing vocals and then work with a producer to make the track sound like a finished master. If you're a writer who doesn't sing, unless you're working with the artist, you have to get in professional singers every single time you want to record a song.

What's the best environment for you to write in?

In this business you don't always get a choice. It could be any environment, but really it's all down to the vibe. As long as you have a great vibe with the person you're writing with, you can write anything, anywhere.

What advice would you give on collaborating?

Obviously, be friendly and open. The key, though, is to be flexible, because everybody has different ways of working and you have to be sensitive to their vibe. You need to be able to adapt your way of working and the way that you function in the studio in order to work harmoniously with the other writer, and hopefully – if you've got a good vibe – they'll be doing the same with you.

How does a typical songwriting session go?

When you get together with a songwriter for the first time, normally you have a chat first, get a chance to bond a bit, before you actually sit down and start writing. Songwriters are very good at opening up and creating a connection as soon as they meet another writer.

I've also worked in Nashville, writing country music, where in my experience the system is different. There, if you've never written with a particular writer before, there's none of that sitting down and having a cup of tea; literally you go into a writing room, shake hands, say hello and start writing a song. A standard session is about three hours. Hopefully, the result at the end of that three hours is a finished song. You then record it live in the room, just voices and instruments – usually guitar and piano – straight into a cassette recorder, and that's what they call a 'work tape' – in other words, a really basic demo. A high-quality demo is then recorded at a later date.

What have you learned from working with other writers?

Michael Garvin, who wrote 'Waiting For Tonight' for Jennifer Lopez, 'Never Give Up On A Good Thing' for George Benson plus several other Number Ones and Top Ten hits, told me that he always tries not just to write a great song but to write a definitive song, a song that will really stand the test of time. I always strive to do that.

Should a songwriter focus on one style of music or learn to write in different genres?

It's actually a benefit for a songwriter to be able to write in different styles. That's my personal belief, and it has definitely worked for me. It stretches you to be able to write in different styles. You can learn a huge amount by taking something that you learned from one style and putting a bit of it into another track. If you can write for different markets, that definitely gives you more chance of success.

What three pieces of advice would you give an aspiring songwriter?

Firstly, write with as many different writers as possible. You have a huge opportunity to learn by collaborating with somebody who's had more experience than you, or is more successful than you, or who comes from a different writer's background, in terms of style or songwriting skill. Although you may be able to write 100 per cent on your own, it's much more fun to write with other people. The songs you write tend to come out better because you're bouncing ideas off other people.

Secondly, surround yourself with good people. I believe that, if you surround yourself with the right people, the other elements will fall into place. A big reason why I signed with Sanctuary was that the chemistry was 100 per cent right between me and Jamie and Deke [Arlon]. You know in your gut when something feels right. Listen to your gut feeling.

Finally, do your own hustling. It never harms anybody to be able to bring in their own opportunities. Sometimes I set up my own writing sessions through networking, sometimes through my publisher, so don't ever be frightened to get out there and do it yourself.

What one thing do you now know that you wish you'd known at the start of your career?

Don't necessarily believe, just because one person has said something negative about a song of yours, that it's the gospel truth, that they're absolutely 100 per cent right. Instead, put it into perspective: it's only one person's opinion in a business full of rejections. When you first start out as a songwriter, you're far more vulnerable and more likely to accept some industry executive's opinion as the final word. They may be right, they may be wrong, but don't let their opinion floor you. You may be able to learn from what they said, or you may choose to discard it, but put any rejection into perspective.

Any writer who truly believes that they have something to offer shouldn't let anybody tell them otherwise. There will be times in everyone's career when they get rejected, and sometimes it *does* hurt. It's those times that you have to get up, dust yourself off and get back out there. Maybe you'll ask yourself the question, 'Why on Earth am I doing this?', but if you truly believe that you have something to give, you'll know the answer, so don't let anybody tell you otherwise. Keep plugging away and something will happen.

Song Craft 12: The Arrangement

The last stages in the creation of a song are its arrangement and production. It would be great to believe that a fine lyric, melody and harmony can stand on their own unsupported, but in today's market a 'complete record' is demanded of the songwriter. Mark Hill, producer/writer with Craig David, concurs: 'It's very difficult to do the traditional demo of an acoustic guitar or a piano and voice. The songwriting process these days includes as much production as writing.'

Prior to the actual studio production, though, consideration should be given to the arrangement. The process of arranging involves the final structuring of the song, choosing which instruments will be used and exactly what each will be playing (ie hooks, melody lines, riffs, harmonies, grooves, bass line, etc).

The main principle behind arranging is that its resultant effect should enhance the song. Ideally, the melody should become more appealing in the context of the harmonies and counter-melodies that surround it, the meaning of the lyric should be conveyed more strongly by being framed and thereby emphasised appropriately, and the rhythmic elements of the song should be expressed clearly so that the groove is clearly defined. A good arrangement should add to a song, not take away from it.

There are even cases when the arrangement of a song results in it becoming

Don Black says:
'The music industry has changed a lot. When I started, it was all about a demo with voice and piano. Songs had to stand up with a melody and a lyric that made sense and rhymed.'

Lamont Dozier says:
'Once we'd established an idea or a feeling, Brian and I would work out the track that we wanted to cut or develop the feeling for the track. Brian was the engineer. We both would then express our thoughts about the track and the music we wanted to inject into it and then relay that to The Funk Brothers, our team of session musicians. Take the bass line on "I Can't Help Myself", for instance. I would pass that idea onto James Jamerson while Brian was telling Benny Benjamin what the feeling of the drums should be. This was the way the workload was distributed. Everything had to be precise; we knew what we wanted when we went in there, and we knew what we wanted to hear. The Funk Brothers would execute exactly what we gave them, and that was invaluable.'

a hit. A particular instrument or riff might be the element that lends to the success of the song – the sax solo in Gerry Rafferty's 'Baker Street', for instance, or the bass riff in Queen and David Bowie's 'Under Pressure', or the clavinet on Stevie Wonder's 'Superstition', or the theremin on The Beach Boys' 'Good Vibrations'. These are all fine examples of the choice and arrangement of the instrumentation enhancing the song.

At this stage, it's important to determine the difference between writing a great song and making a great record. Frankie Goes To Hollywood's 'Relax' and Madonna's 'Erotica' are both examples of great records, but arguably they can't be considered examples of great songwriting. As Glenn Tilbrook of Squeeze maintains, 'The acid test for me isn't whether the song's tricky or not; it's whether it works when you play it on its own, just guitar or keyboards. I know that's an old chestnut, but it's true.'

So, before proceeding to the subject of how to arrange and produce a freshly written song, it's important to understand that the song must first be objectively evaluated – is it, after all, a good song? Songwriter Bill Padley explains the trap: 'It's very dangerous to spend hours and hours working on some great keyboard sound when you actually should be working on whether the chorus is good enough to begin with.'

The difficulty sometimes lies in assessing when the songwriting stops and the arranging begins. In dance, R&B and hip-hop, where the backing track is based on a groove or constructed in the studio, this line is blurred completely as the song is often not finished until the backing track has been more or less written. There's no definite cut-off point, but essentially, once the melody, lyric and basic harmony are down, the songwriting is over. Here, the process of preparing a song for live performance or recording is what can be arguably termed as 'arranging'.

Brian Holland says:
'The Funk Brothers were very important to expressing our songwriting ideas. They were real avid professionals and great musicians in their own right. Collectively, they were unbeatable. They knew how to take directions, first of all, and they understood what to do once they got them. We knew these guys; we knew their best positions. Like in a baseball game or football squad, once you know your positions, you know how to deal with your craft.'

Mark Hill says:
'The arrangement plays a big part in my songwriting process – the way I produce guitars, for instance. I love nylon-string acoustic guitars; I love the sound of a nylon-string being reversed, because it produces a weird rhythmic quality and strange texture. I love the warm tremolo sound of the Fender Rhodes, too. As soon as I play something that I think sounds really good, it will often be because I've used it 100 times before, even though I didn't mean to. I believe the old adage "If it ain't broke, don't fix it." There's no point in trying to be weird just for the sake of being different.'

THE ART OF ARRANGING

Every song is unique and will demand or inspire different choices and arrangements of instruments and sounds. Arranging can be a very creative process and can demonstrate the distinct personality of the arranger, as with Nelson Riddle's much-lauded arrangements for Frank Sinatra's songs, such as 'Come Away With Me'.

The key areas that need to be considered when arranging are:

- The style of music;

- The structure;

- The tempo;

- The rhythm;

- The instrumentation;

- The vocal delivery.

Each of these elements is a variable that can affect the final production. The first – the style of the music – will dictate the choice of instrumentation, the manner of recording, the structure, the rhythm – in fact, everything to do with the arrangement.

Next, as discussed in 'Song Craft 5', a particular structure will help to express a song more effectively than another might, so it's worth experimenting with various arrangements until the most fluid, concise and effective order is found.

The tempo of a song is crucial; Coldplay's 'Yellow', for instance, was almost never released because it lacked the right feel until the track was sped up a couple of bpm and everything settled into place and the song clicked. So, experiment with

Dan Hawkins of The Darkness says:
'Many bands don't excite me that much because they don't have any guitar solos or musical breaks. The musicians are there solely as a platform for the song; they're not made an integral part of the song. With a guitar solo, you can take a song somewhere completely different than could ever hope to be reached with a vocal line. The guitar solo definitely makes a real difference to the way The Darkness arrange their songs. We take great care that the solos are in the right place and are played for the correct amount of time. Before we record a song, we'll generally have been playing it live for quite a while, and we'll leave the guitar solos completely open every time. We'll try different ideas, and only at the very last minute will the solo be finalised in the studio. The key to the success of a guitar solo is that it's not too planned. It should have the same excitement on the recording as when you're playing it live.'

different playing speeds. Often the tempo at which the track was written is slower than would be most effective. One trick is to increase a track's tempo up until it begins to sound odd, then pull back a little. That's often the ideal tempo for the song.

The rhythm creates the groove of a track, which – as highlighted in 'Song Craft 10' – is sometimes as important a factor as the melody or lyric in how well a song succeeds. You need to choose the appropriate sounds and the most effective beat to make sure that the song moves a listener but doesn't drown out the other elements of the song.

The instrumentation, which could range from a standard acoustic guitar to a barking dog, should be selected with due care and attention to the needs of the song. The sonic landscape you create should always help to evoke or enhance the mood, emotion and feel of the core elements of lyric, melody and harmony.

Finally, you'll need to consider the vocal delivery. Would the song best be sung by a male or female singer? How is the central emotion of the song most effectively conveyed, through screaming or by whispering? Is the attitude of the performance appropriate? Is it over the top or underplayed? These and numerous other questions need to be asked. Refer to 'Song Craft 11: The Vocal' for more detailed information concerning this subject.

GUIDELINES FOR ARRANGING

There are certain basic guidelines that can be followed to create the most effective arrangement, as follows:

- Ensure that no parts of the arrangement detract from the listeners' focus on the melody and lyric. Background parts shouldn't clash with the vocal and the instrumentation and the tempo should fit the mood of the lyric.

Bill Bruford says:
'Serious music writing has everything to do with the composer's imagined future for the style or genre in which he's working. To a degree, the mechanics of the music – the actual notes on the stave, the chords and the bass parts – are only a means to a stylistic end. Without a definable approach, which over time can coalesce into a style, the writer's efforts, chameleon-like, will just blend into the landscape of the era rather than stand out as a beacon or lighthouse for others. When Miles Davis's music became the backbone of the Birth of the Cool movement, for instance, it was conceived as a reaction to all the fast bebop playing that had largely alienated an audience. He slowed it all down. Miles had a definite plan. With pop, the plan is the universal song, the great lyrical or musical hook. Jazz, on the other hand, is perhaps more to do with an approach, or a new angle on things. Until I'd figured out what I was about as a musician, where I stood in the scheme of things and what it was that I was trying to offer the listening community in general, I didn't have much hope of writing an effective pop, rock or jazz album. Once you have a plan, though, the notes are relatively easy.'

- Keep it simple. When arranging, less is more. Aim to have relatively few parts in the song but make each one musically interesting. Listen to Norah Jones's album *Come Away With Me* and Arif Mardin's production and arrangements to hear the results of adopting this philosophy.
- Adapt the instrumentation so that it's always relevant to the song's progress.

- Make sure that as many elements of the arrangement as

White Wisdom
By Francis Eg White

1. First and foremost, don't give up that instrument you learned at school. It won't be useful for all forms of pop music, but there's no way you can lose as a songwriter from having mastery of one instrument, preferably the piano. So, if you have given it up, take it up again before it slips away completely.

2. You can choose to start writing a song with a lyric or a melody or simply jam around some chords, but in my experience the best songs start with the lyric, as this provides a definite direction for the mood or story of the song.

3. Don't work for more than four hours straight, unless you're in a very positive and productive mood.

4. Be inspired by others. If you find yourself stuck for ideas, try putting other people's songs into a great big creative mixing pot and taking bits from all of them to create your own song. This can often give you an idea that's new and surprisingly different from your original songs.

5. Work with other writers who contribute interest or different ideas to your own writing. When a complete idea comes to you, however, working alone usually produces the truest and most honest outcome.

6. Avoid writing a song that consciously appeals to another group of people or to someone other than yourself. It normally sounds cheap and your intended audience will see the falsity in it. You'll lose your moral anchor. Instead, aim to create something that pleases you first.

7. Never set out to write a hit song. You'll simply pressurise yourself with such an impossible goal and will then find yourself unable to write a single word or note.

8. When writing, try to establish what state of mind you're in and what feeling you'd like to inhabit you that day, and then follow that one. It's very hard to push against your own feelings.

9. Expect days when you don't seem to get anything of value from a writing session. In retrospect, I've always been surprised by how many half-baked ideas from such 'non-days' come in very useful at another time and session.

10. Enjoy songwriting as much as you can.

possible are hooks in themselves. Don't add superfluous instrumentation for the sake of filling out a song.

- Make sure the lead melody lines don't clash. With regard to the vocal line, the instrumental arrangement is crucial. The natural tendency of a listener is to focus on the vocal line, and while a harmony should enhance it, a different single-line melody or highly unusual sound played alongside it can distract from it. To avoid things sounding too busy, pay attention to the number of melody lines playing at the same time. Rhythm instruments and short repeated parts or riffs tend to be less of an issue as, by virtue of their repetition, the listener quickly accepts them as part of the musical landscape and therefore refocuses his or her ear on the principal melody.

- Allow instrumental space for the vocal. It's important to highlight the vocal and create expectation and tension in relation to it through the use of space in the arrangement, such as by making sure that instruments drop out, drop in volume or play more simply during the main vocal line. Meanwhile, try using fills to bracket the vocals, ending when a phrase starts and beginning when the phrase finishes.

- Be sure to provide sufficient sonic space for the vocal. This tends to be an issue only with non-percussive instruments, such as guitars, saxophones and keyboards, which tend to occupy the same sonic space (ie frequency) as the vocal line and consequently make the vocal less distinct. It's therefore worth experimenting with moving the instrumental parts up or down an octave to keep the 'vocal window' free. This can also be achieved through panning, applying different volume levels and some well-considered EQ.

- Avoid over-arranging. It's always better to let a song breathe.

SONG CRAFT 13: THE PRODUCTION

'Production is all about getting the best out of a song.' – Steve Lironi, producer

The production process – ie the recording and mixing of a song – is the final stage in the creative process. It's at this time that all the elements of the song – lyric, melody, harmony, rhythm and arrangement – are brought together in one complete audio package. Ideally, the production should not only represent the song, honestly and exactly, but also enhance the core song itself. Production is truly a matter of the sum of its parts being greater than the whole.

> *'A well-produced track gets the emotional impact of the song across much stronger.'*
>
> *– Francis Eg White*

Today, production is an integral feature of the songwriting process, as Jem Godfrey from Wise Buddah explains: 'It's inevitable now that songwriters have to be able to produce as well. When you start recording your own material onto Logic or Cubase and begin mixing it, by that very definition you're producing your song.'

The prominence of production in a songwriter's skill repertoire is as much a consequence of advances in technology as it is of the demands of the industry. In today's market, it's extremely rare for a publisher or record company to consider listening to the traditional demo of an acoustic guitar or a piano and voice. With studio technology being so affordable and accessible,

Steve Levine says:
'The producer holds a project together and works with artists to produce that unique vibe. Obtaining this vibe is something that cannot be quantified, because a song really works when the production is indivisible from the song; the listener shouldn't be able to hear the joins between song and production. A great production doesn't have any feeling of intrusion; it's just there. When things work well like that, producers rarely get the credit for it; but when things go pear-shaped and the record sounds like a disaster, then the production gets noticed. Imagine, if you will, that a successful song is a swan gliding along the top of the water while underneath, wiggling furiously, are the legs. That is the production. It's exactly when everything is perfect and runs like clockwork that often producers have worked the hardest to make it do so.'

the bar in demo quality has been raised immeasurably – a song has to be presented as a finished record. 'These days,' points out songwriter Frank Musker, 'there's so much product out there that musical quality is not enough.' A song can't merely have the potential to be a hit; the *demo* has to sound like a hit.

The problems arising from this set of circumstances are twofold. Firstly, a brilliant songwriter won't necessarily be a natural producer. As Tim Hawes of Jiant Productions admits, 'I've always been able to write a song, but putting that into technology and making something sound great is another skill entirely. It takes time.' Unfortunately, many songwriters don't take the time to learn the craft of production. Technology is a wonderful tool, but learning how to use it can be a terrifying prospect to the uninitiated.

Secondly, for those songwriters who *are* talented producers, production can become a false vehicle for a song. A great production can blind a writer to the inadequacies of their song. As a consequence, the market is flooded with highly produced but mediocre songs.

GETTING IT RIGHT TO BEGIN WITH

As I mentioned earlier, the most important element of production is to have a good song to start with. It's very important that you don't let yourself be distracted by the technology at your disposal. In many producers' experience, a great song will almost produce itself.

'You're a songwriter, and as such you must be careful not to get caught up in the production before you've finished the song. It's very dangerous to spend hours and hours working on getting a great keyboard sound when you actually should be working on whether the chorus is good enough to begin with. Our advice is to get a template of the track down, write your song and then, after all that, tart it up as a producer. Don't do it the other way around.

Colin Emmanuel says:
'My attitude as a producer is that the artist comes first. I'm not that concerned about placements and record sales and demographics and all that business. I see my role as giving the artist a song that represents them, allows them to feel comfortable and enables them to express their true selves. If I'm lucky, they'll learn something in the process about themselves or push themselves into an area they'd not thought about before. At the same time, I have to walk the fine line of keeping the label happy and giving them a record that they feel they can exploit and that's not too specialist. I try to give major labels a view into the R&B world without making them feel uncomfortable, yet allowing people from the street or in the club still to appreciate the integrity of what I'm doing without feeling that the music has sold out.'

We've witnessed so many people getting completely lost in hi-hats and filter sweeps on basses when actually the chorus isn't good enough to begin with. Then, because of the fancy production, the track sounds quite good, but they forget that actually the song is not very good. Get the song right before you start getting lost in production. At the end of the day, a great song is a great song is a great song. Tweaking production is the easy bit; writing a great song is the hard bit.'

– Wise Buddah

LEARN THE CRAFT

It's a good idea to take the time to learn how to produce your own material. The home studio equipment that's available today enables you to produce better-quality recordings than ever before, but the lack of knowledge and experience possessed by many of its users is largely responsible for the creation of an avalanche of average, bland recordings. 'The problem is that producers aren't getting the apprenticeships that people like myself had, of working in studios and actually being there and seeing what the microphone does and hearing what difference even a cable can make,' observes producer Steve Levine. He advises that aspiring producers should 'read and learn as much as possible about recording techniques, then work with as many people as you can, because if you're working on your own, you're never going to learn beyond your means; you'll only ever learn your way of doing it. It's often simply lack of experience that squeezes every ounce of life out of a song. People normalise every audio file, finalise every track and add so much compression and reverb that in the end the song may be really loud but there's no soul left in it. It just sounds like mush. The song has to battle so hard to come out from under the 19 plug-ins that have been used on it that it's simply suffocated.'

It's crucial, therefore, for songwriters to take responsibility for their songs and give them the best possible chance of success. When it comes to creating your own quality productions, you have two choices: either you can learn how to produce yourself or you can hire a professional producer. If you intend to

Pete Kirtley says:
'You have to learn the skill of production to get your songs cut, because the A&R guys these days can't hear a song only played on a guitar and sung.'

Colin Emmanuel says:
'Fitting a record into a trend is the very last element of production. It is more important to get the song right.'

develop your own knowledge of production, there are many great books available on the subject (see the 'Recommended Reading' section in 'Body: Essential Information For Songwriters'), as well as magazines (such as the UK's *Sound On Sound*) and music-production courses (such as the one run by the UK's Academy of Contemporary Music).

Alternatively, if you can afford to hire the services of a professional producer, this will usually guarantee good results. However, it's important to find the right producer for your song, so it's worth doing some research in order to establish the one who is most appropriate for your track, has the necessary experience and appears to be the most committed and who understands your vision. The easiest ways of contacting producers are either via recording studios themselves, via their managers or record companies (if they're more successful) or via producer organisations such as the Music Producers Guild in the UK.

A third option is to team up with a producer as an official writing partner. There are countless talented producers out there who are also skilled at producing backing tracks but are in the need of good top line writers and lyricists. This style of partnership can work very well, as there is a balancing of skills, the cost of the production is shared and both parties' commitment to the song is assured.

Guy Chambers says:
'The sound of a record has always been as important as the song itself, ever since the days of Elvis and Frank Sinatra. These days it's almost pointless to play a record label the traditional demo. The demo is dead. There was a time you could present a song with just a piano and a voice and someone would make a decision purely on that, but it's simply not like that anymore. I wrote some really beautiful songs with Neil Hannon of The Divine Comedy for Laura Michelle Kelly, but they were very ambitious and required large orchestral arrangements, so we had to put in a great deal of work before we could even think of playing them to anyone.'

Frank Musker says:
'The best songs are always those that can be stripped down to a singer and one accompanying instrument. Whether you use a guitar, a piano, an Iranian nose flute or just your imagination to write your songs, don't confuse production with writing. Putting up a great-sounding drum loop and playing a chord on a pad sound – even if it's a sample of a full symphony orchestra – for ten minutes and calling it a song just doesn't cut it, I'm afraid. Now, don't get me wrong, Pro Tools is an amazing invention and we wonder how we ever got along without it, but it is nonetheless a production tool, not a songwriting one. Quincy Jones, the legendary producer, once uttered the immortal line, "You can't polish a turd," and it's true. There are many great songs that have become hits without the aid of stellar production but very few great productions that have turned an average song into a standard. Console yourself when your fingers are bleeding on the frets from having played your idea 300 times with the notion that it takes human energy to call in the muse, and no machine, no matter how advanced or expensive, can do what only you can do in your own absolutely distinctive and personal way.'

TARGET THE PRODUCTION

Whether you're a professional songwriter or a self-contained artist/writer, when you're writing a song you need to identify your target market and make certain creative choices to satisfy its expectations. The approach to production should simply be an extension of this thinking.

> 'When you get involved in the production side, target your audience like you should have done when you started writing the song. Who is it you're making this production for? Who are you trying the pitch the record at? If you're trying to pitch it at Robbie Williams, don't make it sound like a dance track. I know that sounds obvious, but some people actually get that badly wrong. They don't listen enough to the person they're actually trying to target their song at.
>
> 'If you're writing a song for Ronan Keating, absorb yourself in Ronan Keating albums and listen to the style of production. Don't try to come up with some brave new sound for him. Unless you're very lucky and clever, an artist isn't going to abandon their previous back catalogue for a new sound. Occasionally it can happen – like "Can't Get You Out Of My Head" with Kylie, for example; suddenly that was the right sound for her – but it's difficult to predict. So, listen to the act that you're writing the song for – or at least the genre that you're writing the song for – then work out the techniques the producers have used and apply them to your songs.'
>
> *– Wise Buddah*

Whether you're writing for yourself or intending your song to be performed by another artist, the direction of the production is fundamental to the overall success of the song.

KNOW WHEN TO STOP

'One important lesson I've learned over the years is knowing when to stop,' confides producer/writer Mark Hill. 'With some of my early stuff, I spent so much time on it that I almost ruined the songs for myself. If you're constantly adjusting the song, in the end you become so sick of it that you have no objectivity left, and then it's really difficult to appreciate it. Now, if I'm happy with a song and its production but something small is niggling me, I'll leave it. It'll be good enough. I'll let the production company or whoever tell me whether it needs work or not.'

This is an important skill for a songwriter/producer to learn. Due to the infinite possibilities presented by the ever-increasing flexibility and functionality of such software sequencing packages as Cubase and Logic, there's a need for moderation and resolute decision-making. There's a very real possibility that your song's progress could be paralysed completely by the almost unlimited choices you have available.

THE COMPLETE PICTURE

For producer/writer Colin Emmanuel, 'Production is all about presentation as a songwriter. You may only get two or three chances before your name is on the list that basically says "not a good songwriter". After that, the industry isn't going to listen, so make sure your production is of the highest quality you can achieve or afford. Show the complete picture of the song. If you have an idea as to how the whole song should go, do it. If it needs strings, put some strings on the track. If you're not capable of recording or mixing a song to how you want it, invest the money and get someone else to record and mix the demos for you. Technology is so cheap nowadays that there's no excuse for making poor-quality demos.'

For the professional songwriter in today's market, production is simply another skill, alongside the ability to compose a melody or write a lyric. In many ways, it's similar to the craft of songwriting. Once you have an understanding of the basic theories and techniques behind the production process, it's just a matter of applying that knowledge, learning from experience and crafting your abilities until you arrive at that magic formula.

> 'In the end, production is strictly gut instinct. Knowing what sounds good is as instinctive for a producer as it is for a songwriter. It's simply about having the confidence to pull up a track and think, "Okay, that's in the pocket."'
>
> – Colin Emmanuel

THE PRODUCER:

STEVE LEVINE

PRODUCING THE SONG

A producer/writer will approach a song very differently to a pure songwriter. A traditional songwriter certainly shouldn't be thinking about the end result in terms of the production; he or she should be thinking about the song and about knocking up a demo that gets across the thoughts they have about the song, but not one that necessarily dots every I and crosses every T.

As a producer/writer, I'm normally further down the line, in as much as I don't have a bunch of songs sitting on the shelf waiting to be recorded. More likely, I'm writing to order – ie the project is defined to some degree. When I worked with The Honeyz, I knew that it was an R&B/pop project. Celena would sing me a melody or have an idea for a lyric. I would say, 'I've got this idea for a groove...' and she'd sing along with it. As we'd develop the song, the line between the demo and the master would disappear completely. It's always a work in progress.

This is a very significant moment between songwriting and record production when the basic song is defined but there are certain things that happen as a result of production that enhance the song. In many cases, these production developments are the very things that people remember about the song. They're the little things that capture the public's attention. This isn't to take anything away from the song, but they can't be separated anymore. That invisible line has been erased. That's why the role of the producer is so important.

The producer is also vital in selecting the most appropriate songs to record. The producer acts as a sounding board, another set of ears for the act. Most artists who write songs for themselves do so because they're satisfying their own personal needs. If the song is so personal that no one gets it, though, it's always going to remain a personal song. As a record producer, it's my responsibility to think of the public at large first, so if an act comes to me with a song that's very personal to them, it might not have occurred to them that it

217

actually applies to 99 per cent of the nation that have also been in a similar situation. It will be the producer's job then to ensure that the ethos of the song applies to the broader public.

Once a song has been selected, it's next a question for the producer of how to produce the song in such a way that it doesn't swamp or kill it. In today's recording world of endless edits, a producer has to be careful that they don't stagnate the production by over-editing and over-deliberating and eventually losing the original feel of the track.

If a song is on an acoustic guitar or piano and it sounds great just like that, it's the producer's job to record that so fantastically that it gets every nuance of the guitar and piano and vocal across. Arif Mardin's work with Norah Jones is a classic example of songs being produced so that every little detail is precise but the songs are never over-burdened with arrangements. That's the mark of a great, really experienced producer. The genius resides in the detail that the listener thinks is so simple. The producer is once again invisible.

AN INTERVIEW WITH ROB DAVIS

How do you prepare for a writing session?

If an artist or writer is coming down to my studio, I like to get the plot beforehand: I like to know what kind of writer they are so that I can prepare some suitable backing tracks. For instance, with someone like Wayne Hector, who excels at ballads and enjoys R&B, I wouldn't work up a hardcore dance track.

Prior to the session, then, I'll have a few backing tracks ready with different vibes for the writer to choose from. And because one needs to be so choosy about what songs to work on, we'll maybe experiment with three or four ideas until we're excited about one of them.

How long does it usually take you to write a song?

If I'm writing a good song with someone, I can have it finished and a quality demo done by the end of the day. That's the advantage of having my studio at home. I worked with Lamont Dozier in my studio for two days and we got two songs finished and another one half finished. Some people might be quite shocked that I can do it in such a short space of time, but I'll only work that hard and fast if the song feels good. If the song doesn't have a vibe, I won't finish it. If it feels only all right, I still won't bother. The songwriting business is so tough that only the best of the best is worth working on. The world and his wife are writing at the moment, so a song has to be perfect nowadays to have even a hope in hell of making it.

Do you find that your best songs are written very quickly?

Not necessarily. Sometimes I'll have a backing track hanging around for a while. I'll bring it up for one writer and their ideas won't work on it, so I'll bring it up with other writers until I find one it works with. Smokey Robinson said it took him seven years to write one of his hits. He must have had a bit of an idea that he liked and just carried it forward, building around it.

What, to you, is the key element in a song?

The lyric is really important for me. I like to come up with a lyric that's left of centre and not too obvious, a concept that hasn't been explored before. All the standard love titles have been covered so many times that, unless you have a really clever twist, the song won't stand out. It is the mark of a great lyricist to

219

be able to express some truism in an original way. A writer like Cathy [Dennis], for instance, is brilliant at spotting lines and ideas in daily life. She comes up with amazing lyrics.

When composing, do you aim to write for a particular artist?

More and more I'm trying to write specifically with artists in mind. I get briefs from Universal and other record companies about who's looking for tracks, and that will guide my writing. If I'm on a co-write, normally I'll discuss a potential direction with the other writer; Cathy, for instance, is quite particular about aiming a song at an artist. In those cases, I'd research the artist's music and find out what their vibe is, then prepare a selection of different grooves and chord changes for Cathy to lay her vocals down and suggest ideas to. Sometimes I'll write a tune that may work for a couple of different artists so I can pitch the track around. It's good to produce a song that could work for a few people in case the targeted artist doesn't want it.

What advice would you give on collaborating?

Personality is the key factor. The songwriting community is actually very small, so it's important to get on well with people. Otherwise you're not going to get anything done and you'll be battling all day.

You need to let everyone put their ideas into a song, and you can't be too stiff about the process of writing. When I worked with Lamont Dozier, he was great, very loose about everything. If I didn't like an idea, he'd try something else, and quick.

Finally, if you're unsure about any ideas in a song, you have to be honest with your partner. A less experienced writer might dive in with an idea that I'm feeling uncomfortable with or that's not truly working. I need to let them know that, or it's a waste of time.

Have you had formal music training?

I had a small bit of music training early on, in classical guitar, but it's really years and years of being in a band and playing live that proved the biggest benefit to my songwriting and musicianship. When you're doing covers of other records, you have to pull them apart, copy the solos and redo all the harmonies. Sometimes I'd have to play a song that I didn't like but, when I analysed it to learn it, I realised it was a lot cleverer than I first thought. You don't notice all the skilful songwriting techniques used by the composer until you pull the song apart yourself.

What's your experience of writing dance songs and working with Paul Oakenfold?

I met Paul late '87/'88, when was A&Ring for a record company called Champion, and he said, 'I know where the whole scene is going: dance is going to be massive.' He invited me to a few of his raves and started coming around to my house, bringing ideas with him. He didn't play an instrument; he just brought other records and would say, 'We'll do a drum track like this and copy it.' We had a few small releases at first, and these developed into bigger projects. It was a big learning period for me at that time.

To write a song over a dance track isn't the same as sitting down to write a normal song; the verse and the chorus have to be very hooky in themselves and credible. Paul was very anti-cheese, so I'd have to make my ideas a little different and off-the-wall-sounding, both lyrically and melodically. Paul has really good A&R ears; while he's not a musician, he could spot a line that was working that I may have missed, or he'd leave tracks running that I'd have taken out. He had an instinct for the requirements of dance.

With dance music, it's important that you don't obliterate the track with too many lyrics and too many sections. The instrumentation is so important to a dance track, since the riffs themselves are what make the track a hit. Often a dance record will have only one chord going through the whole piece, and as a songwriter I still have to make the melody lines interesting over that. Consequently, melody writing is very difficult in that kind of musical environment. Maybe I'll need to come up with only one vocal hook, but I always like at least a verse and chorus vibe in my dance material and – if I can get it in – even a middle-eight. So, when I'm given a dance backing track to write vocals over, I'll occasionally put other temporary chord sequences over it just to be able to write more involving melodies.

How do you create the grooves for your own backing tracks?
If you want to work really quickly, there's a program called Stylus that's wonderful for throwing up ideas for a great groove. Whatever bpm you want, you can ReCycle it, so you can have an R&B groove if need be or a 130bpm dance beat. That's inspiring, because I can then fling out ideas and mess around with chords very quickly.

Where do your lyrical ideas come from?
I keep books and books of titles and ideas to trigger off songs. They come from magazines, books, daily papers, films, conversations, etc. If I'm taking a train into town and I'm waiting for a while, I might go into WHSmith's and look through all the magazines with my little book and write down anything that catches my eye. Out of 20 lines, I might find one that has potential.

What's the story behind 'Can't Get You Out Of My Head'?
Back in 2000, Cathy Dennis spent a couple of days in my studio. The first day we wrote a song that was OK. In fact, it was produced a couple of years ago, but it wasn't a killer hit. The second day we were going through a dance vibe, and I had several drum dance grooves up with chord patterns that I'd pre-

programmed. Cathy started singing, 'I just can't get you...' and the song developed from there. I started doing the 'la la la' bit, and then I put together the bridge chord change. The insistent off-beat bass hits had been done before in other songs, but I built these on two bass sounds: the Triton organ plus a sub-bass line playing the same pattern underneath. In about two hours we had the whole track done. We vocalled it and produced everything that very day. It was one of those songs that come together very quickly.

We were both very conscious about crafting the arrangement and trying not to make it obvious. We were pulling it around until it had an unusual structure that made the track stand out. It started with the chorus, then went to the 'la la la' bit, then went to the middle-eight, then came back to the chorus, then the second bridge extended a bit longer and so on. It certainly wasn't the standard verse-bridge-chorus type of song; it was more off the wall. I remember I played it to a couple of people when it was first recorded and they remarked, 'Where's the hook?' I replied, 'It's all hooks!'

After we'd finished the track, Brian, my manager, ran with it and eventually Jamie Nelson went mad over it for Kylie. Fate had played its hand. Kylie was a great package for the song, and the video was brilliant as well. When Cathy and I did 'Can't Get You Out Of My Head', we weren't even thinking of Kylie, but the whole product just clicked.

In the case of Kylie, the song just zoomed her up and made her massive at the time, but even a bad artist could have come through with a good song like that.

What advice would you give an aspiring songwriter?
Firstly, don't get hung up over songs. Learn to move on. I practise yoga, and it's taught me the art of moving on. If someone doesn't like a song of mine, I won't ponder on it; I'll just move on to the next idea. That keeps me fresh as a writer. So many writers over the years have said, 'This is my one big song!' and they re-demo it and re-demo it. My reaction to this is, 'Why are you demoing something three times if it wasn't good in the first place?' In an industry based on 99 per cent rejection, the art of moving on is a vital philosophy.

Secondly, unless the melody feels great straight away, don't settle for it. Keep pushing and twisting and turning and moving the melody – for example, by taking it higher and lower in less obvious places, or by changing to a particularly odd chord. In the bridge of 'Can't Get You Out Of My Head', for instance, there's an augmented chord; a lot of musos notice it, but it's not that obvious to the average listener. In a standard Oakenfold dance track, I could never get away with an augmented chord, so that's one of the tricks that made that song stand out.

Thirdly, don't become stressed about where the writing is going. You can easily get caught up in forcing the process too much. You'll get there by what feels good to you, naturally. Function off your gut reaction.

Finally, you need to be really, really picky with your ideas. Don't go for the first thing that grabs you. Many inexperienced writers settle on half-decent ideas or deceive themselves as to the quality of a particular song. It's about developing the ears to recognise if a song or idea is good enough. Great ears come with experience.

Song Craft 14: The Hook

'We used to do a lot of radio jingles and are firmly of the belief that a jingle is a 30-second song and a song is a three-minute jingle.'

– Bill Padley, Wise Buddah

The hook is the lifeblood of the popular song. It's the part that's catchy, that reaches out and grabs the listener and is easily remembered. Hooks are the reference points that keep the listener focused and interested in a song, and by virtue of their power and appeal they encourage recognition and repeated play.

A good hook should have tremendous impact. It should be able to conjure up the entire song when heard. It should even sound good when played on its own, completely separate from the rest of the song, such as the guitar riff from Lenny Kravitz's 'Always On The Run', for instance.

Hooks are essential in contemporary commercial music. In fact, pop songs are ideally built solely from hooks. The first priority of a publisher, when assessing a song in today's market, is to establish if the song has a strong enough hook to capture the attention of a saturated market. While the primary job of songwriters is always to write decent songs, it's also vitally important that they create as many suitable hooks as possible in a completed song.

There's a philosophy that you can never have too many good hooks. Paul McCartney's 'Live And Let Die', for instance, could be considered an extreme and highly successful example of this philosophy, where every element of the song can be considered a hook in itself, from the string section to the guitar lines to the vocal parts to the changes in musical style.

Jiant (Pete Kirtley and Tim Hawes) say:
'The reality with songs today, particularly pop songs, is that we live in a fast-food nation. Every aspect of life is about the quick fix. So, when it comes to capturing the attention of the A&R representative at the record or publishing company with a song, you have only a minute to deliver the hook, with all the musical trimmings. The dilemma sometimes with providing the entire song in the first minute is that the song's effect is rather like a McDonald's hamburger – very tasty but over all too quickly and without any lasting appeal – whereas the songs regarded as standards tend to have a greater depth, requiring several listens before they permanently fix themselves in the listeners' heads.'

WHERE'S THE HOOK?

There are many different types of hook. While there's the obvious hook of the chorus, a song can have other, more subtle hooks whose influence can grow with repeated listens. While the principal aim is to create a hook that hits the listener over the head, it's good to remember that softer, less obvious hooks can generate a prolonged appeal in a song. This is why pure pop songs come and go so rapidly – their appeal is immediate but the obvious hook wears thin after a while.

The different types of hooks to consider, then, include the following:

1. Structural
2. Vocal
3. Instrumental
4. Lyrical
5. Rhythmic
6. Production

Structural Hook

This is more usually referred to as the *chorus*. It's repeated regularly throughout a song and is remembered by the listener by virtue of its repetition. The chorus is the high point of the song and therefore should be singable. It's here that the song's appeal lies.

Vocal Hook

This is the sung melody and is generally what the listener goes away singing, but it need not always occur in the chorus. The Beatles' 'Hey Jude', for example, is

Mick Leeson says:
Your song will have lots of competition all along the line, so you want to make it stand out from the rest. It may sound old fashioned, but don't ever underestimate the power of the hook. A hook is not just a 'Boom Bang A Bang' chorus; it is anything that catches the ear. 'Knock On Wood' has a memorable brass intro, a great verse, but the big hook is the four drumbeats inserted between the 'knock' and the 'on wood'. Simple but irresistable. A downbeat song like Roland Orzabal's 'Mad World' repeats the same lyrical phrase twice in each verse – a hook. It also needs a very singable bridge because the delivery of the phrase 'mad world' is appropriately anticlimactic.

Hip-hop understands hooks. NWA's 'Express Yourself' is based on one of the greatest funk bass riffs ever, courtesy of Charles Wright's band. 'Rappers' Delight', ditto, with Chic's 'Good Times', ditto, with one of the all-time-great hard-rock riffs via Aerosmith.

Hooks can come from all kinds of riffs – 'Cars', 'Ashes To Ashes', 'Lady Madonna' – or memorable sounds – the voice of Roy Orbison, the 12-string guitars on The Byrds' 'Mr Tambourine Man' – or killer titles – 'It's Raining Men', 'Walk Like An Egyptian', 'Turning Japanese'. But mainly they're just little pieces of repetition, invention, idiosyncracy, or even something as basic as 'Yeah, yeah, yeah, yeah' – like in 'Man On The Moon' by REM. No one would accuse REM of mindless, pappy pop, but they understand the medium and the power of a hook.

full of great vocal hooks, in particular the 'na na nas' and McCartney's screamed 'Judey Judey Judey!' in the outro. Or how about Marvin Gaye's continued repetition of the vocal chant 'What's goin' on?' in the track of the same name? Or the 'Woo-hoo!' calls in Blur's 'Song 2'?

Instrumental Hooks

The key melodic phrases in a song might be expressed in some manner other than vocally and yet still stick in the mind. The repeated instrumental riffs that run through many great rock and funk songs are often those songs' most memorable parts. Have a listen to the opening guitar riffs to The Rolling Stones' '(I Can't Get No) Satisfaction', for example, or The Red Hot Chilli Peppers' 'Under The Bridge', or the bass line of Michael Jackson's 'Billie Jean', or the keyboard figure in Soft Cell's version of 'Tainted Love'.

Sometimes the riff or figure can venture beyond its typical short length and the instrument itself and/or its melody line can become the hook, as is the case in the violin part in The Bluebells' song 'Young At Heart' and Slash's extraordinary guitar solo in 'Sweet Child O' Mine'.

Lyrical Hook

Sometimes it will be the lyric itself that hooks a listener. The strength of a song's story might remain with a listener even after the melody or the exact words have faded. Bobbie Gentry's 'Ode To Billie Joe' is often cited as an example of this. Many of the songs of Woody Guthrie, Bob Dylan and Billy Bragg also fall into this category, where the message of a song is more important than its melodic vehicle.

A key line in a song might grab the listener's attention beyond anything else, such as the line 'Drove my Chevy to the levy but the levy was dry' in Don McLean's 'American Pie' or 'On a bed of nails she makes me wait' in U2's 'With Or Without You'.

The hook can even be a strong title, such as the shocking but humoured 'Too Drunk To Fuck' by The Dead Kennedys, John Lennon's 'Come Together', Roberta Flack's 'Killing Me Softly With His Song' and Little Richard's 'Tutti Frutti'.

Rhythmic Hook

The hook can even reside in the groove or rhythm of a track. It could take the form of a very simple beat, as in the powerfully communal stomp of Queen's 'We Will Rock You', or be something more complex, as in Prodigy's 'Smack My Bitch Up'. Alternatively, the hook could simply be the quality of the groove, as demonstrated on Stevie Wonder's 'Masterblaster (Jammin')'.

Production Hook

Particular sounds can evoke certain emotional reactions and, applied creatively

– along with the lyrics and melody – can help to generate the mood and emotion of a song. The production itself can even become a hook for the listener.

One of the most effective production hooks is any sound that no one has heard or used before. Throughout the 1960s and '70s, the development in studio technology helped to create many hits through the use of new musical effects, such as flanging and phasing, both of which featured heavily on The Small Faces' 'Itchycoo Park'. Then the 1980s saw the first application of sampling in a commercial track, on Paul Hardcastle's international hit '19'. Later, the 1990s witnessed a proliferation in the use of the Vocoder following Cher's massive worldwide hit 'Believe' as a result of her voice being processed to great effect on that device in the song.

Nowadays, with the proliferation of affordable home-studio technology, there's a whole plethora of sounds at the songwriter's disposal. The main points to consider when applying interesting sounds in the production of a song are:

- The sounds you're using are available to everyone else, so they won't necessarily be unique and result in a hook;

- You need to ensure that your chosen sound doesn't become more important than the song itself. No matter how great the sound is, it won't make up for a poor song.

Having made that second point, a distinctive sound *can* help with getting a song recognised. This applies particularly in the dance genre, as demonstrated by such tracks as Underworld's 'Born Slippy' and Voodoo And Serano's 'Blood Is Pumpin'', both of which are instantly recognisable due to their synth sounds.

THE ART OF THE HOOK

Writing and using hooks in a song is a matter of judgement and crafting. The three key points to remember, however, are:

1. Simplicity
The best hooks tend to be simple and direct. The strength of simplicity is apparent in every example, from the opening guitar jangle on Prince's 'Kiss' to the repeated 'Help' in the chorus of The Beatles' song of the same name.

2. Moderation
A song can be made completely of hooks, from the vocal line to the guitar riff, to the bass part, to a recurring piano figure, to an

instantly recognisable beat using distinctive production sounds. The factor to be careful of here, though, is that too many hooks vying for the listeners' attention at once can lead to confusion and destroy the effect of the song.

3. Everything Counts

A well-crafted song should have no unnecessary parts; every element of the song should add to the track. Padding for the sake of padding is pointless. While too many conflicting hooks can be distracting, a song constructed intelligently with hooks that blend and enhance each other is the ultimate goal of every songwriter and producer.

'I can remember playing [Kylie Minogue's "Can't Get You Out Of My Head"] to a couple of people when it was first recorded and they remarked, "Where's the hook?" I replied, "It's all hooks!"'

– Rob Davis

THE SONGWRITERS:

WISE BUDDAH (BILL PADLEY AND JEM GODFREY)

WRITING FOR RADIO

Due to our previous experience of radio jingles, we're firmly of the belief that a jingle is a 30-second song and a song is a three-minute jingle.

Working in radio stations for years, subliminally we've become disciplined in the way that radio stations work and the kind of songs on the air that sound good. As musicians, we mentally took note of what worked, what techniques stood out, and questioned any song that worked but we didn't know why. After five years, that knowledge became ingrained in us as songwriters. We don't even talk about these things; we'll automatically do a four-bar there, then perhaps consider that something's four bars too long, so we'll take that out. We have a mindset for radio. We know what to lock into and what's going to sound good on the air.

This doesn't mean we have a formula, of course; it's not like A follows B follows C. It's more an inherent ability to self-edit very well.

The most crucial element in a good pop song is a killer hook-chorus. This is the absolute tip of the pyramid of the song. From there on down, a good pop song needs a strong vocal performance, a memorable melody for the rest of the song, an underlying energy and the overall production must sound good and punchy.

We then get our radio hats on for the placement of the chorus. Because we both used to program radio stations, we know exactly what will happen when a record arrives on the desk of a radio programmer. Often their reactions to songs are, 'This is too long; I won't put this on' or 'That takes a long time to get to the chorus.' Unfortunately, there is no formula for the perfect length of a song, even though some people say that pop songs should be 3 minutes 30 long. The real point is that a song should be as long as it needs to be, so if you find yourself bored at around 2 minutes 10 seconds, get out and make the song 2 minutes 10 seconds long.

There are subtle tricks for producing a good radio record – for instance, at the start of songs we tend to put in a four- or eight-bar loop of the beat of the chorus as an intro so that production departments at radio stations can loop them, should they want to make a promo out of a track or use it as a lead-in if there's a featured artist on. There are many tricks like this that you can use to make your song more appealing to a radio station in general, such as making the intro long enough – a comfortable time – for a DJ to talk up to the vocal. Anything that eases the passage of the song across the radio programmer's desk and onto the radio can only be good for you.

An Interview With Chris Difford

When did you write your first song?
I think I must have been about 13 years old. I had a beaten-up guitar and some words I'd written while sitting by a stream. I was curious and swamped with imagination but had no style or direction.

What did it feel like?
It felt fascinating – and to tell the truth, feelings were not yet something I understood, so I just did what was intended.

How long did it take you to get your first success?
It took about three years to get from meeting Glenn [Tilbrook, Chris's bandmate in Squeeze] to having something we knew was going to do well. 'Take Me I'm Yours' was our first real hit, in 1978/'79.

Describe the process you went into when you wrote that song.
I just put pen to paper and it happened. There was no planning involved, no inner secret.

How do you inspire yourself to write?
I sit down and let it all happen. It comes to me; I don't go to it. The feeling is like being washed by the hands of another. And then I have some tea and toast.

How do you come up with titles for your songs?
I beg, steal and borrow from across the universe.

What's the quickest/longest time it has taken you to write a song?
Quickest is four minutes. Longest is four and a half. A day, maybe. Time is not a factor when writing.

What's the most important thing in a song for you?
The last chord. And the words.

What's your personal favourite song? And why?

'Some Fantastic Place', because it means so much to me to remember a friend in this way. Glenn lifted the roof with his tune. It was all very emotional.

If you could write one song in the world, what would it be? And why?
'Circle Game' by Joni Mitchell, because it sums up my life today, yet she wrote it when she was very young. Her gift of foresight is stunning.

How do you split the writing in a song when you collaborate?
I always work on the words. It seems to be my natural home.

Do you recognise when you've written a hit song?
No, I seldom do, or did, or need to. I just write what I like to read.

How many songs do you write per year?
It's not about numbers; it's all about feelings. When I feel like it, I write.

How many songs do you reject?
None.

How do you keep track of all your ideas?
On my laptop. It is my friend.

Who would you most like to collaborate with? And why?
Shawn Colvin, because I love her voice, and her writing. She touches the parts other girls cannot reach.

What advice would you give on collaborating?
Be polite and always be open to ideas. Keep a clean hanky in your pocket and never open the window without asking first.

How do you cope with writers' block?
I live on the ground floor.

What mistakes have you made that you would advise aspiring songwriters to avoid?
Thinking too much about how good I might have been, rather than doing the job in the right way. Don't be lazy; don't be late.

What one thing do you wish you could have known at the start of your career as a songwriter?
How to tune a guitar.

Why did you want to be a songwriter?
Because being an office clerk wasn't going to feed my habit of want. I could not accept anything other than what I became.

How did you survive prior to your success? What forms of work did you do to support yourself?
Ducking and diving by trade.

Why do you think you're successful? What traits have made you successful?
Luck and destiny. Meeting Glenn.

How is piracy affecting you as a songwriter?
I've taken to wearing big boots and a sword to combat this, and it seems to work. What's mine is yours, in many ways. We all must learn to share in the world. Greed will only promote sadness.

What three pieces of advice would you give an aspiring songwriter?
Don't give up. Don't stay up too late. Don't get caught up in computers.

SONG CRAFT 15:
THE ART OF COLLABORATION

'We wrote a lot of stuff together, one on one, eyeball to eyeball...playing into each other's noses. The demand on us was tremendous. They would want a record, a single, every three months, and we'd do it in 12 hours in a hotel or a van.'

– John Lennon

For a songwriter, the act of collaboration can be one of the finest and most productive experiences. Music history is overflowing with hit songs from the prolific partnerships of (to name only a few):

Bacharach and David
Rodgers and Hart
Leiber and Stoller
Lennon and McCartney
Holland, Dozier and Holland
Jagger and Richards
Elton John and Bernie Taupin
Rice and Webber
Chinn and Chapman

Ali Tennant says:
'Prior to my experience with Rod [Temperton], my writing schedule was back to back every day with different people. Even though in hindsight this may have been to the detriment to the quality of my songs, I'm now realising a whole host of benefits from collaborating with so many people in such a short space of time.

'First and foremost, it made me extremely productive. Working with different types of songwriter pushed my songwriting in totally different directions and broadened my approach. As a consequence, I can now adapt very easily to how another writer works, since I'll often have worked with somebody else who has used a similar creative formula. This helps me deal with the typical everyday situation of a professional songwriter of going into a room with a stranger and having to come up with a song within a couple of hours.

'Furthermore, instead of the one singular way of writing that I used to use, I now have a selection of methods to apply to any given situation. And by associating with people that are better than me, I've been able to aspire to and reach higher levels of songwriting.'

Stock, Aitken and Waterman
Cathy Dennis and Rob Davis

For the professional songwriter, collaboration is the norm. With today's song market being so competitive, career writers can't afford to settle for anything less than the best. One look at the contemporary charts reveals that the majority of tracks have been the result of collaborative efforts. Consequently, it's important for a songwriter to understand the demands of collaborative writing and the ways in which the process can be made more efficient, productive and personally fulfilling.

ARE TWO HEADS ARE BETTER THAN ONE?

'I'm a believer in the two-man team – the Jagger/Richards, the Lennon/McCartney – one of whom is good at one thing and the other is good at another thing. They push and shove until they come up with a song idea that gets them both going.'

– Bill Bruford

There's nothing wrong in going solo as a songwriter. In fact, writing on your own can produce the best results. Also, the songs will be uniquely yours, there'll be no arguments and you'll receive 100 per cent of the royalties. Even if you're in a partnership, some songs will warrant singular attention because they arrived complete and another person's input would just spoil the fundamental vibe.

Billy Bragg says:
'One of the things about being Billy Bragg is that, when you're in the studio, you have to write the words, come up with the music, play the song, do the vocals, design the sleeve, make the tea and then buy everyone sticky buns, so if you run out of steam, everyone's just sitting there, looking at you. Whereas when you're with a band and everybody is collaborating, you can afford to go out and clear your head, do something else and then come back and pick it up again, because you know that, while you're out, the rest of the guys are going to be working on it.

'After 20 years of me writing in my own sweet way, it was nice to have The Blokes in the studio with me, to have their input. Some of the songs we wrote I wasn't convinced by, so one time, when I was ill for three days, they went back in the studio and re-recorded them in a completely different style and convinced me that they were good songs. When they'd done that, I had to go back and write completely new lyrics for them as I'd only written half-arsed lyrics because I didn't really believe in the songs. But they damn well knew it! They raised the bar!

'Collaboration can be very fruitful, particularly if you've been writing on your own for a long time, as I have been. Equally, there are times when you've got the guitar and you've got the idea and you've got to run with it. You have to work out how to get these ideas, or "shapes", down on paper. It's like a canvas: sometimes you're trying to paint something that's impressionistic rather than picture-perfect. In the end, it doesn't have to look like that subject, but it has to evoke that subject in the viewer's eye. Not all paintings show exactly what they're about; with some you have to step back a bit and look again. You have that same opportunity to do that with songwriting.'

Furthermore, there are a number of disadvantages to collaborating. Firstly, you'll have to compromise on musical and lyrical ideas, which may lead to a dilution of the song or your particular style. Secondly, you're reliant on somebody else to complete the song with you, and this might prove an obstacle to finishing a project and moving on. Thirdly, artistic differences can result in arguments, while disagreements on the splitting of the publishing royalties can end up in frozen assets and hefty court fines. Finally, there's the difficulty in finding a writing partner to begin with.

None of these potential problems is insurmountable, however, and many are avoidable or outweighed by the numerous benefits of collaboration, which include:

- **A balancing of talents.** One writer might have a knack for writing lyrics while another might be more skilled at composition or production.

- **Increased productivity.** With two writers, there should be at least a doubling of output, if not more, due to the increased opportunities for inspiration to strike.

- **Objective editing.** A writing partner provides a constant source of feedback and criticism that's less subjective than your own.

- **Nurturing of personal growth, both commercially and artistically.** Oscar-winning lyricist Don Black appreciates this

---

Jiant (Pete Kirtley and Tim Hawes) say:

'When collaborating, we would advise you not to get too precious with your own ideas, which can happen if you tend to write on your own. Take the time to prep the chorus section, but don't get too attached to it because you have to be prepared to give the artist a bit of breathing space in which to get involved and to offer their own suggestions. Sometimes the artist will write a better melody. In those cases, keep your alternative chorus for another opportunity.

'The key benefit in collaborating either with an artist or another writer is that you're able to bounce ideas off one another. This is excellent for those moments when you're not certain about a section or an idea. Then the other person can provide feedback, inspiration or alternative ideas. Otherwise, songwriting can be a lonely old game. It's very hard to actually have the confidence and belief in what you're doing from start to finish.

'Furthermore, collaborating will spark off very different ideas as the result of two personalities working together. Jiant's success is based upon the very different opinions and attitudes of two writers. We basically disagree on everything! One writes with the guitar, for a start, which offers a different perspective straight away, while the other tends to write from the perspective of the keyboard. This is good for a song. If you're going to have a partner, there's no point in having someone who things like you because your ideas and direction will be the same. In any great partnership, there needs to be a little friction – Lennon and McCartney being the archetypal example. The tension results in different creative ideas being born that can then be fused together to produce a song that's unique.'

benefit: 'I've worked with maybe 100 different composers and I think each brings a new voice to me. If I sit down and write with Marvin Hamlisch, he brings out something in me, a different colour of lyric writing than if I write with John Barry or Jorgen Elofsson.'

- **New techniques.** Collaboration can inspire fresh ideas and break restrictive writing habits or introduce you to different techniques.

- **New styles.** Working with different people provides the opportunity and encourages you to write in different genres and forms of music.

- **Discipline.** Writing with a partner disciplines your writing habits, since you're compelled to come up with ideas and you have to prepare for planned writing sessions.

- **Greater opportunities for success.** By virtue of increased industry contacts and access to greater opportunities, your chances of success are effectively doubled. Furthermore, in such a competitive industry, it's important to have personal support. As Colin Emmanuel affirms, 'If you're in a partnership or in a team, it can be a lot easier as you have a comrade in arms.'

- **More social.** Songwriting can be a lonely business, so sharing the creative experience can be very enjoyable. Gary Barlow, artist and songwriter for Take That, admits, 'I love to co-write. Sharing the birth of a song is so exciting.'

FINDING THE PERFECT PARTNER

'You walk in every day and you find yourself with a new wife.'
– Wayne Hector

It's clear that an effective writing partnership can be an extremely beneficial arrangement, but where do you find your perfect partner?

Like any form of relationship, choosing a collaborator can be a long and problematic process. Much of it is down to luck. Elton John took his first step towards a world-famous collaboration when he answered a classified ad for a songwriter in a London music paper. Poet and lyric writer Bernie Taupin responded to the same ad and this led to the pair meeting each other and forming one of the most successful writing partnerships in music history.

Successful collaboration is similar to searching for the perfect spouse. There's a whole range of personalities, expectations, personal habits, previous experiences, egos and lifestyles to understand and deal with. On top of these, there's also your partner's musical and literary influences, business knowhow and attitude.

So where do you look? If you were looking for romance, you might visit a bar or a nightclub or join a singles' society. Similarly, if you're a songwriter searching for musical interaction, certain places and events are ideal for encountering similarly creative souls, as follows:

- **Live gigs.** These provide the best opportunity to meet possible collaborators, enabling you to meet and evaluate musicians of all styles in a very social environment.

- **Music publications.** For example, *SongLink International*. As described above, this is how Elton John and Bernie Taupin met.

- **Recording Studios**. These are great places to meet producers, particularly if you're a vocalist, lyricist or top-line writer.

- **Industry events,** such as the Ivor Novello Awards. These provide ideal occasions for meeting professional songwriters and striking up a rapport.

- **Music colleges.** Young, eager and talented students will always be looking for career opportunities.

- **Songwriter societies.** The British Academy, for instance, provides a list of possible collaborators for all their members, as well as arranging regular networking events.

MAKING THE RELATIONSHIP WORK

'The reason why my and Elton's partnership has survived the test of time is that we are very diverse characters and we communicate on different levels.'

– *Bernie Taupin*

Communication is the key to effective collaboration.

Like any other relationship, the only way to make your relationship with your partner work is to make sure that you communicate your feelings, thoughts and ideas clearly and respectfully. Below are ten pieces of common-sense advice designed to help in a collaborative situation:

1. The most important thing is to have respect for each other as writers. Respect your partner's talents, abilities and input as much as you would want them to respect yours.

2. Don't be precious or over-sensitive or believe that you're always right. You need to leave your ego at the door. Keep in mind that both of you are trying to create the best song possible, so don't defend something simply because you wrote it.

3. Listen to each other. Don't merely hear; *listen* to your partner's views and actively consider them rather than leaping to a decision by yourself.

4. Provide constructive criticism. There's a huge difference between saying, 'That's awful' about a song and saying, 'I think that line could be stronger.' Criticism is much easier when delivered in an atmosphere of mutual respect. The criticism and editing of ideas is a necessary part of the creative process, and a good partner shouldn't let a flaw in a song be ignored. This is one of the primary benefits of collaborating, so you need to maintain a professional attitude at all times.

5. Work with someone with whom you're compatible. Don't discount working with people active or with tastes in other genres of music, but consider collaborating with a person who has similar values.

6. Be sure to acknowledge your partner's talent and compliment their good ideas when they have them. If you dish out a perpetual stream of negative comments, over time this will cause them to ignore your comments and suggestions.

7. Be open to each other's ideas. There's no harm in trying out a suggestion. Nothing's set in stone at the songwriting stage, so you have nothing to lose by giving it a go. You'll either prove yourself right or be pleasantly surprised.

8.   Work with someone who has skills and strengths in different areas of songwriting than yours. There's much to be gained from collaborating with a writer who complements your own talents, particularly a greater chance of producing a song that's strong on all sides. There's also less chance of arguing.

9.   Make sure you turn up at writing sessions prepared. Have two or three ideas to play with and fall back on. Then, if nothing sparks immediately, you can try your prepared suggestions. There's nothing worse or more uncomfortable than a 'dead' writing session.

10.   Always keep your writing partner informed. Make reasonable efforts to contact them if you wish to adapt one of your joint works, and never bring in a third person without informing your original writing partner first. This is one reason why you should make sure that your contact details are always kept up to date.

Methods Of Collaborating

It will be helpful for you to find out your partner's preferred mode of working so that you can manage your expectations of the relationship. For instance, do they like...

1.   **Writing lyrics or music alone, then getting together later?** This is for writers who feel more comfortable with getting something solid down before developing it, or for the lyricist who favours writing to a finished melody. This style of collaboration is ideal for correspondence composing.

2.   **Writing together in same room as you?** This method allows for immediate results and can be exhilarating, but it can also be quite threatening, especially for people with less forceful personalities. Compatibility is important with this method of working, and it helps if you can establish each other's most creative period of the day and how often per week they're able to work.

3.   **Writing to an assignment?** With this method, you'll first

need to establish the purpose of writing. If you intend to be commercial in your aims, you'll need to decide on the market you'll be writing for. Certain songwriters, indeed, can't create without an artist in mind. If this is the case with your partnership, you'll need to research the artist in question so you can then tailor something to their style.

4. **Writing organically?** This is the freest form of composition, but it needs to be carefully managed carefully or a writing session can quickly become unfocused and unproductive. As I mentioned earlier, make sure you have

Wayne Hector says:
'I always have the business aspect sorted out before a writing session. There's no point in walking into a room without an understanding of that, or you could write the best song in the world and have it sitting on a shelf for two years while you argued about who wrote which part. From the start, I want to know how many people are in on the writing and what the splits are going to be. If you get three people in a room, it's obviously a three-way split, but you tend to find that there are people out there who don't think in that way; one writer might create all the music and insist that they get 50 per cent and the remaining 50 per cent for the lyrics is to be split between the other two writers, for instance. I don't want to work like that. When you're in the creative process, you realise that everything you do affects what the other person does, and vice versa. Everybody is equally responsible for a song; even the person who wrote only two words is as responsible as the person who wrote the melody. Maybe those two words are genius lines. Occasionally a person simply adds a vibe to a session that helps everyone else create. You have to be open-minded about collaboration.

'Often I'll sing melodies, put all my ideas together into a song and then take it to a composer to finish off. Although I could hire musicians to play the other parts and get 100 per cent of the publishing of the song, it's always about what's going to make my song a great song. I would prefer to involve another writer in the creative process. Remember the songwriters' adage: You can have either 100 per cent of nothing or 50 per cent of something.

'On the creative side, I would advise all songwriters to be prepared to give a little ground when collaborating. Think of it as being like a marriage. You walk in every day and you find yourself with a new wife! You go through that whole awkward process of learning how to give and when to take. I often see that struggle going on in younger writers, and they reveal an immaturity in their craft when they're not aware of the moment to give someone else a little leeway. Never forget that you can always go back to the song afterwards and go, "Well, do you really think that lyric was better?" Collaboration isn't about egos; it's about writing the best song possible. Even if you're a genius and can write a song all on your own, I'd still recommend collaborating. As much as a writer thinks he knows, there's always more to learn about songwriting. You'll always find some idea that you've never considered; you'll always meet somebody who has a different angle on writing. You can learn from every single person you work with. That's why co-writing is as important as anything else in the songwriting business.'

Lamont Dozier says:
'One perfect example of a definitive Holland/Dozier/Holland collaboration would be "Reach Out (I'll Be There)". Brian started out with this Russian melody, as I call it, and then that's where I joined in and we'd leave Russia and go to funkland with the "If you feel that you can't go on…" section before going to the streets for the next section. Once the track had been established, we then shared our opinions about the melody. After we were comfortable with the melody, the idea and whatever title we had, we then passed it on to Eddie so that he could complete the lyrics.'

a few ideas and/or titles prepared in advance in case inspiration doesn't strike.

With this style of collaboration, the creative chemistry is particularly important. You'll often begin a session with a conversation about what interests both of you – current events, musical tastes, etc – in the hope that an idea for a song will develop from there. This is the method most often employed when collaborating with an artist.

Other considerations when working with another writer include the following:

- Does your collaborator have aspirations to be a recording artist? This question is more important than it might seem. If they do want to be an artist, naturally they might want to hold onto the best songs. This could become an issue if there's an opportunity for another artist to record and release this material. You don't want great songs to be held back in the hope that your partner might get signed one day.

- When do you bring in a third party to work on a piece? You have to be sensitive about when it's appropriate to call in another writer to help finish a song.

- Who's going to arrange the demo recording session? And who's going to foot the bill? This second point is also true with songwriting competitions – who will pay the fee? And how will any winnings be split?

- Finally, what industry connections do each of you possess? How are you going to co-ordinate the promotion of the track?

WRITING WITH SUCCESSFUL SONGWRITERS

If or when you get an opportunity to collaborate with a successful writer, the expectations and presumptions you'll have before your first session might be quite nerve-racking. However, it helps if you consider that they'll be as concerned as you about how the session will run. You might be in awe of them, and nervous about your capability of proving your creative skills, but they'll be equally under pressure to produce the goods so that you don't question their validity as a successful songwriter. A good writing session is about making everyone comfortable enough to create.

Writing Splits

The final but most crucial element to get right when collaborating is the agreement on the copyright split. Arguing over percentages can destroy a promising or successful relationship. There are countless examples of ruined partnerships, escalating court costs and frozen royalties simply because the split on copyright was either not agreed at the time or not recorded in writing.

Collaboration agreements are dealt with in more detail later in 'Heart: The Business Of Songwriting'.

Here's some advice from Wise Buddah on the subject of splitting copyright:

> 'Experience has taught us two rules. The first applies where there are only one or two artists joining us on a writing session and the second applies to writing with a band.
>
> 'It's impossible to measure someone's input at the time of writing a song. The situation where writers are arguing, "Well I wrote that word" or "Well, I did that melody and the bridge, so I deserve this much" usually results in a fight. You can't work like that. If an artist comes in and maybe doesn't contribute a huge amount but is very animated in discussions and offers their opinions, this is still a vital part of the songwriting process, because if that person hadn't been there, the song wouldn't have happened that day. If the artist sits on the sofa and doesn't come up with anything for half an hour, then we'll just get on with it. In fact, in one case an artist fell asleep on the sofa!
>
> 'So our rule is quite simple. How many people were in the room? Four? Then that's 25 per cent each. If it gets ludicrous and there are three or more members of a band, that doesn't work the same way and rule two applies. In those cases, we say the band can have 50 per cent and we'll have 50 per cent. Otherwise we end up with nothing in return for our efforts. If you were to work with the 12 or more members of Blazing Squad, for instance, you'd earn bugger all from a hit song!
>
> 'This is such a fair system that no one ever complains.'
>
> – *Wise Buddah*

The professional songwriting community in general works on the principle of splitting the publishing *equally* based on whoever was in the room at the time of writing the song. This system is considered to be the fairest and most practical way of dealing with the issue.

The important thing to remember is not to take the matter for granted when working with another writer. When a song is a hit, the introduction of money does a great deal to distort the memory, and the truth quickly becomes a point of view rather than a matter of fact. So, the three most vital things to remember when collaborating are:

1. To discuss the copyright split before or immediately after the writing session;

2. To agree to a fair and practical system;

3. To put the agreement in writing.

Once the business discussions are out of the way, everyone is then free to create without fear of complications.

Collaboration is a fundamental part of the craft of songwriting. The challenge of finding an appropriate writing partner and making sure that the business side is taken care of is more than compensated by the increased productivity, additional opportunities and improved quality of songs.

THE SONGWRITER:

BARRY MASON

WORKING WITH OTHERS

I really believe that collaboration – as far as you want to take it – really improves your chances. Rejection is certainly much easier to handle with a partner to share the pain, maybe over a drink or two as you curse our cruel and merciless business!

Let's say you've written and demoed your own song. First, play it to two or three *not* very close friends. And don't cough over the dodgy bits! When the demo has played and your friends have finished criticising it, ask yourself, 'Is my song really as good as I thought?' Somehow, a demo played in front of relative strangers sounds quite different. If you feel it can be improved, instead of going back to the drawing board – something I personally find quite difficult – why not collaborate on it with others?

When I give lectures on songwriting and the young writers play their songs, I'll hear maybe one song with a good melody and ordinary words, and another with great words and a too-predictable tune, and perhaps even a super-professional-sounding demo, but no real song. Once I heard an ordinary demo by a wonderful girl singer; her lovely voice was wasted. Just for a moment I mused, 'Imagine if they could all get together. The good melody writer and the fine lyricist – they agree on one good idea and work together on it until it's tight. Then they offer it to the great singer as a vehicle to sell her voice. She learns the song and all three of them fine-tune it until it fits her like it was written for her,' which it almost was. 'They then approach the guy with the great demo sound and studio setup and do a deal for a share of the song instead of money. They work together – listen to his ideas – until he produces a great demo. They let no one be precious or afraid to offer constructive suggestions, but they don't shoot each other's ideas down. Stream-of-consciousness outpourings can contain seeds of greatness, so they just fish around and gently coax them out. Then all the team work together on preparing a good presentation for a record company, from CD design to biography. They try to get a deal – not just for the song but for the whole package: writers, singer and studio producer...'

OK! You're right. I'm well over the top. But I couldn't stop there; I had to see how it turned out. Now where was I? Ah yes...

'I'm sure our team between them know a great local hustler who could sell fridges to Eskimos. They ask him/her to try and place the product for a piece of the action. If there's no joy with a record company, they approach a local businessman, buy him a drink and let him hear their beautiful demo and meet their sexy – and by now much more confident – singer. When their hustler finishes raving about their demo and says, "Why don't they have records like that in the charts?", they tell him that, for a modest investment, he can help them to rectify that by starting his own record label – maybe set one up on the internet. They even have a cool label name ready, incorporating *his* name! They tell him a record label is easy to set up. This song he's raving about could be his first release.' We all moan about how tough the business is, but there *are* those type of guys out there with bundles of readies who would love to be a part of it.

Now, I know by now you're thinking I've got totally carried away, and you're right, but I'm just trying to illustrate a point. One thing we all know to be true is that a piece of something is better than all of nothing.

However, that's not the only reason for collaboration. Maybe you're not a musician. So write or co-write lyrics. You can then work with great musicians and, inspired by their wonderful playing, co-write melodies.

I believe that the struggle of creation, like many things in life, is more fun if you share it. In other art forms, it's difficult, if not impossible, to work with someone else: two people do not normally paint a picture; writing a book takes so much discipline and must be so lonely, sitting for hours and – as someone much cleverer than me once said – facing the terror of the virgin page. Songwriting is made for collaboration – pooling the strengths of talent, youth, ambition, endless energy and enthusiasm. Most important of all of these is raw talent, and there's tons of it out there, untapped and waiting to burst onto the scene.

Alternatively, why not contact veteran successful writers who might be glad and flattered to be coaxed back into writing songs instead of playing golf and railing at rap?

Roger Greenaway, a great writer and one of my favourite people, wrote many songs with me. We would meet at his home or mine, and after the first of many cups of tea we would say, 'Well, no matter if we write a good song or not, what a wonderful way to spend the day.' And it always was. When you and your co-writer have worked all day and a new song is born, it's an act of creation. The song didn't exist prior to that morning. Sadly, most people live and die and never create a thing. So be proud of yourself and the songs you create.

An Interview With The Darkness

How do you go about writing a Darkness song?

DAN: There's maybe a misconception about The Darkness that we're a riff-based band. That's not actually true. Everything we've ever written has always been song-based. If it works on an acoustic guitar and the whole band gets excited about it, even before we've cranked it up, then we know we have a great idea to work from. Generally, the riffs come after having finished the song acoustically.

In the past, we've found writing the riff first to be more difficult. Justin gets more turned on by original chord sequences and so prefers that I create a solid platform for him to sing over. Then the fight begins where I try and outdo his vocal lines with guitar riffs. That method always worked with The Smiths – the constant battle between Morrissey and Johnny Marr's guitar. The vocals and the guitar are both fighting for the same space in the song, and that's what makes our songs sound exciting.

More often than not I'll present a whole bunch of music – backing tracks and arrangements – for Justin to sing over. If he's inspired by an idea, we'll take it forward and the band will add their contribution to make it sound like The Darkness. There are many songs, however, that don't make it simply because Justin isn't inspired by them.

JUSTIN: The whole process can be quite hard sometimes because Dan gets excited about almost the polar opposite of the things that I do. I like songs with a vibe, songs that are instant and playful. I just want to jump around and go, 'Hey!' Dan gets more inspired about the heartfelt and darker aspects of music. Luckily for the band, Dan has a huge output of ideas, chord sequences and sections of songs for me to get excited about. Most of the time I need only apply a vocal and lyrics. Occasionally, of course, I might contribute the odd unforgettable riff of my own, as in 'I Believe In A Thing Called Love'.

I tend to play the melody first on a keyboard and then work the lyrics out later. That's why our melodies sound so strong: they're not simply the result of me vocalising; they're carefully written and constructed. In The Darkness, it's about the song first and foremost.

How do you choose the songs to work on?

JUSTIN: The songs are the result of a collective Darkness songwriting partnership. If one person out of the four doesn't like an idea, it's usually out. This is because they won't play it with enough conviction to actually justify its inclusion. Hundreds and hundreds of songs are therefore left unfinished, but the ones that survive are strong.

DAN: In such an environment, I can't be selfish with the music that I write. I don't expect anything to come alive until Justin or the rest of the band have been inspired by it. I'll go to the band with 10 or 15 pieces of music, and maybe five of them the band will work on, maybe just two of them Justin will end up liking enough to sing on and write lyrics to, maybe one of those two will be a song that we end up playing live, and then only one or two of those new live songs will make the album.

JUSTIN: That's our quality control. We have four different people – four different sets of taste; four different criteria – so if a song manages to pass all that, it'll be a good song. This is the reason why all the band share the publishing rights: everyone has had an input. Songwriting isn't a simply a matter of writing; it's also a matter of editing an idea as a band and saying, 'That's good,' 'That's bad,' 'That helps,' 'That doesn't.'

DAN: Although Frankie might not feel like he has anywhere near as much input as myself and Justin in the early creative stages, he plays a very important role as the Devil's advocate. He has a very good ear for what works and what doesn't. He also presents the band with new song ideas that have then been developed into such hits as 'Love Is Only A Feeling'.

In a band situation, you can never assume you've got it completely 100 per cent right. You need the confidence, though, to take your idea to the other members. It's very easy to take their criticism personally, so it's important that you don't get too sensitive about it all. With Justin, I don't have to hold back anything; when we can have an argument about a song – and we quite often do – I'll tell him very clearly why I don't like a particular idea of his, and it's then up to him to convince me why he wants to do it like that.

JUSTIN: It's important not to shy away from such an ego battle, because the best music comes from these confrontations. Besides, I'm always right!

Is there a secret to writing rock music?

JUSTIN: Predictability is the key to writing great rock songs. The audience have to know exactly what's coming so they're ready for it, ready for the chorus. If there's a little surprise in the song, it's usually because the song almost acknowledges that there was a surprise coming. In rock, it's really important not to surprise anybody.

Rock music is also about attitude. We always saw ourselves as a stadium-rock band. We always used to say that we were bringing the stadium experience to the pubs, and that eventually we will reverse that and we will bring the pub experience to the stadiums. Pub rock and stadium rock are actually the same thing: anything that connects with a pub crowd will connect with a club crowd, will connect with an arena crowd and will connect with a stadium crowd.

Is there a secret to writing good rock lyrics?

JUSTIN: I've discovered that honesty is the best policy in songwriting. Being honest in your writing is actually very rewarding. In every other aspect of this business, you're basically living a lie; you're projecting yourself in a way that's not necessarily you. You get misunderstood. People think you're rich when you're not. They assume things, and you never really get the opportunity to show them the truth. The only way you can do that is through a song, because that's one area that can't be manipulated by the media. It's recorded, it's out there and people are listening to it. Songwriting is the only opportunity you get as a performer to be yourself.

Where does your inspiration come from?

DAN: I get to that zone and it doesn't matter how stressed I am: if I'm playing on a guitar, with the aim to write a song, I forget about absolutely everything.

There's actually a song on the new album that was the result of a dream I had. I was dreaming about the time Paul McCartney said he wrote 'Yesterday' from a dream, and then my dream was me writing a song in my sleep and then waking up. But the thing is, I actually woke up when I was supposed to wake up, and I remembered the chords and the melody!

Does being in a band make songwriting easier?

DAN: Songwriting is an art unto itself and completely separate from being in a band. A great song isn't going to happen when you're running around, making a load of noise, having long hair, pulling girls and imagining you're performing at Wembley Arena. The Darkness always took time away from the rehearsal studio and away from everything else to write songs. We have what you might call the 'office', a place that's our round table, where we write the songs. Then we've got the 'play area', which is our rehearsal room, where we get the ideas up to scratch. Then we have the 'fantasy made reality' realm, where we play on stage and act as rock gods.

It's very easy to make a loud noise and create a great riff, but it's not very easy to turn that into a great song. If you've written a good song to start with, it doesn't matter how loud you crank your amp, how much you run around; you can't destroy it. You cannot kill a good song. And believe me, we've tried.

Song Craft 16: Writing A Hit Song

Songwriting is a craft, and a songwriter needs to take the time to perfect that craft. Once a song has been written in its first draft form, the process of creation is over and the crafting begins. As Stephen Sondheim once very famously said, 'It's not the writing; it's the re-writing.' Like any piece of art – a sculpture, painting or poem – it's the attention to detail that counts, the care that has been taken to ensure that the piece is finished off properly and evokes perfectly the vision of the creator.

This process is about being objective and honest with yourself. It's about being able to step back from your work, like an artist from his easel, and analyse exactly what's working and what's not working in the song. And it's at this stage that songwriters need to be able to disconnect themselves from their personal input into the piece and discard any element that doesn't work, however much effort it took them to create in the first place. This is a difficult but vital part of the songwriting process. And if you're not convinced by an idea, section or song, then get a second opinion.

'Be honest with yourself. Listen to your track. Listen to people's opinion of your track. Play it to your mates. Now, some people would say, "What do your mates know?", but at the beginning that's all you have. We have our parents' opinion and we have our friends' opinions, and they are the buying public, so if they have an opinion, listen to it, take it seriously and look at the song again.'

– Wayne Hector

Wise Buddah (Bill Padley and Jem Godfrey) say:
'We achieved our first hit with [Atomic Kitten's] "Whole Again". It was our first release and it was cut about a year after we started writing together as Wise Buddah. But we don't count [our songwriting careers] as a single year from the moment we decided to be professional songwriters; we count it as 20 years, because we've been learning all the time up until that point. We'd always been musicians alongside the radio work, so we'd had our grounding in playing at pubs and holiday camps with nobody watching. It may have taken a year dedicated entirely to writing, but all the experience and learning up to that point was just as vital as that one year of focusing.'

The art of rewriting is that of being able to look at the small faults as well as the large ones in a song. If the chorus is too weak or the structure is disjointed then make the necessary adjustments, but after you've done that, look closer. Is every word, every note, every chord exactly right for the song?

As an example, here's the first line of the lyric from my song 'Roses On My Table', about a lady who would rather have the simpler things in life and more time with her man than be lavished with gifts and material things and see him less:

> I'd rather have roses on my table than diamonds on my neck,
> Share whisky in the moonlight than sip red wine alone in bed.

There's nothing essentially wrong with this lyric as it stands: it's evocative, to the point and a strong opening. As Don Black observed, however, the 'share whisky in the moonlight' line is slightly at odds with the intended vision of the lady in question; it's a touch uncouth and lends a hard, almost coarse quality to her feminine character. The lyric would be improved and made more memorable perhaps by softening this image and maintaining the romanticism that's suggested by the rest of the lyric:

> I'd rather have roses on my table than diamonds on my neck,
> Walk barefoot in the moonlight than sip wine alone in bed.

It's in such details that great songs are born. Yet it's important that you don't deliberate forever on minute changes. There needs to be a balance between

Eddie Holland says:
'There were certain songs that we recognised as hits once we'd written them and we were very, very excited about them. We knew they were smash records. The reason why I felt "Baby I Need Your Loving" was nothing to write home about at the time [it has since been recognised by the BMI for having over 5 million airplays in the USA alone] was because no one urged me to finish it. It was just sitting there, lying there on this tape.'

Jem Godfrey says:
'It almost makes it quite stressful, being at Number One, because then you're thinking, "How are we going to follow this up?" The interesting thing is that you'd written that song a year ago, so you're probably another 30 songs in by this point, all of which you think are better than that one, but no one has got them yet.'

Bill Bruford says:
'The hardest thing is to get started, and the second hardest thing is to keep going. Try to complete something – anything – rather than have bits lying around. Don't pre-judge the composition; it might turn out to be good for Kylie Minogue or your first symphony, but it will be neither if you don't let it find its own way to a conclusion. Let it tell you what kind of composition it's trying to be. At all costs try to get it played by real musicians, at least in rehearsal; there's a big difference between that nifty software program you're using and five guys in a room trying to make your music live and breathe.'

constructive crafting and paralysing perfectionism. In most songwriters' experience, the best choice is always their gut reaction.

THE TOP TEN COMMON SONGWRITING FAULTS

To help you in your self-examination of your songs, below are ten of the most common faults to beware of:

1. No Structure

The song fails to progress logically or effectively. Strong sections are left too late or not prepared for. Sections are missing, such as a bridge. If there's a lack of structure, there's nothing for the listener to latch onto, in terms of recognition, and they'll lose interest or simply become frustrated with the song.

2. Song Is Overlong

This is the result of poor editing. If a song is too long, no matter how good it is, the listener will get bored. It's far better to leave the listener wanting more than have them switching off. Listen to the track yourself, up to the point when your ears begin to wander. *That's* where the song should finish, so either restructure, cut out sections or speed up the track.

3. Weak Hooks

Do you have a killer chorus? Is the melody strong enough that a

---

Ali Tennant says:

'Rod [Temperton] was emphatic in telling me, "Take time over what you believe in" and "Don't rush things out." When I'd first arrived, I was of course eager to impress him, saying, "I've just come back from Denmark and have written 14 songs in a week!" Rod's response was, "Why did you do that?"

'I immediately thought he expected me to have done more, but what he meant was, how could I possibly write 14 good songs in one week? He was adamant that it didn't work like that; he said, "What's important, Ali, is that you come home after a week and you have one good song, maybe, out of three that you've written. That's what songwriting is about. That one good song needs to be crafted. It could be your 'Thriller' or your 'Rock With You'."'

'In that moment, I understood how important it is to take time when writing. Quality is so much more important than quantity. As songwriters today, we're constantly pushed to create – publishers are rushing us to get 50 songs done by next week – but it's not about that. Rod showed me his CD of active songs that he had working for him. You'd think Rod Temperton, now in his 50s, would have thousands of songs working for him. No. He has a little over 100 songs working for him right now. That's all he needs. But every single one of those songs is a smash.

'Since that writing session, I've taken my time. I've slowed down on writing projects and given more time to each individual piece instead of banging out ten in a week, which no longer makes sense to me.'

listener will remember how it goes five minutes later? Are there enough hooks – instrumental, vocal, rhythmic, production? If not, go back to the drawing board and write a better melody or instrumental hook.

4. Bland Lyrics

Make sure that the lyrics aren't insipid, tedious or obvious. Avoid clichés and unnecessary adages. If the words aren't relevant to anyone, or don't convey an understandable message, there'll be no connection between the song and the listener. Either rewrite the lyrics or co-write the track with an experienced lyricist.

5. Wrong Tempo

Some songs simply won't work when they're played too fast or too slow. Experiment with the best tempo until the song starts to groove.

6. Overkill

Too many ideas or too much instrumentation will drown a song. Let a song breathe; include an instrument or vocal line only if it enhances the song. Remove anything that sounds excessive from the arrangement.

7. Eternal Intros

If a main hook takes too long to get going (generally speaking, longer than 30 seconds) then you'll need to consider restructuring it or the listener will have lost interest by the time the song has gained momentum. Unless it's a characteristic of the genre (eg chillout or trance), an overlong intro will destroy a song's chance in the commercial market.

Frank Musker says:
'The quality that truly sorts the men from the boys and the women from the girls is the ability and the willingness to rewrite. Even though you might have had a truly blinding flash of inspiration initially, check that you haven't just padded out the rest of the song because you were in such a hurry to finish it. This requires honesty and objectivity, and these are hard elements to come by when you're in the full flush of childbirth. Don't succumb to post-natal depression, however, if you're not getting the reaction to your song that you'd hoped for. To be a truly great song, every bit must be as good as the best bit. Don't fall into the trap of believing that, because you've written a brilliant chorus, you can get away with a dodgy verse. That's why co-writing is so useful, because it gives you an inbuilt quality control during the creative process. If your idea is a stinker, you'll soon be able to tell from the look of disgust on your partner's face.

'Also, you must develop the ruthlessness to murder your darlings. Be prepared to sacrifice the bit that only you love and everybody else hates. Even though at the time it might seem sacred to you, it might also be the thing that's stopping an otherwise great song from being a hit.

8. A Song Of Verses

The songwriting world is littered with capable verse writers, but there are very few skilled chorus writers. Does your song *really* have a chorus? If not, call up the Melody Police and write a chorus that stands out from the rest of the song.

9. Not Being True To Yourself

As Steve Harley, songwriter/artist with Cockney Rebel, advises, 'Be true to yourself. Only follow trends if you want a brief professional life.' If a song isn't written with passion or from the heart, it will sound false and unconvincing. Make sure that you write songs for yourself and that they're songs you want to hear. Honesty makes for the best songs.

10. Following All The Rules

You've followed every songwriting rule to the letter and you're wondering why your song still isn't a hit? That's because there's no formula to writing a great song. There are guidelines to creating a song, but that's all they are: guidelines. It's the imperfections and differences that make a song unique and successful. So remember: obey, ignore and contradict anything you've read in this book and see what works for you!

Jiant (Pete Kirtley and Tim Hawes) say:

'[Hear'Say's] "Pure And Simple" took two years to come out. While we hoped it was a hit song, the first time Simon Cowell listened to it, he rejected it outright. It wasn't until Pete Waterman heard it and remarked, "This is a smash record! You could play this on a biscuit tin," that people within the industry started to take notice. Simon Cowell even called us back, saying that he actually did like it and could he have it for his new project, Girl Thing?!

'So it's extremely difficult to know when you have a hit song, especially when you might have to wait several years before it sees the light of day, and you're working in an industry that's ruled by opinion, where one person saying yes may change everyone else's mind! Furthermore, you can mislead yourself as to what you think is a great song, because when you play a song 40 times in a day, you go through a whole process of "Is it good? Yes, it's good. No! It's crap. I'm useless. No, that's brilliant." You just confuse yourself and you can no longer see the wood for the trees.

'Prior to "Pure And Simple' being a hit, we had a show reel which had some of our best songs on it, and people were always positive but non-committal. As soon as "Pure And Simple" was a hit, we went around the record companies with the same show reel again, and all the songs were immediately picked off because we'd had that one single hit. The music business is a very subjective environment, and as a songwriter you live and die by someone else's opinion.'

'Good music is good music and doesn't have to fit to a formula.'

– Colin Emmanuel

THE HOLY GRAIL

'We're all in search of the Holy Grail. We always want to find the better song. If you try and do that, you always come up a loser. It's the ones where you just sit there and they come naturally [that end up being hits]. And they only come along once every three or four albums.'

– Elton John

The quest for writing the great song is a matter of dedication, drive and talent. It's also a matter of persistence and luck. It could almost be considered a numbers game. As the publisher Deke Arlon explains, 'I've met lots of songwriters over the last 30 or 40 years, and the problem is that they actually believe that everything they write is worthwhile. If you write 30 songs a year and two or three are really good, you've done well. If you have a 20-year career, then you have 60 good songs. If, out of those 60, one is a standard – one is a "Born Free" – then you've done very well indeed.'

Guidance From The Godfathers Of Motown

Brian Holland:
'Follow your dream.'

Eddie Holland:
'You first have to have a strong belief and a dedication to what you do. Try to be creative in what you do. Some people creatively believe in writing for themselves and only themselves. My philosophy is a little different: I choose to write for other people, meaning that, if I have an idea that I believe in, it's important that that idea is done in such a way that it becomes universal. To me, it's a little self-indulgent to say, "I'm doing this for me and I don't care if no one understands this but me"; many creative people take that position, and I think that can be a downfall. I believe that we must be creative and true to ourselves, but true to ourselves in an unselfish way, by giving people your creative ideas in a way that relates to them, in your own way.'

Lamont Dozier:
'Don't listen to people who tell you that you can't do it, or that you're wasting your time, or any of those things that people say to discourage you. You can't be thin-skinned in this business, because we're dealing with the business of rejection, and the first thing you have to become is hard-headed and stubborn about it. Be driven and be faithful to the music and the music will be faithful to you.'

HOW DO YOU KNOW WHEN YOU'VE WRITTEN A HIT SONG?

Justin Hawkins, vocalist and songwriter in The Darkness, believes that 'Recognising hit songs is a bit of a black art. You have to learn from experience.' For many songwriters, it's an instinctive feeling, as Pete Kirtley affirms: 'When I hear a great song, it excites me so much I get that tingle, that connection, a chemistry. It's a feeling inside.'

So, until you get that 'feeling' with a song of your own, your best policy is to keep writing songs and keep perfecting your craft. The key thing to bear in mind at all times is that songwriting is a form of expression, and that the concept of a song being a hit should always come second to this ideal. So, write with the purpose of expressing yourself and let success come to you. As Bruce Springsteen once said, 'The only trick to writing a new song is that you have to have a new idea. And to have a new idea, you have to be a bit of a new person. That's where the challenge is.'

George Michael accepting his 1996 Ivor for Songwriter of the Year from Brian May and Paul Gambaccini

Chris Difford admiring his Ivor for Best Song Commissioned for Film/Broadcast in 1998 for 'The Flame Still Burns'

Barry Mason was bestowed with The Jimmy
Kennedy Award at the 1997 Ivor Novello's

Lyricist Don Black speaking at the 1999 Ivor Novello Awards

A rare glimpse of pre-Ivors preparations in 2001

Craig David and Mark Hill celebrate their three Ivor Novello Awards for Best
Contemporary Song ('Seven Days'), the Ivor's Dance Award ('Woman Trouble')
and Songwriters of the Year 2000

Stevie Wonder (Special International Award 2000) with Dave Stewart and Annie
Lennox

Academy President Sir Tim Rice presents Benny Andersson and Bjorn Ulvaeus
with their Special International Award in 2001

2001 Songwriter of the Year, Dido, with Sting, who had been awarded an Ivor for International Achievement

Elton John with Paul McCartney at the 1999 Ivor Award Ceremony

Brian Wilson covets his Special International Award 2002

Paul McCartney rejoices
at his induction into the
Academy Fellowship,
1999

U2 entering the Grosvenor Hotel, London, prior to being bestowed an Ivor for Outstanding Song Collection 2002

Michelle Escoffery (with co-writers John Hammond Hagan and George Hammond Hagan) proudly holds her Ivor Award for PRS Most Performed Work in 2002 for Liberty X's 'Just A Little'

The Darkness, jubilant as ever, receiving their first Ivor Novello for Songwriters of the Year 2003 (L–r: Ed Graham, Justin Hawkins, Frankie Pollain, Dan Hawkins)

The author (far right) with (l–r) Brian Holland, a fan, Lamont Dozier and Eddie Holland, prior to their interview for *Heart & Soul*, London, 2004

HEART

THE BUSINESS OF SONGWRITING

HEART: THE BUSINESS OF SONGWRITING

INTRODUCTION

'The next big thing is a good song.' – Brian Epstein

The song is the heart and soul of the music business. It's the one thing that can make or break an artist's career. As songwriter Mitch Murray observes, 'Performance and sex appeal alone won't sell records worldwide for any length of time. Only good songs will.' Yet the dominant role of the song doesn't preclude it from the dictates of business and other influence.

> *'The fact is that a great song is just part – albeit a fundamental part – of a total experience that involves a record, a video, an artist and their public persona, etc. When someone says they love that song, they're really talking about the total emotional impact of all the above.'*
>
> *– Frank Musker*

The craft of songwriting doesn't function in a vacuum. It would be wonderful to write songs for their own sake, but as the songwriter Wayne Hector is well aware, 'You can't help but be shaped by the industry to a certain extent because, at the end of the day, it *is* an industry. You have to provide something that people want.' Creativity is very much a part of the real world. Your songs could generate millions of pounds per year, so as a songwriter you need to consider yourself as a business as well as a creative force. Consequently, an understanding and appreciation of the business of songwriting is as necessary as the craft of songwriting itself if you're to capitalise on any success.

> *'I wish I'd learned more about the industry, more about how politics and the industry works early on, because it shows you where to walk and where not to walk.'*
>
> *– Ali Tennant*

This section of *Heart & Soul* offers an introduction to the business side of songwriting. It by no means covers everything in this highly complex and constantly evolving industry, but it does touch upon the essentials that a songwriter needs to know in order to survive in the music business – a business that, in the late author Hunter S Thompson's view, is 'a cruel and shallow money trench, a long plastic hallway where thieves and pimps run free and good men die like dogs. There's also a negative side.'

Getting the business side of your songwriting sorted early on in your career could save you a great deal of heartache and money, so if you need further information on any particular topic, you should either contact the British Academy, speak to a dedicated music lawyer or read one of the more business-orientated music-industry guides, such as Allan Dann's accessible *How To Succeed In The Music Business* or Donald Passman's definitive *All You Need To Know About The Music Business*.

THE ATTITUDE OF THE SUCCESSFUL SONGWRITER

'Jack Tinker, a famous theatre critic, once said to me, "There's people with so much talent around but very few people with the right temperament." I think that's right, because as a songwriter you have a lot of failures in your life. You could write 100 songs and not one of them gets cut, or you get a success and then you write another 50 that don't happen. You need a certain character to keep going on with that rejection all the time.'

– Don Black

The business of songwriting is extremely competitive. Later in this book, David Stark notes in his piece 'A Rough Guide To Song Plugging' that in Nashville alone there are an estimated 50,000 songs pitched each year to fewer than 100 major-label acts. In this sort of environment, it has to be understood that rejection is almost inevitable. It is the norm. Success for even the greatest of songwriters can take years. As songwriter Pete Kirtley points out, 'There are so many other people doing it that you have to be prepared to commit totally, to the point where you're going mad.' Perseverance, therefore, is the single most important characteristic of a successful songwriter.

To able to foster such resilience, you need to be totally passionate about your craft. Don Black advises all songwriters that they must have 'fire in their belly', something with which Lamont Dozier agrees: 'Don't listen when people say you can't do this thing or you're wasting your time. You can't be thin-skinned in this business, because we deal in the business of rejection. You've got to be hard-headed, stubborn and driven. Be faithful to the music and the music will be faithful to you.'

Aside from the rejection aspect of the industry, a songwriter also needs to understand that the music business's reaction to a song might not necessarily be logical. Indeed, quite the opposite, according to Bill Padley of Wise Buddah. 'Just because you've written something that's good doesn't mean that other people will get it, and that's a hard pill to swallow. Myself and Jem [Godfrey] will write a song that's inherently good, and then we'll play it to the record company or a publisher and they won't like it. That doesn't mean that the song isn't good; it just means that that individual doesn't get it, although other people might. I wish I could have known at the start of my career how illogical the business can be, because that would have saved me a lot of heartache.'

The varied reactions of the industry can be very frustrating for any songwriter. 'There's no accounting for taste,' rues Colin Emmanuel. 'Beauty is truly in the eye of the beholder. You can write something that you feel is the best song in the world but no one gets it. A label might release it, but then no one buys it. It's down to individual taste – something you have no control over.' Consequently, a songwriter simply has to accept that they'll have no influence over a song once it's written and released.

> 'I don't like my music, but what's my opinion against that of millions of others?'
> – Frederick Loewe

THE CAREER PATHS OF A SONGWRITER

Songwriting opens up a world of career opportunities for those with the right temperament, opportunities and talent. The obvious career paths in contemporary music are either as a writer/performer or as a professional songwriter collaborating with other artists. These are perhaps the most glamorous choices, but they're also the most over-subscribed, so it's worth considering alternatives.

Consider composing for musical theatre, for example. This can be in the form of original music for plays or whole scores for musicals.

Film and television is always on the lookout for good media composers to provide theme tunes or incidental music. Hollywood is the Holy Grail for a media composer, but local TV networks and production companies provide regular work, good experience and occasionally considerable creative flexibility.

The commercial world provides writing opportunities in the form of jingles and background music for commercials. If you choose to follow this route, you should consider working for both radio and TV, but don't overlook the potential of the internet or the corporate market to provide work. Writing music for websites, company identities and promotional videos can be very beneficial in providing experience and an early income.

Finally, with the proliferation of more advanced computer games, there is a burgeoning demand for both songs and instrumental music for video games.

Yet, in spite of all these potential career paths, the reality of being a songwriter remains tough:

- Competition is fierce.

- When starting out, income is low or non-existent, as well as erratic. (For the precious few, though, the rewards can be astronomical!)

- Objective standards for evaluating artistic competence do not exist. In other words, excellence in the craft of songwriting might or might not be rewarded.

- Success, once achieved, is difficult to sustain. This is where having a strong network of contacts and good business relationships can help you significantly.

Commitment to the craft of songwriting is vital if you're to achieve any degree of success. However, to put 100 per cent of your energy and effort into a field where your excellence might not be consistently recognised is to court anxiety and insecurity, which in turn will undoubtedly have a negative impact on your creative abilities as a songwriter. A wiser attitude – for the good of your soul, if not for the size of your bank balance – is to consider having another field of expertise as a career supplement to your dream job of being a songwriter. In other words, you need to find ways to balance your creative commitment with a means of surviving – ie a lifeline career.

These two elements, creative commitment and lifeline career, will be different for everyone. One person's creative commitment might simply be to have the time to write a song for a loved one, while another's might mean having a lifestyle that's flexible enough to allow for day-long writing sessions. A lifeline career, meanwhile, could be anything from being a private music tutor or part-time secretary (ie having a job that's not hugely lucrative or ambitious but serves your basic needs by being flexible) to being in a highly demanding and well-compensated position, such as a lawyer (ie a career that's restrictive in terms of time but provides sufficient security and money for you to chase your music dreams). What matters most is not how you define these two elements but how well you learn to balance them in your life. Discovering the right lifeline career – ie one that provides both the security and flexibility you require to function – can certainly ease your progress to becoming a full-time songwriter.

There's a wonderfully informative and practical book on this subject written by Ronda Ormont and titled *Career Solutions For Creative People*. This guide assists all kinds of creative people in finding their lifeline career and is essential for anyone struggling to balance their artistic goals with career security. Through exploring key skills, values and motivations, Ronda instils in the reader a vision of a creative and financial balance as a means of thriving, not simply surviving, as a songwriter.

COPYRIGHT IN 60 SECONDS

WITH PATRICK RACKOW (STEELES LAW)

'The copyright is your most valuable asset.'
– Guy Fletcher, songwriter and former chairman of the Academy

Many people who make, or seek to make, their living out of creating music appear to have only a hazy notion of what copyright is and what it means to them. They know that, if they compose music or write songs, their work can be protected by copyright, but many seem uncertain as to how and when such protection arises. At almost every music-industry seminar or surgery at which creators are present, the question will arise, in one form or another: 'How do I copyright my work?' What follows is a very brief introduction to copyright, outlining how and when it arises.

WHAT IS COPYRIGHT?

Copyright is the right to authorise or restrict the making of copies of literary or musical works. It allows authors and composers the right to control who issues copies of their works. Copyright is a monopolistic right, allowing the creator to control the exploitation of the copyright work – which, in the case of music, means controlling who may record, broadcast, perform the work in public or issue copies to the public, whether by way of sheet music, sound carrier or electronically. These are known as the 'restricted acts'.

> **Mark Fishlock says:**
> *'I've never assigned copyright in a single one of the songs I've written for the music-production or language courses. I grant a synchronisation licence, which lists the titles and allows the songs to be used for the specific purpose for which they were commissioned. From the client's point of view, they have all the freedom they need, while the composer retains the opportunity to become involved in income from other potential uses. For example, many of these productions revolve around a character, such as Robby Rabbit, Danny the Dragon or The Little Detectives. There's always the possibility that one of these characters becomes so popular that it's made into an animation series for television, or even a Harry Potter-type global franchise. If the songs are used...ker-ching!'*

Copyright is also a property right – hence it's also known as 'intellectual-property right' – and the United Kingdom has traditionally given primary importance to the protection of copyright as an economic right.

WHAT CLASSES OF WORKS ARE PROTECTED?

The class of works protected by copyright are:

- Literary, dramatic, musical and artistic works;
- Sound recordings, films, broadcasts and cable programmes;
- Typographical arrangements of published editions.

The classes of works described above are said to be 'independent', so that, in the case of a CD recording of a newly written song, there are two separate and distinct copyrights. The first one is in the underlying composition and the second is in the particular recording of that composition. It's perfectly possible – and, in fact, is quite usual – for the two copyrights to be owned by separate individuals or companies. The copyright in the recording is that which is exploited (and usually owned) by record companies, and the copyright in the composition is owned by the composer or songwriter or his publisher. Consequently, when people talk of 'publishing' in relation to musical works, they're referring to the copyright in the composition.

WHEN DOES COPYRIGHT START?

Copyright in a musical work arises automatically once the work has been recorded either in writing or by some other physical means, including making a video, tape or CD recording of the work, as well as the more traditional notation of a music score. So, if a British citizen walks along the street, whistling or humming a new masterpiece, and someone else is listening and copies it down, the original creator will *not* be able to take action to prevent that third party from exploiting the new work under the law of copyright. Until the work is recorded in material form, no copyright protection exists.

WHO OWNS THE COPYRIGHT?

Usually the creator of a work is the first owner of any copyright in the work. The exception to this will be if the creators are employed and create the work in the course of their employment. An example of this would have been the staff writers for the old Tin Pan Alley publishers, who were paid a weekly wage to write songs whose copyright was owned by the publisher.

The copyright in and to a sound recording will be first owned by the person who made the arrangements for the recording. Thus, if you're recording some of your songs at a studio with a third-party producer, it's important to ensure that the producer acknowledges that you're the owner of the copyright in and to those recordings. It's always best to get such acknowledgement in writing in order to prevent claims of ownership emerging from the woodwork in the event that your composition is a smash hit.

Since copyright is a form of property, the author can transfer all or part of his copyright in a work to another party, such as the PRS (Performing Right Society) or a publisher. This means that the creator of the work doesn't necessarily have to be the copyright owner.

How Long Does Copyright Last?

Copyright protection for a literary, musical or dramatic work in the UK lasts for 70 years from the end of the year in which the creator dies. This means that not only will the creator benefit from the property rights given by copyright but so will his or her immediate heirs. Works that are written by more than one person retain the protection of copyright until 70 years after the death of the last surviving co-writer. Once copyright protection has expired, works are said to be in the 'public domain', which means that anyone may exercise the rights formerly held by the owner of the copyright without requiring consent or having to pay.

Copyright in sound recordings lasts for 50 years from the end of the year in which they were first released. Consequently, from 2005 many recordings by the rock 'n' roll artists of the 1950s, including Elvis Presley, will come into the public domain. However, the compositions embodied in these recordings will still attract copyright protection.

What Are Moral Rights?

These consist of three basic rights:

1. **The Right Of Paternity.** This is the right of a creator to be properly identified with his or her creation as the author/composer. It applies when a musical work has been commercially published, issued to the public as a record, included in a film that has been issued to the public or

shown in public, or where a work has been adapted and any of the above has taken place in respect of its adaptation.

2.   **The Right Of Integrity.** This is the right of creators to object to the derogatory treatment of their works. It gives them the right to object to and prevent third parties from changing their works by taking parts away or adding to them. The right of integrity does not cover issues concerned with the context in which works are presented, however – for example, as the soundtrack to a snuff movie or in a porn film – but only to presenting a work as a whole. This right is particularly important with regard to samples.

3.   **The Right To Prevent False Attribution.** In the same way that creators have a right to be identified with their works, they also have a right *not* to be identified with works that aren't theirs and that, by wrongful association, might trade upon their reputation and diminish it.

Moral rights arise with copyright, but in order to be protected by the Paternity Right, you must first assert it. These rights are not assignable to third parties and are thus, quite literally, the inalienable right of every creator entitled to copyright protection under UK law. However, instead of requiring creators to assign their moral rights to them, publishers simply insist that they're waived by the creator.

COPYRIGHT AND TITLES

It should be noted that there is no copyright in a title or an idea, although an action might be taken if a composer believes that his or her work has been 'passed off' by others as their own.

PROTECTING YOUR SONGS

WITH RICHARD TAYLOR (THE SIMKINS PARTNERSHIP)

'One of the greatest achievements of the last 500 years, and one of its greatest contributions to civilisation, was the establishment of the concept that a creative person's idea is his own property and can be protected by the law. This notion is now under serious threat. A songwriter's living is being undermined.'

– Frank Musker

Under US copyright law, musical works need to be registered at the Library of Congress in Washington, DC, in order to achieve full protection under the US Copyright Acts. In the UK, however, there is no system of registration of musical works necessary in order to give them statutory protection. Consequently, in the event of a dispute over authorship, ownership or originality, there is no standard method in the UK of proving that one work was in existence before another.

One well-known and inexpensive process of proving this is to seal a copy of the sheet music and/or lyric (manuscript or printout), or a tape or disc copy of a recording of the music concerned (a demo will do), in an envelope and post it back to yourself by recorded delivery. This provides a method of dating that's generally regarded as conclusive. It's important to remember that the sealed envelope should never be opened, except as a formal step in the course of legal proceedings. Therefore, it's necessary to keep a duplicate copy for reference so that in future you'll have an easy way of remembering exactly what the sealed envelope contains. This process should be repeated separately for each individual work. The receipt from the post office, as well as the sealed envelope, need to be kept together.

Alternative ways of providing an authoritative date include depositing a copy with a bank manager or a professional adviser, but neither of these is likely to be as cheap as the recorded-delivery or registered-post method.

In the recent case of *Miles v ITV Network*, the postal method of establishing date came under scrutiny. In this case, it was a format idea for a TV series rather than a recording of a song that was the creative work in question. There was a dispute between two parties about who had first come up with the format idea. A sealed and dated registered-post envelope containing a written description of the essential components of the format was opened before forensic experts on both sides. The claimant went so far as to challenge the authenticity of the package concerned. He claimed that it was somehow retro-dated. Mr Justice Laddie found against the claimant on this and ruled that the proof of dating was sufficient evidence to protect the party who had gone to the trouble to provide himself with this evidence in order to protect his ideas against just such a claim.

NOTE: The registering of a title with the MCPS and PRS (as is required of their members) does not create copyright in the notified work.

WEBSITES OFFERING COPYRIGHT PROTECTION

There have been in recent years a number of web initiatives inviting songwriters to register their songs for a fee with a promise of protection. However, Keith Lowde, Director of Sounds Obvious Ltd and Head of Business at the Academy of Contemporary Music, advises that 'None of them have been accredited by the Academy, the MPA or the Law Society, and there are no legal cases that I know of that have relied on any registration of this type. The law states that a musical work is "in copyright" as soon as it is available in some material form. The problem lies in proving that you own it. Registration with any organisation is only evidence of registration and has no more legal validity than sending a copy to yourself by recorded delivery. Both could be accepted as evidence of "claim" to ownership in a court and would be put alongside any other data available, such as publication, dated computer files, evidence of witnesses, etc. These websites protect nothing.'

PERMITTING THIRD PARTIES TO EXPLOIT YOUR WORK

Music publishers prefer to take their interests in songs from writers by way of assignment, meaning that there is a transfer of ownership of the copyright. In many cases where an individual project is concerned, however, the creator of the song might be able to achieve the required commercial objective by granting a licence. This method can establish who is entitled to what shares of exploitation while allowing the creator to retain their ownership of the copyright in the musical work.

Where a songwriter doesn't know about the company offering to exploit their musical works – particularly where the company is based in a foreign country – the creator should offer an exclusive licence. This is so that the contract can include a condition that, if it turns out that the offered service is either not carried out or is unsuccessful, the licence can be terminated and ownership doesn't have to be disputed or expensively recovered. If, however, the offered service is indeed successfully provided, the contract will entitle the company to retain the agreed share in the income.

WORKING WITH PRODUCERS

When working with recording producers or production teams on making recordings of a particular song or lyric, it's important to be aware that the result of such a collaboration will be the creation of recordings that are separate copyright works from the songs concerned. Accordingly, there needs to be a separate agreement setting out who will own the copyright in these recordings, and how the collaborators will share in any earnings that might flow, should the recordings turn out to have a commercial life of their own.

WHEN DOES COPYRIGHT INFRINGEMENT OCCUR?

Any person who, without the permission of the copyright owner, carries out or authorises someone else to carry out any of the restricted acts may be liable for what is known as 'primary infringement of copyright'.

In addition, a person may be liable for secondary infringement if he assists in copyright infringement by such means as handling or selling infringing copies, or by providing apparatus or premises for an infringing performance.

WHAT CAN BE DONE ABOUT INFRINGEMENT?

Copyright infringement is both a civil wrong and a criminal offence. Criminal sanctions are theoretically available but practically unlikely (as seen in the recent attempts made by record companies) and the cost of bringing a private prosecution (ie one that's funded by the creator or his publisher) is prohibitive. This leaves civil remedies.

The first step towards identifying that someone has infringed your rights is to give notice of the fact, invite them to desist and ask for their proposals to compensate you. If this is met with no response, a flat denial or a derisory offer, the next step is an application to the court for an injunction in order to prevent the infringer from continuing in their actions, together with a claim for damages and/or an account of profits. However, before such action is taken, it's important that you make sure you have a strong case, both musically (by consulting a musicologist) and legally (by consulting a lawyer experienced in dealing with copyright disputes), since any legal proceedings will be time-consuming and costly.

THE EFFECT OF PIRACY ON SONGWRITERS

'My adage is that you can't go into Tesco's or Sainsbury's, fill your shopping trolley up and walk out with it, unless you want to get arrested, and it's the same with music. Someone has worked very hard to make it. You owe it to them to buy it.'

– Steve Levine

The songwriter earns their sole income through the exploitation of the copyright of their songs. Piracy is damaging the very heart of the music business – ie you, the songwriter – so it's your responsibility as a songwriter to educate the listening public in this issue.

Producer Steve Levine explains the import of the current situation: 'There's a big education needed in saying piracy is theft. It may be fun and a laugh for some, but ultimately it destroys what you love. Most people perceive record companies and big conglomerate monsters as money-grabbing machines who don't deserve their money, but what they're forgetting is that it's the artists, producers and songwriters who suffer the most.'

THE INCOME OF A SONGWRITER

*'So few people make any money out of music that it's important to get the
publishing side of your business as good as you can get it.'*

– Don Black

Thanks to the principles of copyright, a songwriter can earn a living from the
use of their songs. There are several potential sources of income that the owner
of the copyright can exploit, either through a transfer of legal ownership (ie the
assignment of the copyright to another party in return for payment) or by the
issuing of licences (whereby permission to use the work is granted in return for
payment, with the advantage that many people can be licensed simultaneously).

The incomes that can be generated through these means are:

1. Mechanical royalties;

2. Performance income;

3. Synchronisation fees;

4. Print and sheet music;

5. Special uses and permissions.

1. MECHANICAL ROYALTIES

Income derived from mechanical royalties is generated from the licensing of the
right...

- to copy the work (ie pressing CDs, downloading);

Bill Bruford says:
*'Songwriting is a considerable second string to any musician's bow. It's very hard to earn a living on a drum
set, and the next best thing – aside from driving a cab – is writing some music.'*

Sharon Woolf says:
'In order to have longevity in the music industry, you have to be able to write songs. That is an absolute fact.'

- to issue copies of the work to the public (ie the sale of CDs, tapes or vinyl in shops);

- to rent or lend the work to the public (ie the renting of videos, tapes and CDs, and library lending).

These three criteria are known as *mechanical rights*, because originally the payments were levied on devices 'serving to mechanically reproduce sound'. In essence, this means that anyone who wishes to record and distribute product containing copyright musical works requires a licence, for which they have to pay a royalty.

In the USA, the mechanical royalty is a compulsory, statutory rate of 7.55 cents per track (or 1.45 cents per minute of playing time, whichever is the greater). However, for economic and political reasons imposed by the record companies, there are reductions in this rate of 75 per cent under a system called *controlled composition clauses* (see Allan Dann's article 'Agreements: A Simple Guide To Publishing Contracts', later in this part). The Harry Fox Agency handles the administration and licensing of mechanical royalties on behalf of publishers in the USA.

In the UK, there is a standard negotiated royalty rate currently set at 8.5 per cent of dealer price (also known as PPD). To give an idea what this might equate to, an album selling at £15 retail might have a dealer price of £8, which works out at a mechanical royalty of 70p. If there were 14 tracks on the album and you wrote one of the tracks, this would entitle you to a 5p royalty per album sale. An album has to sell 100,000 copies for it to be classed as a gold album, for which you, the writer, would then receive £3,500.

In the UK, the MCPS (Mechanical-Copyright Protection Society) licenses these rights. It also collects the mechanical royalties generated and distributes them among its writer members. Writers and publishers of music are eligible for membership of the MCPS if their music has been copied, or is due to be copied, onto CDs, records, computer games, films or DVDs, etc. Writers who have assigned their works to a music publisher don't usually need to join the MCPS, as the publisher – who will now be the copyright owner – will collect the mechanical royalties on their behalf and pay them according to the terms of their publishing agreement.

PERFORMANCE INCOME

This is income generated from the licensing of the right...

- to perform the work in public (concerts, pubs, restaurants, etc);

- to communicate the work to the public (including broadcasting, broadcasting on demand and use of music on the internet and interactive services, including satellite and cable transmissions).

These rights are collectively referred to as the *performing right* and, in the USA, are assigned by the writer either to the BMI, ASCAP or SESAC and, in the UK, to the PRS. The primary role of all these collection societies is to collect royalties from music users who regularly perform publicly, broadcast or include music in their services.

In order to make royalty payments to its members, these societies need to know what music is being played. With an estimated 8 billion public performances every year in the UK alone, it's impossible to track every one, so statistical methods are used, based on actual performance information, to distribute royalties. The performance analysis is calculated through a combination of sample listenings to radio stations, cue sheets from television stations and set lists from venues, commercial discos, clubs and pubs. The system is obviously not 100 per cent accurate (although certain sources, such as BBC1, BBC2 and ITV, log each transmission), but it's the most efficient currently available.

In terms of potential earnings for a song being performed in the UK, the PRS will collect royalties based upon its usage and context. In 2004, a three-minute song on a local radio station earned approximately £1. This increased to £40 or so on national radio, £150 on BBC TV and £200 on a commercial television station, such as ITV. For live concerts at venues over a designated size, the earnings represented a respective share of three per cent of gross box-office receipts.

SYNCHRONISATION FEES

Income generated from use of musical works in films, commercials and other forms of audio-visual media are termed as being *synchronisation fees*. These are usually licensed by the publisher, or they can be managed by the MCPS (UK) or the Harry Fox Agency (US). The actual fees are negotiable and can be anything from a few hundred pounds up to tens of thousands, depending on the song and the context of the usage. As a guideline, for a major film using a hit song or standard, the 'synch fee' could be around £10,000–£20,000, while if used on a commercial on national TV it could generate upwards of £30,000–£50,000. A truly great song can attract even greater awards – for instance, Louis Armstrong's 'What A Wonderful World' was recently licensed for advertising use to MCI in the USA for around $1 million a year.

It should be noted that these fees are in addition to any performance royalties that a song might earn through repeated broadcasts, so a popular commercial can represent an extremely lucrative income source for a songwriter.

PRINT AND SHEET MUSIC

Historically, this was the economic hub of the music-publishing business. At one time, print music was the sole source of a songwriter's income, with millions and millions of copies of sheet music being printed and sold. Today, sales printed sheet music account for a tiny fraction of a songwriter's earnings. The royalty is typically around 12.5 per cent of retail, which equates to a few hundred pounds of income, as now only a few thousand copies of sheet music are sold.

SPECIAL USES AND PERMISSIONS

These additional sources of income are usually based upon a negotiated fee and include reproduction of lyrics in literary publications, use of the song in stage shows, karaoke usage and use of the work on merchandise products, such as T-shirts, mugs and birthday cards.

THE ADVANCE

This income is as a consequence of a songwriter assigning their rights in a work or works to a publisher in return for a lump sum. However, it is in lieu of future earnings from the above income streams (ie it is 'recoupable') and so should not be treated as 'free' money but as a non-repayable loan. The advance can range from £1 to hundreds of thousands of pounds, depending on the status and success of the songwriter in question and the details of the deal (ie a larger royalty share for a smaller advance is often recommended by managers and lawyers). The function of the advance is to allow a songwriter to concentrate on their craft and to develop their careers without the everyday financial concerns or commitments.

ROYALTY TRACKING

Since there are so many different income streams, each of which can originate from a multitude of products, projects and countries, the publisher has a mammoth task in keeping track of all of its potential income. In order to monitor their catalogue effectively and ensure payment, many publishers employ dedicated royalty trackers.

Essentially, a royalty tracker's job is twofold:

1. To ensure that publishing income is collected and paid out correctly (and on time) to the projects on which and clients for whom they're working.

2. To act as a contact point for clients who believe that they haven't been paid correctly and consequently to retrieve the missing income.

Some would say that it's the tracker's job to generate a profit by finding 'missing money' that would otherwise never make it to the writer or publisher. To a certain extent, this is true, but only in the sense that it's a highly beneficial by-product of the role. The definition of 'tracking' should be that of checking or monitoring and, eventually, correcting and collecting. More often than not, the tracker's haul will either help to reduce an advance or, if the client is recouped, generate more income for the writer. Royalty trackers are a cross between a private investigator and an auditor; they are the police of the music-publishing industry, righting wrongs and making sure that you, as a songwriter, get your dues.

For further details on the collection societies and the requirements for membership, refer to 'Songwriter Organisations And Societies' in 'Body: Essential Information For Songwriters'.

Jiant (Pete Kirtley and Tim Hawes) say:

'As a songwriter, you'll have to be prepared to take knocks on your songs. Rejection happens all the time. It's part and parcel of the music business. So it's crucial that you understand exactly what your aims are as a songwriter; whether it's money or success or recognition, this business comes with a price. If it's money that you're striving for, then you have only to work out the maths to realise that songwriting is generally not the most lucrative job in the world. The myth of the millions of pounds that you could earn from this business is a fantasy. It is a reality only for the elite few.

'Due to piracy, market division and the high-speed turnover of music, it's no longer enough to have a Top Ten single in the charts. As we write this, the current UK Number One single had to sell only 26,000 copies to reach the top slot! If you were the co-writer of that song, your earnings would be only a couple of thousand pounds, from a song that you might have put months, or even years, of hard work into.

'Consequently, it's not enough just to write a song and feel great about that. If the song is a hit and the act interested in it doesn't have international priority, it's not worth giving that track to that act. International potential is crucial if you're going to earn a good living as a songwriter. We've taken this philosophy to the extent of developing our own artists so that Jiant can obtain a bigger commitment on any album released.'

THE BUSINESS TEAM

'No man is an island, and no songwriter these days can function successfully without teamwork and input from others.'

– Frank Musker

The choice of the business team surrounding a songwriter is central to the successful exploitation of their work. Understanding what each member does and why it's necessary to have them on your side allows for the most effective and efficient handling of the business elements of songwriting. More importantly, the right choice of team will free you, the songwriter, to concentrate on the creative aspects of songwriting.

The three key members of this team are:

1. The publisher;
2. The lawyer;
3. The manager.

1. THE PUBLISHER

'My attitude as a publisher in this business is to always encourage talent, and it's my job as a publisher to discover songs that will appeal to a broad range of people.'
– Deke Arlon, CEO of Sanctuary Music Publishing

The publisher is just as significant to the songwriter as the record company is to the artist. The publishing business is founded on the copyright of the song, whereas the record industry is based on the copyright in the recording. Thus the primary responsibility of a publisher is the development, protection of and remuneration for the use of songs in recordings and live performances.

The publisher offers a number of services within this remit, and while self-publishing is certainly an option, there are several benefits to having a publisher if you're serious about being a songwriter.

The first role that a publisher performs is *administration*. The company will work with the collection societies and ensure that its catalogue of songs are registered in all territories, that their use is monitored and protected and that the monies from their use is collected and appropriately distributed.

The second role of the publisher is *exploitation*. This is to do with the active promotion of individual songs to generate income from use in performing artists' recordings, live performances, sheet music and any other appropriate audio products, such as musical cards, ringtones, etc. Furthermore, a publisher looks to place songs in an audio-visual context, such as films, TV programmes, adverts, games and multimedia, and to create additional income from synchronisation licences.

The third service of a publisher is *creative*. This refers to the development of a songwriter's, composer's or lyricist's talent through collaborations; introducing them to new songwriters; providing encouragement and support as they develop their skills; offering advice and guidance in any aspect of their career; developing and raising their profile as a creator and facilitating their relationship with record companies and artists.

The fourth function of the publisher is *investment*. This covers the financing of a songwriter via advances (which can be recouped from future earnings) as well as the development funding in terms of providing either the resources or the money to record demos or set up a home studio. This can also include help with financing live work, legal fees, music equipment, general overheads and any promotional costs, such as travelling to music conventions or songwriting sessions. All of this will be recoupable from future income streams but not repayable by the songwriter.

The final key function of the publisher is *protection*. The publisher will monitor the use of a song and ensure that its copyright is not breached, taking action against any infringement that does occur.

There are several categories of publisher. Some specialise in a particular genre or style of music, such as classic or contemporary. The three main types of publisher are major, independent and self-published, and they can be loosely defined as follows:

- A major publisher (such as BMG Music Publishing) does everything 'in-house' and will usually be integrated within a multinational entertainment corporation, like Sony. The benefit of signing with such a publisher is that they tend to have a great deal of clout within the business and have solid publishing connections, globally. However, the downside is that they own hundreds of thousands of copyrights, and unless you're phenomenally successful, your work might be neglected.

- An independent publisher (such as Hit & Run Music Publishing) will be smaller, based in one country and likely to outsource certain services. They can still maintain international reach through sub-publishing deals with wholly owned subsidiaries, majors or other foreign independents. The principal advantage signing to an independent publisher is that more attention will be given to your work and career development. However, the independent publisher's influence in the industry to obtain cuts and synch fees may be less due to its lower profile, weaker connections and restricted opportunities. Furthermore, the potential funding might not be as generous as that derived from a major publisher.

- Self-publishing (also known as self-administration) has the benefit that you maintain ownership of copyright and therefore garner all the rewards for the use of your songs. However, this has to be weighed against the greater workload in terms of administration, the lack of funding and the onus on you alone to promote your catalogue and create opportunities for exploitation and collaborations. This approach is more suited to writers with a track record but who would benefit from personally handling their copyrights, or writers who don't need money up front and can afford to hire an administrator.

Each of these types of publisher is as valid as the others, and a songwriter's choice will be determined both by personal preference and what offers are actually on the table. The key point to remember is that, like signing a record deal as an artist, having a publisher isn't a songwriter's ultimate goal; it's only the beginning. A publisher can provide much-needed kudos and financial backing, but as songwriter Wayne Hector acknowledges, 'With a publishing deal, you're through the door, but that's just the first hurdle. Don't expect them to do it all for you. You still have to be prepared to put in the legwork yourself.'

2. THE LAWYER

Lawyers who specialise in the music business perform a greater function than simply looking through contracts and advising their clients about their rights and the law. A good music lawyer is often very involved in the structuring of deals and helping to shape the writer or artists' career. A good lawyer who is respected and has strong connections within the industry can use these affiliations to introduce a writer to the right people, help get them deals and even promote their songs to publishing companies, artists and record companies.

There are as many styles of lawyers as there are people. Aside from ensuring that a lawyer is competent and has the necessary expertise and experience, choosing one is mostly a matter of personal taste. Ideally, their personal clout should also be such that they can help you to develop your career as a songwriter. A lawyer with good relationships within the industry will get deals done quicker, with the minimum of fuss and hopefully at the maximum possible benefit to you.

A key consideration will be the fees each lawyer charges. In the UK, these are typically worked on an hourly basis, ranging from £80 to £500 per hour, the norm being between £100 and £300. (It's worth noting here that some lawyers may withhold billing until after a deal has been signed.) In the US, some lawyers tend to charge a percentage rate (around five per cent) against a deal, whilst others work on the basis of 'value billing', with a retainer or hourly rate attached, depending on the size of the deal and the amount of work involved.

Another factor to take into account when selecting a lawyer is any potential conflicts of interest. For example, your chosen lawyer might also represent the publisher to which you're signing. In this case, it might be best to obtain an independent representative instead.

Finally, when appointing a lawyer for a particular project, make sure you discuss their fee, the estimated commitment in terms of time and a ballpark figure for the final cost. Then obtain a written fee agreement. This will hopefully forestall any nasty shocks at the end of a contract negotiation.

Whatever your decision, don't underestimate the influence and benefits that hiring a good lawyer can impart alongside the basic contractual dealings.

3. THE MANAGER

Performing artists and bands certainly need managers to handle and guide their careers. The adage that a great band with a bad manager will get nowhere, whereas a bad band with a great manager can become Number One around the world, is very true. In the career of a songwriter, however, the role of a manager hasn't always been so crucial. The songwriter is a more independent creature and not so reliant upon the services that a manager provides. In today's climate, though, songwriter managers are becoming more common, and the arrangement between the two is proving to be very beneficial.

The role of the manager with respect to a songwriter is very similar to that of a band or artist manager, but the emphasis is generally different. A good manager can expand a songwriter's career to its maximum potential: they can help in advising on major career decisions, such as which publishing company to sign to and which artist to approach; they can offer objective opinions on your creative work; they can network for you and promote your services to the industry; and they can handle all the administrative work and generally organise your business diary.

Songwriter Rob Davis explains why he values having a manager: 'A manager is essential for me because I'm very lazy in the area of hustling other writers and record companies. Some writers are very good at that aspect of the business. Diane Warren is; she'll drive record companies bonkers just by ringing them up and insisting that they use her song. I could never do that. That's why I work with Brian, my manager. He's excellent at pitching songs, dealing with labels, working with lawyers and sending out invoices – all the essential pieces I don't have time for. Also, Brian tends to hold onto songs of mine that I wrote five years ago, because he still thinks they're hits and will keep slogging them to record companies, whereas I'm sick of them. As a songwriter, you need people like that to grip onto your songs and believe in them.'

The MMF (Music Managers Forum) is an organisation that exists to assist and support the role of music managers within the industry. Below is a list of guidelines supplied by the MMF for songwriters deciding upon a suitable manager:

FINDING A MANAGER

WHEN SHOULD YOU APPOINT A MANAGER?

1. Generally, the sooner the better. A manager has a role to play right from the beginning of your career. On the business side, he can liaise with professional advisers (such as lawyers and accountants), organise promotion and talk to potential record and publishing companies, and on the creative side he can assist you in deciding what songs to record and the selection of producers and artists.

2. Many songwriters can manage themselves, but even if they have the capability to do so, they would benefit from having somebody else representing their interests, somebody to be (at different times) a spokesperson, a diplomat, an authoritarian, a headmaster, an organiser, a mediator, tough, charming and compromising.

3. Having said that, if you don't find that right person, don't despair and don't feel you must take second best. You'll be able to survive for a while without a manager, and the management functions and responsibilities can be

undertaken by a mixture of yourself, your solicitor, your accountant and your publisher. Don't get impatient; at some point, you'll find the right person. It's better to wait than to make a wrong choice that will cost you later on.

APPROACHING POTENTIAL MANAGERS

1. Do some research. Talk to your musician friends; read any relevant publications; speak to your solicitor, accountant, agent and any people you might know who work in record or publishing companies; ask for recommendations. After you've done all this research, draw up a list of names. It doesn't matter at this stage whether it's a long or short list.

2. Don't send out circular letters. Just like you do, managers trash most (if not all) circulars. And don't make any cold approaches; you'll have a much greater chance of success if either you or somebody on your behalf makes a personal approach.

3. A prospective manager should be sent the following:

    •   Most importantly, a tape of your BEST songs – even if they're just demos. Initially, you should include on the tape only between two and five songs, NO MORE. It's important to make an impact. The manager will have neither the time nor the inclination to listen to any more at this stage;

    •   A short biography – nothing too long or pretentious – complete with song reviews, if you have any.

4. You don't have to make up a package that would impress a Saatchi & Saatchi executive, but it must be presentable to catch the eye.

5. The package should be sent to the prospective manager either by you or by the person making the introduction, such as your solicitor, accountant or agent. Don't be too pushy.

6. Wait to hear back from them. Don't phone them just a few

days after you've sent them the package; wait at least a week. They're busy people – or, at least, they should be if they're successful managers. Again, any decent manager should have the courtesy to respond to your letter anyway in due course. Just give them time. At some point, however, it might be an idea either for you or a representative to put in a phone call to prompt a response.

7.   Hopefully you'll get their response, and hopefully it will be a positive one. If this is the case, now is the time to meet the prospective candidates. Before making a decision one way or the other, you should meet them at least once, and hopefully more often. The first meeting should ideally be at their office, so that you can see them at work. After that, you should go out for a drink or a meal and then, perhaps, invite them to a gig or a rehearsal. You might introduce them to your solicitor and/or accountant and/or any record-company friends so that you can get an opinion from these people.

8.   If you're lucky, you'll have several managers showing interest in you. If this is the case, you should then draw up a list of each candidate's weaknesses and strengths and compare the candidates by reference to the various questions listed below.

FACTORS TO TAKE INTO ACCOUNT

When assessing a particular manager, ask yourself the following questions:

- How experienced a manager is he/she?

- Has he/she successfully managed other songwriters?

- What is his/her background? Has he/she worked for a long time in the music industry? If so, for whom? How helpful will that experience be?

- Does he/she generally have a good reputation?

- Is he/she primarily a 'business manager' or a 'creative manager'?

- If he/she currently manages other artists or songwriters, how long have those other artists been represented by him/her? Do those relationships appear to be successful and happy ones?

- How affable is he/she? Will he/she be able to get on with – for example – the publishing-/record-company staff?

- Where is he/she based? If this is outside your town, will it become a problem to you?

- What other commitments and distractions does he/she have (both business and personal)?

- Is he/she ambitious and keen to succeed by seeing you enjoy commercial success?

- Does he/she use competent and well-respected solicitors and accountants?

- Does he/she have good contacts with promoters, agents, merchandisers, journalists, publicists, etc?

- Does he/she have working relationships with other managers in other countries, particularly America?

- Do you like him/her as a person? Can you easily contemplate working closely with him/her for many months?

- Do you respect his/her musical tastes and opinions?

- Is he/she capable of taking on responsibilities? Making tough decisions? Being a good negotiator?

- How organised does he/she appear? Does he/she have a proper office? Secretarial and administrative assistance? Does he/she appear to return phone calls? Deal with correspondence? Maintain proper financial records?

- Has he/she previously worked with your record company or music publisher (if you have one, or, if not, the companies you'd like to sign to)?

- How old is he/she?

- How committed to the music industry is he/she? Is he/she just dabbling for the fun of it or does he/she approach his/her job with real conviction?

- Does he/she actually like your music? Does he/she have his/her finger on the pulse of current musical tastes and developments? Does he/she know of the 'in' producers, for example?

- What are his/her resources? If you go through lean times or have debts to pay off, will he/she help you out by lending you money?

- What sort of management agreement does he/she contemplate? For how long? At what rate of commission?

You shouldn't expect any manager to fulfil all these criteria. You'll be doing well if you feel positive about just half of them. And even after going through this exhaustive process, there's no guarantee that you'll have chosen the right manager. The artist–manager relationship is just like any other personal relationship: some last forever, some for just a short while.

When obtaining a publisher, a lawyer or a manager, the when, where and how is a matter of timing, networking and gut reaction. There's no point in considering any of these until you have a product to promote, so your first move is to write some songs and record a strong demo.

The next step is to network within the industry and discover who would be interested in or suitable for your work. Recommendations are the best method for finding likely candidates, and you'll discover that certain names will regularly pop up in conversation.

Your task is then to meet and promote yourself to these people, attract their attention and decide who is best for you. The final choice for your business team will be a combination of references from other people and gut instinct.

Then, once your business team is in place, you'll be free to concentrate on being a solely creative songwriter, safe in the knowledge that the business side is being professionally and competently handled.

AGREEMENTS: A SIMPLE GUIDE TO PUBLISHING CONTRACTS (AKA EXCLUSIVE SONGWRITER AGREEMENTS)

BY ALLAN DANN

I'm a songwriter. But, in stark contrast to some other contributors to this book, I'm a very unsuccessful songwriter. To be fair, I mostly write musicals, comedy shows, etc, and I've been a PRS writer member since the early 1970s. I've also tried to write commercial songs from time to time, however, and I should come clean straight away and say that my sole contribution to the first 50 years of the UK singles chart (celebrated in 2002) was one (yes, one!) word of one (yes, one!) hit song. So, if you're an aspiring writer, do as I say, not as I do!

Luckily, I do have a day job, as the Business Affairs Manager of a leading international publishing company (which means that I draft the agreements). When I first tried to get a job in the music business, back in the 1960s, I wrote around to lots of publishers and record companies, telling them I was looking for a worthwhile career in the music business. After a very short while, the truth dawned on me and I started telling other hopefuls, 'Make up your mind. You can either have a worthwhile career or you can be in the music business.'

A lot has changed since then, however. I'm pleased to say that the music business is now more of a...well...business. That's good and bad news for songwriters. What you need to know is that the deals offered to writers now are much better than they were in the 'old days'. In general, though, today's companies have less money and fewer staff, which simply means that fewer writers are being signed. If you want to get signed, you really have to be a producer or a working singer/musician, or both, even if writing is what you're best at.

This article is about what you might be offered in an exclusive (ie 'blanket') songwriting deal. If you already know some of what's below, I apologise, but there will be someone else reading this who might not, so please bear with me. The first question you might ask is, 'Why sign a blanket songwriting agreement at all? Why shouldn't I keep my options open?' I can't argue with the logic, and yet virtually all currently active and successful songwriters have exclusive publishing deals. As a writer, you want to be able to get on and do what you do, having someone you trust handling the business side.

Even writers who had success years ago tend to put all their songs through one particular publisher. That's always assuming that their hits didn't come so long ago that they had to assign them to the first publisher for life of copyright. As explained earlier in this book, copyright in the UK now lasts for 70 years from the end of the year in which the writer dies (or, if you wrote the words and music with someone else, the year in which your co-writer dies, if he lives longer). So do your heirs a favour and try to co-write only with people who are younger or healthier than you!

Back to the subject: why sign an exclusive agreement with a publisher? OK, it's mostly about money, but surprisingly it's not *only* about money. If you're just starting out as an artist/songwriter, you have to ask yourself – as well as your lawyer and your manager, if you have them – 'What do I want out of a publishing deal?' Do you just want to impress your friends by saying, 'Hey, I've been signed up by Megahit Music Ltd'? Fine, but that's not a lot of good unless someone else inside the business is so impressed that on the strength of it they give you a record deal or production/remix work, or whatever it is you want.

If you're an artist and you haven't already got yourself a record deal, a publisher might very well be able to help you get one. Even so, no matter how good he might be, he might spend a lot of time (ie money) trying and still not succeed. So, in this scenario, he won't be able to risk giving you much money, and he'll expect better terms. If you do end up having a hit song or signing a record deal, the publisher licks *your* boots, not the other way around. (Actually, no bootlicking should be required on either side, but at least you'd be in an equal, or superior, bargaining position.) In either of the above cases, it's usually money versus the other commercial terms.

So what's on offer? There now follows a run-down of what actual money and terms you might get these days. If you're not a writer looking for a publishing deal (or a better one than you have now), fast-forward to the penultimate section of this piece.

1. Money (Advance Payments Against Royalties)

Suppose you haven't yet written the hit or signed the deal but the publisher thinks he can get you a record deal, or a cut with a major artist on one of your songs, or a gig producing and co-writing with someone big. Even in this case, he (or she) won't expect to pay you no advance at all, and you certainly should never have to pay the publisher anything – not a penny. Instead, the deal will be what's generally known as a *development deal*. He might pay, say, £10,000–£20,000 advance royalties on signature of the agreement, or in two chunks, or maybe a certain amount a month for, say, six months. However, you should be able to get him to commit to paying you a further advance once you've signed to a label, then perhaps a bit more when the first album comes out, and then more again as 'chart bonuses' if your singles or albums make the Top 40 or better in the UK and USA, and maybe some other countries. This can add up to quite a lot of money in total, if you become reasonably successful.

If you've already written a hit song or signed a record deal for at least one album, guaranteed (I mean you've definitely got it, signed it, started recording the tracks, etc), you could possibly put a nought on the end of the figures in the penultimate section. For a dance act with a deal but no release yet, the advance will depend a lot more on the industry buzz as to whether a track that's done well on white label or has made the club charts is likely to sell to enough of the general record-buying public to make it a top seller.

The important thing about advances is that they are non-returnable. You'll never be expected to pay them back – unless, perhaps, to buy yourself out of the deal if it all goes wrong, but this should be entirely at your own discretion. (Incidentally, there's a school of thought that says that the more a publisher has paid you, the harder he'll work on your songs or your career. For the most part, this really isn't true. If at any given time he thinks he can promote you or your songs, he will. If he doesn't, he won't.)

Two types of advance you might be offered are *rolling* and *min-max*. With a rolling advance, whenever the publisher finds he's recouped all the advances up to that point, he pays another one, usually the same amount again. This might last for the first two years of a three-year deal, or even all three years of the term, provided that the publisher then has a good long retention period (see below) in which to get back any advance he might have had to pay towards the end of the term.

With a min-max deal, the advance for the second and third years will be a multiple of what you earned during the first year but subject to a minimum and – surprise, surprise – maximum limit. The minimum is usually about half to three-quarters of the advance for the first year, while the maximum is usually about one and a half times to twice the advance for the first year. The publisher should take account of the money he or his sub-publishers have received in the previous year but not yet paid you (ie 'pipeline income'), since it can take over a year, and sometimes a lot longer, for money to reach you from the time of a performance or the sale of a record.

2. Royalties (Your Share Of The Spoils)

These days, if you get a record deal or the hit first, you should look for about 75 per cent of mechanical royalties (on sales/pressings of records or on distributions/downloads from the internet) and the same from synchronisation licences (derived when your songs are used in films or commercials) and in ringtones, computer games and compilation shows, such as *Mamma Mia* and *We*

Will Rock You, etc, which are sometimes licensed by the PRS. Your share will again be roughly 75 per cent overall for these and other performances and broadcasts of your songs, but if you're a PRS member you'll get half the royalties directly and the publisher will then (once he's recovered the advances) pay you half of his half – ie you get 75 per cent altogether. The publisher might want to recover the advance from your half, too. This should be determined at the negotiation stage.

In any event, if you qualify for membership of the PRS, you should join as soon as possible. Ask them about the matter; they're very helpful. Otherwise, your publisher can collect your share for you (and usually pay it to you, even before he's recovered the advances), but there are places in the world where your publisher's sub-publishers or the PRS themselves simply cannot collect if you're a non-member, so don't miss out!

If you don't want an advance, or only very little, and you've already got the hit or the record deal, you could get as much as 85–90 per cent from a publisher on all income. If you *didn't* get the hit or record deal first, though, you're more likely to get about 60–70 per cent. However, there's one vital thing you need to know about your royalty: is it derived 'at source' or on 'receipts'?

The figures I've quoted here should be derived at source worldwide, which means pretty much what it says. So, on a 75/25 deal, if $100 are earned in the USA (after the usual collecting-society commission has been deducted), you get $75.

The alternative is a receipts deal. Here, if your publisher gets only, say, 75% from his USA sub-publisher, he has to pay you only 75% of that, which works out at about $56. This isn't crooked or unusual, but it's a lot less than the at-source figure – whereby your publisher and his USA sub-publisher have to divide up between them the 25% that's left – so it really is crucial that you know what you'll be getting.

Incidentally, if you want the publisher to work on your songs – try to get them onto new recordings and into commercials, films, etc, and not just nationally but around the world – then he'll want a better cut on the resulting royalties and fees from those uses. This is because a lot of his efforts will come to nothing, even if he has the best contacts in the world. That's just the nature of the business. Try to ensure that he gets the better percentage only when he or his sub-publishers have actually gone out and secured the use themselves, not when he picks up what are termed 'windfall' uses, which just happen anyway to hit songs from time to time.

I just mentioned sub-publishers. Virtually all UK publishers have sub-publishers, although it's possible for a UK publisher to collect via the PRS and MCPS, who do collect from other collecting societies abroad but (reasonably enough) take a percentage for their trouble. Alternatively, a publisher can join most of the foreign collecting societies directly, which cuts out sub-publishers but means he has no one 'on the ground' outside the UK who can promote the songs, chase up non-payment, handle problems with registrations, etc, in the language of the country concerned (unless he pays someone to do this in each country).

Only the international publishers with their own people in most of the significant countries of the world can offer really competitive at-source deals (ie if pushed, they could pay you, say, £80 or more out of every £100 in sales from a country like Chile or Hungary). Of course, if a smaller UK publisher is successful enough, he or she might sign a deal with one of these companies, keeping maybe five or ten per cent himself and paying you the rest, after he's recouped the advance he paid you.

3. Term (How Long Are You Signed For Exclusively?)

For a songwriter or a writer/producer who isn't also an artist, this could be a straight three-year period, with advances guaranteed on signing and at the start of the second and third years, or a rolling advance. If you're a recording artist, or you hope to be, it will usually be one year, plus your publisher would like two options of a further year each. For each option he'll expect to pay another royalty advance (generally the overall amount he undertakes to pay in each year gets maybe around 25%–50% higher each year). This goes hand in hand with...

4. Product Commitment (Your Side Of The Bargain)

If you're a recording artist, or you're hoping to be, then this is usually one album per 'year'. If you're thinking, "I don't like the way he's put "year" in inverted commas,' then you're right to. If the album doesn't get released within the expected year, which is especially likely with the first one if you haven't even got a record deal yet, then the 'year' usually runs for up to three years, or until the album is released. So, a three-year deal could run for nine years, although this would be very unlikely.

If you're not signed as an artist or hoping to be, then the product commitment is likely to be the rough equivalent – say, ten songs (maybe fewer) per year released on singles or albums on a 'major' or 'significant' label in the UK of which you should have written a minimum of, say, 80 per cent (so eight songs wholly written by you would do). This 'target' applies to artist albums in the previous paragraph, too.

If you're not an artist but you're already getting cuts on your songs and you're happy to be paid one advance on signature for a three-year exclusive deal, it's possible that the publisher won't insist on a product commitment at all.

Still awake? Good. Time for the retention period...

5. Retention Period (How Long The Publisher Keeps Your Songs)

The first thing to note here is that this isn't the same as the term (ie the period during which you're signed exclusively); it's usually a lot longer. It could be a set period of years starting when you sign to the publisher, or it could be a set period of years from the end of the term. If the term runs on a bit, then the additional retention period might not start for, say, five or six years. If you're in the driving seat, look for roughly ten years' retention in total (agree to make it longer only as a trade-off for a better royalty or bigger advance). If you're in the passenger seat, expect 15–20 years and maybe even 25, but try to avoid it being for 'life of copyright'.

It's fair to assume that you and your music will enjoy a second burst in popularity in about 12 years' time, so if you can get the rights back by that time, you'll be in a position to sign a better deal on them – either with someone else or, equally possibly, with your own publisher – when the songs start to earn real money again.

'What about the songs that never see the light of day?' you ask. 'Does the publisher keep them on the shelf for 20 years?' Don't panic. There will always be songs that don't get used by you or anyone else. Generally, a year or two after the term you'll have the right to claim these songs back and give them to someone else or rewrite them or whatever. If you didn't have this right, the agreement could be considered to be a 'restraint of trade' – ie it would prevent you from making the most of your assets. The case of *Schroeder v Macauley* back in 1974 established this.

Finally, note that it's possible, if you're in a strong position but you don't need the advance or any promotion, to enter into a short-term 'administration' agreement with a publisher. Here he just looks after your songs for, say, three to five years on a very high (for you) royalty rate and with no extra retention period (although he will want the right to collect anything earned during the term but paid during the year following the term).

And that's all there is to it...almost. So, what else might there be?

Making Demos

If the publisher has an in-house studio, you might be able to persuade him to make your demos there, or else let you make them there. He'll probably pay for studio time and an engineer, while the cost of hiring singers, musicians and equipment will be open to negotiation. It's quite possible that someone might want to release one of the demos commercially or use it in a film, game, etc. If so, who owns it? Fifty-fifty between you and the publisher might well be fair, but it's something to consider.

Moral Rights

You'll be pleased to know that you have the rights of paternity and integrity in your songs. As explained earlier, in 'Copyright In 60 Seconds', this basically means that you have the right to be identified as the writer and not to have your song messed about with. The publisher's agreement might ask you to waive these rights, or else to exercise them if he asks you to, but not against him.

(Incidentally, it's not clear exactly where a cover version of your song that you don't particularly like becomes a 'derogatory treatment' that can be stopped by you or your publisher.)

Consents

Your publisher won't want to pay you a lot of money only to find that you're so picky about uses of your songs – cover versions, uses in commercials, ringtones, games, etc – that he can't make anything out of them. You should have the right to veto anything to do with sex and drugs (but not rock 'n' roll) or violence, while you might also be able to insist on your consent for other, less contentious uses, 'such consent not to be unreasonably withheld or delayed'. Otherwise, in general, the stronger your bargaining position, the more you can uses you can reject.

Your consent should also be required for new versions of your song, sometimes including versions recorded with foreign lyrics. Foreign-lyric writers in each major country frequently used to get a share of royalties on the original UK hit version, even if their version was never released, in which case the local income had to be from sales of the original. These days, however, this isn't the problem it used to be.

Key Man Clause

If the publisher runs quite a small operation, you might be able to insist that, if the person who liked you and signed you leaves the company, you have the right (subject to repaying any advances that are unrecouped) to terminate both the term and the retention period.

Termination

You should also be able to terminate if the publisher goes bankrupt or fails to account to you on time and after a 30–60-day 'cure period', following written notice from you.

There are two important points to remember about termination, however. Firstly, when your publisher's rights end, all his sub-publishers' rights should expire, too (although ideally he shouldn't be able to sub-publish your songs anyway, except as part of his general catalogue). Secondly, the agreement should contain a re-assignment to you of your songs if the publisher goes broke. You don't want to find that the company's been sold and the new owner doesn't think he has to pay royalties to you.

Assignment Or Licence:

As soon as one of your songs exists in tangible form (eg on a manuscript or recording), you own the copyright in the song. Most publishers take an 'assignment' of your songs, which means that they technically become the actual owner of anything you write during the term. You might be able to insist on a licence instead, whereby you give the publisher the right solely to exploit and collect on the songs while you remain the owner, which will put you in a stronger position if there are any problems. In any event, if you're a member, the PRS becomes technically the owner of the performing and related rights to your songs.

Controlled Composition Clauses

I have left this almost until the end because it's more of a fact of life these days than a bargaining point. Briefly, if you sign as an artist to a record label, they'll expect to have to pay your publisher only 75 per cent of the statutory royalty rate in the USA and Canada to use your songs on your records. What's more, this will be 75 per cent of the rate (a set amount in cents per track) that was in effect when you delivered the record or when it was first released. The rate has been going up every year or two, so a song on a record released several years ago might be earning at only half the current rate now, even though it's still selling well. Not impressed? There's worse…

- The record company will pay that rate only on albums with a maximum of around 11 tracks, so if yours has 13, each of the two extra tracks will earn less money again;

- If you've recorded a couple of cover versions of old songs and the writers of those want the full 100 per cent rate, the extra comes out of the total payable to your songs, so less again per track;

- The record company will want to pay publishing royalties only on the number of records for which you get paid your artist royalty. This might be a lot fewer than normal, thanks to the small print in your recording agreement.

At this point, I should say that, if you get the publishing deal first, you could ask your publisher to say no to these terms, and he could; the extra would come out of your artist royalties. As you'd normally recoup the advances and get paid much sooner under a publishing contract than a recording contract, this would make sense. However, many writer/artists don't like to rock the boat in case it blows the record deal. If your publisher is prepared to accept these terms, he might offer a bit less in advances, especially when they're related to US income, as there will be significantly less.

All Your Eggs In One Basket?

In general, it's regarded as preferable not to sign your songs to the music-publishing arm of the record label to which you're signed – not always easy, but not always a bad move, either, as the major labels and their publishers work quite separately (sometimes remarkably so). However, try to steer clear of signing songs to your record company if it's a smaller organisation. If the record company doesn't bother to account properly to their sister publishing company, you don't get paid. What's more likely is that they will 'cross-collateralise' your publishing royalties against your record deal, which means that you might not see any publishing money until you've recouped all your record advances, recording costs, tour-support expenses, etc.

Renegotiation

After your first big hit, you'll almost certainly be able to negotiate better terms for the future by offering an extra album or an extra year of exclusivity. Don't forget that, if the first album does OK but the publisher can't really risk paying the advances for the next album, you can always renegotiate downwards for a year if the alternative is you being dropped and possibly not finding another deal. This, of course, applies to record deals, too.

SO, IN A NUTSHELL, WHAT'S A GOOD DEAL?

'Unsigned' Artist/Writer

Advance: £10,000–£20,000 for first year plus other advances on releases, etc, and slightly more if publisher takes up option for second and third years.

Term: one year plus two one-year option periods.

Product commitment: one album per year, 80 per cent of which must be written by you.

Retention: 15 years in total.

'Signed' Artist/Writer

Advance: five to ten times the above.

Term: the same.

Product commitment: the same.

Retention: ten years in total.

A Final Note

Only the biggest publishers can generally afford the second sort of deal listed above, but this means that, even if you're successful, you'll still be a medium fish in a big pond. Some writers are more than happy with their 'major' publisher, especially if they have a long-standing relationship with one person in the organisation.

However, many writers would rather sign to a small or medium-sized publisher where, even if their act has gone a bit 'cold', they'll be pretty well guaranteed the publisher's attention. As I said at the start of this piece, it depends on what you want and what you need.

It also depends on whether you get on well with the people at the company. From your side, a balance of confidence and deference will go down well. It's no good being too self-effacing, but if you've just written your first song and you're already practising your Ivors acceptance speech for next year, you might be seen as being a trifle forward.

To finish roughly where I started, I've been signed to a more or less exclusive songwriting deal with the company I now work for that has now been running for 36 years! It started out as a 50/50 receipts deal with life-of-copyright retention. I think it's time I renegotiated! Then again, with only one hit in 36 years, perhaps my bargaining position isn't as strong as it could be. If you're an aspiring writer, I hope you make it a great deal more quickly than I have.

Good luck!

SONGWRITING AGREEMENTS: A PIECE OF THE PUBLISHING?

BY GUY FLETCHER, FORMER BACS CHAIRMAN

For as long as I can remember, I've heard certain producers and artists ask for a 'piece of the publishing'. Famously, when a well-known singer was in his first flush of success, his manager would always ask for a piece of the publishing if he was to record a new song. More recently, a female singer has been known to ask for a share in a new song before taking it into the studio. In common with many businesses, it has always been necessary to sweeten some individuals who have the clout to demand it. Legitimate businessmen call it 'leverage'. However, it can be considered a form of blackmail.

The practice of giving away bits of your songs to artists, producers, programmers and managers is now so widespread that it's becoming an essential part of being a songwriter. The truth is that it's practically impossible to get many current artists to record a cover without sharing the writing and/or publishing income with them. Sadly, however, many new writers are going into these deals without really knowing enough about copyright and are suffering needless long-term losses as a result.

We should consider the reasons why this should be the case. Firstly, short-term thinking amongst the record companies has created a market that requires a large number of new groups and singers to feed it. The economics of becoming a hit artist are such that most new performers have difficulty in recouping their record-company advances, and so don't achieve much in the way of artists' royalties. One way in which they can really make some money out of their hits, however, is by writing and/or publishing them. This is fine if they're great writers – and, of course, there are a few who are just that – but the majority of contemporary hit records are produced by teams of people comprising the artist, a producer (or team of producers), maybe an independent programmer/arranger, the songwriters and, at the end of the line, remixers. Most are paid fees and royalties, but it has become common for all of them to share in the song and receive a slice of the publishing pie. The upside of all this activity is that there are many more opportunities for talented writers to get involved in hit production than ever before. The trouble is that less experienced writers aren't always sure how they should protect their rights and their income in these team-driven situations.

So let's think positively. This way of doing things isn't going to go away, so we have to come up with a good business model for writers to follow when they're faced with this type of deal. Here's my proposal.

A document format should exist that allows the original writers of a song to assert who actually wrote the song and who is to share in its income. This should be written in plain language and signed by all participants at the time that the work is created. Simple enough, you might say, but it must deal clearly with a couple of crucial issues. Firstly, it must establish the difference between owning the copyright and simply earning some money. As a writer, you're perfectly at liberty to share your income with whoever you like, but you don't have to give a share of the copyright; it's your most valuable asset, and you shouldn't share it with anyone except a real co-writer or a *bona fide* publisher who will enhance its value and your career.

Secondly, the document should assert the moral right of the songwriters so that only the proper writing credits are given. This could help ameliorate the ridiculous practice of 10 or 11 'writers' being credited for a song actually created by one or two people. The rule should be, 'Give income if you have to, but not credit or copyright.'

Another reason for the necessity of a clearly written agreement between writers of a composition can be seen in the growing number of legal actions caused by arguments over the origination of songs and ownership of the resulting copyrights. Most actions don't make it to the courtroom; the antagonists settle by negotiation and are usually subject to non-disclosure agreements to protect errant celebrities from bad publicity. Nevertheless, the old saying 'Where there's a hit, there's a writ' has never been more true.

There have always been writers who actually steal other people's work, and such outright plagiarism probably exists in today's business. But that's not what concerns us at the Academy. In the main, we believe that most legal wrangles between group members, writers and their production and management teams can be avoided by simply getting agreements in place at the time songs are created. Often there are a number of people present in the studio when songs are being written, finished, fine-tuned or changed during production, and one further problem here is that there is often a long gap between the creation of a song and its subsequent release. Memories as to who did what can be unreliable.

Another factor here is that there might be several different publishing deals in existence amongst the team, each one requiring recoupment of an advance. In short, it's a recipe for disaster.

These arguments could be eliminated by the provision of a simple document that could be used to give an accurate record of who wrote a song and the agreed split of the proceeds. It should assert the names of the creators (ie the copyright owners) and record their shares in the work, and it should also provide an opportunity for the creators to enter into a simple commercial arrangement and allocate a share of their income to contributors, such as producers or artists, who might have enhanced the value of the song by their input. Everybody named in the agreement then signs at the bottom. This document would then provide irrefutable evidence if, at a later date, there's a disagreement.

It really is unwise to rely on a verbal agreement made while you're working in the studio. Perceptions of the importance of bits of arrangement, lyric changes, riffs or remixes can change over time. Friendships and important musical partnerships are put at risk under these circumstances, so why not avoid the argument entirely? Put it in writing!

AGREEMENTS:
COLLABORATION AGREEMENTS

'Whoever wrote it owns it.' – Pete Cornish (Westbury Music Consultants)

When two or more people sit down together to write a song, the last thing on their minds will be any consideration as to the kind of contractual relationship they want to have with their co-writers. Songwriting is a creative and artistic pursuit and, even with commercial success as its goal, business should have little influence within the writing environment. Considerations of percentage splits, creator rights, warranties and other contractual points are purely academic until a good song has been written in the first place. Songwriting is a fragile enough creative process without these concerns intruding.

However, a complete disregard of these matters can be equally destructive. There are countless examples of songwriters making presumptions on copyright splits or relying on indefinite verbal agreements that have then ended up in assets being frozen, costly out-of-court settlements or expensive legal proceedings and the termination of otherwise highly productive and successful writing partnerships. For the sake of a moment's focused discussion and the small amount of time it takes to sign a simple collaboration agreement, millions of pounds and countless heartaches could have been saved.

While it's acknowledged that a verbal agreement is contractually binding under law, there have been so many cases that have ridden on the opinion of one songwriter versus another (eg the Spandau Ballet case) that it's strongly recommended that any agreements are formalised in writing, whether this be as a formal contract, a letter or – at the very minimum – an email exchange.

As highlighted in 'Song Craft 15', the key point is not to take the agreement on copyright for granted when collaborating with another writer. When a song is a success and starts to generate income, the influence of money can greatly distort memory and truth. This is why a writer should always follow these three simple guidelines:

1. Discuss the copyright split before or immediately after the writing session.

2.   Agree to a fair and practical system.

3.   Get the agreement in writing.

THE PRINCIPLES OF SPLITS

The reason why it's best to agree the copyright split of a song before or immediately after its creation is that there's no value to the copyright at this stage, so writers can decide on their share according to their individual contribution or an agreed system. When money becomes involved, human nature often takes a nasty turn and sadly people can argue over a consideration as small as one per cent.

The actual division of ownership of a song can be made as complex or as simple as you want. There are an infinite number of ways to split the songwriting 'pie', although there are some established systems that can save writers arguing over what a particular contribution equates to as a percentage and destroying an otherwise promising or successful relationship.

Most professional songwriters adhere to the 'in the room' principle, whereby, if there are two people in the room at the time of creation, the song is split 50/50; if there are four, each person receives 25 per cent, and so on, regardless of the concrete creative contribution of the individuals. One writer might have had every single one of his ideas rejected, for instance, but those ideas might have served as a catalyst for other ideas that were accepted. Lennon and McCartney maintained this principle throughout their career, even when they weren't in the same room!

Another standard method is to divide the song into lyrics and music, writers of each being awarded 50 per cent. This is a very valid system when the contributors' skills are similarly divisible.

The situation where a song is almost complete and another writer is brought in to put together the finishing touches could require a different arrangement still. Many professional writers consider that, whatever their contribution, it's worth giving such a third party an equal share in order to get the song finished and made into a hit song. It could be considered just as fair to offer 25 per cent if, for example, a song was complete except for a bridge or a second verse. Whatever the original writer's decision – and technically it's their decision to make – it's courteous and professional to let the finishing writer know what's on offer.

Another common writing situation occurs when two writers have written and completed a song and then a third person is brought in to improve it. This requires a simple act of negotiation between the relevant parties. Complications occur, however, when either of the original creators is unaware of the rewrite. If an original contributor isn't informed, he or she is legally entitled to their original 50 per cent share. Whatever split is agreed with the other writer, the original creator's share can only be reduced by consent. It's vital, therefore, that all writers are kept informed of any rewrites – and this applies equally to the new writers. As Steve Levine observes, 'What's happening more and more now – and this is where producers and songwriters do need to be careful – is that, because projects are being passed around to hundreds of producers, it's conceivable that fragments of a song may have been written in a previous incarnation. You need to be very careful about that, so you have to have the conversation, "Are we starting from page one? Or are we already on page three?" I lost a lot of money due to a song having been previously worked on by another producer without my knowledge. My advice is always to check if there are any skeletons in a song.'

With regard to bands or groups, there are a number of options. You could follow U2's lead and split everything equally between the members of the band (although Bono understandably gets sole credit for writing the lyrics). Their attitude seems to be that a group is a group; everyone lends to the sound, and if it's a success, everyone has contributed.

Alternatively, the splits could be agreed on a song-by-song basis, depending on who has written the song, since a band's job is to arrange their parts around the basic song and as such the members derive their income from their performance and from record sales. The songwriter, therefore, should be fully rewarded for their creativity, as the writing element is separate to those of performance and arrangement (eg The Who's Pete Townshend and Ian Anderson of Jethro Tull are credited as the songwriters in their respective bands).

There is a valid argument, however, for a halfway house whereby the songwriter or songwriters retain all copyright in the song but the actual songwriting income is redistributed amongst all the group members in order to reflect their contribution to the arrangement and ultimate success of the song. This is a principle applied by Travis's Fran Healey, for example. It could be considered to be the fairest method if there are one or two key creators within a group, especially as many bands are likely to split up or change members before achieving success. It should therefore be the right of the original creator to keep control over their own songs.

Whatever the final decision within the band, it needs to be formally agreed and put down in writing. (This latter principle was adopted by Spandau Ballet, but unfortunately it wasn't agreed in writing and led to a very costly court hearing.)

A further consideration with regard to income splits is relevant when a producer, session musician or any other individual makes a significant contribution to a finished song. This is often the case when a song is being recorded and a particular instrumental part in the arrangement becomes a significant hook, such as the sax solo on Gerry Rafferty's 'Baker Street' or the violin part in The Bluebells' 'Young At Heart'. Again, here it's imperative to make a note of the level of contribution and the agreed share of income. If you're employing a session musician or producer, any contribution they make should be considered work for hire, and you should get them to sign an official confirmation that they received payment in return for their services and therefore will make no future claims to the copyright. However, their contribution might be so significant that the writer feels conscience-bound to offer a share of the income (or copyright) in lieu of the originally agreed fee. The legal action surrounding the aforementioned Bluebells song, where the session violinist made claims to copyright in the song, should be warning enough for any successful songwriter to get their affairs in order.*

Finally, it occasionally happens that a person rewrites a song substantially without permission, gets it recorded and the new version then becomes a hit, at which time this unsolicited collaborator demands a share of the copyright. This happened with Leiber and Stoller's 'Hound Dog', for instance, which was originally recorded by Mama Thornton but later picked up by a lounge singer and performed in a version with altered lyrics, and it was this version that Elvis Presley heard and later sang. In this case, the new version was considered an 'unauthorised adaptation', and the uninvited co-writer received neither reward or credit.

JOINT WORKS

Under normal co-writing circumstances, the writers create a *joint work*, which means that the collaborators each have undivided and equal interests in the song. In most cases, this means that one writer may not authorise any dealing with the rights or adaptations of the original song without the consent of all the other owners. When the two distinct components of a song – the lyric and the instrumental musical work – have been created independently of one another, then – based on a recent decision from the High Court about joint works with regard to the case of *Brighton v Jones* – there's a precedent that they can still be used separately thereafter. So, if the author of the lyric and the composer of the

---

* 'Young At Heart' was a hit for The Bluebells in 1984 and again in 1993, when it was used in a Volkswagen advertisement. In July 2002, Bobby Valentino – who played a violin part on the song – was awarded a share of the music copyright in the song, after originally being paid £75 for playing on the recording. The unsuccessful defendant, Bluebell Robert Hodgens, maintained that he was the composer of the violin part and the owner of the entire music copyright in the song. The High Court, however, found that the three requirements for joint authorship were satisfied. These requirements are that (a) there must be a collaboration in the creation of a new musical work; (b) there must be a 'significant and original' contribution from each joint author; and (c) the contributions from each author must not be separate.

music have each created their contribution in isolation, not only could the lyricist invite someone else to create a different musical score but, equally, the composer of the music could invite a new lyricist to create a different lyric.

THE AGREEMENT

Again, the complexity of collaboration splits means that a formal written agreement is required. While the best solution is a contract drawn up by a recognised music lawyer, this isn't necessarily the easiest, most economical or practical. As indicated earlier, the written agreement itself need not be complicated, but should at the very minimum cover the following points:

- The name of the song(s);

- The names of the contributors;

- Their respective shares in the copyright of the song(s);

- Whether that share is in respect of words only, music only or words and music (eg 'Matthew Bould 25 per cent [words]/Sarah Mole 75 per cent [words and music]').

There might also be a separate provision in the agreement to divide the income generated by the song(s) to reflect contributions from other individuals.

The document should then be signed and dated by all contributors and a copy should be held by each for future reference.

While this might seem like a great deal to consider, it's to every songwriter's benefit that these matters are discussed and agreed at the earliest possible convenience, given how important such decisions can be in the years to come. The ideal solution is a formally standardised agreement to which all professional songwriters can adhere. Until such a thing exists, it's up to you to take responsibility for your welfare as a songwriter.

Promoting Your Songs: The Basics

'My advice to all songwriters, great and small, rich or poor, happening or becalmed, veteran or novice: if you want your songs to live and be heard, you have to focus on getting your stuff recorded.'

– Frank Musker

The truism 'You don't get a second chance at a first impression' is particularly relevant within the music industry. Aspiring songwriters need to understand that the manner in which they promote their work is vital to their chances of success. However great a song might be, if it's not presented professionally and correctly, it's very likely to be passed over by the very people who could make it a hit.

There are several areas that require attention when promoting your work. These include:

- Presentation

- Quality

- Career goal

- Targeting

- Profile

The easiest, most effective and surprisingly oft-disregarded area to address is the first of these: presentation. After working so hard on writing, crafting and recording a song, it's amazing how few songwriters pay any attention to how they package their masterpiece. The sheer quantity of demos that a publishing or record company receives means that only the most competent and professional approaches will be considered. So, rather than shooting yourself in the foot, take the time to present your work in the best possible light.

- Send in your demo in CD format. Old formats such as cassette suggest that you're not committed to your craft and aren't willing to invest adequately in your career.

- It's generally considered best to include only three songs on the demo. Any more than this can be overkill. If the publisher or record company is interested, they'll ask you for more examples. Obviously, put your best song first on the CD.

- Present the CD in a professional-looking package – ie with a cover and label. There's no need to go over the top, but handwritten packages look messy and suggest laziness.

- Include a typed copy of the lyrics where appropriate.

- Put your contact details on every item – the letter, the CD and the CD case – as they'll often get separated. Also, as an additional precaution, be sure to include a copyright notice – ie '© John Smith 2005'.

- Enclose a covering letter. This should be brief and to the point and ideally should include full contact details and some information about what genres you cover, past experience, any key success, etc. Avoid telling your life story, though!

- Make sure you use the correct postage and send it all in a protective envelope.

- If you intend to send your demo as an MP3 via email, it's wise to ask the record company or publisher if this is OK before you do so, as some don't accept them.

Mick Leeson says:
'Hits are the cream, the tip of the iceberg visible above the water. In the days when singles were singles, out of 100 weekly releases, maybe four would make the charts. That meant 96 songs in the bin. And they were thought good enough to spend time and money on – ie potential hits. Below them would be several hundred demos classed as "maybes" that some A&R man would keep in his drawer, waiting for the right artist. And below them would be demos that a publisher would like but still wouldn't have an artist or label interested in them, and so on down the food chain, to the unlistened-to demo in every publisher's office.'

The key to effective presentation is to be clear, concise and professional while avoiding overdoing it at all costs. The publisher Christian Ulf-Hansen comments, 'I'm not impressed by photographs or biographies and I hate receiving a foolscap pack of mostly superfluous information. If it's a singer/songwriter, a CD-sized photo is sufficient. What's most important is the quality of the song and the quality of the vocal demonstrating it.'

The quality of the demo is always going to be its most important factor. As I indicated earlier in this book, the affordability and proliferation of home-studio equipment and the extremely competitive nature of the music business means that recordings have to be of the highest standard possible. Solo singers shouldn't just sing into a mic but use a guitar or piano accompaniment, at the very minimum. Bands should ideally go into a studio to produce their demo, since drums are difficult to be properly recorded elsewhere. There's no need to remortgage the house to fund a demo recording, but it does need to be an excellent thumbnail sketch of the song. As Christian Ulf-Hansen recommends, 'Keeping it simple is the key.'

One factor that will influence both the demo and its presentation is your actual career as a songwriter. Bob Clifford, commenting in the Academy's member magazine, *The Works*, advises, 'People sending material should decide beforehand how they want to be regarded: as a writer for other people, as a performing artist or leader of a band, or even if they're interested in writing library music.' This is an important point, as it will affect how you present yourself. Firstly, being clear in your career direction will help those receiving your demo to deal with you effectively and efficiently. Secondly, your career goal will dictate how the package is designed; where singer/songwriters are concerned, for instance, the entire package should combine musicality with a professional attitude, a strong sense of image and a unique but potentially commercial sound. If you're just a songwriter, however, you don't need to concern yourself with image and instead can focus on the commercial appeal of your music.

Once the product and package is right, the next step is to target the promotion effectively. 'The worst way of all [to promote yourself] is to send in material blindly,' observes Justin Sherry at Palan Music.

First of all, you'll need to research your market, as different publishers service different styles of music. Boosey & Hawkes, for instance, specialises in more 'serious' music, including classical and jazz, so there's no point in sending a pop demo to them for consideration.

It's also extremely important that the package is addressed to someone by name and to make sure that the recipient is interested in your style of music. Again, it's a waste of time and money to post a pop demo to an A&R person who's into hardcore dance or hip-hop.

This is where networking comes in. You need to find out who in a record or publishing company is responsible for listening to demos, what types of music they're looking for, how best to get a song to them and even whether or not they're looking for music in the first place. You can find this out by networking and via word of mouth, or by making use of music directories or the internet, or even by phoning up the companies themselves to obtain this information. There are even magazines (eg SongLink) and websites (eg www.taxi.com) that provide insider information on who to send demos to (see the following section, David Stark's 'A Rough Guide To Song Plugging', for further information).

Ideally, you should get to the stage where the industry comes looking for you, instead of the other way round. This will come from raising your profile, or that of your songs, enough to attract serious interest. Networking is one way of achieving this, by getting your name known in the right circles, as explained later in 'The Art Of Networking', while working with other artists and successful songwriters is another. As Justin Sherry points out, 'The best thing people can do in promoting their songs is to try to team up with successful writers or maybe a band on a roll and get their opinions and interest.' This approach is dealt with in 'Working With Artists'.

A third effective method is to use the infinite resources of the internet, and Jake Shillingford explains how to go about this in 'DIY On The Internet'.

Finally, performing the songs live, either by yourself or with a gigging band, is still one of the best promotional tools in the business, and Tony Moore explains why in 'Protecting Your Songs: The Benefits Of Live Performance'.

While all the above can feel like a tremendous amount of work and an obstacle to you focusing on songwriting, it's important to remember that the music business isn't just about writing a good song; you have to sell it, too.

Wayne Hector says:
'Be prepared to stay up late at nights to write. This business is about investing in yourself. It's about investing time. Then, when you finally get money, it's about investing that money in yourself. When Ali [Tennant] and I signed our first publishing deal, we took every penny of that money, but we bought nothing. Instead we flew around the world and paid out to write with whoever we could get to write with, seeking any opportunity. To be a serious writer, you have to be willing to commit time and money to your career.

'After that, it's about investment in the song itself to make it a hit. I don't know how you can control that. Everybody looks for a way, but there are so many factors involved beyond writing a great song. It encompasses making sure that you're honest to your writing in the first place. This leads to creating a good song to promote. Then you must search for every single opportunity in order to place that song with an artist. Then, once you have the song placed, you have to run down the A&R person and push for it to be a single, and on and on and on. That happens with every song that you will ever write. Even when you're doing really well as a writer, you'll still have to chase everybody down. Even when the song is great, maybe the production doesn't turn out well, or the mix isn't particularly good, or radio don't like it, or radio love it but the public don't. There are 1,001 hurdles to success. If you truly want to be a professional songwriter, you just have to keep going for it, keep going for it, keep going for it. Invest in yourself and hopefully someday a song of yours will break through; the opportunity will come and the doors will open.'

A ROUGH GUIDE TO SONG PLUGGING

BY DAVID STARK,
EDITOR AND PUBLISHER OF *SONGLINK INTERNATIONAL*
(WWW.SONGLINK.COM)

The art and business of song plugging has been around since the days before music was electrically recorded onto metal cylinders, back to the late 19th century, when the early music publishers would hawk their sheet music to music-hall artists and the popular entertainers of the times. The hope was that these artists would perform the song on stage and thereby influence their audience to buy a copy of the printed score for the endless enjoyment of the entire family on the traditional home parlour piano.

Later, from the early 1900s to the classic years of Tin Pan Alley and beyond, the stereotype image of a successful publisher/song plugger was as a flash-suited, cigar-smoking hustler with a wink and a smile who would invite the artists of the day into his cubicle-like office in Denmark Street, wherein one or more of his stable of his neatly attired composers would 'demonstrate' their new songs on the battered office piano in the hope of securing an agreement by the artist, or their agent, to perform said song on radio and record. This method of plugging continued virtually unchanged even up to the 1960s and '70s, when many of the Academy's most esteemed members can testify to selling their songs by playing them live in their publishers' offices to visiting artists and agents, often resulting in huge international hits.

Of course, the format of the song 'demonstration' has changed radically over the years, from sheet music and live performance to shellac acetates (the original demo discs) to cassettes, digital CDs and finally the MP3s of today's age of broadband delivery. And, as the music industry exploded internationally from the mid-1960s onwards, so did the demand of music publishers and songwriters for regular contact information for the ever-increasing number of artists and projects to whom they can pitch their wares.

Publisher's tip sheets, or 'pitch lists', have been around for over 30 years in one form or another, originating in New York and, more prominently, Nashville as photostat monthly listings of artists, their A&R managers and current song requirements. The first independent tip sheet on this side of the pond was *UK Songplugger*, launched in 1982 by Tim Whitsett, an American who had previously worked for Chrysalis Music and other publishers over here. The three-page, beige-coloured A4 newsletter quickly became essential reading for every publisher and professional songwriter and led to a lot of cuts with such artists as Cliff Richard, Elkie Brooks, Shakin' Stevens and all the myriad acts of the era who depended on outside songs.

It was through Tim that I first became interested in the concept of song plugging, being an occasional songwriter (and drummer) myself who also happened to work in the industry, having started out at Dick James Music before becoming International Press Officer at Decca and MAM Records and going on to edit various music-industry trade and pro-audio publications. I always had an interest in who was writing and producing for whom and kept a close eye on *Songplugger*, as it became when Tim sold it to a London-based publisher in the late 1980s, before returning to the States to live. In fact, Tim had earlier given me first option on acquiring it outright, which I had to decline as I didn't feel confident about starting up on my own and had just accepted a prestigious job with *Billboard*'s offshoot Music And Media in Amsterdam. However, when I returned to the UK in 1990, I ended up working for the small company that had bought *Songplugger*, which I subsequently developed into more of a mini-magazine. As luck would have it, the company was eventually taken over and I had to make a quick decision about whether to carry on working there under new management or to strike out on my own and create a new publication within the same framework.

Thus I launched *SongLink International* in September 1993, with the encouragement and goodwill of many publisher friends and songwriters who promised to subscribe, and who have faithfully done so ever since (thanks, folks!), not to mention – and just as importantly – the support of the record companies, artist managers and producers whose leads are, of course, the backbone of the service. I'm delighted that *SongLink* has been the starting point for many hit songs and covers around the world by artists of virtually every different genre and nationality. The biggest success to date is probably Christina Aguilera's smash 'Genie In A Bottle', co-written by Pam Sheyne, who spotted RCA's lead for the then-unknown singer in *SongLink* and alerted her LA-based co-writers, David Frank and Steve Kipner, about the project. The rest, as they say, is history, resulting in Ivor Novello Awards and many other industry honours. Christina's follow-up hit, 'Come On Over, Baby', was also a direct pitch through *SongLink*, by Swedish publisher Air Chrysalis Music, while *SongLink* leads have also led to cuts with such names as Oleta Adams, Tom Jones, Diana Ross, Mis-Teeq, *NSync, Sonique and many locally famous artists in various territories. In recent years, this has included the inevitable flush of *PopStars* and *Pop Idol* winners and finalists.

So, how do you get to place songs with major artists, have worldwide hits and enjoy Christmas in Barbados for evermore? The truth is that it's tougher than ever these days for 'pure' songwriters – ie those who don't produce or co-write with the artist, which has developed to be the industry-standard arrangement over the past decade – to get a look in. Hit songwriting is very much a team effort these days, as the writer credits (those tiny names in brackets) of so many chart entries will testify: the writers, the producers, the A&R person, the promotions guy and even the tea-lady all like to claim a slice of the songwriting cake, as do the artists, who are invariably given an automatic writer credit whether they had anything to do with the song's creation or not.

However, luckily there are still opportunities out there for talented songwriters; you just have to do your research, be businesslike in your approach and have the confidence, belief and – most of all – luck to fulfil your ambition. Oh, and a truly great song (and a great demo) helps as well. There are no rules in this business, and the exciting thing is that nobody knows (except possibly a few marketing gurus) what will be topping the charts in six months, a year or two years' time, so why shouldn't it be your song, if you believe in it strongly enough? Of course, that's you and 1,000 others with the same dream; the competition is absolutely immense, and anyone in their right mind would balk at the hurdles that have to be jumped in order to achieve a major or even minor cut. These days it's often a highly political process, especially in the States, where even the best song in the world can be bounced off an album if the manager, A&R executive or producer has other ideas and interests, inevitably of a financial nature.

Luckily, though, there are easier routes to securing a cover with the right material, and *SongLink* has had much of its success in mainland Europe, where good old-fashioned A&R still exists in Germany, the Benelux countries, Scandinavia, Spain, Italy and even Greece. Record companies in these countries are usually very receptive to well-produced commercial demos, either in English or to be translated into their own language, and if they hear something they like, they'll usually get straight back to the writer or publisher with the good news. Names like Patricia Kaas (France), Monica Naranjo (Spain), Tik Tak (Finland) and Hi-5 (Greece) don't mean much in the UK but have earned good money through sales and airplay for many UK writers and others who have songs on their major-selling albums. Additionally, quite a few US writers have also commented recently that getting a few covers of various songs released in Europe can be financially as rewarding as getting one big cut in the States.

Meanwhile, the most intensely competitive market is that microcosm of the music industry at Nashville, where an estimated 50,000 songs or more are pitched each year to fewer than 100 major-label acts. But if you don't live on or visit Music Row on a regular basis, you can forget about getting a cut there. However, for a small group of British songwriters, such as Roger Cook, Chris Eaton, John Peppard and Steve McEwan, the proof is in the country charts that success is possible for overseas writers.

In conclusion, here are a few tips for any budding songwriters looking for a way into the industry:

1. Make your demos as good as possible within your budget, with particular emphasis on using the best possible vocalists if you don't sing (and even if you do!) and on making sure that the vocals can be heard clearly above the track. A great vocal can really help to sell a song. Beware of using factory preset keyboard and drum sounds; there's nothing worse than hearing a demo that sounds like it was recorded on a 1980s calculator. These days, the trend is for a live feel with authentic sounds.

2. Listen to what's in the charts, get familiar with your targeted artists' styles and try to tailor your songs specifically to them, in their usual keys. Play your song in various styles and tempos to see what will suit them – and it – best. Great lyrics are also paramount; if you can't come up with original ideas, great storylines and interesting middle-eights yourself, find yourself a co-writer who can.

3. Do your research. Read *Music Week* and *Billboard* to get a feel of what's going on in the industry, who's moving where and which new artists are hot. Also, there's a monthly roundup of publishing and A&R news and moves listed at www.songlink.com. If you're serious about pitching your songs, you'll know which publication to subscribe to, but be warned: we vet all unpublished writers and can only accept those with the most commercial and potential hit songs.

4. Try to network with industry professionals at the many seminars, events and showcases arranged by industry organisations like BACS, MCPS–PRS, the Musicians' Union, ASCAP and BMI (the two US rights societies, both with offices in London) and others. Be professional in your approach: print up some business cards and don't be afraid to say that you have a great song they should listen to, but make sure you ask for their permission if you plan to send it by MP3 rather than CD.

5. When sending demos by CD, make sure your contact details are printed or clearly written on the sleeve or plastic case and the CD itself. Send the lyrics plus a brief accompanying letter with details of the track, the writers and any other relevant

information, but don't send pages of boring biography, write in multicoloured inks, wrap your CD lovingly in acres of bubble-wrap and miles of clear tape, or staple the envelope to high heaven. These are usually ominous signs that the music inside is going to be complete crap!

6. Don't expect an immediate response. If someone likes your material, they'll usually get back to you pretty quickly, even if it's just to say, 'Nice songs,' and no more. Otherwise, wait at least a week or two before following up, ideally by email. If you're extremely lucky, you might receive a call or email asking you to put the song 'on hold' – ie agree not to pitch it to other artists for an agreed period of time. This is no guarantee of a cover, however, so you'll have to go with your gut feeling regarding the artist's potential, especially if they're unknown.

7. If you're serious about selling your songs and winning an Ivor Novello Award or three, don't give up. Keep writing and keep in touch with as many industry professionals – and successful songwriters – as you can and pump them for their opinions, feedback and advice. Keep up your standards and try to raise them each time you write or make a demo, as your song will have to stand out among hundreds of superbly recorded publisher and pro-writer demos.

8. Above all, keep believing in yourself. If you've got it, your songs will do your plugging for you.

PROMOTING YOUR SONGS: THE BENEFITS OF LIVE PERFORMANCE

BY TONY MOORE,
PROMOTER OF THE BEDFORD CLUB

'One thing you can't download is a live performance.'
– Mark Hill, producer/writer with Craig David

Legendary songwriter Sammy Cahn, when asked what came first, the lyrics or the tune, used to reply, 'The phone call.' It's an anecdote that still raises a wry smile today, yet songwriting as a craft has changed dramatically since his day. Yes, the phone call still gets made, but these days it's usually to one of a very few production teams somewhere in Scandinavia who have the ear for a contemporary commercial production and a reputation for churning out hits.

Since the 1960s, there has been an exponential growth in songwriting. The fact is that we now live in a giant global village with hundreds of thousands, if not millions of songwriters competing for the tiniest imaginable outlets. True, the vast majority of these writers aren't of a professional standard, and of those that are, very few will have the X factor that unlocks the door to success. However, the industry has battened down the hatches under a barrage of unsolicited CDs and tapes delivered by the truckload, MP3 attachments clogging up email accounts and streams of phone calls arriving daily from hopefuls believing that they deserve a chance for recognition. One last bastion of opportunity to promote yourself is the live circuit, though even that is now diminishing rapidly.

For perceptive writers, a live performance of one of their songs can help to mould it. What seemed like a perfectly acceptable 60-second intro can suddenly feel like a lifetime in front of an audience who don't agree. Likewise, it can suddenly become apparent that 16 repetitions of the final chorus is too much when you notice people's attention drifting. You can always judge how right you got it by the reaction afterwards. Believe me, after six years of running the Kashmir Klub, the best songs, artists and writers *always* stand out and people want to know about them.

Playing live doesn't always mean performing your own songs. There are thousands of bars, hotels and clubs around the country in which musicians play well-known songs simply to provide ambience and light entertainment. Those songwriter/performers who undertake this kind of paid work should use it as a way of truly appreciating what can be great and eternal about well-written songs. Whether you play a Beatles songs or a Frank Sinatra song, you'll notice that they've passed the test of time with flying colours, sounding as fresh and inspirational now as they did the day they were released. However, the years in between have also added a certain familiarity that means the melodies and words have lodged in the psyche of the world's population.

If you're playing at one of these kinds of venue, try slipping one or two of you own songs into the set and see how they feel there. Obviously, they won't have the power and weight of a song that people know really well, but if you've written a great song (and all songwriters should be aiming to write only great songs) it will catch people's ears. Its very freshness will draw some of the audience's attention. See how it feels when you play your songs. Do they stand up to the competition of the rest of your repertoire, lyrically, melodically or rhythmically? Can you be honest enough to judge the quality of your work against the standards that have been laid down over the last 50 or so years?

Be open and perceptive. Successful songwriting is about channelling universal truths through personal interpretation. There are as many different styles of songs as there are individual composers and authors, so always try to be original while not sacrificing a song's mass appeal. If your song has mass appeal, this doesn't mean you'll be an instant millionaire, but if you touch a nerve that really moves people, you'll have achieved your aim as a creative communicator. Leonard Cohen is just as valid as Noel Gallagher despite the fact that the people who appreciate the music of each may be different in age, lifestyle and numbers. However, if you sit in a bar with a guitar or a piano and play 'Wonderwall' by Oasis followed by 'Suzanne' by Cohen, you'll notice that they don't sound out of place next to each other. That's because they're both great songs, and by the time you strip away the production and present them as they were written, at an acoustic level, they have much in common. They're just *right*. The magic is there, and it is everlasting.

Songwriting is an art, and like all art it has value only because a very few people have a gift to make something truly special. The argument still rages about whether you're born with the gift or whether you can learn it, but I feel that it's a mixture of both: you must have an innate sense of creativity to start with, but you can – and you always should – learn as you progress. Paul McCartney and John Lennon had the gift at an early age, while others can take years to find it, but the development of a songwriter depends on experience and instinct.

One of the greatest places to experience music, both as a listener and as a contributor, is on the live circuit. It may well be the case that the intensity and non-stop workload of playing in Hamburg in The Beatles' early years were instrumental in accelerating the development of McCartney and Lennon's abilities. After all, they performed something like eight hours a night, every night of the week, playing all the hits of the day as well as the classics of the time. They learned what worked. Their early original material was a reflection of all the music that they realised people enjoyed and responded to. As their career took off, their original songwriting talents matured and evolved. So the live circuit might well have played a vital role in the history of The Beatles – not only as performers but as songwriters, too. Today the modern-day equivalents of the Hamburg Kaiserkeller and Star-Club are still out there in various guises, and no one should be too proud to learn their craft in these environments while earning an income at the same time.

Another advantage to being out there and playing live is that you're showing the world what you do and giving yourself the opportunity to make connections with others in the business. You'll meet other performers and writers. It might be the chance meeting with a lyricist drinking in the pub who loves your melodies that leads to the formation of the next John–Taupin relationship. You might casually remark that you fancy writing some material in a different style only to find another writer at the venue who thinks like you and becomes another writing partner.

The other great thing about playing live is that you never know who might be in the audience. Many of the A&R executives that came to see an act at the Kashmir Klub ended up signing someone else on the bill as well. It's great when they call you simply because they saw you unexpectedly and were blown away.

So, remember: be the best you can, listen to constructive criticism, develop your songs through live performance and get your music heard.

Promoting Your Songs: The Art Of Networking

'If you think you've got what it takes, don't be ashamed to bang on the right door. If you think you have a great lyric that Guy Chambers would love, get it to him, because Guy and any other top songwriter are always looking for good ideas.'

– Don Black

Sadly, success in the music business isn't simply a matter of being a great songwriter. In today's industry, you also need perseverance, people skills and an ability to network.

Networking is merely fashionable term for an old methodology. Networking is essentially the forming of any relationship, alliance or communication with others in the music business. This could start as simply as a conversation with another writer in a music shop about what software sequencer he uses. He might then invite you to his recording studio. You perhaps end up writing a few songs together. He then might get signed as an artist and decide to use one of your co-writes for his first album. The song is released as the first single and shoots to Number One. Suddenly you're the hottest new songwriter on the block and everyone wants to work with you – all because you struck up a conversation and developed a working relationship.

While this process might take several years, the above example makes it clear why networking is so important. A songwriter can't succeed in a vacuum. In fact, all business is done through networking, not only within the music industry but in every feasible configuration of commerce.

The Three Factors To Success

Say, for example, that your car broke down. Would you automatically pick up a copy of the *Yellow Pages* and pick an unknown car mechanic at random or contact someone you know first or who has been recommended to you? In most cases, you'd probably favour someone you know or has been recommended to you.

The music business works under exactly the same philosophy. Consequently, the music that gets recorded and released isn't always the best; it's that which has been written by the most connected songwriters.

Taking talent for granted, therefore, a songwriter's ultimate success within the industry is determined by three key factors:

1. Who you know;

2. What you know;

3. Who knows you.

In other words, opportunities for success will come about if you have the right connections with the right people who can open doors for you, get you gigs, pass your CD on to an artist or publisher, etc. In order to do this effectively, you need to understand the workings of the music business, who's in and who's out, and which companies are most appropriate to you and your music. Then, and most importantly, the industry needs to know *you*. Otherwise, no one's going to take you seriously and it will be next to impossible to get anywhere.

WHEN AND WHERE

Networking should be something you do constantly. You should be networking every time you meet someone, whether at a party, pub, social event or work. Obviously, there will be certain situations when networking is particularly important, such as at gigs, business meetings, music-industry shows or conventions. At such events, you'll need to be consciously active in your approach. Even so, you can never predict where the golden opportunity will come from, so be vigilant at all times and keep on developing and maintaining contacts.

EFFECTIVE NETWORKING

The skill of networking lies in your ability to relate to other people – your interpersonal skills. For some people this is a natural talent, while for others introducing themselves to and socialising with new people presents huge difficulties. However, there's no need for a personality transplant to be able to network effectively. In fact, any attempt at pretence immediately comes across as insincere or false. In any networking situation, honesty and an appropriate sense of humour are your most valuable tools.

It's also helpful to remember that most people are insecure, too, so make it your responsibility to dispel their insecurity by taking an active role in engaging in conversation. By simply looking your contact in the eyes, focusing on them and smiling, you'll have done much of the work in fostering a potential relationship.

Beyond this there are a few simple dos and don'ts that will ensure that any meeting goes smoothly and you're remembered by the other person:

Do...

- ...ask the person's name, and then remember it. A tip here is to use the person's name in conversation immediately, and to continue to do so repeatedly.

- ...be polite. This is a simple thing, but so many people forget. Stand out from the crowd.

- ...use positive, open body language. Keep your arms uncrossed, face the subject and smile every so often.

- ...take an interest in the person. Ask them what they do and why they happen to be at the event or venue. By asking general questions, rather than those that have simple yes/no responses, you can keep them talking. If you begin to run out of conversation, use the environment around you to bring up mutual topics for discussion.

- ...sense when a conversation is coming to a logical conclusion. This is crucial. The worst thing to do is draw out a meeting or conversation that has obviously run its course. Give the other person an opportunity to move on.

- ...keep the door open for future discussions. Ask them for their business card (and make notes after the conversation about who they are and what they looked like, along with one or two notes about what you discussed) and, if appropriate, suggest a potential follow-up meeting. If this involves a phone call, make sure you call them when you said you would.

- ...let the other person know that you enjoyed speaking with them. There's no need to be over-exuberant at this point, but a simple 'It was nice to meet you' goes a long way.

DON'T...

- ...begin with a negative comment – eg, 'Isn't this champagne awful?' This will immediately give the other person a poor impression of you.
- ...begin a conversation with 'Where do I know you from?' if you've obviously never met the person before.

- ...talk about yourself continually. Show more interest in the other person. Find out what you can about them and then use this knowledge to shape the way you eventually promote yourself to them. It's often better to give detailed information about yourself at a later date.

- ...forget all the basic social etiquette – ie don't look over their shoulder and talk to other people passing behind them (although it's fine to acknowledge others with a smile or a wave); try not to give off a sexual vibe; don't forget their name repeatedly. And don't say saying anything negative about anyone else who might be present. You don't know who they know or might be friends with.

The idea is to make sure they remember you and would be happy to meet you again. There's much to be said for a good firm handshake, an air of confidence and a sense of humour. And when you meet people for a second or third time, a good tip is not assume that they'll remember who you are. If they don't remember you, don't be offended by the situation; just gently remind them who you are as you're re-introduced. They'll appreciate this as it means they won't lose face.

One final tip for effective networking: on those occasions when you know in advance who you're going to meet, try to acquire some background information on the person. For instance, if you know you have a meeting booked with an A&R executive, it would be useful to know what type of music they like, who they've signed to their label and who they like and dislike. By demonstrating your knowledge of them, they should be flattered, and it shows that you're serious about your job. Making others feel important is always a good approach in any line of business.

For a successful career in the music business, building a strong network of people is crucial. Networking is far-reaching and its results can be profound, unexpected and often welcome. Someone with whom you carry on a seemingly insignificant conversation at a party might well prove to be your most valuable ally in the future. Only with hindsight will you realise the influence your networking had on your own success.

'For a young songwriter setting out and trying to achieve success, we can't stress enough the importance of networking. It goes without saying that you can have great songs and sit in your bedroom forever, but if you don't get out there and meet people and make the right connections to get the breaks, they're never going to be more than that. It's not enough just to be skilful at songwriting; to succeed as a songwriter, you need a combination of determination, networking and luck: absolute single-mindedness about having to make a living out of music, a gift of the gab and the good fortune of being in the right place at the right time.'
– Pete Kirtley and Tim Hawes, Jiant Productions

As a songwriter, you'll need to work hard on being a positive, approachable and generous person. Talk to everyone, everywhere. Cultivate your people skills, because your charm and enthusiasm are tools of influence that are as invaluable as your skills as a songwriter. No matter how talented you might be, if others don't enjoy being around you, working with you and being part of your network, you won't succeed.

DIY Via The Net

By Jake Shillingford

Doing It On Your Own

The true essence of punk rock, the DIY ethic, is now finally attainable. In 1977, the fanzine *Sniffin' Glue* claimed that all you needed to form a band was three chords and a guitar. Today, all you need is three chords and a broadband modem.

Punk tried to be autonomous and change the music scene forever but couldn't fight the powerful majors, with many acts eventually signing to them and losing control of their ideals along the way. It had the agenda but not the armoury. In the meantime, the industry was developing new digital formats and ultimately more revenue. The 1980s saw analogue change to digital and the industry grew even more powerful, putting out countless reissues.

The picture is very different now. These days the music industry is desperately trying to restructure in order to survive. But now, the very artists it nurtured with financial, marketing and promoting machinery can bypass this system with the use of digital media, digital distribution and low-cost digital recording equipment, ultimately competing directly within the industry itself.

I became interested in autonomy in 1986 when my first band, My Life Story, released 'Home Sweet Zoo', our debut single, on a label that we'd set up in a bedsit in Southend-on-Sea, Essex. Five hundred 7" singles with hand-coloured sleeves went out to the clamouring masses.

Fast-forward 14 years and I found myself in New York without a band or a record label. My Life Story had disbanded with three farewell shows at the Camden Underworld after six Top 40 singles, three albums on three separate labels and the best part of £1 million spent on us (most of which was spent by Parlophone Records). I needed a new direction, I needed to perform, I needed to write and, most of all, I needed a chance to develop my career without the fear of being moulded into something I didn't want to be or dropped altogether. Although I was unsure of my musical direction, after being in a 12-piece mini-orchestra, I knew that I didn't want to be restricted by the prohibitive contracts that record labels offer.

These are the factors that motivated me to create ExileInside, a self-financing business model that has allowed me to continue to be creatively free, able to define my own release schedule and communicate directly with the fans, ultimately involving them in the music-making and release process themselves. Basically, I'm turning fans into A&R men!

I chose the name ExileInside for my project because it was an oxymoron. It defines the sense of feeling trapped and uncomfortable in your own skin and the inability we sometimes have in expressing ourselves fully. I wanted to try to get these feelings across in songwriting, but ironically this moniker has also taken on a secondary meaning: that of using the infrastructure of the music industry but operating completely outside it.

Record companies have never been so out of step with the times. Until only recently, they failed to understand how technology can help music, in fact railing against it when peer-to-peer and file-sharing networks took control. The irony is that, by creating the digital format, the industry eventually lost control of it through the proliferation of CD burning and the rise of sites such as Limewire, Napster, etc. The MP3 format and its delivery mechanism was developed outside the music industry, and this is why record companies have been trying to control digital media and ultimately make money from it. It made a huge amount of capital from reselling its artists when the digital CD came out in the 1980s, and now, paradoxically, money is now being lost through the advancement of that very technology.

Just when people started to realise the internet was going to be more than the CB radio of the 1990s, My Life Story released the first UK internet-only single in August 1999. The song was accessed using Windows Media Player, then a beta version. We wanted to increase our database of fans by giving the song away for free while ensuring that they provided us with their email address for future correspondence. This proved a powerful tool for the band at the time, and I came to realise the potential of direct communication with the fans. I was always a big advocate of fan clubs and loved the feeling of being part of something inclusive and exciting, and I felt that the internet could offer everything a fan club could do but more. Being a Mac user, I was more than slightly frustrated that I couldn't access the song myself, but we had to start somewhere!

A couple of years later, while living in New York, I was writing with my friend Aaron Cahill, who had created many of the My Life Story string arrangements. We wanted to see if we could come up with whole songs together rather than Aaron just bolting on parts to my material. The problem was that I was near Central Park and Aaron was living in Finsbury Park, London. We developed a technique of emailing musical parts of songs in MIDI file format to each other using the same sound source – General MIDI instruments – as well as exchanging lyrical ideas. We took the precaution of installing the same software and sounds on my laptop as well as Aaron's host computer, so we were hearing the same arrangements. Two people hovering over a mouse in a studio never works, in my opinion, as someone has to be the controller/programmer, and I found that, by emailing updated versions of song files to one another, the songs took on new directions and left us with lots of spare parts for remixes.

Deciding on lyrics transatlantically was also an interesting process. Aaron would quite often email me stream-of-consciousness passages that I would pick through and make sense of in my other world.

Another friend who played a key part in the inception of EI was Anthony Hill, an original member of My Life Story. Having spoken to him about what I wanted to do, he became my first 'Investor Angel' and EI was born. I've always been fascinated by the great era of music hall and vaudeville, when productions would receive patronage from the wealthy theatre lovers and benefactors. The term 'Investor Angels' came from that time. My idea was to garner financial support in a similar way, so I learned a bit of HTML and designed a very basic website from a friend's office in the shadow of the World Trade Center. I then contacted the remaining names on the My Life Story database and begged them for money.

The EI philosophy is: 'Made for the people; paid for by the people.'

I asked for a minimum investment of £500 per person. In return, they would receive regular packages which included an 'Investor CD' containing exclusive demos, remixes of EI music, free merchandise, free entry and AAA passes to EI concerts, and of course the satisfaction of being part of this exciting venture. Also, their initial investment would be returned once the album had sold in sufficient quantity. I felt that this figure was big enough to put off potential time wasters yet small enough for anyone who wanted to be involved.

The demographic of the Investor Angels turned out to be multifarious. We have students, bank managers, mechanics and even a silent investor on board who works for a multinational record company!

The advantage of being autonomous is that the scheme allows me to have closer relations with the fans and investors. Even now, I'm canvassing their opinions on singles releases as well as marketing ideas for the next album. I've already received many helpful and inspiring suggestions relating to this venture.

I'm also able to involve fans more closely in our projects by utilising their individual talents and skills. These fans are referred to as 'Alpha Members', and I've had much valued help and advice from them in many fields, including help with the IT side of the website, translation of the site into different languages, and sleeve and web artwork. I want to engender a sense of community and involvement with all those who take an interest in ExileInside. I've always loved the old idea of exchanging favours and lending one's skills to each other for the common good, a chicken for a loaf of bread.

Investor Angels are also encouraged to interact with the band, usually via email. However, I started a small club night – Club Exile – during the making of the first album at which investors could meet and discuss the project. In conjunction with Gary Robertson from the Sister Ray record store, myself and guest DJs reflect the influences that have shaped the EI sound from the decks.

My main musical influence came from the budget I had at my disposal! I quickly discovered that the cheapest production techniques come from electronica and the dance scene, so I armed my spare room with a computer, music software and samplers, and these tools shaped the sound of ExileInside. Using dance sounds and samples for strong melody- and lyric-based music was a challenge but, by default, gave us our sound.

The ExileInside website is the beating heart of all our operations. The project, however, is not wholly based on digital distribution and mail order; I've slowly secured licensing and distribution deals around Europe and the rest of the world to stock EI in record shops. Even though I make only half the amount from retail stores that I do from online mail order and digital downloads, I feel that the record shops' role is changing, in that many independent stores offer advice and education to record buyers that the worldwide web cannot provide in the same way. My CDs out there in the field also serve as glorified flyers; once someone has bought a CD in Geneva, for instance, an insert will invite them to the website, where they can download free songs and other goodies, and hopefully from then on they'll buy directly from www.exileinside.co.uk.

Furthermore, online distribution is like the mother of all Nectar cards: details of every purchaser are stored on a database and one day I imagine hanging a James Bond-style map of the world on the studio wall displaying the city location of every purchaser. Eventually I'll be able to target our gigs to specific areas where there is a swell of customers and expand on those localised areas. I've already noticed that word of mouth has increased online sales in certain towns and cities.

Everyone is getting iPods for Christmas, and more people will be listening to music in MP3 or IAAC format. I believe that, because of this, websites will become the new record sleeves – somewhere that a fan can get everything else associated with their favourite band. Even today, the artist/songwriter is no longer bound by the traditional necessity of signing to a record label to be heard or seen; you just need creative and supportive friends and a dedicated web designer. After all, musicians have traditionally hung around artists, and vice versa. The art-school refectory suddenly becomes your marketing and image-making machine.

Another benefit of setting things up on your own is that you can secure your pension in music. As I get older, I hope to work on new acts, record and produce them and release them as ExileInside develops from being a band into a label. Many artists, after the stigma of being dropped, have historically been unable to continue to ply their trade. Bands like Marillion and Simply Red have disproved this philosophy, of course, becoming role models for future dropped acts.

However, there's still a question mark over whether new up-and-coming bands have the force of presence to utilise this technology. The future is to be written by such bands as Japanese rockers Electric Eel Shock, who are preparing investors and applying the ExileInside model for when they leave their current label.

According to the IFPI (International Federation of the Phonographic Industry), the global value of recorded music sales has dropped over $6.2 billion since 1999. At the same time, less and less money is being spent on developing and nurturing new talent and investing in longevity. I believe that if U2 or REM were signed now there would be a good chance that they'd be dropped after their first releases. Most record companies operate on a success rate of less than ten per cent, which means that nine in ten acts fail to recoup their advance. In order to achieve significant sales, a record company invests an immense amount of cash in marketing, and an act has to sell hundreds of thousands of records if they're to recoup this. It's not uncommon, therefore, to have acts sell well over 50,000 records yet still be dropped. In comparison, in order for ExileInside to be a going concern, I'll need to sell only between 5,000 and 6,000 albums, which is a very realistic target.

The infamous Robbie Williams/EMI deal shows the direction in which record labels may be heading to survive. No longer can record companies simply be the catalyst for putting out records; they need to share in all forms of income – copyright on the songs, record sales, merchandise and touring revenue. As a result, the record label has an even bigger stake in image, presentation and creativity and can now hold the artist to ransom if he or she is not completely commercial. I truly believe that we're entering an age in the history of music when the artist will either be completely owned by a label or totally out on his or her own.

If you want to get your hands dirty and delve into the EI DIY manual of selling music on the internet, I suggest that the five key philosophies to adhere to are as follows:

1. Investigate a way to raise capital. The more gigs you do, the bigger your fanbase, the more emails you have, the better your chances of getting people to put money into your project.

2. Groups don't need to be made up of just musicians anymore. Treat your web designer, sleeve artist or producer as the fifth member of the band. Remember: a favour for a favour; a chicken for a loaf of bread.

3. Employ a dedicated company to process your online credit-card transactions. Try WorldPay (posh) or PayPal (cheap).

4. Hang onto your ego. You're never going to end up on *Top Of The Pops* with this venture, but frankly, these days, who cares? Remember that you'll be selling small quantities in countries all over the world so you'll be invisible to the chart radars, nationally. On the other hand, your profit margins will be massive compared to those of a normal label.

5. Work. It's impossible to explain the agony of filling in an expenses spreadsheet when you've just come off stage, but that's what I have to do a lot of. Don't let the business side of this venture stifle your creativity. After all, you can now release a record whenever you want. So plan carefully and release product often to keep your fans interested. Also, maintaining an online diary every day will make sure that people keep visiting your site.

GETTING CUTS:
WORKING WITH ARTISTS

'The recommended route to getting a cut on a record today, as a pure songwriter, is by writing with an artist. This is down to the intricate politics and economics of the publishing and music business. Collaboration is very much an integral part of writing pop music, both on a creative and commercial basis.'
— Pete Kirtley and Tim Hawes, Jiant Productions

You've written an amazing song that's perfect for Tina Turner, or maybe Joss Stone or Whitney Houston. The problem is, how do you get it to her when she's surrounded by countless other successful people – the best writers in the business and the best producers, who are also pitching their songs? There's an infinitesimal chance that a CD sent via the post might reach her, but it's highly unlikely that it will get through all those layers of people.

On the other hand, you've been invited to a small time gig in a local bar by a no-name singer without a record deal. As an aspiring professional songwriter, is it worth your time attending? Or should you concentrate on artists who are already recording and releasing hits? However unlikely this no-name singer might be, she could be a future star. After all, no one knew who Whitney was when Arista Records showcased her in Los Angeles before she was famous. The record company invited some of the best songwriters to a showcase gig and many didn't turn up. Thus an amazing opportunity was missed by many as Whitney went on to have a staggeringly successful music career.

Another example is Mariah Carey's most frequent collaborator, Ben Margulies. Ben is now a highly respected and in-demand songwriter/producer, but at the time of Mariah's first breakthrough album he was totally unproven. So, how did he get the gig? He had started working with Mariah when she was just 17 years old in a makeshift recording studio and helped her build her career.

The problem for most songwriters is that, once an artist has become successful, they have so many middle men creating barriers between them and the world that it's almost impossible to pitch a song to them. The answer is to get in on the ground floor: meet the artist when their career is developing and be part of that development phase. Hopefully, as the artist's career takes off, you'll have become so integral to their success that you're pulled along too.

Once you've achieved success as a professional songwriter with one artist, opportunities for collaborating with other artists tend to follow. Working with an artist is very similar to collaborating with another songwriter, but there are several things that you can do as a songwriter to ensure that a session with an artist goes well. Songwriter and artist Ali Tennant explains: 'When I'm asked to write for someone in particular, I tailor it to them. I try to befriend the artist and make sure they're comfortable. Then I find out more about them and bring the song out of them, crafting it from them, stamping their personality on a song so that they have something they feel they're part of.'

This skill of discovering the identity of the artist and weaving it into the fabric of the song is an important one for the professional songwriter to have. Producer Colin Emmanuel describes his approach to working with artists: 'Confidence, hunger and self-belief are the three personality traits I look for in any artist that I work with. I also look to see if they have a game plan. I get many artists that come through my studio who have incredible talent but don't honestly know what they want to do or why they're doing it. They lack artistic identity. This identity is what ultimately sells the artists, sets them apart from the competition, and that's why the identity should come from the artist, not the record label.

'So, if I'm working with an artist for the first time, I'll arrange a meeting with them to establish their identity before undertaking any writing or recording. This is vitally important if they're an emerging talent as it's rare to find an artist who is completely self-assured in their direction. So I'll talk to them, one to one, and get to know them. Nine times out of ten, what the label has asked for and what the artist really desires are completely at odds with one another, so I'll look to find the middle ground, the one result that will please both artist and label.

'Above and beyond that consideration, I'm also searching for an angle that hasn't been worked before. The music business is so competitive that I need to bring out the unique feature of that artist. In order to do this, I go through a research-and-fact-finding mission prior to the session.

Rick Nowels says:
'I continued writing songs with the vague notion of being a solo artist. One of these songs was called "I Can't Wait". I put the track together with my friend George Black and I ended up playing it for Stevie Nicks in Los Angeles. The next night I was in the studio with Stevie, collaborating with her on the song. Jimmy Lovine heard it and encouraged us to finish it. It would become my first Top Ten hit. Jimmy was gracious enough to allow me to produce other tracks on the album that would become Rock A Little. Danny Goldberg, who had worked with Stevie, was managing Belinda Carlisle, the lead singer of The Go Gos, who was making a solo record. He hooked up a meeting with Belinda and myself and I got the producer gig on her record. I had two months to come up with the songs and in this time I co-wrote "Heaven Is A Place On Earth" and "Circle In The Sand" with my friend Ellen Shipley. "Heaven..." was Number One in 20 countries around the world and "Circle..." became a huge worldwide hit also. Suddenly I became known as what the business calls a "writer/producer". It was better than being a "guy with a lot of songs, trying to get a band together".'

'I would have heard the artist's previous material up front, if there is any. This gives me the musical grounding I need to establish their past form and present direction. I'll then look for my angle on the artist by talking to them and finding out what they're about – not necessarily from a musical point of view but a total overview of their life: what makes them laugh and what makes them cry; what they enjoy doing and what turns them off. I'll ask them what films they've seen and what they thought of them, what the last record they bought was, what music they're really into – and I mean *really* into, because there are loads of people in hip-hop and R&B who enjoy Oasis or Coldplay or The Foo Fighters but would never admit it in front of their peers. It's exactly those little things that the artists keep to themselves that provide the angle for a producer. I can take each little bit and mould them all into a particular formula or genre, resulting in a track that both the artist is proud of and the label wants.

'A case in point is Jamelia. Dropping her off at her home in the car one night after a session, I was flicking through the radio stations and some classical music came on and she expressed her fondness of it. That was the first nugget of musical gold that set in my brain. Another day, she turned up for a writing session and her choreographer had been saying that she was having difficulty dancing to R&B because she was basically a "bashment girl" [ie into ragga and its specific style of dance]. That was the second nugget of musical gold for me. I now knew that she was comfortable moving to ragga rhythms and that she was into classical music, so I began to blend those two styles to create her sound. It's this attention to detail of Jamelia's life that makes her sound unique.

'In this respect, an identity can't be falsified as it's generated by the artist's own personality. When I get an artist like Beverley Knight, who knows why, what and where, there's no time wasted in pinpointing the artist's musical identity; we just get on with it. As a producer and songwriter, it's my job not to change what they do but simply to highlight what they have.'

Jiant (Pete Kirtley and Tim Hawes) say:

'As working songwriters in this day and age, there are certain creative restrictions imposed, depending on the style of artist you're writing for. One of the services provided by Jiant Productions is to write songs for people who don't have the ability to write songs for themselves but maybe have the charisma, connections or vocal talent to succeed as pop acts. This is nothing new in the music business; prior to The Beatles, it was standard practice for a team of writers to provide the songs while artists performed them, without the need to have the credibility of penning them themselves. Elvis, Aretha Franklin and Frank Sinatra were all such non-composing artists, but they were certainly never considered lesser artists because of this.

'Now the public look down on manufactured pop acts, because these days being a pop star is so accessible to every kid on the block. Fifty years ago, the children growing up would never dream of going to an audition; it wasn't a talent that they considered having. Nowadays, every man and his dog can audition. You don't have to be that talented to get a Number One. It was perfectly acceptable, years ago, for the singer to be the singer and the writers to be the writers. Nowadays, to get real credibility, an artist needs to be seen to be writing their own material.'

In summary, the ability of a songwriter to work and write with an artist is crucial, since it's arguably the best route to getting a song recorded and released. A songwriter therefore needs to work with artists early in their career, and when collaborating the focus has to be on expressing the artist's unique identity.

GETTING CUTS: WRITING TO BRIEFS

'I want a cross between Judas Priest and Atomic Kitten.' – Record-company brief

Writing to briefs is an acquired and necessary skill of the professional songwriter looking for cuts. Record companies today – particularly those operating in the pop genre – require a specific sound for their acts and circulate 'briefs' describing their requirements to songwriters, who can then pitch tracks in the style of past hits or of two or three recent successful songs blended together. This means that a songwriter not only has to present demos of a certain quality and presentation level to get a look in, but they also have to create to precise guidelines.

The same is true in other spheres of the commercial music industry. Writers of music for advertisements and films are also given briefs outlining the exact length of the music required, the genre, the type of sound and, often, the instrumentation as well.

A brief will contain a description of the required piece of music and a deadline for submission. This deadline can sometimes be so extraordinarily tight that, once a brief comes in, the songwriter must deliver the finished song in a matter of days, and sometimes even as little as three hours, in order to take advantage of the opportunity.

The actual descriptions of briefs vary considerably, from the obvious to ambiguous to the outrageous. 'When briefs are distributed in the music industry, few executives honestly know how to articulate their needs or provide a new or fresh direction to work towards,' explains Jiant Productions' Pete Kirtley. 'The briefs are usually restricted to references to a recent track that's been successful. Whatever the brief says – for example, "Gareth Gates looking for New Radicals with Justin Timberlake" – it always comes down to one thing: "Write another hit like the last one."'

Wise Buddah describe their experience of writing to briefs: 'As we come from a radio background, we're very big on briefs. The more specific the brief, the easier it is to write a song to and the better the result. If somebody says, "We want a second single for artist X and it has to sound like a cross between Y and Z, with a bit of W thrown in," that's the best type of brief, although it's rare for anyone in A&R to be that specific. We used to do a lot of radio jingles and we'd often get briefs from client saying, "We want a jingle for blah and it has to sound really green with a bit of blue and with a touch of yellow." This sort of brief meant nothing in real terms, but if they provided a specific brief saying, "We want a jingle that sounds like that track by that artist," that resulted in a far better track for them.

'The briefs in pop music generally come in the form of "We need a single for this artist and it has to be up-tempo, a bit like a cross between this track and that track." Whilst not emulating the previous hits, at least we have a direction to work in'.

In order to be able to work to briefs effectively, therefore, a songwriter needs to be adept at translating a record company's description and reading between the lines. For songwriter Wayne Hector, it's about doing the right research for a project: 'It's doing what I call "homework", which is basically listening to what the record company have said and listening to the feel of the artist's previous music. After I've been listening to that for about a week and I'm in that mindset, I find it easier to write in that direction. For instance, I did a swing album last year with Matt Dusk, and basically I listened to Nat "King" Cole, Frank Sinatra and Tony Bennett for two months before I even started putting pen to paper. By that time, it had sunk in a little bit and we were in that mentality to write great swing songs, like "On The Street Where You Live".'

However, success with briefs doesn't always mean following the description to the letter. This is why Pete and Tim of Jiant Productions don't always submit tracks that match the brief precisely, instead sometimes purposefully going against the grain: 'The trick with briefs is to completely contradict them,' explains Pete. 'If the record company is looking for something in the vein of "Believe" by Cher, then every writer will go in and produce lukewarm, watered-down versions of that track. They'll get the singer to sound exactly the same and use the Vocoder to death. This approach rapidly becomes very uninspiring, as the A&R teams end up hearing 40 or 50 versions of the same kind of non-song. Consequently, if you present a track that's completely left or slightly right of expectation, it will stand out. The absolute fact is that, no matter who the artist is, whatever their style, a hit is a hit, and when the artist or whoever hears it, they'll want your song. They'll make it work for themselves.'

However, Pete and Tim are quick to point out that, if the sound or song is too novel, the company will fear the track won't sell and might still reject it, so the balance between giving a record company what they want and providing them with a track that's fresh and unexpected is a fine one.

> *'Sometimes you can be so focused on pleasing somebody else that a track becomes obviously manufactured. "Can't Get You Out Of My Head" was a lot more self-indulgent because we didn't have anyone in mind when we wrote it.'*
>
> – *Cathy Dennis*

Here are eight key skills that a songwriter needs in order to be able to write successfully to briefs:

1 .Be adept at translating other people's requirements;

2. Understand the medium you're writing for – ie records, TV, adverts or film – as this will give the 'employer' confidence;

3. Stay current with music in all popular genres;

4. Be aware of the specific audience you're targeting;

5. Maintain a strong network so that you're on the receiving end of the record company's mailing list for briefs;

6. Be willing to research new styles of music;

7. Develop your skills in a studio so that you can work up demos quickly;

8. Be able to work to a deadline.

GETTING CUTS:
GETTING MUSIC INTO FILM AND TV

BY IVAN CHANDLER,
SORCERER OF SONG, MUSICALITIES LIMITED

The focus for promoting music in television and film productions has become more important for composers and publishers in today's marketplace. This is not only because of the increase in the number of television channels and independent film production, which has created more opportunities for music creators, but also because of the limited opportunities available for placing 'outside' songs with recording artists, who mostly have their own production teams. However, film and television work has always been attractive for composers, particularly, for the following reasons:

- The kudos;

- The credits (mostly in films);

- The licence (or 'synch') fees;

- The residuals, such as PRS income;

- The spin-offs, such as soundtrack albums.

But how do you go about placing music in the audio-visual arena in the first place? Unless you're very lucky, with a lot of hard work!

The whole area has become extremely competitive and TV producers are spoilt for choice, being inundated with CDs that mostly don't get heard. After all, every producer has many other aspects of the production to look after; choosing music is just one part of the production process.

As in life, in the entertainment field people often make choices based on personal recommendation, and I've often been working on a film where, after suggesting various composers for the score, the director nevertheless decides on someone he or she has known for years. It's mostly where the staff of a production company have a problem with licensing their first choice of music that they start making calls to publishers, composers (and their agents) and, of course, music advisers and supervisors. Therefore, the need to be ready with a good package is fundamental, as decisions often need to be made quickly – on many occasions, by the next day!

However, just because you find an opportunity, don't tarnish your reputation by sending in something inappropriate. When I ran Motown's publishing company in the 1980s, record producers and A&R managers would appreciate it when, after contacting me for a song for a particular artist, I would say that I really didn't feel I had anything that was quite right. Naturally, at the same time, if I genuinely felt I had something that might suit, I would make a point of sending just one title. No one wants to be sifting through a whole bunch of material that doesn't fit the brief.

The most crucial aspect of television and film work is that of copyright. Rights clearances for TV and film producers can be become quite complex, so – for example – don't submit a track that contains samples unless you know that all the other parties involved will approve their usage and provide user-friendly terms.

Also, as I point out regularly to record companies who send me tracks with big orchestral backings, the Musicians' Union require a payment of £208 per player when a record is used in a feature film where all media clearance is required.

So, if you feel that your music really has potential for film or television, where do you start?

- Conducting some research into what's up and coming in production can bring many new openings for composers and publishers.

- Subscribing to *Screen International*, *Broadcast* and various tip sheets is an excellent way of finding out what's going on in production and of giving you the chance to get in early with your pitch.

- The PACT directory, available from the Producers' Alliance for Cinema and Television (www.pact.co.uk), gives details of many independent UK production companies.

- If you have the time and money, attending international film and television festivals can provide a great opportunity to network and meet producers and directors outside the confines of offices and film sets.

- Present your material professionally and creatively.

- Don't expect responses immediately, so do follow up after you've sent your demo, but don't pester anyone. Being quietly persistent is the key. Try to arrange meetings so that your face gets around. If no one appears to want to take a meeting, casually drop by the company's offices one day. Make sure you take another copy of your demo.

- MP3s and/or website links are becoming the favoured way by which people listen and access music, but if you choose this route then make sure that the person to whom you are promoting material is able to work in this way. Furthermore, try to find out who is the key person responsible for choosing the music at the production company. This is often the director, but if there's no music supervisor involved, the key person may be the producer, the music editor or even the post-production supervisor.

- Finally, concentrate on one area of music. Even though many composers are capable of working in a variety of genres, a lot of people in the business tend to relate particular styles to individual composers.

When the opportunity arises and you're asked to submit, deliver on time with the right music and within the given budget.

Once you have your foot in the door and have received your first commission or have placed your first track, you're then in a position to develop the relationship and introduce other facts about the music you have to offer. You might also be able to negotiate better terms, depending on the producer's available budget and distribution arrangements.

Above all, there's so much music around today that's predictable, safe and unimaginative that, if you present some music that's exciting, inspirational and produced to the highest standards, this should give you an edge. But unless you can get it heard, it might as well stay on your hard drive.

There are so many people trying to get into writing music for film and TV that you must be passionate about the music you're promoting and determined to be successful. Moreover, you must be prepared to stick at it however long it might take because, while the film and television industries run a lot more efficiently than the music business, they're also very unpredictable.

THE SONGWRITER:

MARK FISHLOCK

WORKING TO DEADLINES

Media composers are used to working quickly. Deadlines are always too soon and even though the project might have been at various stages of development for many months, it's incredible how often the composer is brought in weeks or even days before the contracted completion date.

Fortunately, I like to work quickly. It leaves no time for prevarication, which has always been a problem of mine. It also guards against over-writing and, when recording the tracks, over-production. Within reason, the first idea has to be the one you go with, and while there will inevitably be songs that could have been better, the strike rate is surprisingly high.

The most intense schedule I've had to face is 44 songs in just under three weeks, from receiving the lyrics to completion of the recording. Generally speaking, the writing is the easy bit and certainly the most fun. Programming the tracks becomes draining by about song number 30, and you really do start to go nuts trying to find new sounds and new arrangements.

I write away from the studio, not least because I know I'll be spending more than my fair share of time in front of that darned computer screen. I also prefer the flexibility of pencil, manuscript paper and eraser to composing directly into the computer. It sounds like it should be the real thing far too soon and I'd miss the physical element of screwing up bits of paper or drawing big black lines though naff ideas.

You can't afford the luxury of writers' block, although on a big job there's a huge difference between a productive and an unproductive day. I always expect more of the latter as the deadline approaches, so being able to pace myself is very important. Like an elastic band on the propeller of a toy plane, fatigue at the end of a project really slows down one's productivity.

All composers have their idiosyncrasies, and at the start of every job I draw a chart. Having to come up with 44 songs in three weeks sounds scary, but for some reason it looks more achievable when it's written down. I number the 'cues', or song titles, and create three boxes for each labelled 'W', 'P' and 'M'. As soon as a song has been written, programmed or mixed, I fill in the relevant box with a luminous yellow marker pen. This may sound like the behaviour of a composer who needs to get out more, but it becomes a huge psychological boost because, as the page turns from white to yellow, there's visible evidence that you're making progress. With that amount of material to produce, it's easy to fall off the schedule and find you still have seven songs to do and only a day to do them, and the final days before a deadline aren't the time to be faced with the most intensive output. The chart makes sure you stay on track and, like opening the windows of an Advent calendar, there's a curious pleasure in counting down the days to the deadline.

I also set myself targets for each working day: three songs, four songs – it depends on the schedule. If I under-perform, I try to catch up the following day. This might sound a bit picky but the only date that counts is the deadline, and there are no allowances made for creative flakiness. Singers will have been booked, the client will probably have flown over from Germany, Spain or wherever, and if you turn up three songs short, you're unlikely to be working for that producer again.

THE COMPLETE SONGWRITER: AN ANTIDOTE TO INDUSTRY SHORT-TERMISM

BY JONATHAN LITTLE

This section considers some of the consequences of the present-day short-termism of major record labels and publishers, who, in all fairness, are beset by increasingly substantial development and marketing costs whenever they sign new talent. Technology has, once again, enabled several traditionally separate functions to be undertaken by a single individual, so that the truly competent songwriter/producer, for instance, can now potentially do everything from create new sounds to master a demo recording, or even produce the final master recording itself. But the demands on such individuals, or songwriting teams, are clearly heavier than ever. A useful case study in this respect is provided by Jiant Productions' Tim Hawes and Pete Kirtley, who won an Ivor Novello Award with their single 'Pure And Simple', written for the TV-generated pop group Hear'Say. The era of the single musical specialism seems to be passing, with the truly successful and long-lived composer-musicians of tomorrow likely to be multi-specialists within their chosen field.

The successful modern songwriter needs to be so much more than a simple tunesmith. Where once the Jerome Kerns and Irving Berlins of this world could present their publisher with the mere outline of their latest number, hammered out on a much-used and -abused upright piano, today a whole string of complex technological and business phases will probably have elapsed before most serious songwriters will dare approach their publisher or, indeed, hand over a song to a record company. As a vital complement to the traditional craft of composition, production and music-business skills are also becoming a necessity in an environment where record companies are increasingly demanding that songwriters present them with a product so polished that it could easily go straight to market. This state of affairs is largely the result of increasing pressure to drive down the now substantial front-end costs that record companies must bear. Gone, therefore, are the days when many publishers and record companies would consider investing a substantial amount of time, effort and lucre in developing many of their newly signed songwriters – and, indeed, in nurturing most of their performers, too.

In the past decade, a new musical culture has been forming, one that owes less and less to individual creativity and more and more to the decisions of multinational music companies over where – or whether – to slot expendable performers and independent songwriters in and out of standardised, made-to-order, market-ready formats. The traditional nurturing of artists and songwriters by recording and publishing companies is increasingly being farmed out to partnerships, small companies and even educational establishments, who, paradoxically, can often least afford to put forward the funds for such endeavours.

The recent TV craze of searching for instant pop stars through much-hyped national talent quests is correspondingly symptomatic of the desire to discover stars who no longer require intensive further training before their careers can be launched. Crucially, from a record company's point of view, such instant stars already have serious media exposure and a solid fan base before they even cross the threshold of a recording studio to cut their first disc. While a singer with the longevity of Cliff Richard might lament this state of affairs, arguing that such a transient and mercenary philosophy to cultivating new talent risks incurring premature performer burnout, this latest corporate attitude to finding and exploiting the talent of singers and songwriters is now so widespread that it seems unlikely to change (although there are indications that a backlash has begun with such bands as Athlete, Keane and The Delays). In an industry already infamous for its fickle treatment of performers and composers, any new device that helps record companies to acquire product with minimal up-front costs is eagerly embraced.

A further manifestation of this phenomenon can be seen in the growing tendency displayed by the 'Big Five' multinational music corporations towards encouraging the licensing and mass selling of the musical product of small independent labels, or else endlessly exploiting the back catalogues of multi-platinum-selling artists (or inventing novel and frequently implausible reasons for assembling compilation albums), often in preference of developing new talent. In such situations, independent labels become the most important A&R sources for the five corporate giants. The competitive need to reduce expensive product-development costs, coupled with the need for greater economies of scale in producing music, are seen as very real commercial pressures.

The public themselves are becoming unwitting conspirators in this general trend, too. Of 2,474 respondents to a *Billboard* magazine poll, nearly 40 per cent reported that, with remastering to improve sound quality, as well as bonus tracks and more extensive liner notes, they see it as good value to purchase an updated version of an album they already own.[1] By sticking to a tried and true musical product, this makes it less likely that the growing number of older and more musically conservative customers, in developed countries at least – such as the USA and Britain – will risk investing in any new product sung by what they see as fly-by-night pop stars. A vicious circle of conservatism is then perpetuated by major record companies, who insist that by repackaging old favourites they're merely delivering what their customers want.

To compensate, the battle for the youth market is becoming characterised by the extraordinarily frenzied marketing of any performer or performers able to generate a sudden and large following. Such short-termism is nothing new, of course; it has been an increasing trend in the pop and general music market for more than two decades. Now, however, it does seem to be reaching an unsustainable critical mass. UK pop songwriter Alison Clarkson (formerly known as the early-'90s performer Betty Boo) has been outspoken in her condemnation of hurriedly formed, audition-based, 'disposable' pop groups, arguing that such formulaic approaches to music-making will ultimately do irreparable damage to the industry. If this trend continues unabated, Clarkson fears, audiences will become very cynical about pop talent, and natural musical evolution could be restricted through excessive product control.[2]

A fine case study of this whole phenomenon is provided by the manufactured British group Hear'Say and one of their leading songwriting teams, Tim Hawes and Pete Kirtley of Jiant Productions. Hear'Say were a group of three girls and two boys – all singers, who danced appropriately choreographed dance routines for each of their numbers – who were the successful finalists in a UK TV series titled *PopStars*, a show aimed at putting together a new, mixed girl/boy band from the best contestants nationwide.[3] Even the producers of the prime-time television series couldn't have predicted the enormous national success of the show, which has subsequently led to eponymous imitators as far afield as Denmark (generating girl band Music Metals) and the US (generating girl band Eden's Crush and rival boy band O-Town), as well as imitators in several other countries worldwide, including Germany (who assembled an all-girl trio in the mould of US chart songstresses Destiny's Child or the UK's Atomic Kitten).

The *PopStars* format originated, in fact, in Australia (delivering up girl band Bardot), but it was the astonishing appeal of the UK version that proved the vital catalyst in demonstrating that the format could be easily transformed into a viable, standardised, global product. And the particular strength of this particular product, moreover, is that it keeps generating more and more product, in the form of both imitators and marketing spin-offs derived from each prefabricated group's music and image. Not surprisingly, then, there was also a follow-up show in Britain aimed at identifying a new solo artist, titled *Pop Idol*, while the Fox Television Network in the US aired its own version of the show as *American Idol*.

As a group, Britain's Hear'Say had the envious reputation of having achieved an instant debut Number One hit with 'Pure And Simple', which was on its eighth remix within a year of its release. Indeed, such was the media frenzy created by *PopStars* that Hear'Say's young fans were primed well in advance to help the ready-made pop act set a UK singles-chart record for the biggest-selling first-week sales tally by a new artist.[4]

Significantly, in addition to selling records, Hear'Say made a huge amount of money – and in an extraordinarily short time – from merchandising, the marketing of products to which their name was linked. In short, merchandising has – perhaps appropriately – been the real bonanza for these manufactured musical 'frontmen', the creation of TV- and record-company executives. On 3 October 2001, it was reported in London's *Evening Standard* newspaper that at least 30 companies had already made licensing deals with Hear'Say by the time the *PopStars* TV series came to its conclusion, in February that year. The lesson is clear: gather revenue any way you can, while you can, in case the fad doesn't last. Indeed, when group member Kym Marsh left Hear'Say due to the 'brutal' rollercoaster pressure of the unrelenting touring, recording and public appearances required by their record company in order to build the band into a 'brand', this initiated a downward spiral that led to the entire group disbanding within two years of its first phenomenal success.

Hear'Say's record label, Polydor (owned by Universal), has easily netted in excess of £100 million ($150 million) from merchandising deals, leaving aside the further income they've derived from sales of singles, albums, concert tickets and airplay. A Polydor spokesperson put it this way: 'Merchandising and endorsement deals have always been an important part of the music business, especially the pop-music business. Hear'Say is an extremely strong brand which a lot of companies want to come on board with.'[5]

The band members themselves also managed to do quite well, allegedly earning around £100,000 a month from such merchandising deals, and of course significant further revenue from their first national tour, their two hit singles ('Pure And Simple' and 'The Way To Your Love'), their debut album, the *PopStars* show and their ubiquitous media and public appearances. Guided by their manager, Hear'Say agreed to have their name linked to everything from cakes to watches, as well as endorsing products by companies such as car manufacturers Peugeot and even the biggest multinational software producer of them all, Microsoft.

In the four decades since the outbreak of Beatlemania, the music marketing machine has not only grown more sophisticated but is now integral to the development of such manufactured bands. Some managers even consider in advance what product band members might most appropriately by able to endorse and factor this into their anticipated revenue streams. And, unlike The Beatles, some contemporary performers are positively discouraged from writing their own songs, on the advice of their managers or their record company's A&R department.

Before Hear'Say came along, Tim Hawes and Pete Kirtley were successful mainstream pop songwriters, when composing both individually or as a team, though their early years in the business had certainly been a struggle, with some hard lessons learned along the way. They've lately written for several established UK Top 40 acts, including The Honeyz, 5ive, Stephen Gately, The Spice Girls and Girl Thing, yet it was only relatively recently that they came to form their own production company, Jiant Productions.[6] They had to set up this company in a hurry in response to the fact that they'd reached a stage where they were working on a regular basis with major labels, who made it clear that they preferred to deal with people who could supply the whole songwriting and production package. Tim and Pete were effectively responding in business terms to a trend that had become recognisable just a few years earlier and US record producer Kashif Michael Jones had pointed out in his 1996 book *Everything You'd Better Know About The Record Industry*. 'In the music industry of the 1990s,' Kashif argued, 'the role of the songwriter who just writes songs and doesn't produce or is not an artist is diminishing rapidly.'[7] Indeed, Tim and Pete not only write songs and produce records now, but they also do nearly all of the administration (the business aspect), as they have no employees. Successful they might be today, but they're working hard for it – seemingly eight days a week, as The Beatles put it.

This phenomenon is symptomatic of the way in which music-industry service organisations are re-inventing themselves in response to changes in the business. Record companies are moving towards becoming solely global marketing and distribution conglomerates, selecting their music and artists from a new group of hastily formed management companies, agencies and production companies. These companies, in turn, control increasingly large rosters of composers, artists, producers and techies (usually sound programmers and engineers), who are leased (usually on a very short-term basis) for any current record- or publishing-company project but are rarely employed directly by a major company.

For the major record labels, the only way of recouping most investments in new artists today is to find those who will sell globally, not just nationally. Like modern book-publishing executives, today's major record-company decision-makers are increasingly reluctant to sign artists who have only national appeal. This fact doesn't bode well for the nurturing of musical individuality and diversity, as global products tend to be homogenised items that belong to no particular culture at all. It's against such a background that modern songwriters must try to tailor and place their songs.

In June 2001, Jiant Productions took up an offer to base themselves in the Academy of Contemporary Music's Rodboro Buildings in Guildford, outside London, from where they run most of their recording sessions today. The ACM is a popular music-education institution, running courses in music performance, music technology and music business, including a two-year intensive degree course integrating all three streams. It is the vision of the founders of the Academy, Pete Anderton and Phil Brookes, to encourage more in-house industry links – such as that with Jiant Productions – for the mutual benefit of both students and industry professionals. (Such harmonious industry/education integration is a long-held government ideal but one that has rarely, if ever, been fully realised).

During talks to the students given by the Jiant team, it has emerged that the practice of professional songwriting differs considerably from student expectations of what the day-to-day craft of modern songwriting must be like. This fact was confirmed, for example, when the songwriting duo held auditions to take on an 'apprentice' and, ironically, had difficulty finding more than a handful of novice first-year degree students with a detailed understanding of how songs are composed and produced for the contemporary pop scene. The need for such industry-education partnerships was never more strikingly demonstrated. Music students might certainly be trained well, even in vocational subjects, but few, it would seem, are regularly exposed to current industry practice at the majority of educational institutions.

Something that students have clearly learned from their interaction with Tim Hawes and Pete Kirtley, however, is that songwriting remains one per cent inspiration and 99 per cent perspiration. The songwriters readily admitted that it took them three minutes to compose the outline of 'Pure And Simple' but three months to put together the track to the satisfaction of record company Polydor. They described how their own workload hasn't been lessened by modern industry structures as, while music publishers are certainly fulfilling their traditional role of helping to place the duo's songs with potential performers, Tim and Pete must nevertheless spend a great deal of time networking with anyone looking for songs. They pointed out that often, when they could be composing, they're on the phone, trying to secure placement of their songs, either off the back of contacts suggested by publishers or, more frequently, through their own vital and extensive network of contacts, in addition to their own managers' efforts.

Completely unlike the traditional notion of a songwriting partnership, where one member specialises in lyrics and the other in music, the members of Jiant fulfil each of the roles equally well. They then criticise and try to improve upon each other's contributions – whether these are lyrical or musical – until, as a team, they feel satisfied with the final product. Tim and Pete are, therefore, the complete antithesis of such famous collaborations as those between Bernie Taupin and Elton John or Tim Rice and Andrew Lloyd Webber, teams whose members almost exclusively stick to their respective roles as either lyricist or composer. While reluctant to talk in too much detail about the mysterious art of song composition, Tim and Pete admit that, 'While our thought processes and musical styles as songwriters are very different, we each bring something unique to the process. We've learned the need for compromise, and together we seem to produce better material than we do separately. It's not the case that one writes the lyrics and one does the music; we want to do all parts of the process and hammer songs out that way.'[8]

Both Tim and Pete started out in the music business as performers and then decided that they'd prefer instead to be songwriters. Tim's manager (also the manager of Hear'Say) first introduced him to Pete, and thus the partnership was born. In the early days, Tim had written three songs for The Spice Girls, and he got his initial publishing deal through this association. It proved to be Tim's first real rung on the ladder. In their first incarnation, these now world-famous representatives of girl power – the ultimate in manufactured pop – were known by the name Touch (ie you can look but you can't touch!). It was while in Woking-based Trinity Studios in 1994, in the midst of co-writing and recording the song 'Sugar And Spice' with the group, that Tim pointed out just what 'spicy girls' they really were – and the name stuck. Tim confides that the major reason his own early bands (and songs) didn't happen is because he didn't then appreciate the need for networking.

While speaking about contemporary pop songwriting, Tim and Pete stress that record companies require you to write very specifically to a brief. In response, they'll first get a vibe about a potential new song, establish the groove of a backing track, then try to 'discover' the chorus – perhaps feeding a singer the lines – and so it builds up. But if you're a pop songwriter, there's very little scope to explore any new genre or any strikingly new sound that the record company hasn't heard before.[9] If this seems ironic in a so-called creative profession, the news gets worse: once a brief comes in, the deadlines these days are so extraordinarily tight that the songwriter must deliver on demand in a matter of days, and sometimes even hours. A delivery time of three hours, for example, isn't unheard of in a studio context. Clearly, today's record companies wait for no man.

On Hear'Say's second album, the songwriting competition was necessarily more fierce. Even though Tim and Pete had been asked to make a significant contribution to the album, other top writers also joined the fray, so that Polydor ended up with about 60 solidly crafted pop tracks from which to choose for the 12-track album. In such cases, at least three-quarters of the songs usually end up coming from sources other than the originally favoured insiders. And it's not always friendly competition, either; with big money at stake, fortunes can turn on musical politics and finance. With large future royalties as the bait, managers, singers and publishers all want a slice of the action. But ultimately – and certainly compared to the performers – each one of the album's songwriters will end up being the least recognised among industry stars and will consequently often feel relatively badly treated due to such lack of recognition in comparison to that of many other music-industry personnel.

So, for most professional songwriter/producers, even those with a huge amount of specialist knowledge in a host of musical, technological and business areas, the industry remains tough and Lady Luck often elusive. Guy Fletcher, former Chairman of the British Academy of Composers & Songwriters, puts it bluntly; 'Most writers who make it into the charts have more than paid their dues with months or years of disappointment and sometimes downright failure.'[10]

The hit track 'Pure And Simple', for instance, was written (in outline) two years prior to release in Tim Hawes's garage, and initially it was rejected by some big names. But for a twist of fate – which hinged on the last-minute interest of an established record producer – the public might never even have heard of the track today. While 'Pure And Simple' is undoubtedly a classically crafted pop song, few would put the phenomenal sales of the single down to the songwriters' – or, indeed, the performers' – talent alone. The huge success of the single represents nothing less than the triumph of marketing over musical raw material. As the media composer and songwriter Mark Fishlock observed of the new industry extreme, the road to stardom is today more likely to be laid down by someone with a marketing diploma, and a performer's songs are 'as likely to be chosen for them as their haircut or the width of their flares'.[11]

With repeated free promotion over several weeks on prime-time British national television, any decent single can't really fail in today's 'everyone can be a pop star for 15 minutes' atmosphere. Such marketing pressure also means that the number of successful pop bands formed entirely by themselves is today declining in favour of production-line pop, where a chosen few artists spend all day being interviewed, touring, performing and recording while their alter egos – the songwriters – spend all day writing, producing, learning new technical tricks and conducting their business. Even the bands that form independently of management and record companies are increasingly meeting on the audition circuit, whereas bands in the past simply got together through a love of creating the same music and then would spend months, rather than merely weeks, honing their sound before approaching a record company. Thankfully, this is a trend that appears to be returning with the recent emergence of such acts as The Libertines, Snow Patrol and Franz Ferdinand.

Undoubtedly, Tim Hawes and Pete Kirtley will write better songs than 'Pure And Simple', as will other similarly competent songwriters, but it's worth remembering that many such songs will never see the light of day, often on the whim of a record-company executive. Alison Clarkson, who also collaborated on 'Pure And Simple', seemed disappointed that she hadn't been asked to contribute more songs for million-sellers Hear'Say, and in an interview went as far as to claim that the song-selection system is now 'very crooked'. She argued that, as owners of their own music-publishing companies, a 'good handful of really high-powered executives' often reject songs not penned by songwriters already signed to their own companies.[12]

Clearly, the next generation of successful songwriters will need to learn as many industry-relevant specialist skills as possible. They will have to be truly clever composers if they're to become commercially successful, because they might well have to operate within the formidable straitjacket of increasingly precise musical briefs while fighting to retain some individuality and artistic integrity. Past lessons show that they will have to network constantly to keep abreast of what record companies want at any given moment in time because, in the new music-industry culture now evolving, the 'suits' still largely dictate to the creators of music, telling them exactly when and where their services are required.

In such a environment, highly skilled and knowledgeable songwriters and artists will have to be able to compose and perform music that is increasingly acceptable to a global audience and be sanguinely prepared to make the inevitable compromises that might dilute or dissipate any musical novelty. And, while also being keenly aware of the pitfalls of financial and legal politics, tomorrow's successful composers and artists will need to keep persisting long after the other 99 per cent have given up and gone home.

NOTES

1   Report carried in the www.billboard.com 'Daily Music Update' for 9 November 2001.

2   In Alexis Petridis's 'The Power Behind Pop', *The Guardian*, Friday Review (23 November 2001). Within this article on who's writing for whom, Petridis gives examples to illustrate the fact that many of the biggest UK chart successes of 2001 were penned by ex-artists who now largely rely on manufactured songsters in order to sell their product to a very young target audience. Interestingly, the decline of investment by major record companies in guitar-based bands continued alongside the rise of management-assembled pop groups, although some industry pundits believe that guitar bands are certain to increase in the coming years.

3   The five members of the group were Noel Sullivan, Danny Foster, Kym Marsh, Suzanne Shaw and Myleene Klass.

4   The single 'Pure And Simple', written by Tim Hawes, Pete Kirtley and Alison Clarkson, sold 550,000 copies in its British debut week. One hundred and sixty thousand units alone were shifted on the first day of release. Clarkson was disheartened by the fact that she never met Hear'Say or, indeed, had any input into how the song could best be shaped for the group. By contrast, she points out, when she was a performer/songwriter in her own right in the late '80s and early '90s, she was consulted by everyone from video directors to art designers.

5   Quoted in Richard Simpson's 'How Hear'Say Hype Is Making Them Millions', *Evening Standard*, 3 October 2001.

6   Such a production company could be established as a limited-liability company or as a sole trader.

7   Kashif Michael Jones (with contributions from Gary Greenberg), *Everything You'd Better Know About The Music Industry* (Brooklyn Boy Books, USA, 1996), p52.

8   Pete Kirtley in an informal lecture on songwriting delivered at the Academy of Contemporary Music, 13 September 2001.

9   At a time when composers are less and less willing to be boxed into narrow musical categories, with all sorts of musical crossovers now possible, record companies seem to be moving in the opposite direction.

10   Quoted in *The Works*, the in-house magazine of the British Academy of Composers & Songwriters, issue 8 (London, 2001).

11   *The Works*, issue 8 (London, 2001).

12   Alexis Petridis, 'The Power Behind Pop', *The Guardian*, Friday Review (23 November 2001).

Seven Survival Philosophies
For The Professional Songwriter

1. **Believe in yourself.** As lyricist Don Black explains, 'You have to be confident in your own ability, that there's only one of you and there's no one else like you. As John Barry once said, a little arrogance in a songwriter is not a bad thing. It doesn't mean that you have to be bolshy and flash, but you have to have the courage of your convictions.' Without this confidence in your abilities, it will be difficult to handle the reality of rejection and you'll be on the floor before you've even started.

2. **Accept the fact of rejection.** Every songwriter experiences rejection at some point during their career. Even the most successful writers have had songs turned down or projects dismissed. The industry is so competitive that rejection is a basic fact of life. As Richard Kerr acknowledges, 'It's much harder today for a songwriter – no matter whether you've had a hit or not – simply to get your songs covered.' Come to terms with this reality. Don't let your passion for the craft turn to bitterness simply because your song has been turned down by the 99th publisher. Keep trying!

Wayne Hector says:
'Success isn't just about taking advantage of opportunities; it's also about persistence and commitment. A case in point is my first Number One record, a song called "Flava", performed by Peter Andre. Now, the day I wrote that song for Peter I had almost cancelled the appointment. I really, really did not want to write. I hadn't slept for a while, I felt completely drained and I simply couldn't be bothered to get up and do the session, but Jackie, my manager, bugged me until I fulfilled the commitment. That was the day I wrote my first Number One. After that, all the doors opened.

'Now, it's very hard for a writer starting off to get those doors opened, because nobody is going to open them for you; you have to make your own opportunities. There are many fantastic writers out there. Some have been discovered but there are so many that haven't. The only difference between those two sets of people is the opportunities they've had, or created. A songwriter has to be determined to push, to knock on doors, to talk to people. The more people you talk to and the more people you give your music to, the more likely that it will happen for you. There's no cast-iron way of getting into the industry but, from my own experience, I can honestly advise a writer to take advantage of every situation that presents itself, even the ones that you don't think are going to be that important.'

3. **Perseverance is your greatest strength.** As Confucius wrote, 'Our greatest glory is not in never falling but in rising every time we fall.' Carrying on writing and persistently promoting your songs is your primary weapon to defeating this cycle of rejection. With the right material, success becomes just a numbers game; luck, after all, is merely preparation meeting opportunity.

4. **Create your own luck.** On the heels of the previous point, you need to be pro-active as a songwriter. Write that song; learn to produce; hire a session singer; record some demos; join the Academy. Then, with the preparation in place, make opportunities for yourself through networking: talk to people; listen out for writing opportunities; make certain people are aware that you're looking for work or have suitable songs available. In the music business, you won't get to where you need to be if you hold back.

5. **Stay true to your vision.** This relates to point one, about believing in yourself. As Stewart Copeland, ex-drummer with The Police, once said, 'There's something very scary about being unique.' If you have a particular musical vision that feels right, pursue it. Writers who self-consciously court approval by following this or that fashion tend to have very short or non-existent careers. Take The Carpenters, for instance. With regard to their unexpected success, Karen Carpenter observed, 'We came out right in the middle of the hard-rock period... It was hard rock everywhere! But we were ready to make our music. And it was such a turnaround, I guess it caught people by surprise.' There are countless further examples of highly accomplished artists who have followed their instinct against the commercial dictates of the music industry, such as Norah Jones and Joss Stone, for whom commercial success was a welcome by-product of their musical vision.

6. **Be objective.** Having the right perspective on your work will enable you to become the best songwriter you can be. It's important, therefore, to develop the ability to edit your own work. As Rob Davis advises, 'For people who want to write songs, I recommend that they become their own A&R person. [They need to] listen to what they've done and judge it against what's happening today and be honest with themselves about its quality before offering it around.'

Furthermore, you need to able to accept constructive criticism about your work. Learn how to deal with positive and negative feedback on equal terms. Listen to the criticism and honestly assess the song in the light of those suggestions before applying whatever changes you consider appropriate. If you're capable of learning from the criticism and enjoying the praise, but at the same time not getting personally caught up in it all, your skills as a songwriter are guaranteed to improve.

7. **Enjoy the experience**. Although it sounds obvious, this is a philosophy often forgotten by many. Songwriting is both a creative art and a commercial business, and you need to learn how to enjoy both experiences for what they are. If you're not getting pleasure from being a songwriter, you're missing the point. You might as well be a lawyer, accountant or sales manager, in which cases you're at least guaranteed to earn a decent living! Every phase of your career is important, from the first song to your first Number One, and every experience is part of your professional development as a songwriter, so enjoy it.

MIND

THE HISTORY OF SONGWRITING

Mind: The History Of Songwriting

Introduction

'I'm always amazed when I talk to young songwriters who aren't familiar with Bob Dylan or John Lennon and who don't have any connection to Joni Mitchell or Leonard Cohen or any of the great writers. To me, it's like being an artist and not being familiar with Picasso or any of the great painters who provided a great foundation to spring from.'

– Sheryl Crow

Every great songwriter acknowledges the vital importance of having an extensive knowledge of music of the past and present. Don Black, for instance, is adamant that one of the key factors in his ability as a lyricist is that he was brought up on the traditional songwriting methods of Sammy Cahn, Johnny Mercer, Lorenz Hart and Stephen Sondheim. 'This provided a great grounding to be a songwriter,' he says. 'To be a lyricist, you have to study all the great lyric writers. You need to understand why their lyrics are marvellous.'

By studying songwriters who have been successful, analysing their techniques, breaking down their song structures and listening to their use of sounds, textures and vocal arrangements, you'll soon begin to recognise the elements that make a song truly great.

'Fall in love with the song. Fall in love with the art of the song and study all the nuances. Study how the great songwriters put their songs together. Why did they do that? Why did they do this? Why is that melody going on? If it emotionally moves you, find out why.'

– Barry Gibb, songwriter and artist

Listening to a wide range of genres will help you to absorb musical influences, blend them into your own compositional style and, from there, to discover or develop your own unique writing identity. Songwriter Wayne Hector expands on this: 'Different musical styles have different formats, structures and tricks that you may not normally think of yourself, so if I had a piece of advice to give any songwriter it would be to listen to the great songwriters. Even if you're not into a particular type of music, listen to it.

New ideas may be brought to your attention that can then be used in your own songwriting.'

Great songs are also a wonderful source of inspiration. Simply listening to them can help to break a creative block. Even more importantly, you should always get pleasure from playing, writing or listening to music, but if you lose that pleasure factor, listening to great songs should remind you why you wanted to write in the first place. Great songs feed great songwriting.

With regard to this point, the following section is dedicated to the evolution of the song and the great songwriters who have featured in its vibrant history. The section 'A Brief History Of The Popular Song' can only hope to provide a summary of the last two centuries of the popular song, but if you're interested in a more in-depth study of the history of the songwriter, I suggest that you take a look at Mike Read's book *Major To Minor: The Rise And Fall Of The Songwriter* (Sanctuary Publishing, 2000).

Similarly, due to the practicalities of space within the book, the songwriters featured in the section '50 Great Songwriters Of The Last 100 Years' have been selected for their individual impact on songwriting and for the purpose of educating the aspiring songwriter. Many remarkable songwriters are missing from these pages, such as Jerome Kern, Neil Young, Willie Nelson and Bruce Welch, to name but a few, along with some of whom have already been covered via their contributions in 'Soul: The Craft Of Songwriting' – writers such as such as Barry Mason, Don Black, Billy Steinberg and Holland, Dozier and Holland. And because the impact of many contemporary artists has yet to be fully realised through the perspective of history, I've omitted writers such as the hugely successful team of Guy Chambers and Robbie Williams, the tragically short-lived but significant singer/songwriter Jeff Buckley, the acoustic songsmith Neil Finn, and even the immensely influential rapper Eminem, an artist who is responsible for taking hip-hop to a worldwide level through his ruthlessly self-aware, humorous and bluntly controversial lyrics that stick to the basic principles of quality songwriting – ie they're about subjects that people can relate to: getting wasted, girl problems, family arguments, etc. As a result, Eminem became the first hip-hop/rap artist ever to receive an Academy Award, winning in 2003 the Oscar for Best Original Song with 'Lose Yourself', featured in his semi-autobiographical movie *8 Mile*.

Many talented songwriters have been similarly honoured with Ivor Novellos and are members of the Academy, and if you're interested in learning more about these writers then visit the British Academy website www.britishacademy.com for guidance. Alternatively, for songwriters who have had a major impact on the American popular song, the Songwriters' Hall of Fame archive at www.songwritershalloffame.org offers wonderfully informative histories and detailed discographies.

A BRIEF HISTORY OF
THE POPULAR SONG

'The history of a people is found in its songs.' – Anonymous

The popular song – being defined as a commercial entity that is sold or appeals to the general public – has a vibrant but relatively short history, evolving a little over 200 years ago from English ballads, psalms and hymns of the oral tradition. English country dances such as 'Greensleeves' and Irish folk songs like 'The Girl I Left Behind Me' formed the bedrock of the popular song, while the Industrial Revolution and colonisation of America provided the impetus for the song to develop into the diverse creation that it is today.

Traditionally, music was bound by the region from which it came, passed only via of mouth. This meant that – particularly in the vast landscape of America – few songs achieved any permanence. Without radio or records, no capability of mass-printing music and the relatively static nature of the general population, there was no easy means of distributing a song, even if it proved popular.

Then the Industrial Revolution of 1800s generated the tools with which to disseminate songs. The invention of the modern printing press, the development of the upright piano and improved transportation provided songs with an outlet for distribution and gave the public an appetite for fresh material. The potential for merchandising and making money from music in this brave new world encouraged the involvement of entrepreneurs, who in turn built an industry around the song.

THE BIRTHPLACE OF THE POPULAR SONG

America is arguably the birthplace of the popular commercial song. Colonial settlers brought with them the psalms and hymns of English life, mostly in little books such as Henry Ainsworth's 1612 collection *Englished Both In Prose And Metre* and the Reverend James Lyon's *Urania: A Choice Collection Of Psalm-Tunes, Anthems And Hymns* of 1761. Other, less Puritanical settlers maintained the English ballad and country dances through word of mouth, and these secular tunes provided the musical base for what was to become the traditional folk music of the southern mountains, which in turn laid the foundations for hillbilly and country music.

As America released itself from the political shackles of Great Britain, so too did its music. By the 1780s, American colonists had established a folk heritage of their own, adapting the lyrics of English melodies to reflect the American conditions and lifestyle. The War of Independence inspired songs of liberty and patriotism, such as 'War Song' and 'The Star-Spangled Banner', while the pride that came from gaining independence prompted the creation of songs of belonging. Most popular of these is John Howard Payne and Sir Henry Bishop's 'Home Sweet Home', a song that could have been written as the blueprint for the popular song, demonstrating simplicity of melody, balance between lyric and tune and uniformity of rhythm.

Perhaps the most significant cultural development for the popular song was the importation of African slaves, who carried with them the rhythms and song traditions of their homeland. This music would eventually give rise to the blues, but prior to that the presence of black people would provide the inspiration for the first commercial vehicle for the popular song: the minstrel show.

The exploitation of the newly independent America's black population was well under way by the 1820s, when Thomas A Rice established the 'Jim Crow', a blackface characterisation that was to become the mainstay of the minstrel show. No longer was music restricted by the limitations of word of mouth; as the minstrel shows began to tour America, so songs were exposed to more and more people. Furthermore, the shows promoted each song individually and credited the songwriter for the music, thus paving the way for the professional songwriter.

'IT ALL BEGINS WITH A SONG' (LAMONT DOZIER)

In 1844, Stephen Foster had his first song published: 'Open Thy Lattice, Love'. This is significant because Foster is considered to be the first full-time songwriter of the popular song. He pioneered the concept of writing down both the lyrics and the music in sheet-music form and attempted to make a living out of having it published. (See 'The First Professional Songwriter', later in this book, for more detail on Foster's life and times.)

The following decade proved to be the breeding ground for the music-publishing industry. With the touring of the minstrel shows promoting individual songs and the increased presence of the parlour piano in homes, allowing families to play and listen to their own choice of music, there was a rapidly growing demand for sheet music from the 1850s onwards. Store owners would print sheet music by local musicians, along with books, posters, maps and stationery. Occasionally a deal was made between the owner and the songwriter whereby the latter shared in the income from the sale of the sheet music. Thus began the business of modern music publishing.

As the music arm of the business grew, these early publishers of the popular song started to employ travelling salesmen to stock their sheet music – along with the usual clothes, household supplies and miracle cures – and sell it to other music shops, individuals and local stores. Salesmen capable of playing the piano would then perform the songs to potential proprietors and customers. From this simple promotional trick evolved a fundamental element of the music industry: the concept of song plugging.

Certain salesmen began to realise the huge returns that this infant music industry could bring in and set up their own businesses that specialised solely in the publishing and promotion of songs. They effectively were their own A&R departments, researching which music was most fashionable and then either writing their own or hiring others to write similar songs. They would then hire an independent printer – or even purchase their own in-house printer – and begin the process of promoting and selling the new songs.

Tin Pan Alley

Following the American Civil War, the music-publishing and songwriting business found its epicentre in New York. All the different genres and local styles of song – from western cowboy trail songs to sophisticated East Coast sentimentals, and from southern honky-tonk minstrel songs to Midwest folk hymns and transportation songs – gravitated to this city, and in fact to one street in particular: Manhattan's West 28th Street, between Broadway and Sixth Avenue.

This area was nicknamed 'Tin Pan Alley', supposedly after a *New York Herald* reporter, Monroe Rosenfeld, heard the dissonant chords and strings of competing pianos through the open windows of different publishers' establishments and in an article compared the sound the sound to a bunch of tin pans banging together.

The reasons why the industry converged here in New York and could be supported on such a scale are fivefold. Firstly, at this time the minstrel shows of the mid-1800s were giving way to more sophisticated shows known as 'vaudeville' and 'burlesque'. These were variety shows, influenced heavily by the European operettas, and provided a range of live entertainment, comedy performances, music and speciality acts. They became hugely popular, and the stars of these shows – singers and comedians such as Fred Astaire, WC Fields and the Marx brothers – required a constant flow of new songs in order to maintain their acts.

Secondly, the theatres in which these vaudevilles began life were situated around New York's 28th Street. These theatres naturally encouraged booking agents, talent agencies and entertainers to establish themselves in the district, and in turn so did the publishing houses in order to service the artistic needs of the vaudeville stars and to promote their song catalogues.

Thirdly, the aforementioned growth in the popularity of the piano as a home entertainment system meant that there was an increasingly strong market for sheet music. In fact, by the end of the first decade of the 20th century, millions of copies of sheet music were being sold every year.

The fourth reason why the market was booming was the simple fact that improved and cheaper transportation – such as the transcontinental railways – allowed for groups of entertainers to perform across the country to huge audiences.

The fifth factor was the method by which songs were now promoted to an artist. In order to be a success, a song needed a vehicle, a star to perform it on the touring vaudeville shows. This meant that publishers had to work closely with the artists themselves.

The setup was simple. A publisher would rent a one- or two-room office on 28th Street. In each room there would be a piano, and from 9am to 5pm songwriters hired by the publisher would tirelessly churn out song after song after song. Once a song had been finished and approved by the publisher, it was the publisher's job to persuade an entertainer to add it to his or her act – in effect, plugging their songs.

At this time, there were no rules or restrictions to song plugging; publishers came up with any number of ways to get a song to an artist directly or via their agent. One publisher by the name of Lou Levy paid an elevator operator 50 cents a day to sing one of his songs, 'Shoeshine Boy', as he worked the lift in a music company in the hope that an entertainer or agent would pick up on it – as they eventually did.

After an artist had agreed to perform the song in their set, the publisher would then arrange for the sheet music to be printed. Often the front cover would feature the name and picture of the artist, which effectively played to the artist's ego and encouraged them to keep the song in their act. Then, while the act was taking the song on tour, the sheet music would be distributed throughout the country via wholesalers or 'jobbers' (essentially, a more specialised species of travelling salesman). The hope was that in each new town, following a performance of the song, the local music store would be flooded with requests for the sheet music of the artist's song.

Through Tin Pan Alley, the working practices of music publishing became defined: a publisher hired songwriters to write songs in a popular style; these were then plugged to a performer; the performer sang them in their act; and the sheet music was marketed to the masses. Consequently, the popular song was shaped not only by public taste but also by the practicalities of business – ie the songs that made the most money were identified and similar ones were then written.

This period in the history of the popular song proved a boom time for music of many different genres, such as the ballads of the 1890s and the rags of the 1900s. Blues and jazz grew in prominence during the 1910s thanks to the introduction of the radio. Then the 1920s ushered in both country-and-western music and the golden age of Broadway, which led to the glorious Hollywood musicals when movies with sound became possible. The mid-1930s found country and folk music making headway in the mainstream, while both the 1930s and '40s witnessed the rise and fall of big bands and swing music.

Tin Pan Alley was dominant throughout all this. It allowed songwriting to become truly a profession in its own right and introduced the concept of songs being created to order for a particular performer. As a consequence of an industry focused on creation, the 'standard' was written into the landscape of popular music.

POPULAR STANDARDS

In music terms, a standard is an instantly recognisable song. It is a song that can be recognised after only a couple of lyrics or a few bars of music. As the Songwriters' Hall of Fame's website states, 'Standards are timeless and embedded in the psyche, reflecting the soundtrack of our lives.' An example of this is Irving Berlin's 'Cheek To Cheek', which opens with the line 'Heaven, I'm in heaven,' or Cole Porter's 'I've Got You Under My Skin', or the Gershwins' 'Summertime'. All of these songs spark immediate recognition in the listener.

Such standards were born of an environment of unfettered creativity and were usually written without the context of a script, storyboard or particular artist (although they were often later included in Broadway shows and Hollywood musicals). The primary goal of the Tin Pan Alley songwriters was to write great songs, of which a select few became adopted as standards by the listening public.

At first, the performance vehicle of such songwriters was vaudeville and variety shows. These forms of entertainment then developed into 'musical revues', performed by a single cast and comprising skits, dialogue and songs based around a single theme. These in turn later became 'musical comedies', with a libretto and a complete narrative thrown into the mix.

In the 1920s, all of these stage formats fused into one: the Broadway musical. This form paved the way for such writing teams as Rodgers and Hart (later Rodgers and Hammerstein, who rose to prominence with the classic Broadway shows of *Oklahoma!* and *South Pacific*). Simultaneously, with the introduction of sound in films and the pioneering talkie *The Jazz Singer* in 1926, the Hollywood musical came into its own over the next 30 years, lifting such musicals as *West Side Story* to the silver screen and catapulting composers such as Stephen Sondheim and Leonard Bernstein into the limelight.

Broadway and Hollywood somehow managed to co-exist, with the stage regularly being the source for stories and soundtracks for the movies. However, the combined effect of Hollywood and radio effectively killed vaudeville. Some vaudeville stars were lucky enough to make a new career for themselves in radio, a medium that publishers soon came to realise could reach millions of potential sheet-music customers, requiring relatively little effort on their part.

The advent of radio also led to the popularisation of ragtime, blues, jazz and country-and-western music. Throughout the 1900s and 1910s, an increasingly fashionable song was the rag, after the style had been inaugurated with Scott Joplin's 'Maple Leaf Rag' and later epitomised in Irving Berlin's 1911 hit 'Alexander's Ragtime Band'. Ragtime – a contraction of 'ragged time' – is a strongly syncopated style of music based primarily on the piano and performed rhythmically in fast 2/4 or 4/4 time. Its beat was completely different to anything that had existed before it. Between 1900 and 1910, more than 1,800 rags were published.

Meanwhile, the blues was creeping into the popular song. Born out of the work songs of the African slaves, the blues was a combination of dramatic gospel hymns and songs recounting the tortured experiences of black people. Such songs were known as 'one-verse songs' and comprised southern plantation folk narratives, emotive improvised sections and heavy harmonic lines. In 1912, WC Handy brought the blues to mainstream attention with his publication of 'Memphis Blues'.

Jazz grew out of ragtime's improvisatory nature and the 12-bar progression of the blues. The form was initially slowed down, as exemplified by Louis Armstrong's work from 1917 onwards, but over time it became more and more complex, introduced more dynamic rhythms, expressive vocals and explorative improvisations and gave rise to a number of stars, including at this time The Paul Whiteman Band, Eddie Cantor and Sophie Tucker. By the mid-1920s, dances such as the foxtrot, the shimmy and the charleston took America by storm and helped to put jazz on the musical map. Popular jazz became a showcase for many Tin Pan Alley standards, including Irving Berlin's 'Puttin' On The Ritz' and Duke Ellington's 'Prelude To A Kiss'. By the 1930s and '40s, Jazz had evolved into big band and swing, the latter genre featuring such stars as Benny Goodman, Count Basie, Ella Fitzgerald and Billie Holiday.

The medium of radio also led to white folk music such as country being heard across America; based on Colonial interpretation of English and Irish folk, this new American genre was immediately embraced across the nation. The radio also allowed for the dissemination of styles and inflections of artists like Jimmie Rodgers, rapidly laying the groundwork for what would become known as country-and-western music.

From the 1880s until the mid-1950s, Tin Pan Alley – along with its UK equivalent, London's Denmark Street, which actually remained a compelling centre for creativity even into the 1970s – had held sway over the popular song. Music publishing *was* the music industry, and the dominant force guiding and creating hits in all genres was Tin Pan Alley. And then...

THEN ELVIS HAPPENED

Elvis Presley made the performance of a song more important than its publication. In other words, a song's success began to be measured not by sheet-music sales but by record sales.

The 1950s represented a significant change to the way in which the music-publishing industry functioned. Radio, DJs and the advent of 45s (singles) meant that publishers were no longer in control of the promotion of a song. Furthermore, the new style of music that Elvis represented, rock 'n' roll, was targeted towards the new phenomenon of the teenager, not the adults who bought sheet music to play at home.

Publishers had a choice: they could cater to the new youth market, wait the new craze out, turn to Broadway or tackle Hollywood to snap up the last big-budget musicals as this format gave way to television, the ultimate form of home entertainment. During this period, the key to survival for music publishers was adaptability. Very few Tin Pan Alley songwriters made the switch to rock 'n' roll, as they found themselves replaced by younger writers of the likes of Jerry Leiber and Mike Stoller. Meanwhile, the publishing companies that thrived were those that followed each dance craze and moved into the emerging record industry. These companies simply signed the emerging stars, who then recorded the songs that had been written by the publishing division of the same company. Publishing, once again, had the industry sewn up.

While this period was tumultuous for publishers and devastating for Tin Pan Alley, it proved a fantastically creative and expressive period for the popular song. The essential difference between Tin Pan Alley and the new emerging sound was that of instrumentation. Rather than the piano, the instrument at the forefront of rock 'n' roll was the guitar, and no songwriter represented this polar shift better than Chuck Berry.

John Lennon once opined, 'If you were going to give rock 'n' roll another name, you might call it "Chuck Berry",' and Berry was indeed the standard-bearer for rock 'n' roll guitar. His fusion of blues and country and western on such tracks as 'Johnny B Goode' and 'Maybellene' effectively erased the line between black and white music, while his lyrics reflected the new cultural developments and attitudes of American society. In the post-war affluence and optimism of the new species of 'teenager', there was a demand for music that represented the lives of these young people, not that of their parents.

The record that many consider to have officially announced the arrival of the rock 'n' roll era is Bill Haley And The Comets' 1955 Number One hit '(We're Gonna) Rock Around The Clock'. This song was typical of the new genre, with a heavy backbeat, simple, driving harmonies and a strong, rhythmic vocals – all true to its roots in the blues of the South. However, it's Elvis Presley who is credited with defining and perfecting that sound.

Presley's performance of 'Don't Be Cruel' on *The Ed Sullivan Show* in 1956 was a turning point that changed the music business forever. The popular song now had a new name, a new audience and a new attitude. For publishers, this meant that there was now a fresh outlet for songs, and professional songwriters such as Leiber and Stoller were put to work writing for Elvis and similar artists. More significantly, the performance of the artist was now the key to a song's success.

To feed this new phenomenon of the teen idol, New York's Brill Building became one of the new homes for professional songwriters. Based around the publishing firm of Aldon Music, this establishment served as a base to a generation of composers who bridged the gap between Tin Pan Alley's musical sophistication and rock 'n' roll's demand for songs about the typical teenage life. Due to a vastly increased turnover in record sales, the Brill Building came to house some of the most prolific songwriting partnerships in the history of the popular song: Barry Mann and Cynthia Weill, Gerry Goffin and Carole King, Howard Greenfield and Neil Sedaka.

Then on 9 February 1964, The Beatles appeared on *The Ed Sullivan Show*.

THE BEATLES HAVE LANDED

The Beatles' appearance on *The Ed Sullivan Show* created an impact equal to that of Elvis. Similarly, the band changed the music-publishing business forever. Their music took America by storm, but significantly it was *their* music. Until the mid-1960s, the majority of successful performers did the performing while the songwriters wrote the songs. Historically, there was a deep divide between the songwriter and the recording artist. All of a sudden, though, here was an act that supplied all their own material. Publishers no longer knew how to go about getting their songs recorded.

Initially, with the first spate of self-contained acts, publishers managed to convince the artist to sign over 100 per cent of the publishing to them in return for them administering and promoting the song. The publishing industry essentially turned their whole business on its head. Publishers no longer tried to place songs with an artist; instead they signed artists with record contracts, gave them a financial advance to guarantee the publisher all the songs on the album and then sat back and watched the money roll in.

It was during this period that the publishing industry acquired a bad reputation. Record companies began to realise that they had taken over many of the functions of the publisher – primarily the pressing, distribution and promotion of the song – but this was now done in the form of a record, now that sheet music now accounted for a minimal percentage of the business. So, throughout the 1960s and '70s, many record companies demanded that acts who signed their record deals also had to sign to their internal publishing company.

When artists came to realise just how important publishing was and how much income it could generate, this arrangement led to disputes and artists began to oppose these restrictions. From the 1980s onwards, the practice became less frequent and the publishing split between artist and publishing company moved more in favour of the artist as a reflection of the reduced activity of the publishing company.

However, this wasn't the only source of disgruntlement for the songwriting community. Brill Building writers such as Carole King became disenchanted by the assembly-line-style production methods that were being adopted and sought to pursue more creatively free and expressive avenues. Such songwriters recognised that, by writing for themselves, they could acquire more control over their artistic abilities and become performers in their own right. And so came about the rise of the singer/songwriter.

THE BIRTH OF MODERN MUSIC

During the late 1960s and early 1970s, traditional folk music rose again to prominence as such songwriters as Bob Dylan, Paul Simon and Joni Mitchell applied powerful socially aware and introspective narratives to simple melodic lines. In the tradition of folk and in reflection of the upheavals that society was experiencing at the time, these songs became the protest songs of a generation.

The popular song had become a weapon in the social rebellion against war, corruption and inequality. While Bob Dylan was a pivotal figure in demonstrating the power of an expressive lyric within a song, James Brown was working hard to reassert and redefine the black identity through his music, largely in response to the assassination of Civil Rights activist Dr Martin Luther King. 'Say It Loud – I'm Black And I'm Proud' became an anthem for African-Americans and exemplified Brown's new form of music, a combination of funk rhythms, smooth melodic lines and powerful statements that its creator dubbed 'soul' music.

Soul had its roots in rhythm and blues, a broad style of music whose influence extended across all genres of the popular song. Writers like Ray Charles and Sam Cooke laid the foundations of the genre, fusing gospel, blues and rock. Meanwhile, in the 1950s Berry Gordy had established Motown

Records, and by the late 1960s the label's songwriting team of Brian and Eddie Holland and Lamont Dozier perfected a sound that dominated the charts with its straightforward lyrics, repetitive hook lines, driving dance beats backed to the hilt with gospel-type singing, strings and horn sections.

Meanwhile, within the domain of white popular music, artists like The Beach Boys' Brian Wilson and The Rolling Stones were taking blues-based rhythm tracks and laying their own style of melody lines over the top. Wilson became primarily responsible for the West Coast surf sound when he combined Chuck Berry-esque guitar lines and beats with sweet, layered pop harmonies. The Rolling Stones, however, were influenced by blues purists like Muddy Waters and T-Bone Walker, and Keith Richards' distorted guitar riffs and Mick Jagger's invective-laden, uninhibited lyrics and singing style served to kick the blues firmly into the realm of rock. Then, in the 1970s, The Beatles took the popular song to an entirely new level with the release of their album *Sgt Pepper's Lonely Hearts Club Band*.

As the technology of recording studios developed, so did the creative possibilities for the popular song. A song's potential came to be limited only by the imagination of the artist. Similar to Elvis's impact of making the performance of a song more significant than its publication, as studios developed so the actual production of the song became a factor in its success. This was perhaps best demonstrated by Pink Floyd, whose popularity arguably was due primarily to the way in which their music was recorded, the sounds of their songs and their Technicolor performances, rather than the performers themselves.

As a consequence, the 1970s and 1980s became ever more diverse and ever more excessive, producing music that sounded completely at odds to the introspective singer/songwriter material and uncomplicated soul music of the previous decade. Rock evolved into heavy metal, prog rock and punk. Soul broke off into funk, disco and dance. Introspective songs were replaced by power ballads and bubblegum pop, with its inconsequential lyrics and buoyant, catchy melodies. This gave rise to a number of successful songwriting–production powerhouses, such as that of Stock, Aitken and Waterman, who based their business model on the artist/songwriter relationship of the Tin Pan Alley and Brill Building eras but acquired far greater control over the creative and marketing elements of each particular project. Meanwhile, country music firmly stayed true to its roots and remained a predominantly song-focused genre, servicing both the singer/songwriter and the more traditional non-composing artist.

Throughout this explosion of popular song styles, the Hollywood musical faded and by the end of the 1980s had virtually died out, with the occasional exception, such as *Saturday Night Fever*. Only New York's Broadway and London's West End survived, maintaining their links to the songcraft of Tin Pan Alley. Contemporary music began to make a mark on the traditional musical, and in 1971 Tim Rice and Andrew Lloyd Webber's phenomenally successful rock 'n' roll production *Jesus Christ Superstar* completed the transition. Since then, musicals such as *Rent, Bombay Dreams* and *ABBA: The Musical* have continued to be inspired by other music genres.

The Popular Song Today

The 1990s and 2000s have witnessed a further proliferation of song styles, including rap, dance, techno and world music. The popular song is now so many things to so many people that it is perhaps impossible to define. It can't be restricted to a simple definition of having a lyric, a melody and a harmony; rather the term 'song' is more an umbrella term for something typical of all types of popular music, from folk to nu-metal, hip-hop to pop.

The spirit of Tin Pan Alley still lives on in Music Row in Nashville, home of songwriters who specialise in writing country music. Other centres for songwriting include London, Chicago, Philadelphia and Boston, each area focusing on a different musical style.

Publishing remains a thriving business, with companies now playing a new role in the life of the popular song. The emphasis in music publishing today is on development deals, whereby the company supports, promotes and funds self-contained bands and singer/songwriters in their early stages in order to sell them to major record labels. In exchange for this, the publisher retains a percentage of the publishing on any songs released. This obviously means that there are fewer opportunities for non-performing songwriters to write songs for performing artists.

Another issue in recent times is the escalation of mass-scale mergers between publishers as various catalogues are bought out and brought under one roof. The effect that this has on the professional songwriter is that their songs become lost amongst a million and one other compositions and have little chance of receiving the dedicated attention that characterised the Tin Pan Alley or Brill Building eras. However, this is the reality of music publishing today.

Without The Songwriter, There Is No Music

The popular song and the songwriter have come a long way since 1844 and Stephen Foster's 'Open Thy Lattice, Love'. A large-scale industry has developed around this originally simple form of lyric, melody and harmony. Billions of dollars have been made and lost; the aspirations and dreams of artists and songwriters have been realized or have been shattered; society has been enriched and shocked in equal measure; people have been moved to tears or action by a single song. Yet, despite all the changes that the music industry has witnessed, despite the shifting emphasis on the songwriter and the publisher, one thing remains unchanged, and that is the importance of the song itself.

THE FIRST PROFESSIONAL SONGWRITER

Stephen Foster was the first person to make a living solely as a professional songwriter. That's not to say that there were no other songwriters prior to his birth, on 4 July 1826 in Pennsylvania, USA. Indeed, men such as Thomas Moore ('Flow On, Thou Shining River', 'There's Nothing True But Heaven') and Thomas Dartmouth 'Daddy' Rice ('Jim Crow') had already established themselves as popular songwriters. However, these men also performed, published, acted as agents, were entertainment impresarios and assumed any other role that might earn them a living. What made Stephen Foster remarkable was that he aspired to be solely a songwriter.

Stephen was a pioneer. Before him, songwriting as an occupation had never existed. Back in the 1800s, there was no music business as we understand it today. Records wouldn't be invented until 13 years after Stephen's death, and the birth of the radio as a broadcast medium was still over 65 years away. The rise in popularity of pianos from 1813 onwards did much to spread and promote the work of songwriters, but there was no organised system of publishers or agents pushing to sell new songs. The concept of performance rights was an alien one to singers and minstrels performing in restaurants, in theatres and at concert recitals.

The only way of earning money as a songwriter was through a tiny five- to ten-per-cent royalty on the sale of sheet music by the original publisher, or through the one-off purchase of a song by a publisher. However, there was very little enforceable copyright protection. America's first copyright law, drafted in 1790, covered only maps, charts and books; it wasn't until 1831 that the composers of music were given exclusive rights to 'printing, reprinting, publishing and vending'. Consequently, the songwriter had no way of knowing whether or not he was being paid for all the copies sold and would certainly earn nothing should other people arrange his works or print his lyrics, or should other publishers put out their own editions of his music.

Into this brave new world, Stephen stepped forth. His first published song, 'Open Thy Lattice, Love', was published by a Philadelphia firm when he was 18 years old. At that time, he was still an amateur songwriter, and from the age of 20 he had to work as a bookkeeper for his brother Dunning's steamship firm in Cincinnati. However, he continued to circulate manuscript copies of his songs amongst various performing minstrel troupes (the principal public outlet for songs in the 1800s) and in 1848 The Christy Minstrels' performance of his song 'Oh! Susanna' led to his first national hit.

Stephen sold 'Oh! Susanna' to a local publisher, WC Peters, for a mere $100, but the song was widely pirated by more than 20 music-publishing firms, who earned tens of thousands of dollars from the sale of sheet music. In that regard, 'Oh! Susanna' was a financial failure for Foster, but he learned two valuable lessons: that there was a great potential for him to earn significant sums from his songwriting, and that he needed to protect his artistic property.

Determined to make a full-time career in songwriting, Foster returned to Pittsburgh, Pennsylvania, in late 1849 and on 3 December signed a publishing deal with the New York music publisher Firth, Pond & Co. While not a particularly favourable arrangement (Foster would earn only two cents for every 25-cent sheet sold), it was at least properly structured and in writing. In fact, his contracts were written out in his own hand and are the earliest recorded existence of a contract between an American music publisher and an individual songwriter. With this act, Foster officially began his professional career as a full-time songwriter.

From the start, Foster worked very hard at his craft and kept a thick notebook in which to draft ideas for lyrics and melodies. His notebooks show that he often laboured over the smallest details, such as where to include or remove a comma from his lyrics. Sometimes he took several months to craft and polish the words, melody and accompaniment of a song before sending it off to a publisher.

To begin with, Foster wrote ballads and dances for parlour singers and pianists, as well as minstrel songs (often referred to as 'Ethiopian' songs) for professional theatrical performers. These minstrel songs had simple melodies and accompaniments, but their lyrics – written in dialect – depicted African-American slaves as simple, good-natured creatures. However, he soon grew ambivalent toward these songs and their dehumanising of the black people, and instead sought to (as he put it) 'build up taste…among refined people by making words suitable to their taste, instead of the trashy and really offensive words which belong to some songs of that order'. He began to offer a different image – that of the black as a human being experiencing all the same emotions as white folks: love, joy, pain, longing. Foster even requested that certain songs be performed in a 'pathetic' style (in the sense of engendering compassion) rather than in the traditional blackface comic style.

Foster's 1849 song 'Nelly Was A Lady' is the first example of a song written by a white composer for a white audience that portrays a black man and woman as loving husband and wife. Foster even insisted on calling the woman a 'lady', a term traditionally reserved for a well-born white woman.

Foster's intention to write the people's music, regardless of their ethnic identity or social or economic class, was an attempt to reform blackface minstrelsy, then the most pervasive and powerful force in American popular culture. He used images and musical vocabulary that would be widely understood by all groups, and it's this that perhaps explains his widespread popularity.

In 1850, Foster wrote his first enduring classic, 'Camptown Races', before composing his most beloved and universally popular song, 'The Old Folks At Home' (later known as 'Swannee River') in 1851. The original version of the latter was entitled 'Way Down Upon De Old Plantation' and used the name of the Pedee River instead of Swannee, but Foster – evidently unhappy with the river's name (as indicated by a double line underscoring the offending word in his notebook) – walked into his brother Morrison's office one day and asked him to suggest the name of a river with only two syllables. Morrison's first suggestion was 'Yazoo', but this didn't appeal to Stephen, who took out a map of the United States and came upon the Swannee River. 'That's it! That's it!', Stephen announced on hearing the name, and thus an insignificant river that empties into the Gulf of Mexico became immortalised in a song.

'The Old Folks At Home' is one of the most popular songs ever published and has endured probably because of its universal themes of yearning for lost home, youth, family and happiness. This song alone earned Foster's publishers upwards of $15,000 – a small fortune.

Ironically, Foster wasn't credited as the writer of 'The Old Folks At Home'. Keen to move into areas other than blackface, Foster made a conscious decision to omit his name from the song, leaving only the name of the performer, Edwin Christy. In hindsight, he realised his mistake and wrote to Christy to amend this error: 'I have concluded to reinstate my name on my songs and to pursue the Ethiopian business without fear or shame... I find I cannot write at all unless I write for the public approbation and get credit for what I write.' Foster's name wasn't reinstated until some 15 years after his death.

During the 1850s, Foster continued to produce non-minstrel hits with 'Farewell, My Lilly Dear' (1851) and 'Jeannie With The Light-Brown Hair' (1854), a song dedicated to his wife, who had left him because of his heavy drinking and bohemian ways. Songs such as 'My Old Kentucky Home' (1853) and 'Old Black Joe' (1860) brought him further popularity and further financial reward, but following the death of both his parents in 1855 his output diminished; he wrote only four new songs that year, and his debts began to increase. Despite his apparent success, the lack of enforceable copyright laws meant that he reaped little benefit from the widespread performance and publication of his songs.

During the Civil War, Foster's popularity waned and his once-promising songwriting career seemed to be at an end. In 1857, he found himself in severe economic difficulties (primarily due to his drinking habits), but rather than succumbing to a day job he calculated the likely future earnings of his current songs and offered all future rights to his publisher for a one-off payment, selling the rights to 36 songs for just under $2,000.

The following year, and riding on his previous successes, Foster then signed another deal with Firth, Pond & Co that gave him a ten per cent royalty and $100 advance for each song. However, although he wrote almost 100 songs during his final years in New York, none were successes, the only exception being 'Beautiful Dreamer', which was written in 1862 and published after his death in 1864.

Stephen Foster died as the result of a fever brought on by his alcoholism. After being confined to bed for days in a hotel in New York's theatre district, he tried to call a chamber maid but collapsed, splitting his head against the washbasin next to his bed. It took three hours to get him to the hospital, and in that era before transfusions and antibiotics, he succumbed after three days.

Foster's only real income had been the royalties he had earned on sheet-music sales. Altogether he made $15,091.08 in such royalties during his lifetime and almost nothing in performing rights, earning on average $1,371 for each of his 11 most productive years. His heirs, Jane and Marion, later earned a further $4,199 in royalties, so that the total known royalties on his songs amounted to $19,290. In today's music industry, Foster would have been worth millions of dollars a year, but he died on 13 January 1864 at the age of 37 with just 38 cents in his pocket and a scrap of paper that read, 'Dear friends and gentle hearts.'

These words would inspire songwriter Bob Hillard, many years later, to write a lyric entitled 'Dear Hearts And Gentle People', which in 1949 became Bing Crosby's 20th million-selling single. In fact, Stephen Foster's songs live on in a multitude of cover versions by artists as diverse as Roy Orbison ('Beautiful Dreamer'), Glenn Miller ('Jeannie With The Light-Brown Hair'), James Taylor and The Byrds ('Oh! Susanna') and Randy Newman ('My Old Kentucky Home'). It was this enormous popularity of Stephen Foster's songs that paved the way for all songwriters to come.

50 Great Songwriters Of
The Last 100 Years

'Listen to The Beatles, by all means, but go further back and listen to The Sound
Of Music *and listen to the sophistication of some of the songs by Irving Berlin and
people like that, because, if you really want to be a songwriter, the nuances and
techniques that they used in their songwriting still apply to today – much more than
we're be led to believe.'*

– Barry Gibb (The Bee Gees)

1. Irving Berlin (1888–1989)

Composer Jerome Kern said of the composer and lyricist Irving Berlin, 'He has no place in American music; he *is* American music!' Starting out as a singing waiter in a café in Chinatown, in 1907 Israel Baline wrote the lyrics to his song 'Marie From Sunny Italy', which was published mistakenly under the name 'I Berlin', and henceforth Israel called himself Irving Berlin. Irving had only an elementary understanding of music; he didn't read harmony and only ever played in the key of F♯. He composed completely by ear, picking out the notes for an arranger to then write down.

Berlin was a hugely popular composer of rags and made his mark with 'Alexander's Ragtime Band' in 1911. Over the next five decades, he went on to compose ballads, dance numbers, novelty tunes and loves songs that defined much of American popular music for the first half of the 20th century. Today, his standards include 'How Deep Is The Ocean', 'Blue Skies', 'White Christmas', 'Always', 'Anything You Can Do, I Can Do Better', 'There's No Business Like Showbusiness', 'Cheek To Cheek', 'Puttin' On The Ritz', 'A Pretty Girl Is Like A Melody', 'Easter Parade', 'Let's Face The Music And Dance' and 'God Bless America'. In total, he published close to 1,000 songs during his lifetime. In an interview, a reporter remarked to him, 'You must have written more songs than anyone else in the world,' to which Berlin replied, 'I don't know about that, but I sure wrote more failures than anyone else.'

Berlin's motto was, 'Give the people what they want to hear.' He had an uncanny ability to know what that was, and unlike many of his contemporary writers he was able to move with the times, keeping up with evolving American

371

taste and style. He admitted, however, that songwriting was never easy for him; he worked hard at his craft and was always genuinely surprised to have written another good song, let alone one that became a major hit.

Regarded by many as the best all-round popular songwriter of the century, Irving Berlin also co-founded ASCAP (the American Society of Composers, Authors and Publisher), set up his own publishing company, built his own Broadway theatre (the Music Box) and was the recipient of numerous awards, including a special Tony Award (1963) and an Academy Award for 'White Christmas' (1942), one of the most recorded songs in history. He died in New York City on 22 September 1989 at the age of 101.

SUGGESTED LISTENING: *The Irving Berlin Songbook* (GRP Records, 1999), which includes recordings by Louis Armstrong, Dianne Schuur, Shirley Scott and Betty Carter.

2. COLE PORTER (1891–1964)

Like Irving Berlin, Cole Porter was unusual amongst the great Tin Pan Alley songwriters in that he composed both the melodies and lyrics to his songs without the standard practise of collaboration. In contrast to Berlin's populist style, though, Porter's songs were sophisticated, chic and risqué. His songs possessed an elegance, wit and artistry that few other composers could match. Critics considered his work rather naughty at the time, and his music did much to push the boundaries of open sexuality.

Neither did Cole approach songwriting with the same focus and studious determination that characterised Berlin's career. Positioning himself as an international socialite who simply happened to write witty songs, he had a very relaxed attitude to being a songwriter. In the 1920s, he wrote many new songs, but the only people who heard them were guests at his parties. His breakthrough came in 1932 with a stage show called *The Gay Divorce*, starring Fred Astaire, for which he wrote the classic 'Night And Day', later revealing that the song had been inspired by Moroccan drums and an Islamic chant.

Porter went on to produce a rich and fascinating body of work, always characterised by his trademark wit and sophistication. His best-known stage works are *The Greenwich Village Follies*, *Panama Hattie*, *Mexican Hayride*, *Leave It To Me* and *Kiss Me Kate*, for which he wrote the standard 'I've Got You Under My Skin'. Equally successful in films, his Hollywood hits include *Anything Goes*, *Rosalie* and *Something To Shout About*. His best-known songs include 'Night And Day', 'Begin The Beguine', 'You're The Top' and 'In The Still Of The Night.' He died in 1964 in Santa Monica, California.

SUGGESTED LISTENING: *Let's Misbehave: A Cole Porter Collection, 1927–1940* (Naxos Nostalgia, 2002). Contains recordings of Cole Porter performing his own material.

3. WC HANDY (1873–1958)

Known as the 'father of the blues', Handy was born in Alabama on 16 November 1873. He starting his professional life as a school teacher before working the Southern Iron Mills and then returning to his career as a music teacher, and was responsible for a catalogue of genre-defining blues records.

Handy is best known as the writer of 'St Louis Blues', and if he'd written just this one song he would still be honoured today, but his portfolio of songs also includes 'Memphis Blues', 'Joe Turner Blues', 'Hesitating Blues', 'Ole Miss', 'Harlem Blues', 'Basement Blues', 'Loveless Love (Careless Love)', 'Chantez Les Bas', 'East St Louis Blues', 'Annie Love', 'Hail To The Spirit Of Freedom' and 'Atlanta Blues'. A strong defender of black music, he raised its profile in the popular consciousness, once stating, 'I think America concedes that [true American music] has sprung from the Negro. When we take these things that are our own, and develop them until they are finer things, that's pure culture. You've got to appreciate the things that come from the art of the Negro and from the heart of the man farthest down.'

Handy was also responsible for setting up the first African-American publishing company, in 1913. He died in New York City on 29 March 1958.

SUGGESTED LISTENING: *Louis Armstrong Plays WC Handy* (Legacy Recordings, 1999, reissue). Guest artists include Velma Middleton, Trummy Young, Barney Bigard, Billy Kyle, Arvell Shaw and Barrett Deems.

4. JIMMIE RODGERS (1897–1933)

From the father of the blues to the father of country music, James Charles Rodgers, who is considered by many to have brought country music to the forefront of American music.

Nicknamed 'America's Blue Yodeller', Rodgers' music was unique for the time, being an appealing fusion of hillbilly, gospel, blues, jazz, folk and popular music. He wrote many songs, including 'Why There's A Tear In My Eye', 'Peach-Picking Time Down In Georgia', 'Hobo Bill's Last Ride', 'Somewhere Down Below The Dixon Line', 'Waiting For A Train', 'Soldier's Sweetheart' and 13 songs he termed 'blue yodels', a distinct style of yodelling that was immediately embraced by the American South.

Rodgers toured the country as a solo act and with vaudeville companies and was broadcast regularly on the radio, becoming a national star by 1929, despite a continual battle with tuberculosis contracted during his childhood. His last recording session for Victor Records was completed on 24 May 1933, for which he was accompanied by a nurse and had to rest on a cot between takes. Two days after finishing the record, he died from a lung haemorrhage. He was buried in Meridian, Mississippi, and is commemorated by one of the biggest memorials in country music.

SUGGESTED LISTENING: *The Very Best Of Jimmie Rodgers* (BMG Records, 1998), which includes Rodgers' quintessential yodel songs.

5. GEORGE GERSHWIN (1898–1937) AND IRA GERSHWIN (1896–1983)

In the 1920s and '30s, critics made the assumption that writers of popular music were incapable of creating serious music. The Gershwins altered that perception completely by ambitiously combining the popular commercial style with the classical genres. Their blending of the worlds of classical, opera and Broadway resulted in *Rhapsody In Blue* (1924), *An American In Paris* (1928) and *Porgy And Bess* (1935), an opera that includes the classic songs 'Summertime', 'Bess, You Is My Woman Now', 'It Ain't Necessarily So' and 'I Got Plenty O' Nuthin'.

George started his career at the age of 16 as a song plugger for a Tin Pan Alley publisher. Five years later, in 1919, he wrote a huge hit song, 'Swanee', with a lyric by Irving Caesar. The song was sung in a show titled *Sinbad* and went on to sell more than 1 million copies of sheet music and more than 2 million phonograph recordings.

In the same year, George wrote his first complete Broadway score for the show *La, La Lucille*, with lyrics by Buddy De Sylva, before collaborating with his brother, Ira, on a string of hugely successful Broadway shows including *Oh Kay!* (1926, including 'Clap Yo' Hands', 'Do-Do-Do', 'Maybe' and 'Someone To Watch Over Me'), *Funny Face* (1927, including 'S'Wonderful'), *Rosalie* (1928, including 'How Long Has This Been Going On'), *Show Girl* (1929, including 'Liza'), *Girl Crazy* (1930, including 'But Not For Me', 'Embraceable You', 'Bidin' My Time' and 'I Got Rhythm') and *Of Thee I Sing* (1931, the first musical to win the Pulitzer Prize and which features 'Of Thee I Sing', 'Love Is Sweeping The Country', and 'Who Cares').

Between them, George and Ira composed some of the most sophisticated popular songs, and they will always be admired for their sheer melodic inventiveness and their ability to appeal to music lovers of all persuasions.

SUGGESTED LISTENING: *Gershwin Plays Gershwin...And Other Great Composers* (Magnum Collectors, 2000), featuring George Gershwin with Fred Astaire on vocals.

6. DUKE ELLINGTON (1899–1974)

Duke Ellington is considered by many to have been one of the most important creative forces in the music of the 20th century, and his writing has influenced every form of music from modern classical through to pop to jazz.

With initial ambitions of becoming a painter, the erstwhile Edward Kennedy Ellington became involved in bands in his early teens. Winning recognition through his own band's nightly broadcast performances at New York's Cotton Club, he built such a profile for his work that in 1931 he was invited to visit the White House and in 1933 even toured Europe – a major event in those times.

Primarily an instrumental composer, Ellington's songs were all originally instrumental pieces, the words being added later by various high-profile lyricists including Bob Russell and Johnny Mercer. Such songs include the classics 'Sophisticated Lady' (1933), 'In A Sentimental Mood' (1935), 'Prelude To A Kiss' (1938), 'I Let A Song Go Out Of My Heart' (1938), 'I Got It Bad (And That Ain't Good)' (1941), 'Don't Get Around Much Any More' (1942), 'Do Nothin' Till You Hear From Me' (1943), 'I Didn't Know About You' (1944) and 'Satin Doll' (1958). He died in New York on 24 May 1974.

SUGGESTED LISTENING: *Duke Ellington's Finest Hour* (Verve, 2002), featuring Duke Ellington performing with John Coltrane, Barney Bigard, Harry 'Sweets' Edison, Johnny Hodges, Paul Gonslaves, Cootie Williams and Cat Anderson.

7. RICHARD RODGERS (1902–79), LORENZ HART (1895–1943) AND OSCAR HAMMERSTEIN (1895–1960)

Composer Richard Rodgers collaborated with lyricists Lorenz Hart and, later, Oscar Hammerstein II to produce some of the most extraordinary work in musical theatre.

In the first decade of his collaboration with Hart, Rodgers averaged two new shows every season, integrating libretto, music and dance. Among the standards the pair wrote during this time were 'My Funny Valentine' (1937) and 'Bewitched' (1940). Lorenz Hart's show lyrics were distinguished by their clever wordplay, intricate rhymes and often sardonic nature.

When Hart died in 1943, Rodgers began a working relationship with Oscar

Hammerstein, which marked the beginning of another dominating creative partnership in Broadway musical history. Together, Rodgers and Hammerstein created the milestone musical comedy *Oklahoma!* (1943), which they soon followed with *Carousel* (1945), *Allegro* (1947), *South Pacific* (1949), *The King And I* (1951), *Me And Juliet* (1953), *Pipe Dream* (1955) and *The Sound Of Music* (1959). Between them, they earned 35 Tony Awards, 15 Academy Awards, two Pulitzer Prizes, two Grammy Awards and two Emmy Awards. In 1998, *Time* magazine and *CBS News* judged Rodgers and Hammerstein to be among the 20 most influential artists of the 20th century, and in 1999 their images appeared on a US postage stamp.

When Oscar Hammerstein passed away in 1960, Rodgers continued to write and collaborated with others for another 20 years, producing further works for theatre, film and TV, including his first solo musical, *No Strings*, in 1962, which earned him two Tony Awards for music and lyrics. He died in 1979 in New York City.

SUGGESTED LISTENING: *The Best Of Rodgers And Hammerstein* (Laserlight, 1994). Includes selections from *South Pacific*, *The King And I*, *Oklahoma!*, *Carousel* and *The Sound Of Music*.

8. JOHNNY MERCER (1909–76)

Mercer was a lyricist *par excellence*. The sheer quantity, fluidity, sophistication and ease with which he wrote lyrics was unparalleled. As the Songwriters' Hall of Fame describes them, 'Mercer's lyrics combine a keen appreciation of American colloquialisms with a profoundly poetic sensibility. At their best, they have a richness and emotional complexity that is simply amazing.'

Mercer wrote hit songs in four separate decades, from the 1930s through the 1960s. In the 1930s, these included 'PS I Love You' (1934), 'Goody Goody' (1936), 'Too Marvelous For Words' (1937), 'Jeepers Creepers' (1938), 'Hooray For Hollywood' (1938) and 'I Thought About You' (1939). In the 1940s, he wrote such well-known songs as 'Fools Rush In' (1940), 'One For My Baby' (1943), 'Ac-Cent-Tchu-Ate The Positive' (1944), 'Any Place I Hang My Hat Is Home' (1946), 'Come Rain Or Come Shine' (1946) and 'Early Autumn' (1949). The 1950s heralded 'Autumn Leaves' (1950), 'Here's To My Lady' (1951, with Rube Bloom), 'Something's Gotta Give' (1955) and 'Satin Doll' (1958). Finally, Mercer came up with 'Charade' in 1963, 'Summer Wind' in 1965 and 'How Do You Say Auf Wiedersehen?' in 1967.

Mercer was the first songwriter to win four Oscars, first for 'On The Atchison, Topeka And Santa Fe' (1946); then for 'In The Cool, Cool, Cool Of The Evening' (1951); in 1962 for 'Moon River' (with music by Henry Mancini) for the film *Breakfast At Tiffany's*; and finally for the title song to the 1962 film *Days Of Wine And Roses*.

Not only was Mercer a talented lyricist but he was also a popular singer with his own radio show, *Johnny Mercer's Music Shop*, as well as an astute businessman. In 1942, together with fellow songwriter Buddy De Sylva and businessman Glen Wallichs, he founded Capitol Records and signed up such artists as Stan Kenton, Nat 'King' Cole and Margaret Whiting. By 1946, Capitol was responsible for one-sixth of all records sold in the US.

Johnny Mercer died in 1976 in Los Angeles, California.

SUGGESTED LISTENING: *The Complete Johnny Mercer Songbooks* (Verve, 1998), a three-CD set featuring recordings by Ella Fitzgerald, Billie Holiday, Sarah Vaughan, Woody Herman, Cleo Laine, Louis Armstrong and Charlie Parker.

9. SAMMY CAHN (1913–93)

A true legend amongst songwriters, Sammy Cahn has been nominated for more than 30 Oscars, winning four, and his songs have been recorded by virtually every major artist there is.

Starting out by writing for vaudeville acts, Cahn first found success in 1935 with 'Rhythm Is Our Business' for The Jimmy Lunceford Band, who used the track as their theme song. However, it was an adaption of the Yiddish song 'Bei Mir Bist Du Shön' for The Andrews Sisters that truly launched his career as a creative artist.

In 1942, Cahn began working with Jule Styne and together they wrote for 19 films between 1942 and 1951. Among their songs during this period were 'I've Heard That Song Before' (1942), 'I'll Walk Alone' (1944), 'Saturday Night Is The Loneliest Night Of The Week' (1944), 'It's The Same Old Dream' (1947), 'Time After Time' (1947) and, in 1948, 'It's Magic' and 'Put 'Em In A Box, Tie 'Em With A Ribbon' for the Doris Day film *Romance On The High Seas*. The pair also wrote 'Let It Snow, Let It Snow, Let It Snow', 'There Goes That Song Again', 'The Things We Did Last Summer', 'Guess I'll Hang My Tears Out To Dry' and the Oscar-winning 'Three Coins In The Fountain' (1954).

If that wasn't enough, Cahn's long friendship with Frank Sinatra led to Ol' Blue Eyes recording almost 90 of Cahn's songs, including 'Love And Marriage' (1955), 'Come Fly With Me' (1957), the Oscar-winning 'All The Way' (1957), 'Only The Lonely' (1958), 'Come Dance With Me' (1959), the third-Oscar-winning 'High Hopes' (1959), 'When No One Cares' (1959), 'September Of My Years' (1959) and 'My Kind Of Town' (1964).

Sammy Cahn died in Los Angeles, California, on 15 January 1993.

SUGGESTED LISTENING: *An Evening With Sammy Cahn* (DRG, 1992), recorded live at the 92nd Street Y, New York, 12–14 April 1972.

10. LEONARD BERNSTEIN (1918–90)

Described on his induction into the US Songwriters' Hall of Fame as 'a titanic force in American music', Leonard Bernstein is remembered for his innovative and highly influential work in Broadway musicals.

In 1944, together with Betty Comden and Adolph Greene as lyricists and Jerome Robbins as choreographer, Bernstein created the smash musical *On The Town*, about three sailors on shore leave for a night in New York. The show contained some of the most popular songs in Broadway history, including 'Lonely Town', 'Carried Away', 'Some Other Time' and 'New York, New York'.

Bernstein's work as a highly respected conductor, classical composer and innovative television presenter kept him away from Broadway for almost a decade before he returned in 1953 with the Tony Award-winning *Wonderful Town*, with lyrics once again provided by the Comden and Greene team, including those for the show's highlight song, 'Ohio'.

Bernstein then began a collaboration with the young lyricist Stephen Sondheim that resulted in the masterpiece Broadway musical *West Side Story*. The show proved to be an unforgettable mix of the classic romantic tragedy of *Romeo And Juliet* (updated to 1950s America), astounding choreography (again by Jerome Robbins, who also directed) and a setlist of songs that stood head and shoulders above most writers' aspirations and included 'Something's Coming', 'Maria', 'Tonight', 'I Feel Pretty' and 'One Hand, One Heart'.

Bernstein wrote only one other Broadway musical following this, the rather unsuccessful *1600 Pennsylvania Avenue*, but the towering achievements of *On The Town*, *Wonderful Town* and *West Side Story* are more than enough to ensure his reputation as a composer of rare distinction. He died in New York in 1990.

SUGGESTED LISTENING: *Leonard Bernstein's New York* (Nonsuch, 1996), featuring selections from *West Side Story*, *On The Town* and *Wonderful Town*.

11. WOODY GUTHRIE (1912–67)

The early years of Woody Guthrie's life were marked by a series of personal losses that seriously affected the rest of his life: the death of his older sister, Clara; his father's financial ruin; and the institutionalisation of his mother. These tragedies might perhaps might explain his truly unique, wry and rambling outlook on life that led to a catalogue of songs that have influenced most subsequent singer/songwriters.

During America's devastating Great Depression of the 1930s, Woody made the journey to California along with countless farmers and unemployed workers escaping the dustbowl of the Great Plains in 1935. Penniless and starving, he hitchhiked, walked and caught freight trains to Los Angeles, in the process developing a passion for the open road that he pursued throughout his life. When he arrived in California, he was met – like so many others – with intense scorn and hatred. The dustbowl refugees were branded outsiders by the local Californians, and Woody's consequent identification with the outsider became part and parcel of his political and social songwriting, as witnessed in such songs as 'This Land Is My Land', 'I Ain't Got No Home', 'Goin' Down The Road Feelin' Bad', 'Talking Dustbowl Blues', 'Tom Joad' and 'Hard Travelin''.

Woody lived and breathed his times like no other writer. A prolific songwriter, his songs, prose and poetry reflected the plight of the everyman as he lived through the Depression, World War II, the social and political upheavals resulting from unionism and the Cold War. His songs are the voice of the marginalised, disenfranchised and oppressed – 'people's songs', as he called them. He created haunting lyrics shot through with honesty, humour and wit as he fought to express his beliefs in the social, political and spiritual turmoil of his times.

Woody was inducted into the Rock 'n' Roll Hall of Fame and Museum and has received numerous awards, including the US Department of the Interior's Conservation Award (1966) and Lifetime Achievement Awards from the Folk Alliance (1996) and the National Academy of Recording Arts and Sciences (1999). He died in New York City in 1967.

SUGGESTED LISTENING: Billy Bragg And Wilco: *Mermaid Avenue I* and *II* (Elektra Records, 1998 and 2000), a collection of Woody Guthrie poems set to new music by Billy Bragg and Wilco.

'Til We Outnumber 'Em: The Songs Of Woody Guthrie (Righteous Babe Records, 2000).

12. Hank Williams (1923–53)

Walking the path laid by Jimmie Rodgers, Hank Williams became the first true star of country music, although he lived life like a rock 'n' roll icon. The leading light on Nashville's Grand Ole Opry throughout 1949, he experienced unparalleled success as country music's pinup singer/songwriter, but his life was that of a man intent on living it to its limits, cataloguing drug and alcohol misuse and marital upheavals.

Despite these tragedies, Hank wrote some of the best-loved pure country songs ever, including 'Your Cheatin' Heart', 'Move It On Over', 'I'm So Lonesome I Could Cry', 'Ramblin' Man', 'Cold, Cold Heart', 'There'll Be No Teardrops Tonight', 'Mind Your Own Business', 'Hey, Good Lookin'', 'Window Shopping', 'I Can't Help It (If I'm Still In Love With You)', 'Half As Much', 'Why Don't You Love Me', 'You Win Again', 'May You Never Be Alone', 'Baby, We're Really in Love' and 'Take These Chains From My Heart'. He died in 1953, but was inducted posthumously into the Country Music Hall of Fame, the Rock 'n' Roll Hall of Fame and the Songwriters' Hall of Fame in 1961.

SUGGESTED LISTENING: *The Millennium Collection: The Best Of Hank Williams* (Mercury Nashville, 1999), featuring 12 hit songs written and performed by Hank Williams.

13. CHUCK BERRY (1926–)

A writer of pounding rhythms, bold melodies and populist lyrics, Chuck Berry single-handedly fashioned rock 'n' roll as we hear it today.

Born Charles Edward Anderson Berry, 'Chuck' developed his highly individualised style, combined with a dazzling showmanship, while playing in his own band, The Chuck Berry Combo. Then, in 1955 he was introduced to the President of Chess Records and cut the record that defined his sound, 'Maybellene', which became one of the most popular records ever, winning a triple crown in *Billboard*'s charts when it reached Number One in the pop, country-and-western and R&B charts.

Chuck went on to forge his widely imitated sound with such songs as 'Johnny B Goode', 'Roll Over, Beethoven', 'Rock And Roll Music' and 'Sweet Little Sixteen'. The Beatles began their career by covering his records, and such popular imitation established Chuck Berry as the singular most influential songwriter in rock 'n' roll.

SUGGESTED LISTENING: *Chuck Berry: The Anthology* (MCA Records, 2000), a two-cd set including 'Johnny B Goode', 'Carol', 'Around And Around', 'Reelin' And Rockin'', 'Memphis', 'Rock And Roll Music', 'Let It Rock' and 'No Particular Place To Go'.

14. BURT BACHARACH (1929–) AND HAL DAVID (1921–)

Together, this writing duo have written many of the most memorable songs of the past century, including '24 Hours From Tulsa' (1964), 'Walk On By' (1964),

'What's New, Pussycat?' (1965), 'What The World Needs Now Is Love' (1965), 'The Look of Love' (1968) and 'Close To You' (1970).

Bacharach and David were key figures behind the career of Dionne Warwick, writing a string of 39 consecutive hits for her over a period of ten years. From the standard 'Walk On By' to 'I'll Never Fall In Love Again' and 'Message To Michael', the quality of their songwriting shone through, winning them a Grammy for Song of the Year when Dionne – along with Stevie Wonder, Elton John and Gladys Knight – recorded the Number One song 'That's What Friends Are For', which raised over $1.5 million for the American Foundation for AIDS Research.

Bacharach and David's work within the movies has also been phenomenally successful. They have been awarded an Oscar nomination for the theme to *Alfie* (1966), written the million-selling 'What's New, Pussycat?' for the film of the same name, had a gold record with Dusty Springfield for 'The Look Of Love' from *Casino Royale*, and were presented with an Academy Award for the song 'Raindrops Keep Falling On My Head' from the 1969 film *Butch Cassidy And The Sundance Kid*.

Over a period of four decades, Burt Bacharach has proven that he truly is a multifaceted composer who can write in all genres of music, having scored hits in contemporary pop, R&B, country, film soundtracks and, with 'Promises, Promises', even Broadway.

Equally, Hal David has reached the highest level of achievement as a lyricist. Even before meeting Burt, he was already an established writer of such songs as 'Broken-Hearted Melody' and 'Johnny Get Angry'. Like Burt, Hal also demonstrated a knack for writing in different genres, providing the lyrics to the smash country hit 'It Was Almost Like A Song'. In the 1980s, he acted as President of ASCAP and in 1999 was the first winner of the Special International Award at the Ivor Novellos.

SUGGESTED LISTENING: *The Look Of Love: The Burt Bacharach Collection* (Rhino Records, 1998), three-CD collection featuring Dionne Warwick, Fifth Dimension, Elvis Costello and Dusty Springfield performing the highlights from the Bacharach/David catalogue.

15. STEPHEN SONDHEIM (1930–)

In contrast to the few but impressive creations of his occasional writing partner Leonard Bernstein, Stephen Sondheim's output was prolific and strikingly diverse. One of the rare writers to have been awarded both Tonys and Oscars for his work across film, television, legitimate theatre and Broadway, Stephen Sondheim is truly a unique creative talent.

Success came quick for Sondheim. Having already garnered a Hutchinson Prize for Music Composition at college and studied with Milton Babbitt, his first work to gain recognition was *West Side Story*. For most writers, such success would be difficult to maintain, let alone exceed, but Sondheim went on to write *Gypsy* with Jule Styne and then the self-penned work *A Funny Thing Happened On The Way To The Forum*, which became a hit show in 1962.

This initial success was followed by an unbroken 30-year run of successful musicals, starting in 1964 with *Anyone Can Whistle*. As a result, Sondheim has won five Best Score for a Musical Tony Awards for *Into The Woods*, *Sweeney Todd*, *A Little Night Music*, *Follies* and *Company*. Every one of these shows also won New York Drama Critics' Circle Awards, as did *Pacific Overtures* and *Sunday In The Park With George*. This latter musical also received the Pulitzer Prize for Drama in 1985, featuring music and lyrics by Sondheim and book by James Lapine.

Aside from all this, Sondheim somehow found time to write the lyrics for *Do I Hear A Waltz?* and Bernstein's *Candide*; to organise revue-style anthologies of his songs on Broadway, such as *Side By Side By Sondheim*, *You're Gonna Love Tomorrow* and *Putting It Together*; to compose film scores for *Stavisky* and *Reds*; to write songs for the film *Dick Tracy* (one of which, 'Sooner Or Later', won him the Academy Award in 1990 for Best Song) and the television show *Evening Primrose*; to co-author the film *The Last Of Sheila*; and to provide incidental music for the plays *The Girls Of Summer*, *Invitation To A March* and *Twigs*.

In view of this, Stephen Sondheim ranks amongst the elite of composers and songwriters and is essential listening for any would-be songwriter.

SUGGESTED LISTENING: *West Side Story: Motion Picture Cast Recording* (Sony Broadway, 1961).

16. LIONEL BART (1930–99)

Fighting the corner for music in the English theatre is Lionel Bart. Duly honoured as 'the father of the modern British musical' by Lord Andrew Lloyd Webber, Lionel was the composer, author and lyricist for the outstanding and much-admired musical *Oliver!*

Despite being unable to read music, Lionel's earliest stage successes included lyrics for the London musical *Lock Up Your Daughters* (1959) and both the words and music for the 1960 hit *Fings Ain't Wot They Used T'Be* (whose film adaptation won six Oscars). Bart then single-handedly restored the faded fortunes of the British musical with his adaptation of the Charles Dickens' novel

Oliver Twist to create the first British musical to enjoy international success since Noël Coward's revues three decades earlier. The show's songs 'Consider Yourself', 'Oom-Pah-Pah' and 'As Long As He Needs Me' have become standards, while the 1968 film version won an Academy Award for Best Picture.

Tragically, this success was marred by Bart's decision to sell the valuable rights to *Oliver!* to finance his ill-fated musical 1965 *Twang*. The decision cost him an estimated £100 million and henceforth he was regularly plagued with debt and an infamous dependency on drink and drugs.

Bart's later musicals – including *Blitz!* (1962) and *Maggie May* (1964) – had little life beyond their London runs, but good fortune didn't entirely elude him; he wrote the title song to the 1963 James Bond film *From Russia With Love* and his own stage musical, the period romp *Lock Up Your Daughters!*, was filmed in 1969 (though unfortunately without his songs, which were replaced by a Ron Grainer score).

At his peak, Lionel Bart was also one of Britain's most successful pop songwriters, penning hits for the likes of Cliff Richard, Anthony Newley, Shirley Bassey and Adam Faith. He was responsible for arguably one of the all-time perfect pop songs, the Number One record for Cliff Richard 'Living Doll'. Screaming Lord Sutch honoured him by saying, 'He composed the classic rock 'n' roll songs for Cliff Richard before anyone else was doing them, before even The Beatles had got out of their nappies.'

SUGGESTED LISTENING: *The Songs Of Lionel Bart* (Empire Music Collection, 1999).

17. JOHN BARRY (1933–)

John Barry dominates the world of motion-picture composition. Always determined to be a film composer from an early age, he developed his musical skills by learning the piano and trumpet as a child, taking a correspondence course in composition and orchestration while serving in the British Army and forming a rock 'n' roll band, The John Barry Seven. Parlophone signed the band, whose first album, *The Big Beat*, was released soon after and followed by a string of singles.

In 1969, however, John managed to acquire his first film assignment, scoring the film *Beat Girl*. While maintaining his rock 'n' roll career, which was going from strength to strength, he wrote the scores for two other films: *Never Let Me Go* and *The Amorous Prawn*. Then, in 1962 Barry's big break came and his ambition of being a successful film composer came true when he was commissioned by the producers of *Dr No* – the very first James Bond movie – to develop the Bond theme tune.

John Barry's instantly recognisable and devastatingly simple arrangement became part and parcel of the James Bond legend, and on the heels of this initial success John scored the next two James Bond films: *From Russia With Love* and *Goldfinger*. The soundtracks of both films were released as albums and became bestsellers. John Barry was now the composer of choice for the Bond franchise. In fact, no other composer has scored more than one Bond movie in the series.

For many writers, such success can also prove a trap as they are stylistically boxed into a specific genre. Barry, however, managed to sidestep this fate and composed musical scores for films as diverse as *The Ipcress File*, *Born Free* and *The Lion In Winter*.

Throughout his career, John Barry has won multiple awards. A Fellow of the Academy, he was also won Best Original Score Oscars for *Born Free*, *The Lion In Winter*, *Out Of Africa* and *Dances With Wolves*. He was also awarded a Best Original Song Oscar for 'Born Free', while his scores for *Chaplin* and *Mary, Queen Of Scots* were both Oscar nominees. He has also won four Grammy Awards, including those for *Out Of Africa* (Best Instrumental Composition), *Dances With Wolves* (Best Instrumental Composition Written for a Motion Picture or for Television), *The Cotton Club* (Best Instrumental Performance, Big Band) and *Midnight Cowboy* (Best Instrumental Theme). Not a bad collection of trophies for a composer who started off composing for a film titled *The Amorous Prawn*!

SUGGESTED LISTENING: *John Barry: The Collection* (Silva America, 2001), four-disc collection featuring 56 instrumental recordings including the themes for *From Russia With Love*, *Zulu*, *You Only Live Twice*, *Born Free*, *Midnight Cowboy* and James Bond.

18. JERRY LEIBER (1933–) AND MIKE STOLLER (1933–)

Leiber and Stoller are arguably the godfathers of rock 'n' roll, popularising what was rhythm and blues to a black audience as rock 'n' roll to a white audience. Lyricists, composers and producers, their influence reaches far beyond their songwriting skills. After several years of writing songs for the recording industry, the pair began to produce music – first the songs they wrote themselves and then songs written by others. They became the first independent recording producers – a now-common job – of their generation, significantly altering the landscape of the music industry in the process.

As songwriters, Leiber and Stoller produced some of the biggest hits of the day, including 'Yakety Yak' (recorded by The Coasters), 'There Goes My Baby' and 'This Magic Moment' (both recorded by The Drifters). It's their work with Elvis Presley, however, that popularised rock 'n' roll and raised their public profile.

Success wasn't handed to them on a plate, however. In an interview with *Rolling Stone* magazine, Leiber revealed, 'We used to go to Mike's house, where the upright piano was. We went there every day and wrote. We worked 10, 11, 12 hours a day.' Stoller continued, 'When we started working, we'd write five songs at a session. Then we'd go home and we'd call each other up: "I've written six more songs!" "I've written four more."' Such speed characterised much of their writing and resulted in their first big hit, 'Hound Dog', which was written in less than a quarter of an hour.

In 1952, Johnny Otis asked Leiber and Stoller to attend a rehearsal of his band and write some songs for them. One of the singers was Big Mama Thornton. When the pair met her, they thought her to be one of "the saltiest chicks" they had ever seen and attempted to capture her personality in song by writing a mean one. The first printable line that came out was 'You ain't nothin' but a hound dog.' Big Mama's recording of the song was a huge local hit in 1953, but when Elvis Presley recorded it in 1957, national success was assured.

Presley was so happy with the success of 'Hound Dog' that he asked Leiber and Stoller to write songs for his movies, including *Jailhouse Rock* and *King Creole*. Since Presley was the most popular singer of his day, Jerry and Mike became the most popular songwriters, leaving an even more tangible legacy than their production accomplishments. Songs such as 'Hound Dog' and 'Jailhouse Rock' defined the new sound of rock 'n' roll in the mid-1950s and will forever evoke that era, remaining popular 50 years after their creation.

SUGGESTED LISTENING: *A Tribute To Leiber And Stoller* (DVD), two-hour tribute show recorded at London's Hammerstein Apollo Theatre in 2001 with performances by Ben E King, David Gilmour, Tom Jones, Elkie Brooks, *et al.*

19. JAMES BROWN (1933–)

The Godfather of Soul has been such a dominant musical force for so many decades that his songs have become an integral part of the fabric of popular-music culture. Artist as diverse as Bruce Springsteen, The Rolling Stones, Prince, Sting and Puff Daddy have all announced their debt to his music. Ironically, his success as an entertainer has perhaps overshadowed his towering achievements as the songwriter of all his hits.

A winner of two Grammy Awards, Brown's work as an entertainer and songwriter was a key factor in mainstream acceptance of R&B music in the 1950s. Beginning with his first significant record release, 'I'll Go Crazy', in 1960, almost every James Brown release has been a chart hit, including 74 R&B Top 20 entries, of which 17 were Number Ones. During his career, Brown has racked up total sales of more than 50 million records. This has as much to do with his dedication to touring (during the 1950s, '60s and '70s he was known to perform as many as 350 one-nighters in a single year!) as with the quality of his songwriting. So strong are his compositions that they each stand out in popular-music history as unique achievements, including 'Papa's Got A Brand New Bag', 'Baby, You're Right', 'Get It Together', 'I Don't Want Nobody To Give Me Nothin'', 'Say It Loud – I'm Black And I'm Proud', 'Get Up (I Feel Like Being A) Sex Machine', 'America Is My Home' and 'I Got You (I Feel Good)'. For these, Brown has deservedly been awarded a Grammy Lifetime Achievement Award and the Award of Merit from the American Music Awards, among others.

SUGGESTED LISTENING: *40th Anniversary Collection* (Polydor Records, 1996), two-disc compilation of quintessential James Brown recordings, including 'Please, Please, Please', 'Lost Someone', 'Night Train', 'Out Of Sight', 'Papa's Got A Brand New Bag', 'Say It Loud – I'm Black And I'm Proud' and 'I Got The Feelin''.

20. BUDDY HOLLY (1936–54)

If Chuck Berry forged rock 'n' roll, Buddy Holly changed the face of it. Born Charles Hardin Holley in Lubbock, Texas, his first group, The Western And Bop Band, was formed in 1955 and was an opening act for the then-unknown Elvis Presley. Soon afterwards, Holley was signed to a record deal and, under the stage name 'Buddy Holly', he recorded 'That'll Be The Day' with his band The Crickets. The song rocketed to Number One in the *Billboard* charts and Holly's brand of loose, jangling guitar and flowing melodies brought a softer edge to the world of rock 'n' roll.

Acknowledged by Paul McCartney as a major influence, Buddy's innovative style and staggering versatility as a songwriter are apparent in songs such as 'Peggy Sue', 'Rave On', 'Oh Boy', 'Maybe Baby', 'It's So Easy', 'Heart Beat', 'Raining In My Heart', 'Every Day', 'Not Fade Away' and 'True Love Ways'. Despite their creator suffering an early death, Holly's songs, originality and legendary drive continue to inspire generations of songwriters.

SUGGESTED LISTENING: *The Very Best Of Buddy Holly* (Prism, 2001), 20-track compilation.

21. BARRY MANN (1939–)

Wayne Hector believes that 'Collaborating is like having a new wife every time,' and in Barry Mann's case, this isn't far from the truth as he married his writing partner, Cynthia Weill. Their songwriting relationship brought them considerable success and they became one of the most prolific and successful of the Brill Building songwriters.

The Mann–Weill catalogue accounts for more than 200 million record sales worldwide, including such songs as 'On Broadway', 'Blame It On The Bossa Nova', 'My Dad', 'Johnny Loves Me', 'Saturday Night At The Movies', 'You've Lost That Lovin' Feeling', 'Walking In The Rain', 'Only In America', 'We Gotta Get Out Of This Place', 'I Just Can't Help Believing', 'It's Getting Better', 'Make Your Own Kind Of Music', 'The Shape Of Things To Come', 'Here You Come Again' and 'Just Once'.

At the end of 20th century, BMI announced the Top 100 Songs of the Century, based on US radio and television play. The Number One song on the list was 'You've Lost That Lovin' Feeling', which had received over 8 million airplay performances, surpassing even The Beatles' 'Yesterday'.

Barry Mann and Cynthia Weill have been awarded over 100 pop, country and R&B awards from BMI including that organisation's 1977 Robert Burton Award for Most Performed Country Song with 'Here You Come Again', along with Lifetime Achievement Awards from the National Academy of Songwriters, the Clooney Foundation's Award for Legendary Song Composition, an Oscar and Golden Globe Nomination for 'Somewhere Out There' and double Grammy Awards for Song of the Year and Motion Picture or Television Song of the Year with 'Somewhere Out There'. And if that wasn't enough, that song also received an Oscar and Golden Globe nomination for Best Song in a Motion Picture.

SUGGESTED LISTENING: *The Barry Mann Songbook* (2001), featuring tracks performed by the original recording artists, including The Diamonds, BJ Thomas, Steve Lawrence, Claudine Longet, The Righteous Brothers, Mama Cass, The Sandpipers and Scott Walker.

22. JOHN LENNON (1940–80) AND PAUL MCCARTNEY (1942–)

Songs like 'Yesterday', 'Hey Jude', 'Eleanor Rigby', 'Here, There And Everywhere' and 'All You Need Is Love' are the foundation stones of what has become the pop mainstream. The Beatles, particularly the songwriting duo of Lennon and McCartney, helped to change both the voice of popular music and the way in which the music industry worked.

The Beatles were one of the first bands to perform their own self-penned material, altering the landscape of music publishing irreparably in the process and opening the gates for a flood of similar artists who both wrote and performed their own material. They took rock 'n' roll and, together with their producer, George Martin, developed it in directions that had never before been anticipated. Through their creative output, they helped to give the youth culture of their time a common voice and shaped the music of the future.

Lennon and McCartney composed a virtually uninterrupted string of hit songs, from their first three trailblazers – 'Love Me Do', 'Please Please Me' and 'She Loves You' – all the way through to 'All You Need Is Love' and 'Hey Jude'. Their historic album *Sgt Pepper's Lonely Hearts Club Band* has been recognised as the greatest album of all time on countless occasions and contains such songwriting classics as 'Lucy In The Sky With Diamonds' and 'A Day In The Life'.

Simply studying and learning to play any of The Beatles' songs is often a songwriting masterclass in itself. Lennon and McCartney displayed an envious knack for creating the perfect pop union of melody, harmony and lyric. Even the most simple-sounding of their songs contain surprising twists and subtle techniques.

Like any of the great songwriters, it's impossible to cover the sheer breadth and magnificence of Lennon and McCartney's compositional achievements here. Suffice to say that in 1979 their unique accomplishments were recognised by the *Guinness Book Of Records*, which awarded them its Triple Superlative Award. Even when that honour was bestowed upon them, the duo had to their credit 41 songs with sales of over 1 million copies each, as well as total sales of over 200 million singles and albums.

SUGGESTED LISTENING: *1* (Capitol–EMI Records, 2000), a compilation of 27 Number One hit singles recorded between 1962 and 1970, with liner notes by Sir George Martin.

23. BOB DYLAN (1941–)

Born Robert Allen Zimmerman, this folk/rock singer/songwriter was popular music's first major social spokesman of the 1960s. Dylan's song 'Blowin' In The Wind' became an anthem for the US Civil Rights movement, and his vast output of songs deal with subjects ranging from the evil of war to the value of Christianity. Musically, Bob blended blues, folk and rock, and significantly his lyrics form some of the first rock words to venture heavily into poetry. He was the musical flag-bearer who told other songwriters that they could sing about vital subjects, express publicly their discontent and use music as a means of changing the world. His messages served as an inspiration to the songwriters who wrote of their anger and despair during the time of the Vietnam War.

Dylan's album *The Times They Are A-Changin'* firmly established him as the definitive songwriter of the 1960s protest movement. The albums that followed, 1965's *Highway 61 Revisited* (which included the seminal rock song 'Like A

Rolling Stone) and 1966's double *Blonde On Blonde*, represented Dylan at his most innovative. With his unmistakable voice and unforgettable lyrics, he brought the worlds of music and literature together as no one else had.

In 1989, Bob Dylan was inducted into the Rock 'n' Roll Hall of Fame. Bruce Springsteen spoke at the ceremony, declaring that 'Bob freed the mind the way Elvis freed the body... He invented a new way a pop singer could sound, broke through the limitations of what a recording artist could achieve and changed the face of rock 'n' roll forever.'

The influence of Bob Dylan's songs is still as powerful and relevant today as it ever was. In 1997, after a year-long hiatus, Bob released the album *Time Out Of Mind*, for which he was awarded three Grammy Awards: for Album of the Year, Best Contemporary Folk Album and Best Male Rock Vocal. In 2004, *Rolling Stone* magazine hailed 'Like A Rolling Stone' as the number-one greatest rock 'n' roll song of all time.

SUGGESTED LISTENING: *The Essential Bob Dylan* (Legacy Records, 2000), two disc collection including 'Blowin' In The Wind', 'It's All Over Now, Baby Blue', 'Mr Tambourine Man' and 'Like A Rolling Stone'.

24. PAUL SIMON (1941–)

In 1964, singer/songwriter Paul Simon and vocalist Art Garfunkel released the album *Wednesday Morning, 3AM*. It remained completely unnoticed until a reworked version of the song 'The Sound Of Silence' was released as a single the following year and rose rapidly to Number One in the *Billboard* chart.

Following this, Simon wrote hit after hit for him and Garfunkel, including 'The Boxer', 'I Am A Rock', 'Homeward Bound', 'Old Friends/Bookends', 'Mrs Robinson', 'The 59th Street Bridge Song (Feelin' Groovy)', 'Scarborough Fair/Canticle', 'Cecilia' and the epic ballad 'Bridge Over Troubled Water'.

Simon revealed a natural ability for creating imagistic lyrics delivered in what became his trademark conversational style of delivery. The frank yet poetic content of his lyrics, blended with Garfunkel's angelic singing voice, quickly raised the duo's profile on the burgeoning socially conscious rock/folk scene of the 1960s that included Bob Dylan, Crosby, Stills And Nash, Cat Stevens and Joni Mitchell.

In 1969, Simon and Garfunkel were awarded a total of five Grammys for their album soundtrack to Mike Nichols' *The Graduate* and another in 1970 for 'Bridge Over Troubled Water'.

Throughout the 1970s, as a solo artist Simon recorded a string of hits, including 'Mother And Child Reunion', 'Me And Julio Down By The Schoolyard', 'Slip Slidin' Away', 'Loves Me Like A Rock' and '50 Ways To

Leave Your Lover.' These tracks demonstrated Simon's willingness to branch out into new musical styles.

Then, on his groundbreaking *Graceland* album, Simon borrowed from the musical traditions of other cultures to produce an eclectic combination of doowop, modern jazz and world rhythms. The album became Simon's magnum opus, becoming an enormous hit with critics and fans alike. The album's hit song 'You Can Call Me Al' was an exciting blend of zydeco, South African mbaqanga (featuring South African artists performing music that until then had never been heard popularly in the Western world) and Simon's more familiar pop/rock sensibility. Winning two Grammy Awards – for Album of the Year and Record of the Year – the album sold over 10 million copies.

Paul Simon continues to push the boundaries of songwriting. In 1991, he released *Rhythm Of The Saints*, an album featuring prominent Brazilian artists, highlighting once again Simon's understanding and deep respect for international talent and its music. He later ventured into Broadway with the musical *The Capeman* before released the hit album *You're The One* in 2002.

Besides his Grammys, Paul has been awarded the Dove Award from the Gospel Music Association and an Emmy Award for a *Paul Simon Special*. His music continues to have an impact on musical culture 30 years after his first hit.

SUGGESTED LISTENING: *Simon And Garfunkel: Greatest Hits, 1972* (Columbia Records, 1993), greatest-hits album including '59th Street Bridge Song (Feelin' Groovy)', 'The Sound Of Silence', 'The Boxer', 'Mrs Robinson' and 'Cecilia'.

25. BRIAN WILSON (1942–)

The legendary producer, arranger, performer and songwriter Brian Wilson has created a body of work that remains one of the most memorable in rock music history. His band The Beach Boys capitalised on the teenage US West Coast life of fast cars and motorcycles, all-American girls and the southern California craze of surfing, a sport that provided the raw material for many of The Beach Boys' early hits, such as 'Surfin'', 'Surfin' Safari', 'Surfin' USA' and 'Little Surfer Girl'. These songs, along with others such as 'Little Deuce Coupe', 'I Get Around' and 'Fun Fun Fun', all became part and parcel of the new American pop culture. Their propulsive, Chuck Berry-style rock 'n' roll combined with sophisticated pop harmonies defined The Beach Boys' sound.

In late 1964, stressed from overwork, Brian Wilson decided to focus completely on writing new songs while leaving the rest of the band to tour. This period of intense songwriting allowed for an upward shift in the sheer innovation and inspired genius of his craft. During this period he produced the pop classics 'Dance, Dance, Dance', 'Help Me Rhonda' and the anthemic

'California Girls' before making the stratospheric leap in artistry with what came to be known as 'the great American album': *Pet Sounds*. Here, teaming up with lyricist Tony Asher, an increasingly reclusive Brian Wilson applied an imaginative use of recording techniques, implementing a host of unique sonic flourishes with the generous use of such offbeat music sources as accordion, theremin, bicycle wheels, kazoo, banjo, glockenspiel and even barking dogs. The result was a masterpiece of modern pop music that included the classics 'Wouldn't It Be Nice', 'Sloop John B' and the ethereal 'God Only Knows'. Paul McCartney, who at that time was competing with The Beach Boys as a Beatle, said in later years that *Pet Sounds* was his favourite album of all time. Wilson had been just 24 years old when he'd written it.

A year later came yet another trail-blazing opus and possibly Wilson's finest track: the three-and-a-half-minute-long 'Good Vibrations'. The song represented pop music at the peak of perfection, being wonderfully expressive and rapturous in tone and thought, with glorious melodies and unparalleled harmonies. Brian referred to it at the time as his 'pocket symphony'.

Following this triumph, however, Wilson began to experience considerable personal stress and artistic frustration and suffered heavily from both physical and psychological exhaustion. It was during this period that he wrote and recorded sessions for the seminal album *Smile*, which remained locked up and unreleased for over 40 years due to his own dissatisfaction with being unable to attain the impossible perfection to which he aspired. In 2004, however, *Smile* was finally released in its entirety to both critical and public adulation. Brian Wilson remains one of the most influential pop music composers of this or any era.

SUGGESTED LISTENING: *Brian Wilson Presents Pet Sounds Live* (Sanctuary Records, 2002), recorded live at London's Royal Festival Hall in January 2002.

26. CAROLE KING (1942–)

Carole King is best known for her spectacular success in 1971 with her best-selling album *Tapestry*, which swept the Grammys, winning Album of the Year, Record of the Year with 'It's Too Late' and Song of the Year with 'You've Got A Friend', while Carole won an Award for Best Pop Female Vocalist. *Tapestry* has gone on to sell over 15 million copies worldwide.

A proficient pianist by the age of four, and already a prolific songwriter by her early teens, King recorded demos, sang backing vocals, arranged recording sessions and wrote and recorded a number of singles that went nowhere. During this time, though, she worked hard at honing her craft.

In 1959, she landed a writing post at the Brill Building and began to collaborate with such musicians as Cynthia Weill, Barry Mann and Neil Sedaka, who happened to be a childhood friend of King's. (In fact, King's songwriting skills had first been noticed when she wrote the single 'Oh! Neil' as a response to Neil's hit song 'Oh! Carol').

Signed to the Aldon Music Empire, Carole, along with her then-husband Gerry Goffin, became a formidable songwriting force throughout much of the 1960s, building a reputation for being a spirited and highly skilled songsmith. King and Goffin's first Number One hit came in 1961 with The Shirelles' 'Will You Love Me Tomorrow', which was followed by a seven-year run of chart successes, including 'Up On The Roof' for The Drifters, 'Locomotion' for Little Eva and 'Natural Woman' for Aretha Franklin.

After her success as an artist in her own right with *Tapestry*, Carole concentrated on writing for herself and released a number of albums including *Music* (1971), *Rhymes And Reasons* (1972), *Fantasy* (1973), *Wrap Around Joy* (1974), *Thoroughbred* (1976), *Simple Things* (1977), *Pearls* (1980), *Speeding Time* (1983), *City Streets* (1989) and *In Concert* (1994). In 1992, she was nominated for a Best Song Academy Award for 'Now And Forever', which she had written for the 1992 film *A League Of Their Own*. She now lives on a ranch in Idaho, occasionally performing live for environmental fundraising events.

SUGGESTED LISTENING: *Natural Woman: The Very Best Of Carole King* (Sony, 2000), featuring 'It's Too Late', 'Jazzman', 'I Feel The Earth Move', 'Will You Love Me Tomorrow', 'You've Got A Friend', 'Nightingale' and 'So Far Away', all performed by Carole King.

27. JONI MITCHELL (1943-)

Joni Mitchell has created an impressive catalogue of musically adventurous songs with lyrics that are deeply personal yet accessible.

The archetypal female folk singer/songwriter, Joni first attracted attention among folk-music audiences in Toronto while she was still in her teens. Soon, a number of well-known folk singers began to record her songs, including Tom Rush, Buffy Sainte-Marie and Dave Van Ronk. Then, in late 1968, Judy Collins scored a massive international hit single with a cover of Mitchell's song 'Both Sides Now'. As a result of this, Mitchell garnered considerable attention for her second album, *Clouds* (containing her own version of 'Both Sides Now'), when it was released in April 1969 and later won her a Grammy for Best Folk Performance.

In 1970, Mitchell released her third album, *Ladies Of The Canyon*, which contained the international hit single 'Big Yellow Taxi'. She followed this with a number of albums that featured her trademark intense introspection, but musically she evolved, with 1971's *Blue* sounding more rock-based and 1974's *Court And Spark* betraying a greater sophistication.

Always a non-conformist, Joni Mitchell is a truly original voice in popular music and in 1995 was the recipient of *Billboard*'s prestigious Century Award for 'distinguished creative achievement'. However, the true mark of her ability as a songwriter is that, despite the intensely personal nature of many of her compositions, her songs still prove versatile enough to have been covered by artists from almost every musical genre, including Bob Dylan, Percy Faith, Amy Grant, Chet Atkins, Frank Sinatra, Andy Williams, Glen Campbell, Tori Amos, The Byrds, Crosby, Stills And Nash, James Taylor, Neil Diamond, Willie Nelson and Bing Crosby.

SUGGESTED LISTENING: *Joni Mitchell: Hits* (Reprise Records, 1996). Guest artists include David Crosby, James Taylor and Graham Nash. Tracks include 'Urge For Going', 'Big Yellow Taxi', 'Woodstock' and 'The Circle Game'.

28. MICK JAGGER (1943–) AND KEITH RICHARDS (1943–)

Perceived as the big bad brother of The Beatles, The Rolling Stones' rebellious image, combined with the hard-edged aggression of their blues-driven music, drew them an eager following amongst the burgeoning teenage scene of the day. (Interestingly, though, their first hit was a Lennon and McCartney song, 'I Wanna Be Your Man'.) However, while their uninhibited and sexually loose attitudes might have appealed to a generation, image is often a temporary phase and their longevity as a band is truly accounted for by the excellence of their compositions.

During the late 1960s, The Rolling Stones pushed the envelope of rock 'n' roll with album after album containing provocative songs replete with sexual innuendoes ('[I Can't Get No] Satisfaction'), drug references ('Mother's Little Helper'), interracial relations ('Brown Sugar') and Satanism ('Sympathy For The Devil'). These albums also included 'Get Off My Cloud' from *December's Children (And Everybody's)* (1965); 'Paint It Black' from *Aftermath* (1966); 'Let's Spend The Night Together' and 'Ruby Tuesday' from *Between The Buttons* (1967); and 'Jumping Jack Flash' from their classic album *Beggars Banquet* (1968).

The band's breakthrough single, '(I Can't Get No) Satisfaction', rocketed to Number One in the US charts for four consecutive weeks on its release in 1965. The song is a blend of a raucous, primeval guitar and scathing, slurred lyrics, and it marked the band's transgression from the classical blues of their formative years to a darker and more sexually explicit rock 'n' roll. '(I Can't Get

No) Satisfaction' embodies what would become the group's signature style and is regarded by many as the greatest rock 'n' roll song of all time.

SUGGESTED LISTENING: *Forty Licks* (Virgin Records, 2002), two-CD compilation of 40 recordings spanning four decades, including 'Wild Horses', 'You Can't Always Get What You Want', '(I Can't Get No) Satisfaction', 'Ruby Tuesday', 'Street Fighting Man', 'Jumping Jack Flash', 'Brown Sugar', 'Tumbling Dice' and 'Angie'.

29. RANDY NEWMAN (1943–)

Songwriter, artist and film composer, Randy Newman has excelled in all areas of music. Considered by the Songwriters' Hall of Fame to be 'one of the most musically adept and stylistically diverse singer/songwriters in the industry today', Randy has enjoyed a phenomenal career. His work on films alone has earned him 16 Oscar nominations, including his first Best Song Award for 'If I Didn't Have You', from the film *Monsters, Inc*. In addition to that, he has received three Grammy Awards, an Emmy for the song 'He's Guilty' (from *Cop Rock*), the first Henry Mancini Award for Lifetime Achievement from ASCAP in 1996, a Golden Satellite Award in 2000 for 'When She Loved Me' (from *Toy Story* 2), an Annie Award from the International Animated Film Society (also for his work on *Toy Story* 2), the Century Award from *Billboard* magazine in December 2000 and the Frederick Loewe Achievement Award from the Palm Springs International Film Festival in 2001.

Randy's compositions can also be heard on such films as *Parenthood*, *Awakenings*, *James And The Giant Peach*, *Pleasantville*, *A Bug's Life*, *Meet The Parents* and *Toy Story*.

However, this is only one aspect of Randy Newman's creative output. As a songwriter, he has been composing professionally from the tender age of 17, enjoying early success with 'I Don't Want To Hear It Anymore' and 'I Think It's Going To Rain Today', while as an artist himself he has released several Top 40 albums, the debut of which – 1968's *12 Songs* – spawned the Number One Hit 'Mama Told Me Not To Come' for Three Dog Night. The same song was later covered by Tom Jones and The Stereophonics and was a massive success in the UK, while Newman's 'You Can Leave Your Hat On' has charted several times and was featured in the international hit movie *The Full Monty*.

SUGGESTED LISTENING: *The Best Of Randy Newman* (Warner Bros, 2001), featuring over 20 recordings by Randy Newman with guest artists Ry Cooder, Glenn Frey, Joe Walsh, Don Henley, Mark Knopfler, Ricki Lee Jones and Bob Seger. Tracks include 'Mama Told Me Not To Come', 'You Can Leave Your Hat On' and 'I Think It's Going To Rain Today'.

30. Sir Tim Rice (1944–) and Lord Andrew Lloyd Webber (1948–)

Tim Rice and Andrew Lloyd Webber, who met and become friends on the London music scene of the 1960s, were the engine of the British stage musical. With Rice writing lyrics and Webber the music, they are responsible for producing such hits as *Joseph And The Amazing Technicolor Dreamcoat*, *Jesus Christ Superstar* and *Evita*. The album of the rock opera *Jesus Christ Superstar* achieved record-breaking sales.

Independently, they have also achieved astonishing results. Rice has provided the lyrics for the smash musicals *Chess* (with music by ABBA's Björn Ulvaeus and Benny Andersson), Disney's *Beauty And The Beast* (with Alan Menken) and *Aida* (with Elton John). Tim has been presented with three Oscars for Best Song so far: his first for 'A Whole New World', from *Aladdin*; his second for 'Can You Feel the Love Tonight' from *The Lion King*; and his third for 'You Must Love Me' (co-written with Madonna), from *Evita*.

Meanwhile, Andrew Lloyd Webber has gone on to work with other collaborators, including lyricist Don Black (*Tell Me On A Sunday* and *Sunset Boulevard*), and his musical output – also including *Starlight Express*, *The Phantom Of The Opera*, *Aspects Of Love*, *Whistle Down The Wind*, *The Beautiful Game* and *The Woman In White* – has so far garnered him seven Tonys, three Grammys, six Oliviers, one Golden Globe, one Oscar and an International Emmy Award.

Suggested listening: *Jesus Christ Superstar* (Decca Records, 2000), cast album on a two-disc set produced by Webber and Rice.

31. Eric Clapton (1945–)

Eric Clapton's achievements as a songwriter and performer are almost without par, as recognised by the fact that he's the only triple inductee into the Rock 'n' Roll Hall of Fame, as a member of both The Yardbirds and Cream and as a solo artist.

Clapton's early years in The Yardbirds and Cream demonstrated his ability not only to absorb the blues of such original artists as Muddy Waters, Bo Diddley and Robert Johnson but to incorporate the emotion of the blues into his style of playing and take blues guitar to a new level of expression. Cream blended neo-psychedelia with fiery versions of classic blues tracks like 'Spoonful', 'Born Under A Bad Sign' and 'Crossroads'. Through his work with Cream, Clapton attained international stardom that was raised to almost biblical proportions, evidenced by the infamous graffito 'CLAPTON IS GOD'.

Clapton's popularity continued beyond Cream and he enjoyed further success with his next band, Blind Faith, who released an eponymous Number One album in 1969. Then, in the following, he struck gold again with the Derek And The Dominos album *Layla And Other Assorted Love Songs*. Despite the overwhelming response to 'Layla', Clapton became a recluse for almost three years after the album's release, eventually making a comeback in 1974 with the Bob Marley cover 'I Shot The Sheriff'. Then, beginning in 1977 with the triple-platinum album *Slowhand* (including the single 'Lay Down Sally'), he wrote a stream of gold and platinum hit songs, many of which featured in his 1988 double-platinum compilation *Crossroads*, which include 73 digitally remastered tracks covering every phase of his career until that time.

Since then, Clapton has continued to surpass his previous successes. His 1989 album *Journeyman* sold more than 2 million and earned him a Grammy for the single 'Bad Love'. Then, in 1992, following the tragic death of his son, he wrote and recorded the Grammy-winning Top Five single 'Tears In Heaven' for the film *Rush*. That same year, his album *Unplugged* – recorded live on the MTV programme of the same name – went straight to Number One and stayed there for three weeks, selling more than 15 million copies worldwide. Its creator earned an astounding six Grammy Awards that year alone.

Clapton won another Grammy for his performance on the track 'The Calling', from Santana's *Supernatural* album, and a nomination for his blues exploration with BB King, *Riding With The King*. He continues to be a relevant songwriter and performer to this day, using the passion of the blues to express the music of his soul. 'The blues are what I've turned to, what has given me inspiration and relief in all of the trials of my life.'

SUGGESTED LISTENING: *Clapton Chronicles: The Best Of Eric Clapton* (Reprise, 1999), featuring 'Tears In Heaven', 'My Father's Eyes', 'Change The World', 'Bad Love' and 'Before You Accuse Me (Take A Look At Yourself)'.

32. BOB MARLEY (1945–81)

Bob Marley is the man who brought reggae to the masses. In the late 1960s, he began recording with prominent reggae producer Lee 'Scratch' Perry, quickly gaining immense prominence in Jamaica as he moved musically from ska to the somewhat slower 'rude boy' music, eventually developing his own innovative brand of reggae and producing the national hits 'Soul Rebel', '400 Years' and 'Small Axe'.

In 1972, Marley's album *Catch A Fire* was his first album to be marketed outside Jamaica, bringing his artless lyricism and infectious rhythms to a wider audience. The album contained such reggae classics as 'Stir It Up' and 'Stop That Train.'

1975 saw the release of Marley's album *Natty Dread* (featuring the classic 'No Woman, No Cry'), while *Rastaman Vibration* was released in 1976 and was followed by another sensational album, *Exodus*, in 1977. The latter were both international smashes, *Exodus* staying in the British charts for 56 consecutive weeks. This album became a classic thanks to several huge commercial hits, including the title track, 'Waiting In Vain' and 'Jamming'. Then, Marley's 1978 album *Kaya* demonstrated a gentler approach to songwriting, yet it found an equal measure of success, especially with the songs 'Is This Love', and 'Satisfy My Soul'.

In addition to becoming a formidable force in the music world, his albums' politically charged messages catapulted Marley into the forefront of a steadily worsening political situation in Jamaica. In fact, his iconic status as a poet and a prophet in his native country had reached such heights that one reporter claimed in *Time* magazine that he 'rivals the government as a political force'.

Bob Marley's music is imbued with its creator's belief in the faith of Rastafarianism, which represented a spiritual alternative to the frequent violence of ghetto life for many poor Jamaicans. As a consequence, Marley's songs gave voice to the day-to-day plight of the Jamaican people. His songs are of faith, devotion and revolution, capturing both his fellow Jamaican's rich spirituality and their impoverished circumstances while managing to retain the strength and pride that pervades their culture. It's therefore little wonder that songs still carry great weight.

'My music fights against the system that teaches to live and die.' – Bob Marley

SUGGESTED LISTENING: *Legend: Bob Marley* (Island Records, 2002), the definitive collection of Bob Marley classics.

33. DON McLEAN (1945–)

Don McLean struggled early in his career to get a deal. His first album was turned down by several labels because he insisted on retaining his own publishing.

Don said he had been inspired by the death of Buddy Holly when he wrote his epic 'American Pie'. A sentimental song about America, it captured the lost American dream perfectly as US citizens struggled with the realities of the Watergate scandal and the war in Vietnam. The irresistible chorus and poetic, Dylan-esque storyline verses carried the song for its unconventional eight and half minutes, and it remained at Number One in the US *Billboard* charts for four weeks, catapulting the album to Number One for over seven. The album also spawned the loving ballad 'Vincent (Castles In The Air)', a track that played daily in the entrance to the Van Gogh Museum in Amsterdam.

Never quite reaching the heady and unattainable heights of success he'd achieved with 'American Pie', Don still wrote some memorable hits, including the Top 30 'Dreidel' and the UK Top 40 single 'Everyday'. To celebrate the turn of the Millennium, President Bill Clinton asked Don to sing at the Lincoln Memorial and attend the Founders' Dinner at the White House, honouring artists and industrialists.

In 2002, NEA/RIAA (US National Endowment for the Arts/Recording Industry Association of America) announced the greatest songs of the 20th Century. Following the inestimable 'Over The Rainbow', 'White Christmas', 'This Land Is My Land' and 'Respect', 'American Pie' was deemed the fifth-greatest song of the century. No small achievement.

SUGGESTED LISTENING: *The Best Of Don McLean* (EMI Gold, 2001). Includes 'Vincent', 'Castles In The Air', 'Crossroads', 'Birthday Song', 'It Doesn't Matter Anymore' and 'Winterwood'.

34. VAN MORRISON (1945–)

Born in Belfast in 1945, Van Morrison is the son of a shipyard worker who collected American blues and jazz records. He grew up to the sounds of Muddy Waters, Lightnin' Hopkins and John Lee Hooker, influences that are clear in his playing and songwriting. As a teenager he played guitar, harmonica and saxophone in a number of small-time Irish showbands, skiffle groups and rock 'n' roll bands before forming an R&B group called simply Them in 1964.

Three years later, Morrison broke onto the scene as a solo artist with the album *Astral Weeks*, a timeless combination of Celtic music, improvised jazz and rhythm and blues. Since then, he has written songs of such unrivalled integrity and vision that his place in songwriting history is undisputed.

Moving musically between his Celtic roots and his passion for the blues, in his songs Morrison found a medium in which to express his deep interest in spiritual matters, as reflected in such albums as *Wavelength*, *Common One*, *Beautiful Vision*, *Inarticulate Speech Of The Heart*, *A Sense Of Wonder*, *No Guru No Method No Teacher* and *Poetic Champions Compose*.

A versatile and prolific writer, Van Morrison has released countless albums, of which his collaboration with John Lee Hooker, *Don't Look Back*, won him a Grammy in 1998. The depth of his lyrics and the soft musicality of his melodies have stood the test of time, as proven by the continued popularity of such songs of his as 'Have I Told You Lately That I Love You', 'Moondance', 'Brown-Eyed Girl' and 'Gloria.'

SUGGESTED LISTENING: *The Best Of Van Morrison* (Polydor Records, 1990).

35. THE GIBB BROTHERS (BARRY 1946–; ROBIN 1949–; MAURICE 1949–2003)

The Bee Gees have been at the top of the pop game for over 40 years, having achieved Number One status in each of the last five decades. Together they have sold more than 110,000,000 albums, including the most successful motion-picture soundtrack album of all time, *Saturday Night Fever*. They have been nominated for 16 Grammy and won nine. Their songs have been covered by hundreds of artists, including Barbra Streisand, *NSync, Wyclef Jean, Kenny Rogers, Destiny's Child, Dionne Warwick, Celine Dion, Al Green, Diana Ross, Oscar Dela Hoya, Luther Vandross, Dolly Parton, Johnny Mathis, Sarah Vaughn and Elvis Presley.

As songwriters and producers, the Gibb brothers are attributed with the unique achievement of having had five singles in *Billboard*'s Top 10 simultaneously, and, as artists, with having had six consecutive Number One singles. Their songs are admired the world over for their indelible melodies, highly crafted structures, inspirational harmonies, affective vocals, boundary-setting production and incredible hooks. In the mid-1990s, The Bee Gees received industry acknowledgment in the form of Lifetime Achievement honours at the American Music Awards, then at the World Music Awards and finally the British Music Awards. Such international admiration is a long way from the local Manchester cinemas in which Barry, Robin and Maurice first performed as little boys in the 1950s. In fact, only Frank Sinatra and Barbra Streisand have had careers that have matched the Gibb Brothers in terms of longevity and continued success and popularity; but what's more significant is that The Bee Gees, unlike those legends, wrote, arranged and produced all their own songs.

SUGGESTED LISTENING: *Their Greatest Hits: The Record* (Universal Records, 2001), two-disc compilation including 'If I Can't Have You', 'Staying Alive', 'More Than A Woman', 'How Deep Is Your Love' and 'Emotion'.

36. BENNY ANDERSSON (1946–) AND BJÖRN ULVAEUS (1945–)

As the songwriting engine behind ABBA, the most commercially successful pop group of the 1970s, Benny and Björn were the ultimate pop songwriter/producers, creating lush, buoyant songs with a melodic immediacy that was enviable.

ABBA (an acronym taken from the bandmembers' first names) first came to light when they submitted the single 'Waterloo' to the Eurovision Song Contest and became the first Swedish act to win the competition. Although the group failed to follow up the hit immediately, having several non-event singles, a year later they released 'SOS', which became an international smash and led the way for a string of hits, including 'Mamma Mia', 'Fernando', 'Knowing Me, Knowing You', 'The Name Of The Game' and 'Dancing Queen', the latter of which was surprisingly ABBA's only US chart-topper.

In 1978, the band was so popular that they made *ABBA: The Movie*. However, the strain on the group's dynamics and internal marriages – amplified by their success – was becoming apparent, and romantic suffering became a core subject for many of the songs featured on the albums *Voulez-Vous* and *Super Trouper*.

While the group officially disbanded after the 1982 release of their single 'Under Attack', the spirit of their music never faded and is still as strong today, highlighting the magnitude of Benny and Björn's songwriting talent. Aside from the continued repackaging of their hits in various compilations, the Australian impersonators Björn Again tour relentlessly to packed-out crowds worldwide; British dance duo Erasure released a covers collection, *ABBA-esque*; 'Dancing Queen' was a permanent fixture of U2's 1993 'Zoo TV' tour; the 1995 movie *Muriel's Wedding* garnered acclaim for its depiction of a lonely Australian girl who seeks refuge in ABBA's music; and, most recently, the musical *Mamma Mia* – based around Benny and Björn's songs – has become a constant sell-out since playing in London and New York.

SUGGESTED LISTENING: *The Complete Gold Collection* (Polygram, 2000), a double disc compilation of all the band's hit records.

37. ELTON JOHN (1947–) AND BERNIE TAUPIN (1950–)

Aside from Bacharach and David, Elton John and lyric writer Bernie Taupin comprise one of the longest running and most successful songwriting teams of all time. Without doubt, Elton John fits the classification of what it is to be a singer/songwriter and was the earliest successful artist of the rock 'n' roll era to make the piano the lead instrument, at a time when the guitar dominated the pop-music landscape.

Born Reg Dwight in London in 1947, by age four Elton could play the piano by ear and went on to study at the Royal Academy of Music at the tender age of 11. Although he failed an audition at Liberty Records, he was given the number of Bernie Taupin, a lyricist. Elton started writing music for the lyrics he was sent, and so the two began corresponding by mail. The pair met six months later and so began one of the most enduring and successful writing partnerships of the 20th century.

Since then, Elton and Bernie have co-written countless hit singles, including 'Rocket Man', 'Levon', 'Honky Cat', 'Crocodile Rock', 'Daniel', 'Bennie And The Jets' and 'Don't Let The Sun Go Down On Me'. Elton's 1997 re-recording of 'Candle In The Wind', sung at the funeral of Princess Diana, became the highest selling single in history within a month of its release.

Between them, Elton and Bernie have sold more than 100 million records. They have both received countless accolades and awards, and in 2004 Elton John's songwriting achievements were recognised further when he received the prestigious Fellowship of the British Academy of Composers & Songwriters in 2004.

SUGGESTED LISTENING: *Elton John, Greatest Hits: 1970-2002* (Island Records, 2002). Guest artists include Luciano Pavarotti, Alessandro Safina and George Michael.

38. NICKY CHINN (1947–) AND MIKE CHAPMAN (1947–)

Nicky Chinn and Mike Chapman represent one of Britain's most successful songwriting teams of the 1970s.

Mike Chapman first met Nicky Chinn when the former was in the group Tangerine Peel. They were brought together under the wing of producer Mickie Most's RAK label and assigned to work with a new group named The Sweet. Following two hits in 1971, 'Funny Funny' and 'Co-Co', the duo revealed a flair for big melodies and nonsensical lyrics.

Chinn and Chapman went on to provide The Sweet with a series of smash records in a progressively harder style, including 'Little Willy', 'Wig-Wam Bam', the UK Number One 'Blockbuster', 'Hell Raiser' and the oft-covered 'Ballroom Blitz'. As The Sweet began to desire more control over their music and Nicky and Mike looked to expand on their glam-rock songwriting talents, they turned to the female artist Suzi Quatro. Their songs for her – including 'Can The Can', '48 Crash', 'Devil Gate Drive' and 'The Wild One' – launched Suzi's career into the stratosphere, and they then proceeded to do a similar favour for a band named Mud. Again, the hits kept coming with 'Dyna-Mite', 'The Cat Crept In', 'The Secrets That You Keep' and the Number Ones 'Tiger Feet' and 'Lonely This Christmas'.

Despite their success with a large number of different bands, Chinn and Chapman remained virtually unknown in the USA. A couple of Sweet tunes had made a small impression, but it wasn't until 1978 that the duo finally impacted on the US charts with Exile's 'Kiss You All Over'. Soon after, Chinn and

Chapman began to concentrate more on personal projects and production. This effectively brought an end to their flow of hit records, although they did make one final charge in 1982 with the smash song 'Mickey' by Toni Basil.

SUGGESTED LISTENING: Suzi Quatro, *Greatest Hits 1* (EMI, 2000).

39. DAVID BOWIE (1947–)

David Bowie has demonstrated remarkable creative skill in being a chameleon of songwriting. A gifted mimic of many musical genres, throughout his career he has adapted his songwriting to the changing musical trends of the industry. Yet, with each stylistic movement, his songs have remained insightful, highly original and eminently hook-laden.

Amazingly, Bowie's early career was undistinguished and he came close to becoming a Buddhist monk before the success of 1969's 'Space Oddity', a song based on the Stanley Kubrick film *2001: A Space Odyssey*. Since then, he has continually re-invented himself, shifting between almost every genre that exists, including hippie, proto-metal, pop/rock, androgynous glam rock, 'plastic soul', avant-pop, electro, dance pop, guitar rock, techno/drum 'n' bass and acoustic folk.

Even when Bowie occasionally fell out of fashion, his influence was still marked in popular music, surfacing in a number of sub-genres, including punk, new wave, goth, new romantic and electronica. For other songwriters, he will remain a great source of inspiration for both his lyrical exploration and stylistic manipulation, and it's hard not to marvel at the sheer breadth of his ability, particularly in tracks such as 'Space Oddity', 'Changes', 'Fame', 'Heroes' and 'Let's Dance'. Few songwriters have had such a significant impact on popular music.

SUGGESTED LISTENING: *Best Of Bowie* (EMI, 2004), a double-CD compilation covering Bowie's career from 'Space Oddity' to 'Little Wonder'.

40. BILLY JOEL (1949–)

Billy Joel is the archetypal piano man, a songwriter who writes for the piano and lives for the piano. Although he has achieved great success as a performer, he has gone to lengths to establish his status as a songwriter first, for which he has been justly recognised through various awards and accolades.

The key indication of Joel's songwriting prowess is the list of distinguished major artists who have covered and had success with his songs.

Such artists who have recorded his material include Barbra Streisand, Frank Sinatra, Bette Midler, Isaac Hayes, Barry White, Kenny Rogers, Dolly Parton and Garth Brooks.

As an artist in his own right, Billy has been a major recording artist throughout the past four decades. Of his 14 album releases, 11 have been certified platinum or multi-platinum and have generated more than 40 chart-listed single hits, including 'Piano Man', 'Just The Way You Are', 'Only The Good Die Young', 'It's Still Rock And Roll, Girl' and 'We Didn't Start The Fire'. In recognition of these achievements, Joel has been nominated for 18 Grammy Awards, of which he has won five, including two each for 'Just The Way You Are' and '52nd Street' and one for 'Glass Houses'. In 1990, he was presented with the Grammy Legend Award.

SUGGESTED LISTENING: *Greatest Hits* (Columbia Records, 1997), four-disc collection covering different periods in the singer/songwriter's career.

41. STEVIE WONDER (1950–)

Born Steveland Morris on 13 May 1950, in Saginaw, Michigan, Stevie Wonder was given too much oxygen in an incubator shortly after his birth and permanently lost his sight. However, this didn't prevent him from becoming one of the most respected songwriters of modern music. In fact, as was aptly said of the man when he was inducted into the Songwriters' Hall of Fame, 'Our expectation of Wonder is different to that of most other artists. He could release ten indifferent, poor, weak or spectacular records over the next 20 years and nothing would change our fixed perception of him and of the body of outstanding music he has produced since 1963.'

Under the name 'Little Stevie Wonder', Morris's first single, 'Fingertips', was a Number One smash and was followed swiftly with such classics as 'Uptight', 'For Once In My Life' and 'Signed, Sealed And Delivered'.

Not only a musical genius, Wonder was a savvy recording artist and invested all the money he had earned in his teens to fund his own studio. As a result, he became the first Motown artist who could call his own shots, allowing him to negotiate a better financial deal and, more importantly, enjoy the freedom to create his music how he wanted it.

Empowered by this freedom, Wonder's creativity as a songwriter exploded. He pioneered the use of the synthesiser in black music while broadening his lyrical concerns to include racial problems and spiritual questions. Playing all of the instruments on his albums and producing himself, he recorded and released a stream of classic soul albums, including *Talking Book* (1972), featuring the polyrhythmic funk of 'Superstition' and the appealing pop ballad

'You Are The Sunshine Of My Life'; *Innervisions* (1973), with the socially conscious 'Living For The City' and 'Higher Ground'; and the double album *Songs In The Key Of Life* (1976), which is regarded as his most ambitious and fulfilling work to date.

Throughout his career, Stevie Wonder has demonstrated a complete mastery of musical forms and instruments. He appears as happy writing a groove-busting reggae track ('Masterblaster [Jammin]') as he is a sentimental ballad ('I Just Called To Say I Love You') or even breathing new life into an old topic ('Happy Birthday'). Consistently at the forefront of black music, he remains one of the most admired songwriters in popular-music history.

SUGGESTED LISTENING: *Song Review: A Greatest Hits Collection* (Motown Records, 1996).

42. STING (1951–)

Of all the songwriter/artists featured here, Sting is arguably most worthy of the description of 'songsmith'. His attention to melody, lyrical development and harmonic integrity have created some of the most affecting and memorable pop songs ever written, including 'Every Breath You Take', 'Message In A Bottle', 'Roxanne' and 'Fields Of Gold'.

From his work with The Police to his career as a solo artist, Sting has demonstrated his trademark ability to blur cultural lines and blend high art with pop. In 2001, he was presented with the Kahlil Gibran Spirit of Humanity Award from the Arab-American Institute Foundation for his 'efforts to promote cross-cultural understanding', in particular through his duet 'Desert Rose' with Algerian superstar Cheb Mami.

Whether the genre is classical, country, folk, jazz, R&B, reggae or rock, he appears equally at ease with each, mixing styles to create a dazzling palette of songs. Every one of his albums contains a masterclass in being a songsmith, particularly the phenomenal *Ten Summoners Tales*, while the 2.5 million-selling live album *All This Time* (which provides fresh renditions of classic songs from his Police and solo years) highlights just how much his songs have become part of the soundtrack of people's lives

In recognition of the impact Sting has made on music, he has received countless accolades, including 16 Grammy Awards, the 2002 Brit Award for Outstanding Contribution to British Music and the Ivor Novello Award for International Achievement.

SUGGESTED LISTENING: *The Very Best Of Sting And The Police* (UTV Records, 1997).

43. Phil Collins (1951–)

Phil Collins' exceptional career as a drummer, singer, composer and producer has so far accounted for over 250 million albums sold (including his work with Genesis), seven Grammy Awards and a catalogue of memorable hits. His body of work has been both upbeat – as demonstrated in songs such as 'Sussudio', 'You Can't Hurry Love' and 'Two Hearts' – and serious, as portrayed on haunting tracks such as 'In The Air Tonight', 'Against All Odds' and 'Another Day In Paradise'.

Collins' debut solo album, *No Jacket Required*, reached Number One in the UK pop charts and remained in the charts for an astounding 123 weeks. Despite such achievements as a songwriter, he is understated in his accomplishments, affirming modestly, 'Behind the drums is where I live, although I do like to visit other places.'

These 'other places' include film scoring, a discipline in which he struck gold with his highly awarded music for the Disney animation *Tarzan*, a film that carried the hit single 'You'll Be In My Heart'.

Suggested listening: *Hits* (Atlantic Records, 1998). Comprises 16 Collins songs, including 'Easy Lover', 'Separate Lives', 'Both Sides Of The Story' and 'One More Night'.

44. Diane Warren (1956–)

A three-time Grammy Award winner, a five-time ASCAP Songwriter of the Year Award winner and a two-time BMI Songwriter of the Year Award winner, Diane Warren is considered to be the most prolific and successful contemporary female songwriter of her generation. Even so, she possesses a common songwriter trait: relative public anonymity. People know the artists who have sung her songs and recognise her songs immediately but wouldn't recognise her on the street.

Warren's songs reflect the essence of being a pop songwriter, replete with fluid melodies, easy tempos and universal lyrical themes, and are the result of a skill carefully honed over 20 years of 12-hour/six-day-a-week writing schedules. This has led to a catalogue of some 800 songs.

A summary of Warren's career reveals an amazing ability to write across a diverse range of musical genres and styles. Her songs have been covered by artists of the likes of Aretha Franklin, Celine Dion ('Because You Loved Me'), Patti Labelle ('If You Asked Me To', also a hit for Celine Dion), Barbra Streisand, Gloria Estefan ('Reach'), Tina Turner, Whitney Houston ('You Were Loved'), Toni Braxton ('Unbreak My Heart'), Aaron Neville, Faith Hill and Tim McGraw ('Just to Hear You Say That You Love Me'), Starship

('Nothing's Gonna Stop Us Now', from the 1987 movie *Mannequin*) and Ricky Martin.

Warren started her career as a songwriter with her father escorting her to music publishers, where she was rejected time after time. To gain entry into the insular music business, she then took a job with a music-industry messenger service, hoping that this would open doors for her, but she was fired two weeks later. Her big break came when a friend helped her to get a staff songwriting job with pop singer Laura Branigan's producer, Jack White. Giving her a French melody written by Martine Clemenceau, Jack asked Warren to write English lyrics. The resulting song became 'Solitaire', a Number Seven pop hit in early 1983.

Since that day, Warren has written hit after hit and broken record after record for songwriting achievements. Her Oscar-winning 'I Don't Wanna Miss A Thing', performed by Aerosmith for the movie *Armageddon*, wasn't only a Number One in the pop charts but simultaneously hit number one in the country charts with a version by Mark Chestnut. Meanwhile, 'How Do I Live?', from the Nicolas Cage movie Con Air, charted for a record-breaking 69 weeks in *Billboard*'s Hot 100 chart.

SUGGESTED LISTENING: *Because You Loved Me: The Songs Of Diane Warren* (Columbia Records, 1998). Johnny Mathis performs tracks including 'Unbreak My Heart', 'Love Will Lead You Back', 'Don't Take Away My Heaven' and 'Set The Night To Music'.

45. MICHAEL JACKSON (1958–)

Once described as 'a true ambassador of what pop music can be', Michael Jackson has recently become so synonymous with scandals and plastic surgery that his songwriting talent appears to have been overshadowed or forgotten.

In a remarkable career of unparalleled musical, commercial and critical success, Michael – along with Quincy Jones and Rod Temperton – is responsible for the best-selling album of all time, *Thriller*, which features the Number One 'Wanna Be Startin' Somethin''', 'The Girl Is Mine', 'Beat It', 'Billie Jean', 'The Lady In My Life' and 'Baby Be Mine' and features Eddie Van Halen, Paul McCartney and Janet Jackson as guest artists.

Even in his youth, Michael was a precocious talent as the lead singer of The Jackson Five. With him at the forefront, the group scored 13 Top 20 singles. His first solo album, *Off The Wall*, was an equal success and offered such pop gems as 'Don't Stop 'Til You Get Enough' and 'Rock With You', tracks that previewed the distinctive rock/soul fusion that became the sound foundation for the quintessential pop album, *Thriller*.

Jackson continued to extend his musical legacy with the follow-up albums *Bad*, *Dangerous* and *HIStory*, proving and maintaining his status as an innovative and original performer and songwriter of the highest calibre.

SUGGESTED LISTENING: *Thriller* (Epic Records, 1982).

46. QUEEN

'Bohemian Rhapsody' has become Queen's signature song, its bombastic, pseudo-opera structure, punched through by heavy-metal guitar, encapsulating their music. The song also came to represent their penchant for musical excess; it took three weeks to record and legend has it that there were so many vocal overdubs that it was possible see through the tape at certain points.

Queen's heady concoction of exaggerated prog rock, heavy metal, vaudevillian music hall, opera and kitschy humour led to the composition of some of the greatest rock anthems ever, including 'We Are The Champions', 'We Will Rock You', 'Fat Bottomed Girls', 'Crazy Little Thing Called Love', 'Another One Bites The Dust' and 'Under Pressure' (with David Bowie). Their influence on subsequent generations of hard-rock and metal bands can be heard in the music of such heavyweights as Metallica, Smashing Pumpkins and Limp Bizkit. However, they have also produced some truly touching songs, such as 'Who Wants To Live Forever' , the hit single 'Somebody To Love' and the fragile acoustic and Live Aid show-topper 'Is This The World We Created?'

Queen were a band built from contradiction – macho and fey, hard and soft, serious and kitsch. They were also unusual in that all four members of the band were writers and each one of them wrote a Number One hit for the band.

SUGGESTED LISTENING: *Greatest Hits 1* and *2* (EMI, 2001).

47. PRINCE (1958–)

A multi-instrumental genius of the likes of Stevie Wonder, Prince had mastered 12 instruments by ear by his late teens. At aged 19, he had signed a contract with Warner Brothers Records for $100,000 and enjoyed unprecedented total control over his debut album, 1978's *For You*.

With this album and the three that followed – *Prince* (1979), *Dirty Mind* (1980) and *Controversy* (1981) – Prince was free to concoct his unique blend of disco rhythms, funky synthesised riffs, rock 'n' roll guitar and sleazy, overtly sexual lyrics. While he had a small hit with 'I Wanna Be Your Lover' in 1979, it wasn't until the release of *1999* (in 1982) that he made his commercial breakthrough. From this album, Prince scored three Top 10 singles – '1999', 'Little Red Corvette' and 'Delirious' – while the album stayed in the *Billboard* charts for a further three years.

Prince's next album was his key to superstardom: the soundtrack to his 1984 film *Purple Rain*, which he had produced, arranged, composed and performed in. The album won him both a Grammy and an Academy Award for Best Original Song.

With each album he has released, Prince has shown remarkable stylistic growth and musical diversity, constantly experimenting with different sounds and textures and paying scant regard to the boundaries of pop, rock, jazz, funk and dance. Instead, he composes his own experimental concoction of sexually charged lyrics and innovative instrumentals.

Acting as writer, producer, arranger and composer for most of his records, Prince has proved again and again to be one of the most singular talents of the rock 'n' roll era. Not only has he released a string of groundbreaking albums, toured frequently, produced albums and written songs for many other artists (including Sinéad O'Connor's 'Nothing Compares 2 U', possibly the most successful of Prince's collaborative efforts), he has found the time to record hundreds of songs that still haven't seen the light of day and remain unreleased in the vaults at his base of operations at Paisley Park.

SUGGESTED LISTENING: *The Hits 1* and *2* (Paisley Park, 1993).

48. STOCK, AITKEN AND WATERMAN

If Nicky Chinn and Mike Chapman ruled the '70s with their brand of glam rock, Mike Stock, Matt Aitken and Pete Waterman ruled the '80s with their take on pop/dance music.

Stock, Aitken and Waterman rapidly gained a reputation for being a slick, well-oiled songwriting/production powerhouse that cranked out hit after hit, becoming the template for many future production houses. In one end went their influences – ABBA, Cerrone, The Village People and all the other Euro-disco of the late '70s – and out the other came ultra-slick, glossy and infectious pop of the highest commercial quality. Their results were loved and loathed in equal measure.

Whatever critics said, the results speak for themselves. Stock, Aitken and Waterman single-handedly launched the careers of Dead Or Alive, Bananarama, Mel And Kim, Rick Astley and the superstar Kylie Minogue with self-aware, over-the-top and commercially rich productions. Tracks like Dead Or Alive's 'You Spin Me Round (Like A Record)', Rick Astley's 'Never Gonna Give You Up' and Kylie Minogue's 'I Should Be So Lucky' are masterful in their demonstration of the art of infectious melody writing and simple chord turnarounds over hi-NRG dance tracks. Their songs are all simple, but deceptively so, as good pop writing can be the most demanding kind of songwriting that there is.

SUGGESTED LISTENING: Kylie Minogue, *Kylie* (Mushroom Records, 1988).

49. U2

With songs like 'Sunday Bloody Sunday', 'Pride (In The Name Of Love)', 'With Or Without You' and 'One', U2 have proven themselves to be songwriters unafraid to wear their hearts on their sleeve. If there is a band that truly believes in the potential for rock 'n' roll to change the world, it is U2. Their songs feature passionate, grandiose musical and lyrical statements on politics and religion, providing a vehicle for Bono's crusade to express his beliefs in song. Whether his words come down with the force of a sledgehammer (as in 'Sunday Bloody Sunday') or are subtle and looser in meaning (as in 'One'), the effect is still the same: U2 write music to emote and move the listener to action.

The flawless combination of Bono's soaring, powerful vocals; the Edge's signature guitar sound of heavily processed, sweeping sonic landscapes; and Adam Clayton and Larry Mullen's driving, hard-rock rhythms have led many to consider U2 as being the epitome of what a band should be: a collaborative effort. The band never rest on their laurels, and anyone who has witnessed them work in a studio has been astounded by the craft, energy and detail that goes into their songwriting as they constantly hone and develop their trademark sound.

Their 1987 album *The Joshua Tree* is perhaps U2's finest hour, providing them with their first US Number One and third consecutive UK Number One in the album charts, setting a record by going platinum within 28 hours. That album – which spawned the US Number One singles 'With Or Without You' and 'I Still Haven't Found What I'm Looking For' – and the group's subsequent tour earned U2 appearances on the covers of respected publications such as *Time* magazine.

SUGGESTED LISTENING: *The Best Of U2: 1980–1990* (Island, 1998) and *The Best Of U2: 1990–2000* (Island, 2002). For an example of perfection in the crafting of an album of songs, however, listen to the classic *The Joshua Tree* (Island, 1987).

50. RADIOHEAD

Radiohead are a band that have made experimentation their songwriting tool. Their innovation and boldness has created a series of albums markedly different from each other but held together by a core vein of angst and alienation.

Thom Yorke's tortured lyrics sung to an epic backdrop of textured guitars has been a theme of theirs since the band's surprise breakthrough single, 'Creep', in 1993. Influenced as much by Pink Floyd and My Bloody Valentine as REM and The Pixies, Radiohead have cultivated their sound from the debut release *Pablo Honey* in 1993 through the deeper, darker and more acoustic compositions of *The Bends* (1995) to the progressive, electronic-tinged masterpiece of *OK Computer* (1997) and beyond into a challenging landscape of minimalist electronica (*Kid A*, 2000; *Amnesiac*, 2001).

Radiohead's quest for perfection in their craft has led to both elation and disappointment in fans and critics alike as the band strive for a near-impossible goal. Yet, in many people's eyes, they have already achieved their goal; the majestic blend of unfettered prog rock, post-punk angst, eerie electronic textures and assured songwriting present in *OK Computer* is considered by many to be their greatest work. Even so, for Radiohead, their quest is far from over.

SUGGESTED LISTENING: *The Bends* (Capitol/EMI, 1995) for crafted rock songwriting and *OK Computer* (Capitol/EMI, 1997) for experimentation.

50 Years Of The
Ivor Novello Awards

With Brian Willey

The 'Ivors' are the premier awards ceremony for the recognition of excellence in songwriting and composing. The ceremony is the only annual event that exclusively honours the source and centre of the music industry's existence and prosperity: the songwriter.

The Ultimate Accolade

Over the years, many of the biggest names in popular music have collected Ivor Novello Awards for their outstanding contributions to music. Elton John, George Michael, Robbie Williams, Kylie Minogue, Madonna, Stevie Wonder, Phil Collins, Travis, UB40, Blur, Queen, Sting, David Bowie, Take That, The Bee Gees, Simply Red, U2, Tom Jones, Avril Lavigne, Coldplay, The Streets and Craig David are just a few of the exceptional artists and bands who have picked up awards.

Perhaps more importantly, the writers behind many of the greatest songs have been honoured for their contributions to music. Holland, Dozier and Holland; Rob Davis and Cathy Dennis; Stock, Aitken and Waterman; and Sir Noël Coward have all been recognised with Ivors, as have many songwriters who might otherwise have gone unrecognised in the public eye but have become part of the musical consciousness of society – the writers of such tracks as 'Delilah', 'Save Your Kisses For Me', 'Kung-Fu Fighting', 'We Don't Talk Anymore', 'Believe' and 'Leave Right Now'.

To a songwriter, an Ivor is regarded as the ultimate accolade. The reason why an Ivor is held in such esteem is that these awards are given by songwriters to songwriters, from one peer to another. The award winners are chosen by a committee made up solely of writers from across the whole spectrum of musical genres, while the ceremony itself is presented by the British Academy of Composers & Songwriters, in association with the Performing Right Society.

This has given the event an integrity and international respect that is fiercely guarded by the Academy.

THE ORIGIN OF THE IVOR NOVELLO AWARDS

The histories of the Academy and the Ivor Novello Awards are inextricably linked. The Academy was first formed in March 1947 as the British Songwriters' Protective Association, before becoming the Songwriters' Guild of Great Britain in the following year. The Guild's main purpose was to increase the broadcasting performance of British compositions, but further endeavours were also to be made in order to ensure enhancement of the British songwriter in general. With regard to this, the concept of bestowing awards was first mooted by Vice-Chairman Eric Maschwitz in early 1948, but it took a further eight years before the project reached fruition. As the work and influence of the Songwriters' Guild grew, full-time General Secretary Victor Knight was appointed in early 1949, and his endeavours eventually brought about the Ivor Novello Awards scheme in 1955.

So why the 'Ivor Novellos'? The answer to this question is simply that, at the time of their creation, Ivor Novello had undoubtedly been the most successful and distinguished theatrical composer of his time. How better to pay tribute, then, than by creating an award in his name to honour British musical excellence?

IVOR NOVELLO

David Ivor Davies was born in Cardiff on 15 January 1893. Being born in the Land of Song helped to nurture his musical talent to some degree, but it was his mother's influence that carried him forward to fame and fortune. He was exactly the son Madame Clara Novello Davies had prayed for: 'It would surely be a boy. And I would have him "made to order", a beautiful "Bubbles" sort of creation with every gift, especially with music in his soul...' Well, she certainly got her wish, and with his mother being a singing teacher, 'Ivor' was immersed in her world almost before he could walk and talk.

At the age of ten, Ivor won a scholarship, as a chorister, to Magdalen College School, Oxford, but when his faultless treble sound eventually broke, the voice of the adult Ivor wasn't what the College had hoped for. Leaving Oxford, he returned to Cardiff, where he taught piano to a few pupils but accompanied and composed constantly.

Ivor was 21 when World War I was declared, and he was in no rush to enlist. What seemed more important was the need for a new patriotic song. He came up with a title – 'Till The Boys Come Home' – and began working on a melody, but he needed help to complete the lyric and asked a family friend, Lena Guilbert Ford, to finish it. From its first performance, the song proved a hit with the public, and by 1915, under its new title of 'Keep The Home Fires Burning', it became a nationally acclaimed song.

In 1916, Ivor joined the Royal Naval Air Service, intent on becoming a pilot, but two disastrous solo flights, both culminating in crashes, determined that he should spend the rest of the War firmly on the ground. He was subsequently posted to the Air Ministry in London, and there he was able to continue composing. By then he had co-written with Jerome Kern the score for the show *Theodore & Co*, along with a number of songs for revues. Other composing co-operations ensued, and Ivor developed a desire to write his own musicals and even star in them.

There was a long way to go before that could happen, however, and Ivor's next 13 years were almost non-musical, although far from unproductive. With his striking good looks, he was frantically busy as a film star and screen writer, both in the UK and in America, where he appeared in some two dozen Hollywood productions. During all that time, his 'musical' dream was still present, but he didn't get his break in this respect until he was 41 years old, and even then it came purely by chance.

HM Tennant was the General Manager of the Theatre Royal, Drury Lane, and was in desperate need of a lavish romantic play. Could Ivor come up with something suitable? On impulse, Ivor said that he could, asserting that he had an idea. The fact that he hadn't any idea didn't seem to matter; that would hopefully come soon enough – and, indeed, it did. Within 24 hours, Ivor had written a synopsis, had it accepted and was given six months to write it, score it, cast it and stage it.

On Thursday 2 May 1935, Drury Lane resounded to the music and songs of Ivor Novello and lyricist Christopher Hassell's *Glamorous Night*. The show, featuring such songs as 'Fold Your Wings' and 'Shine Through My Dreams', was to prove a huge hit.

After this success, there was no stopping Ivor. *Careless Rapture* followed a year later, and then *Crest Of The Wave* in 1937, featuring the rousing song 'Rose Of England'. Probably his best-loved show, *The Dancing Years*, opened on 23 March 1939 and surely had the finest selection of songs from the Novello/Hassell partnership, including 'I Can Give You The Starlight', 'My Dearest Dear', 'My Life Belongs To You', 'Waltz Of My Heart', 'Wings Of Sleep' and 'The Leap Year Waltz', all of them possessing magical words and music.

In all, Ivor staged four spectacular musicals, all at Drury Lane and all in the space of five years – an unheard-of achievement. Only World War II put an end to that success; the show closed on 1 September 1939, marking the end of the London run and the end of Ivor's association with Drury Lane.

Ivor and his company then went on tour the provinces with *The Dancing*

Years, returning to London in 1942, but this time to the Adelphi Theatre. 1943 saw his show *Arc de Triomphe* open at the Phoenix Theatre, but it was also a year that brought a disastrous incident into his life. Wartime fuel restrictions prevented Ivor from driving his beloved Rolls-Royce – his only relaxation at weekends – as often as he wished, and that year a fan conned him into fraudulently obtaining petrol, a complicated story that finally came to head in April 1944. He may have been naïve and innocent of actually committing a crime, but nevertheless he was pronounced guilty and sentenced to imprisonment for two months. An appeal was made which reduced the sentence to one month, but nothing could have been worse for him than incarceration in Wormwood Scrubs. It emotionally broke him, and he needed much help to recover from the indignity of such a penalty.

After D-Day, in the autumn of 1944, Ivor persuaded ENSA to let him go to France and Belgium with his theatrical company to entertain the troops. They stayed for eight weeks and would have remained longer but for engagements already arranged back home.

Perchance To Dream was the musical for 1945, the London Hippodrome was the venue and the lyrics and music were all Ivor's own work. The show is perhaps best remembered for the songs 'We'll Gather Lilacs' and 'Love Is My Reason'.

When the War ended, Ivor took the show on tour in South Africa. On his return he began work on *King's Rhapsody*, his final musical with Christopher Hassell as lyricist. The show opened at London's Palace Theatre on 15 September 1949 and proved to be yet another triumph, particularly its main song, 'Someday My Heart Will Awake'.

In the summer of 1950, Ivor underwent a serious operation, followed by intensive treatment. No details were given but, when he returned to the stage, he was noticeably more frail. He appeared in *King's Rhapsody* until Boxing Day and then left for a holiday in Jamaica to recuperate in the tropical sunshine of Montego Bay.

Ivor came back to London earlier than expected, straight into a British winter. There were several reasons for his early return. Firstly, his new show – *Gay's The Word*, with lyrics by Alan Melville – was opening at the Saville Theatre in February, and its first night was an event he could not miss. Secondly, *King's Rhapsody* had been revived and Ivor was due to take over the role of 'King Nikki'.

The winter of 1950/1 was harsh and Ivor caught a chill. Three weeks later, on 6 March 1951, only three hours after he'd left the theatre, he suffered a coronary thrombosis and died. He was just 58.

The day of Ivor's cremation at Golder's Green was dry and blustery, but at least the sun shone on the many thousands that thronged the approach roads. Eyewitnesses accounts attest that the route was lined three-deep with people for several miles. It was as if every member of every past audience had come to say farewell to their beloved idol, who was known to them simply as 'Ivor'.

His name is continued to be revered by the Academy in its presentation of the Ivor Novello Awards, a lasting tribute to an actor, composer, film star, lyricist, manager, matinée idol, pianist and playwright, a man whose work brought happiness to the hearts and memories of countless millions.

THE AWARDS

The televising of the first presentation of the awards ceremony, at the Theatre Royal, Drury Lane, on Sunday 11 March 1956, proved to be the awards' one and only television appearance. The occasion was a picture of comfortable respectability, with 'Salad Days' winning for the Year's Most Effective Musical Play Score and Eric Coates's *Dambusters* theme winning in the Light Orchestral category. While the winners didn't allude to the revolution that was about to take place (1956 was also the year that Bill Haley And The Comets' '(We're Gonna) Rock Around The Clock' was released in the UK, marking the beginning of the modern rock era in Britain), the coincidence of the Ivors being inaugurated in this year is auspicious. During the 50 years that have passed since then, the Ivor Novello Awards have gone on to reflect ever-changing tastes in music, identifying and acclaiming British music writers of all genres.

One of the first Ivor Novello Awards presented was given to Tolchard Evans and Larry Kahn for their 1955 composition 'Ev'rywhere', which won in the Year's Most Popular Song category. Since that award, over 1,000 Ivor Novello statuettes have been handed out to deserving songwriters. Paul McCartney has received the most, acquiring an impressive collection of 20 bronze statuettes...so far. He is followed by his writing partner John Lennon with 15, and then Lord Andrew Lloyd Webber, with 14. Freddie Mercury, though, is the first writer to receive two awards for the same song – 'Bohemian Rhapsody' – in different years: first in 1975 for Best-Selling British Record and then, 16 years later, at the 1991 Awards for Best-Selling A-Side.

The most awards any writer has received in one evening is three. The first time this occurred was in 1978, when The Bee Gees won International Hit of the Year for 'Staying Alive' and Most Performed Work and Best-Selling A-Side for 'Night Fever'. Six other sets of writers have also achieved this feat: Stock, Aitken and Waterman in 1987 with 'Never Gonna Give You Up'; Mick Leeson and Peter Vale with 'Would I Lie To You?' in 1992; Reg Presley with 'Love Is All Around' in 1994; Brian Higgins and his writing team in 1998 with 'Believe'; Mark Hill and Craig David in 2000 for 'Woman Trouble' and 'Seven Days' and as Songwriters Of The Year; and Rob Davis and Cathy Dennis for 'Can't Get You Out Of My Head' in 2001.

In 1995, the Ivors recognised two formidable acts of the Britpop era when, for the first and only time, a joint award was given for Songwriter(s) of the Year to Blur and Oasis. Stock, Aitken and Waterman set another precedent within this category by being the only writers to be awarded it twice: once in 1987 and then again in 1989.

The categories of the awards have changed dramatically over the years, and this is often a good indication of changing fashions. Ivors have been given for Best Novelty Song, for Best Composition in a Jazz or Beat Idiom and for Outstanding Light Orchestral or Other Non-Vocal Composition. In 1966, Geoff Stephens' 'Winchester Cathedral' was recognised as Britain's International Song of the Year, highlighting the widening influence of British writers on a global scale, while in 1997 the first Independent Dance Award was presented to Tim Kellett and Robin Taylor-Firth for their track 'You're Not Alone', recognising the impact that dance had had on the music business. Once, however, a track defied all categories: David Lee and Herbert Kretzmer's 1960 hit 'Goodness Gracious Me'. The writers of this song were presented with an award boldly entitled Any Work Which In The Opinion Of The Judges Is Worthy Of An Award But Which May Not Necessarily Be Governed By Existing Categories!

Novelty songs have also played their part in the Ivors, featuring prominently during the first five years of the ceremony, with the classic 'Nelly The Elephant' by Peter Hart and Ralph Butler winning in 1956. Throughout the 1960s, such songs continued to appear intermittently, along with 'Flash, Bang, Wallop' by David Heneker in 1963 and 1966's memorable 'Hav Yew Gotta Loight Boy?' by Allan Smethurst. The last time a novelty song was awarded in its own category, however, was in 1971, when Benny Hill's song 'Ernie' won the award.

It would be another 22 years before a novelty record again featured in the Ivor Novellos ceremony. However, on this occasion the song wasn't recognised for being the best novelty song; in 1993, 'Mr Blobby' by Paul Shaw and David Rogers actually won in the Best-Selling Song category! Then, in 2000, Paul Joyce scooped the award for Best-Selling UK Single with 'Can We Fix It?' by Bob The Builder.

Although the awards ceremony has been going strong for the past 50 years, one constant factor remains, and that is the unconditional respect of the world's greatest songwriters to the Ivors.

'I remember coming here the very first time with my mates John, George and Ringo and sitting back there. Just little kids, we were, younger than my kids are now. It was just fantastic to be part of this whole songwriting thing... The Ivors are the greatest awards, the greatest thing for songwriters.'

– Paul McCartney on receiving an Ivor Novello Fellowship Award, 2000

Each Ivor Novello award takes the form of an elegant, bronze, 12", 7lb 2oz statuette depicting Euterpe, the Greek muse of music and lyric poetry. The design was created by Hazel Underwood and it is one of the heaviest and most valuable awards in showbusiness circles.

THE TOP 10 IVOR NOVELLO WINNERS AFTER 50 YEARS OF AWARDS

PLACE	NAME	NUMBER OF AWARDS
1	Sir Paul McCartney	20
2	John Lennon	15
3	Lord Andrew Lloyd Webber	14
4	Sir Tim Rice	12
5	Sir Elton John	11
6	Robin Gibb	11
	Barry Gibb	11
	Maurice Gibb	10
7	Tony Macauley	8
	Sting	8
	Mike Stock	8
	Bernie Taupin	8
	Pete Waterman	8
	Matt Aitken	8
8	Lionel Bart	7
	Leslie Bricusse	7
9	George Fenton	6
	George Michael	6
	Michael Kamen	6
	Phil Collins	6
10	Mike Batt	5
	Don Black	5
	Roger Cook	5
	Roger Greenaway	5
	Les Reed	5
	Paddy Roberts	5
	Barry Mason	5

BODY

ESSENTIAL INFORMATION FOR SONGWRITERS

BODY: ESSENTIAL INFORMATION FOR SONGWRITERS

INTRODUCTION

A thorough knowledge of the music business and where to get the necessary information from is as crucial to the success of a songwriter as is the craft of songwriting itself. Questions of 'Where to perform?', 'Which competitions are worthwhile?', 'What organisations should I join?', 'What's a "mechanical royalty"?' and 'Where can I find a good publisher?' are all relevant and need answering. This section of *Heart & Soul* aims to provide you with the answer to all these questions and more.

Comprehensive information on songwriting competitions, industry organisations, showcases, further-reading resources and where to get contact information on music publishers are all covered within this section. However, if a question remains unanswered – for instance, you might need legal advice and want to be directed to a recommended lawyer – then ideally you should become a member of the British Academy of Composers & Songwriters and make use of their knowledge and resources. The Academy offers dedicated services for the songwriting community, including seminars and workshops, bi-monthly news and feature publications, web promotion and legal and business advice.

'Everyone who writes should be a member of the Academy,' recommends David Ferguson, Chairman of The Academy. 'Not only does it provide unparalleled opportunities to network with your peers, as well as a growing list of member services, but it's also the place where your voice will be heard.'

If you wish to join or have any questions, contact the British Academy of Composers & Songwriters at:

British Music House
26 Berners Street
London W1P 3LR
Tel: +44 (0)20 7636 2929
Fax: +44 (0)20 7636 2212

Email: info@britishacademy.com
www.britishacademy.com

Alternatively, the internet is a wonderful resource for gathering information on the music business and several recommended internet sites dedicated to the needs of songwriters have been listed within this section.

Finally, as is highlighted in the section 'Heart: The Business Of Songwriting', networking is a key factor in creating opportunities, and meeting the right people is vital to furthering your career as a songwriter. To this end, the contact details for a broad cross-section of songwriters' organisations have also been provided. Along with their specialised services, many societies offer advice or further information, songwriter showcases or career-guidance seminars, such as the MMF's highly recommended training seminars on the music business that run monthly around the UK. For further information on these, contact:

MMF Training
Second Floor
Fourways House East
57 Hilton Street
Manchester
M1 2EJ
Tel: 0161 228 3993
Fax: 0161 228 3773
www.mmf-training.com

'Body: Essential Information For Songwriters' closes with lists of suggested listening and reading, plus a comprehensive glossary of songwriting terms.

SONGWRITER ORGANISATIONS AND SOCIETIES

This section contains a comprehensive list of the key organisations and societies of which a professional songwriter should either be a member or at least aware. Each writer's needs will be different, so it's important to be aware of all the choices available to you and when it's appropriate to join certain organisations. Each organisation's web address has been provided so that you can obtain further information on membership conditions and services. The contact details are correct at the time of going to press.

ASCAP (AMERICAN SOCIETY OF COMPOSERS, AUTHORS AND PUBLISHERS)

ASCAP is a membership association of nearly 200,000 US composers, songwriters, lyricists and music publishers of every kind of music. Through agreements with affiliated international societies, ASCAP also represents hundreds of thousands of music creators worldwide. ASCAP is the only US performing rights organisation created and controlled by composers, songwriters and music publishers, with a board of directors elected by and from the membership.

> ASCAP (US Office)
> 1 Lincoln Plaza,
> New York
> NY 10023
> USA
> Tel: +00 1 (212) 621 6000
> Fax: + 00 1 (212) 724 9064
>
> ASCAP (UK Office)
> 8 Cork Street
> London W1X 1PB
> UK
> Tel: +44 (0)20 7439 0909

Fax: +44 (0)20 7434 0073
Email: info@ascap.com
www.ascap.com

THE BRITISH ACADEMY OF COMPOSERS & SONGWRITERS

The largest composer/songwriter membership organisation in the world, representing the interests of over 3,000 UK writers and composers, the Academy numbers Britain's leading songwriters amongst its members and honours the best of them at the annual Ivor Novello Awards. It also holds writing and business workshops designed to help develop new talent and is able to offer advice on contracts and agreements. Contact the Academy at:

British Music House
26 Berners Street
London W1P 3LR
UK
Tel: +44 (0)20 7636 2929
Fax: +44 (0)20 7636 2212
Email: info@britishacademy.com
www.britishacademy.com

BMI (BROADCAST MUSIC INCORPORATED)

BMI is an American performing rights organisation that represents the interests of more than 300,000 songwriters, composers and music publishers in all genres of music. It is non-profit-making and was founded in 1940 to collect licence fees on behalf of the American creators and copyright holders it represents, as well as those creators who choose to be represented in the US territory by BMI, rather than by ASCAP.

BMI (US Office)
320 West 57th Street
New York,
NY 10019-3790
USA
Tel: +00 1 (212) 586 2000
Email: newyork@bmi.com

BMI (UK Office)

84 Harley House, Marylebone Road
London NW1 5HN
UK
Tel: +44 (0)20 7486 2036
Fax: +44 (0)20 7224 1046
Email: london@bmi.com
www.bmi.com

BMR (BRITISH MUSIC RIGHTS)

The BMR promotes the rights of British music composers, songwriters and publishers through lobbying UK government and EU institutions, education, PR and staging events. Its member organisations are the Academy, the MPA and the MCPS–PRS Alliance.

BMR
British Music House
26 Berners Street
London W1P 3LR
UK
Tel: +44 (0)20 7306 4446
Fax: +44 (0) 20 7306 4449
Email: britishmusic@bmr.org
www.bmr.org

BPI (BRITISH PHONOGRAPHIC INDUSTRY)

The BPI is the British record industry's trade association, representing thousands of British record companies, from the largest corporation down to the smallest label. It is committed to supporting record companies, fighting piracy, lobbying government, raising money for charitable causes and promoting the value of music.

BPI
Riverside Building, County Hall
Westminster Bridge Road
London SE1 7JA
UK
Tel: +44 (0)20 7803 1300
Fax: +44 (0)20 7803 1310

Email: general@bpi.co.uk
www.bpi.co.uk

JAZZ SERVICES

This organisation was founded to promote the growth and development of jazz within the UK.

Tel: +44 (0)20 7928 9089
Fax: +44 (0)20 7401 6870
Email: admin@jazzservices.org.uk
www.jazzservices.org.uk

MCPS (MECHANICAL-COPYRIGHT PROTECTION SOCIETY)

The MCPS is the UK collection society that collects, administers and distributes mechanical royalties generated from the recording of music sold on various formats, which it then distributes to its writer and publisher members. The society is also very active in lobbying government on copyright issues. In recent years, the MCPS merged with its sister collection society, the PRS – thus becoming the MCPS–PRS Alliance – in order to improve efficiency for both societies' writer members.

MCPS–PRS Alliance
Copyright House
29–33 Berners Street
London W1T 3AB
UK
Tel: +44 (0)20 7580 5544
www.mcps-prs-alliance.co.uk

MMF (MUSIC MANAGERS FORUM)

The MMF, formed in 1992, represents the interests of UK artist managers in the music industry. The society runs comprehensive and highly recommended training courses on all aspects of the music business throughout the UK and acts as an advice centre for managers. It also produces a regular magazine, *The Forum*, and runs an informative and active website. The MMF also has international branches.

MMF
1 York Street
London W1U 6PA
UK
Tel: +44 (0)870 8507 800
Fax: +44 (0)870 8507 801
Email: info@ukmmf.net
www.ukmmf.net

MPA (MUSIC PUBLISHERS' ASSOCIATION)

The MPA represents the interests of UK music publishers to the government, music industry, media and public.

MPA
Third Floor
20 York Buildings
London WC2N 6JU
UK
Tel: +44 (0)20 7839 7779
Fax: +44 (0)20 7839 7776
Email: info@mpaonline.org.uk
www.mpaonline.org.uk

MPG (MUSIC PRODUCERS GUILD)

The MPG promotes and represents all individuals active in the music-production and -recording professions. It's a professional organisation that represents those engaged in collective and individual creative contributions to the production and recording of all genres of music and media-related activities.

MPG
PO Box 32
Harrow HA2 7ZX
UK
Tel: +44 020 7371 8888
Fax: +44 020 7371 8887
Email: office@mpg.org.uk
www.mpg.org.uk

MU (MUSICIANS' UNION)

Founded in 1893, the MU has represented and protected UK musicians of all types for over 100 years.

> MU National Office
> 60/62 Clapham Road
> London SW9 0JJ
> UK
> Tel: +44 (0)20 7582 5566
> Fax: +44 (0)20 7582 9805
> Email: info@musiciansunion.org.uk
> www.musiciansunion.org.uk

PCAM (PRODUCERS AND COMPOSERS OF APPLIED MUSIC)

PCAM is a UK-based membership society representing composers who write music for advertising, TV programmes and other audio-visual media.

> Tel: +44 (0)906 895 0908
> www.pcam.co.uk

PRS (PERFORMING RIGHT SOCIETY)

Established in 1914, the Performing Right Society is a non-profit-making membership organisation of composers, songwriters, authors and publishers of music of all styles, including classical, pop and jazz, as well as music for films, adverts and TV. The essential function of the PRS is to collect and distribute music royalties on behalf of its members. See also the entry for MCPS.

> MCPS–PRS Alliance
> Copyright House
> 29–33 Berners Street
> London W1T 3AB
> UK
> Tel: +44 (0)20 7580 5544
> www.mcps-prs-alliance.co.uk

SESAC

SESAC is a performing rights organisation with headquarters in Nashville and offices in New York, Los Angeles and London. It was founded in 1930, making it the second-oldest performing rights organisation in the United States. SESAC's repertoire – once limited to European and gospel music – has diversified to include today's most popular music, including dance hits, rock classics, the best of Latina music, the hottest jazz, the hippest country and the coolest contemporary Christian music.

> SESAC Headquarters
> 55 Music Square East
> Nashville, TN 37203
> USA
> Tel: +00 1 615-320-0055
> Fax +00 1 615-329-9627

> SESAC International
> 67 Upper Berkeley Street
> London W1H 7QX
> UK
> Tel: +44 (0)20 7486 9878
> Fax: +44 (0)20 7486 9934
> Email: rights@sesac.co.uk
> www.sesac.com

SONGLINK INTERNATIONAL

This is a monthly newsletter, magazine and website designed to connect songwriters and publishers with artists, co-writers and companies who are looking for songs on a global basis.

> SongLink International
> 23 Belsize Crescent
> London NW3 5QY
> UK
> Tel: +44 (0)20 7794 2540
> Fax: +44 (0)20 7794 7393
> Email: info@songlink.com
> www.songlink.com

MUSIC PUBLISHERS

If you want to obtain a comprehensive and up-to-date listing of music publishers, there are a number of websites, books and industry organisations that will provide contact details and other relevant information, either for free or for a fee. This section contains brief descriptions of the best of these services in both the UK and the US.

FOR THE UK...

Here, the best resource for finding a music publisher is the MPA, who provide an online listing of their member publishers for free, while a more detailed hardcopy version is available for a small charge from the MPA office. This membership list contains a genre breakdown for individual publishers and an indication of those companies that accept unsolicited materials. For more information, refer to the MPA's website at www.mpaonline.org.uk.

The drawback with this resource, however, is that it features only publishers that are members. For a complete listing of UK publishers, the definitive guide is the annual *Music Week Directory*. This provides comprehensive contact details and contact names (but no indication of genre preferences) of all UK music publishers. It also has sections on record companies, accountants, lawyers, recording studios and every other business associated with the music industry. It currently costs £65 but is free when a subscription to the magazine is taken out. For more information, contact:

Music Week Subscription Department
Tower House
Sovereign Park
Market Harborough
Leicestershire LE16 9EF
UK
www.musicweek.co.uk

For The USA...

The US equivalent of the *Music Week Directory* is the highly recommended Musicians' Atlas, available (at a price) from www.musiciansatlas.com. This annual directory links songwriters and artists to thousands of music businesses and key industry contacts in more than 25 categories and includes a comprehensive listing of publishers. It has the useful feature of indicating genre preferences and an indication of those companies that accept unsolicited materials.

Meanwhile, a free online resource specifically dedicated to singer/songwriters can be found at www.singer-songwriter.com. The list contained on this site isn't comprehensive, but it does provide useful descriptions of the selected publishers. Alternatively, there is a similar free listing, along with company descriptions, on the very helpful www.musesmuse.com website.

SONGWRITING COMPETITIONS

Songwriting competitions are a great option for promoting your songwriting talents. They can offer feedback on the quality of your songwriting, provide welcome cash prizes and/or recording equipment and open doors to high-profile writing opportunities, publishing contracts and chart success. Most importantly, in a business that can appear impenetrable to the outsider, competitions are open to anyone.

Songwriting competitions are also a fantastic opportunity for lyricists and writers of less commercial genres. Some have categories for Lyrics Only, World Music, Folk, Gospel, Children's and Instrumental, among many others.

Some competitions are free to enter, while others charge an entry fee to cover the costs of administration and prizes. These fees are sometimes reduced for multiple entrants. One tip worth remembering is that it pays to check the deadlines for application, as certain competitions have a reduced fee for early entry.

The focus of these events is the song. While this means that simple piano/vocal demos have a good chance of succeeding against professionally produced songs, it's still important to apply the same rules of presentation and production in competitions that you would when preparing and recording a demo destined for a publishing or record company. Make sure that the song is recorded to the highest possible standard, that the lyrics are printed legibly and that your contact details are listed on everything. First impressions count just as much with a competition judging panel as they do with A&R executives.

WORDS OF WARNING

- As with any aspect of the music business, remain cautious when entering a competition and protect your rights at all times.

- On entering, be certain that you have proof of copyright on your material (ie original recordings, lyrical notes and a version of the song posted to yourself by recorded delivery prior to entry).

- Keep copies of anything you send in, including the original entry form, in case you need to prove your involvement in the competition.

- Establish the legitimacy of the competition. Does it have a long history? Who is sponsoring it? Is it backed by the music industry? What have previous winners gone on to achieve? What prizes are being offered? There are many songwriting competitions, and the majority of them are legitimate, but it pays to be aware of where you're sending your songs. Firmly established and respected competitions include that hosted by the Academy, Song Search UK, Unisong (in association with *SongLink International*) and the John Lennon Song Competition.

- Always read and make sure that you fully understand the terms and conditions of entry. It's important to be cautious when signing any document that relates to the publishing of your song. If you're uncertain about any aspect of an agreement, seek legal advice.

- Finally, some competitions offer a prize of a publishing deal. This is great news – and congratulations if you do win one – but do ensure that this is the best publishing company for you and your song. First, check that the publishing company is well established and has the necessary resources and contacts via which to place your song with an artist, and always refer to a music lawyer before signing such a deal. If your winning song is that good, you might be best off shopping around before you sign over any rights to a publishing company.

Having said all that, don't get paranoid to the extent that you don't enter any competitions. As with everything worthwhile in life, it's about taking risks. While they can't guarantee a worldwide Number One hit, songwriting competitions are a great way of getting a foot in the music industry's door.

Listed below is a selection of songwriting competitions that were running at the time of publication. For a comprehensive listing of songwriting competitions, refer to the British Academy website at www.britishacademy.com or visit www.musesmuse.com.

Good luck!

SONG SEARCH UK

Song Search UK is a competition organised by the British Academy of Composers & Songwriters that gives writers the opportunity to showcase their writing talents across a range of different styles and have their work heard by key people in the UK music industry.

Categories: Pop, Contemporary Pop, Rock/Guitar, Country, Ballad, Easy Listening and Contemporary Christian.

Entry Guidelines: Open to all writers, published and unpublished. Songs must be entered on CD or cassette and accompanied by a typed lyric sheet.

Prize: Significant cash prize; fast-track entry into selection process for Eurovision Song Contest; covermount on *Music Week* magazine and invitation to the prestigious Ivor Novello Awards.

Entry Fee: Yes.

General Closing Date: September.

Further Information: visit www.britishacademy.com or call the Academy on +44 (0)20 7636 2929.

UNISONG CONTEST 2004

The Unisong International Song Contest offers prizes and real opportunities to new and developing songwriters around the world. It is officially partnered with *SongLink International*, amongst others.

Categories: Pop Ballad, Pop Uptempo, Rock, Country, Acoustic/Folk, Urban/R&B, World/Reggae, Gospel/Contemporary Christian, Children's, Instrumental/Jazz, Social/Political and Lyrics Only.

Entry Guidelines: A professional recording is not required to enter. Songs are judged on quality, craftsmanship and listener appeal and not on production or instrumentation. Lyric entries are judged on content, form and originality.

Prizes: Selected winners appear on a special limited-edition CD and one Grand Prize winner wins a trip to write new songs with established professional songwriters. A cash prize is awarded to each category winner and a year's membership to *SongLink*, *Taxi* and *American Songwriter*. Professional song critiques are also available to all entrants.

Entry Fee: Yes.

General Closing Date: November.

Further Information: visit www.unisong.com.

GREAT AMERICAN SONG CONTEST

Created by songwriters, the Great American Song Contest is designed to benefit every songwriter, lyricist and music composer who participates. One of the key features of this competition is that every entry receives written feedback on their songs. Winners retain all rights to their songs.

Categories: Submissions are requested in nine categories: Pop, Rock/Alt, Country, Contemporary Acoustic/Folk, R&B/Hip-Hop/Rap, Christian/Gospel, Instrumental, Special Category and Lyrics Only.

Entry Guidelines: Three typed lyric sheets and a CD or cassette recording of your unpublished or self-published work must be entered along with an application form and entry fee.

Prize: Cash prize plus songwriters' pack including membership to *Taxi*, vouchers and computer songwriting software. Every entry receives feedback.

Entry Fee: Yes.

General Closing Date: November.

Further Information: visit www.greatamericansong.com

COOCH MUSIC AMATEUR SONGWRITING CONTEST

Established in 1999, this competition announces itself as the first amateur-only songwriting contest. It offers an outlet for amateur songwriters of any age to get their songs heard and win publishing contracts and prizes that are designed to help further their careers in the industry.

Categories: Rock/Alternative, County, Pop/Dance, Folk/World, Rhythm and Blues, Hip-Hop/Rap, Gospel/Inspirational, Latin, Novelty/Comedy/Children's and Lyrics Only.

Entry guidelines: Songs of up to five minutes' duration can be submitted for this competition. All songs must be original and be submitted on cassette or CD, accompanied by an entry form, lyric sheet and entry fee.

Prize: Winners receive a variety of music-industry publications, a Fender guitar, computer software and a publishing contract from J Cooch Music.

Entry Fee: Yes.

Closing Date: December.

Further Information: visit www.coochmusic.com.

THE JOHN LENNON SONGWRITING CONTEST

This international songwriting contest began in 1997 and is open to amateur and professional songwriters.

Categories: Rock, Country, Jazz, Pop, World, Rhythm and Blues, Hip-Hop, Gospel/Inspirational, Latin, Electronic, Folk, Children's and Lyrics Only.

Entry Guidelines: The recording of each entry, which should be no longer than five minutes' duration, is judged on its originality, melody, composition and lyrics (where applicable). Neither performance nor production values be considered during the adjudication process.

Prizes: Include a publishing contract from EMI, Yamaha studio equipment and $20,000 for the Maxell Song of the Year. In 2004, one winning songwriter's band was selected by Warped Tour to tour and perform for one week on Warped Tour '05.

Entry Fee: Yes.

General Closing Date: September.

Further Information: visit www.jlsc.com.

THE UK SONGWRITING CONTEST

The organisers of this well-established UK songwriting competition work hard to generate industry interest and obtain media attention for the songwriters involved.

Categories: Pop, Rock/Indie, Dance, Jazz/Blues, Folk/Country, Christian/Gospel/Faith, R&B/Hip-Hop/Rap, Lyrics Only, Instrumental and Miscellaneous.

Entry Guidelines: Entries should be provided on CD or cassette and accompanied with typed lyrics, the entry form and a fee. Songs are judged on their composition, lyrics, melody and originality. The quality of performance and production is not a consideration. All entrants retain their ownership rights and all copyrights to all songs submitted.

Prizes: 2004's prizes included publishing deals, subscriptions to www.taxi.com, songwriting computer software and promotional and career-development packages.

Entry Fee: Yes.

General Closing Date: June.

Further Information: visit www.songwritingcontest.co.uk.

PACIFIC SONGWRITING CONTEST

The main criterion of this New Zealand-based competition is excellence in expression. It's sponsored by an opera singer with a passion for original music and those who create it. There are neither promises of chances to be heard by the 'big boys' nor product to be given away as prizes.

Categories: Rock/Metal/Indie, Pop/Contemporary Ballad, Rock/Indie, Spiritual/Gospel/Inspirational/Sacred, R&B/Hip-Hop/Rap, Country, Café Scene (Acoustic/Folk), Dance/Electronica, Jazz/Blues, Instrumental, Lyrics Only, Political, World and Open.

Entry Guidelines: The competition is open to all nations, genres and both amateur and professional songwriters. There is no age limit.

Prizes: Cash prizes totalling NZ$25,000 (£9,400). In 2005, two iPods are to be given away on the 500th and 1,000th entry opened.

Entry Fee: Yes.

General Closing Date: March.

Further Information: visit www.pacificsongwritingcompetition.com.

Nashville Song Search

A songwriting competition with a heart, this song search, while not promising big cash prizes, does offer excellent networking opportunities while aiming to raise money for Nashville's Crisis Center charity.

Categories: Ballad, Uptempo, Traditional Country, Crossover/Pop Country, Folk, Perfect For Diamond Rio, Christmas Holiday and Under 18 (in which category writer and co-writer[s] must both be under 18 years of age).

Entry Guidelines: The competition is open to all nations and both amateur and professional songwriters.

Prizes: Flight to Nashville, networking and collaboration opportunities, guaranteed feedback from Universal, Warner–Chappell, Sony and EMI, and mentoring sessions with professional country songwriters.

Entry Fee: Yes.

General Closing Date: June.

Further Information: visit www.nashvillesongsearch.com.

Song Of The Year

Song of the Year is an international contest encouraging the art and discipline of songwriting. Its primary aim is to find great songwriters while helping them to network with professionals in the music industry. A portion of the proceeds support VH-1's Save The Music Foundation. Song critiques are available on request.

Categories: Pop, Rock, Electronic/Dance, R&B/Hip-Hop, Country/Americana, Adult Contemporary, Christian Contemporary/Gospel, Folk, Instrumental/Jazz/World and Lyrics Only.

Entry Guidelines: Open to all songwriters.

Prizes: Cash prize, plus songwriting products and review by BMG.

Entry Fee: Yes.

General Closing Date: Monthly.
Further Information: visit www.songoftheyear.com.

INTERNATIONAL SONGWRITING COMPETITION

This is an annual songwriting contest whose mission is to provide the opportunity for both aspiring and established songwriters to have their songs heard in a professional, international arena. The ISC has the most prestigious panel of judges of all the songwriting contests in the world, and in the past this has included Sean 'P Diddy' Combs, Darryl McDaniels (Run-DMC), Aaron Lewis (Staind), Macy Gray and Paul Asher (Co-President, Sanctuary Artist Management). The competition offers exposure and the opportunity to have your songs heard by *the* most influential decision-makers in the music industry.

Categories: Pop/Top 40, Rock, Country, AAA/Roots/Americana, Blues, Instrumental, Folk/Singer-Songwriter, R&B/Hip-Hop, Jazz, World, Gospel/ Christian, Children's Music, Dance/Electronica, Lyrics Only, Teen (18 years old or younger), Performance (judged on performance as well as on songwriting).
Entry Guidelines: Amateur and professional songwriters and musicians are invited to participate.
Prizes: Cash prizes totalling $100,000.
Entry Fee: Yes.
General Closing Date: October.
Further Information: visit www.songwritingcompetition.com

AND OF COURSE... THE EUROVISION SONG CONTEST!

The Eurovision Song Contest is a glitzy television song competition between musical acts representing countries of the members of the European Broadcasting Union. Individual member countries submit their entries and the contest is put to a mass public tele-vote. The competition offers immensely entertaining viewing but is perhaps less about the song today and more about politics and performance. However, here are ten interesting facts about the Eurovision Song Contest:

1. The Eurovision Song Contest was first staged in Switzerland in 1956, when Lys Assia from Switzerland won with 'Refrain', beating Belgium's marginally less cheerful 'The Drowned Men Of The River Seine'.

2. The UK is the most successful Eurovision nation, having won five contests and finished second an astonishing 15 times.

3. More women than men win the Eurovision Song Contest, with an average of one man winning for every three or four women.

4. In 1967, Sandie Shaw's barefoot rendition of 'Puppet On A String' gave the UK its first victory. Rolf Harris commentated.

5. From 1977–2003, Greece voted for Turkey only three times. However, in 21 years, Cyprus has given a maximum 'douze points' to Greece no fewer than 11 times and Greece has returned the favour nine times.

6. According to a study by the University of Leiden, the most used words by Eurovision fans in connection with the song contest are 'ABBA', 'Eurovision', 'Dana' and 'Leandros'.

7. Obscure tongues have surfaced in the competition on numerous occasions. In 1989, Switzerland's entry was sung in Romansch and Lithuania's song 'Strazdas' was sung in a west-Lithuanian dialect. France has also attempted to win with songs in Corsican and Breton, and in 2003 Belgium came second with a song in a made-up language!

8. So far, the most covered Eurovision hit is 'Volare', with artists such as Dean Martin, Al Martino, Marino Marini and David Bowie all recording cover versions of the song.

9. The most commercially successful pop group of the 1970s, ABBA, won the 1974 Eurovision Song Contest with 'Waterloo', while Britain's answer to ABBA, Bucks Fizz, won in 1981 with the fewest number of top three scores (12, 10 or 8 points).

10. Belgium has been voted last a record number of eight times and in 1962 was the first country ever to score 'nul points'.

UK entries for the Eurovision Song Contest are officially organised by the BBC, although entry may be gained via Song Search UK.

Songwriter Showcases

'It's essential to play new songs live. You might think you have a Top Ten hit on your hands – maybe another "Stairway To Heaven" – but if the crowd doesn't think so, you perhaps need to go back to the drawing board.'

– Gareth Huggett, Minifish

There are three main reasons why gigging is important for a songwriter.

1. A performance provides you with the opportunity to air your songs and get them heard by the general public, sometimes creating the buzz that attracts interest from record companies and publishers.

2. Live work provides the best forum for getting your songs critiqued in terms of the response they elicit, the effectiveness of their arrangement and each track's potential for success.

3. The experience of playing live or hearing your songs played live is a great thrill, the reward for all the hard work that has been put into the writing and rehearsing of the material.

There are many songwriters, however, who don't possess the desire or the ability to perform their own songs live. If this is true of you, consider forming a band to play your own material. Being able to write songs is a rare talent, and consequently there are countless musicians who are in need of strong material to launch their performance careers.

Below, Kizzy Donaldson, Membership Manager of the Academy, provides several tips to make the most of your live experience. 'As a songwriter,' she affirms, 'the live music scene provides a fantastic opportunity to have your music heard by fresh ears, helps you to define your sound (what works and what doesn't), gains you a strong following and can possibly attract the interest of publishers. It's safe to say that, as a budding songwriter, you can't rely merely on your music being played in the MiniDisc/CD player of an A&R executive or the fact that you know someone who has access to the right circles. With respect to this, the live music scene shouldn't be seen in isolation but rather as one of many vehicles available for promoting your songs, not just to publishers and managers but to the end consumer as well.'

Here are Kizzy's tips for getting your music heard by the people you want to hear it on the live circuit:

- Research gigs in your locality. Visit the venues, familiarising yourself with the acoustics, equipment, format of the night, etc.

- Make sure you send a demo that's well produced together with a well-written biography and – without going overboard – a professional photograph. If you can't do this yourself, find someone who can do it for you.

- Get to know the promoter and build a relationship. This could lead to a regular platform, becoming a headliner and referrals to A&R representatives.

- If you feel that you're not a strong enough singer to do your songs justice, find a willing vocalist to sing them for you.

- Don't rely on the promoter to attract an audience for you; you'll need to market yourself. Start by designing flyers to distribute to your friends, family and target audience. After you've started showcasing your material, creating a mailing list is an excellent way of developing a following as you can then effectively notify those on it of forthcoming events. And if you don't already have one, it would be wise to get yourself a website. Most ISPs give you sufficient space to build a basic one or, alternatively, you should be able to buy extra web server space from them.

- If you have an EP or album available, find out if you can sell it at live events or, alternatively, shamelessly plug it while on stage. (This is one reason why it's necessary to have a website, in order to sell the product.) Also, make sure that your CDs have your relevant contact details on them.

Having chosen the most appropriate venue and booked a gig, all that remains is to rehearse, produce the flyers and posters, promote the night, create some media interest, organise the equipment and transport, play well and enjoy yourself!

The UK Songwriter Showcase Scene

The variety and constantly evolving nature of the UK live music scene thwarts any permanent or comprehensive listing of venues dedicated to songwriters. However, the next section lists a small selection of singer/songwriter venues in the UK that are well-established and offer a good opportunity for writers to perform their works. The information is accurate at time of going to press, but of course venues change, close or move on, so if you're interested in performing live you'll need to research possible venues in your local area through music magazines, local newspapers and websites dedicated to the music scene, such as by visiting www.acousticunderground.org.uk if you live in Edinburgh or www.acoustica.tv if you live in Manchester.

UK Showcase Spotlight (With Kizzy Donaldson)

London

DUBLIN CASTLE/HOPE & ANCHOR

The Dublin Castle and Hope & Anchor are organised by Bug Bear Promotions and have been running for approximately eight years. These showcase events give unsigned acts taking their first steps on the gig circuit a platform from which to be heard by industry figures and, hopefully, to obtain a recording or publishing deal. A&R representatives from both major and independent labels and publishers regularly attend both events. Bands such as Travis, Madness, The Libertines, Keane and McFly have all played at the Dublin Castle and been subsequently signed, while the likes of Gillian Welch and Toploader have graced the stage of the Hope & Anchor.

The crowds at these events are right across the board, from students to city workers, band members, musicians and industry figures. The type of music such events tend to attract is punk, rock, guitar, indie and soul, although they're open to all genres of music.

The Dublin Castle has a capacity of 140 and is a serious rock venue, with a large PA, and it has the added bonus of being in Camden Town, which is the central hub of A&R activity in London. The Hope & Anchor, on the other hand, is a smaller, more intimate venue. It is quite old-fashioned, with a low ceiling, and you can almost imagine U2 performing there (as they did very early in their career) – very rock 'n' roll.

The promoters of both these establishments state that their PA systems are superb.

The format is simple but fair: three acts play slots of 30 minutes each, while the headliner gets 45 minutes. It's also worth noting that Radio 1 DJ Steve Lamacq is a strong supporter of the Dublin Castle and frequently pays it a visit (think networking!). If you submit your biography and CD to these establishments, someone there will endeavour to get back to you – which is more than can be said for most publishers.

In a nutshell, the Dublin Castle and the Hope & Anchor are showcases that give a good platform for talented singer/songwriters seeking to gain recognition. They both have a great sound and a relaxed atmosphere and are ideal venues for new bands starting out.

Hope & Anchor, 207 Upper Street, Islington, London N1
Tel: 020 7354 1312
Email: bugbear@btconnect.com

Dublin Castle, 94 Parkway, Camden, London NW1
Tel: 020 7485 1773
Email: bugbear@btconnect.com

BARFLY ACOUSTIC AT THE BARFLY

Barfly Acoustic is another showcase event for singers and songwriters eager to be discovered and, hopefully, signed. It has earned a reputation over the last five years for having the best unsigned artists showcasing their material at events there, regularly in front of managers, labels, publishers and the media.

The promoter of the Barfly, Terry Kirby, describes the showcase event as 'manic, edgy, with loads of youthful energy between the performer and the audience. The audience and the artist connect; they become part of the show. [It's] almost like a club.' He goes on to describe the venue as a 'hotbed of new talent that no one has seen; fresh blood'. He prefers to view the Barfly as a venue that reflects what's already happening in the UK, as opposed to hosting new music.

The crowds that go to the Barfly are keen followers of music who like to be kept up to date with fresh new talent and can visit as often as three or four times a week.

The likes of Craig David, The Cure and The Darkness have all performed at the Barfly, and the venue attracts a healthy supply of publishers, managers and agents, making it one of the premier places in which to showcase material.

Although the Barfly traditionally has a reputation of being a rock/indie venue, it's open to all types of music and its organisers encourage songwriters in all genres to send in their demos. Its experienced promotion team receives approximately 100 demos per week and holds weekly A&R meetings at which they discuss their quality. They also spend a significant amount of time scouting showcases and gigs around the capital and beyond for unsigned talent.

The Barfly has been running for ten years and stages live music seven days a week.

> **Barfly/The Monarch**, 49 Chalk Farm Road, London, NW1
> Monday to Sunday, 7pm until late
> Tel: 020 7691 4244
> www.barflyclub.com

Demos should be sent for the attention of Barfly Bookings, 109X Regents Park Road, London NW1 8UR. Include contact information, biography and any press coverage. All demos received are heard. For feedback on your demo, call the Promotions Office on the above number between four and six weeks after sending it in. The best time to call is between 12pm and 6pm on Tuesdays and Thursdays.

THE BEDFORD

The founder of this showcase event, Tony Moore, used to run a hugely successful showcase at the Kashmir Klub. The Bedford is a continuation of this and hosts a variety of events, featuring performances from both emerging and established artists, including Guy Chambers, Thunder and James Fox, to name just a few that have appeared there. It attracts a diverse crowd of people from all ages and backgrounds that enjoy live music.

When asked to describe his events, Tony says that the idea is 'to create an experience that's both intimate and captivating. The philosophy is to create an atmosphere where music is given the utmost respect.' He also welcomes a diverse range of music – 'the more eclectic the better' – and if that doesn't entice you to play at the Bedford, Tony states that their PA system is 'one of the most hi-spec PA systems of any venue'.

The Bedford allows for great interaction between artist and audience, providing a location from which the latter can buy artists' material and join mailing lists.

Due to the fact that there is a limited number of days that music is put on there, the Bedford's organisers are looking for material of a 'certain standard' that can fit with the style of events they hold. Bearing this in mind, it would be a good idea to do a bit of research into the showcase events at which you'd like to perform before sending in your demo.

The Bedford, 77 Bedford Hill, Balham, London SW12 9HD
Tel: 020 8682 8940 (table bookings)
www.thebedford.co.uk

Events are held every Wednesday (in the Tavistock Room) and every Monday, Tuesday and Thursday (in the Theatre). Doors open Monday and Tuesday at 8:30pm, and 7:30pm for a 9pm start all other days. Entry is generally free entry, but refer to their website for more details. To get a gig there, send your CD and bio to the Booking Team at the above address.

OTHER RECOMMENDED LONDON SHOWCASES

12-BAR CLUB

Possibly one of the best acoustic venues in central London, this club has a long and respected history. The venue itself has much character and is an essential venue for any singer/songwriter or acoustic act.

12-Bar Club, 23 Denmark Place (off Denmark Street), London WC2
Contact Andy Lowe: 020 7916 6989

BIG NOTE AT THE HOPE

A very 'vibey' acoustic club run by an enthusiastic and supportive promoter.

Hope And Anchor, 207 Upper Street Islington, London N1 1RL
Contact Marc Johnson: 020 7704 2689
Email: marc@bignote.co.uk
        big.note@lineone.net
www.bignote.co.uk

KINDRED SPIRIT

Stages R&B, jazz, soul/neo-soul, hip-hop/MC and poetry.

The Rhythm Factory, 16–18 Whitechapel Road, London E1 1EW
Email: info@kindredspirit.org.uk
www.kindredspirit.org.uk

Events are held every third Monday of the month. Doors open at 8pm for an 8:30pm start.

PUSH GETS LAZY

Stages R&B, jazz, soul/neo-soul, hip-hop/MC and poetry.

The Light, 233 Shoreditch High Street, London E1 6PJ
Tel: 07939 623 837
Email: pusha@tiscali.co.uk
www.pushents.co.uk

Events held every first and third Sunday of the month, 5pm–12am.

LIVE

Stages R&B, jazz, soul/neo-soul, hip-hop/MC and poetry.

Suga Suga, 187 Wardour Street, London W1
Tel: Lish on 07940 380 941 (guest list)
    0207 434 2118 (table bookings)
Email: jade@jade-inc.net

Events held every Monday. Performances start at 9:30pm–10pm, then 10:30pm–11pm. Door closes 10:30pm. Over-18s only. Send demos to:

Live c/o Music Matrix, 11 Bear Street, London WC2H 7AS.

SINGERS AND POETS

Bug Bar, St Matthew's Church, Brixton Hill, London (opposite the Fridge)
Tel: Jackie Darling on 020 7924 9294/07930 619 302

Events held every first Wednesday of the month. Free before 8pm.

SINGERS' NIGHT

The Spot, 29 Maiden Lane, Covent Garden, London WC2
Tel: 020 7379 5900

Events held every Sunday, 9pm–12am.

TALL POPPY PRESENTS

The Goose, 360 Wandsworth Bridge Road, London SW6
Tel: 020 8408 0777 (table bookings)
Email: man@tallpoppyrecords.com

Events held every Thursday. Free before 8pm.

EDINBURGH

THE LISTENING ROOM

The Blue Blazer, Spittal Street/Bread Street, Edinburgh EH3 9DX

Offers a strong programme of visiting and resident songwriters in a well-appointed pub with excellent beer and food and no amplification. Events take place between 8pm and 10pm, including one hour of floorspots and a main guest. The Listening Room is presented by Acoustic Underground and events are hosted and managed by Chris Brown. Tel: 0131 551 3448. Email: loudmouthchris@yahoo.co.uk.

ACOUSTICA!

Cabaret Voltaire, 36–38 Blair Street (formerly the Peppermint Lounge), Edinburgh EH1 1NQ
Tel: 0131 220 6176
www.cabaret-voltaire.co.uk

Between two and five acts are showcased here every Monday by different promoters from 7:30pm–11pm. To play at Acoustica, email jay@cabaret-voltaire.co.uk or talk to the promoter on a Monday night.

OUT OF THE BEDROOM

Upstairs, **The Waverley Bar**, 3–5 St Mary Street, off Royal Mile,
    Edinburgh EH1 1TA
Tel: 0131 478 5541
Email: info@outofthebedroom.co.uk
www.outofthebedroom.co.uk

'Out Of The Bedroom' nights run every week night from 9pm until midnight and there is a policy of original music only. Performers simply turn up at 8:30pm for a slot. There is a house guitar, keyboard and PA as well as a weekly prize draw, with the option of performances being taped and reproduced.

GLASGOW

THE ACOUSTIC AFFAIR

Tron Theatre, 63 Trongate, Merchant City, Glasgow
Email: info@acousticaffair.co.uk
www.acousticaffair.co.uk

A series of excellent, intimate acoustic concerts. Past guests include James Grant, Cosmic Rough Riders and Lush Rollers.

THE GLASGOW SONGWRITERS,

Scotia Bar, Stockwell Street, Glasgow (every Tuesday, 9pm)
Jaspers Bar, Midland Street, Glasgow (last Tuesday of the month,
    with open mic for non-members)
Email: contact@glasgowsongwriters.freeserve.co.uk
www.glasgowsongwriters.org.uk

MANCHESTER

ACOUSTICA

Blazing Rag, Mossley
Tel: 01457 837184
Email: info@acoustica.tv
www.acoustica.tv
Every first Thursday of the month, this pub venue plays host to songwriters, acoustic bands and poets. Interested performers should attend by 8:30pm for a slot.

LIVERPOOL

FOLK OFF

Stamps Bar, Crosby, Liverpool L22
Tel: 0151 286 2662

This showcase occurs every third Monday of every month and is available only to booked acts. It's a popular showcase that has featured acts such as Cicero Buck, Jont and Damien Rice.

FREE & EASY

Touchwood, 32–36 Church Road, Waterloo, Liverpool L22
Tel: 0151 928 5656

This open-mic night, held every Thursday night from 9pm, offers a chance for acts interested in playing at Folk Off a showcase to obtain a future booking.

NOTTINGHAM

ACOUSTIC ROUTES

The Golden Fleece, Mansfield Road, Nottingham
Tel: 0115 9472843

This is one of Nottingham' s longest established and most popular open-mic sessions. Interested performers should just turn up and play or book one of the half-hour slots. Solo musicians through to full bands are catered for with top-quality sound equipment. The showcase is held every Monday and Tuesday, with performers booking in from 8pm.

FRAMPTON'S BAR & BISTRO

11 St James's Terrace, Nottingham.
Tel: 0115 9411947

This open-mic night is held on the second Tuesday of every month, from 9pm. The venue gives songwriters a platform to perform their own songs and, at the time of writing, provides one free drink for performers!

BRIGHTON

FREEBUTT

Freebutt, 1 Phoenix Place, behind Phoenix Art Gallery, Brighton, BN2
Tel: 01273 603974
Email: freebutt@zelnet.com

Established as one of the premier small music venues in Brighton, the Freebutt stages ska, punk, emo, rock, acoustic, electronica, hip hop and saccharine pop, while upstairs there is a kitsch haven of music, moody lighting and sofas in the Penthouse. Music is staged seven days a week.

HEALTHY CONCERTS

www.healthyconcerts.com

Launched in Brighton in 1994, Healthy Concerts' friendly open houses continue to build a new audience for genuinely unplugged acoustic music. They have been recognised by artists and audience alike as the new home of acoustic music in Brighton, and Healthy Concerts is at the very heart of an expanding network of listening rooms.

THE US SONGWRITER SHOWCASE SCENE

The vastness of America's music scene prevents any attempt at a comprehensive listing of venues dedicated to songwriters. Therefore, if you're interested in performing there, you should research your local area using relevant music magazines and local newspapers. Alternatively, visit www.musesmuse.com, www.acousticmusic.com or obtain a copy of the highly recommended *Musicians' Atlas* from www.musiciansatlas.com. This 368-page annual directory links songwriters and artists to thousands of music businesses and key industry contacts in over 25 categories, including a comprehensive listing of clubs and venues. Here's a small selection of appropriate venues to get you started.

NASHVILLE

THE BLUEBIRD CAFE

This venue has gained a worldwide reputation for presenting the best original country and acoustic music seven nights a week. Performers don't generally play cover songs. Musicians don't jam here, and songwriters frequently are accompanied by just one guitar or piano.

For further information, visit www.bluebirdcafe.com.

SAN FRANCISCO

STRINGS ACOUSTIC MUSIC VENUE

Strings is a non-profit-making music showcase space located in the San Francisco Bay Area. For seven years its organisers have put together weekly shows featuring the best acoustic fingerstyle guitarists, songwriters and acoustic bands available. Strings is one of the premier acoustic music spaces on the West Coast.

For further information, visit www.strings.org.

DENVER

SWALLOW HILL MUSIC ASSOCIATION

Denver's home for folk, roots and acoustic music, the Swallow Hill Music Association was established as a non-profit-making organisation in 1979 and has grown to become the second-largest folk- and acoustic-music organisation in the United States. Swallow Hill serves as a regional resource for the presentation, teaching, preservation and encouragement of folk music and dance.

For further information, visit www.swallowhill.com.

PHOENIX

LONG WONG'S ON MILL

And intimate living-room-style bar that books music nightly. Touring acts often open here for popular local acts.

For further information, visit www.longwongsonmill.com.

LITTLE ROCK, ARKANSAS

ACOUSTIC SOUNDS CAFÉ

This is a smoke-free, alcohol-free, listener-orientated, coffeehouse-style acoustic-music venue that presents shows routinely on the second and fourth Fridays of each month. Programmes may include traditional, Celtic and/or contemporary folk, pop, bluegrass, jazz, blues or other styles of music appropriate for a family audience.

For further information, visit www.acousticsoundscafe.org.

LOS ANGELES

14 BELOW

This is a very popular, 300-capacity venue at which bands play nightly. The styles performed here range from rock to alternative, acoustic, world music, R&B and reggae.

For further information, visit www.14below.com.

CAFÉ BOOGALOO

An intimate yet funky café that books music nightly and claims to be the best blues venue in the South Bay area.

For further information, visit www.boogaloo.com.

ATLANTA, GEORGIA

EDDIE'S ATTIC

Eddie's Attic has become a popular proving ground for aspiring artists and accomplished musicians alike, with a superior sound system and excellent acoustics that made the venue an instant hit with music enthusiasts. Much praised for the music room's listening policy, the Attic draws both fans and artists from all over the world and continues to be the premier acoustic-music venue in the South. On any given night, music lovers can hear performing songwriters playing their own particular brand of music in an intimate setting. The Attic welcomes all kinds of original, live music and embraces the diversity that allows independent music to thrive.

For further information, visit www.eddiesattic.com

NEW YORK

THE POSTCRYPT COFFEEHOUSE

The Postcrypt Coffeehouse, established in 1964, features professional, amateur and student performers throughout the academic year every Friday and

Saturday night from 9pm to 12:30am. Admission is always free and open to all. As one of the country's longest running campus coffeehouses, Postcrypt is the home of diverse music – including and extending beyond blues, folk, jazz, rock, country and *a cappella* – as well as performance art, poetry, comedy and storytelling. It stages live acoustic music from both local and national acts, and when the organisers say acoustic, they really mean it: there are no microphones. Some of the more well-known artists who have graced the stage there include David Bromberg, Jeff Buckley, Shawn Colvin, Ani DiFranco, John Gorka, Patty Larkin, Lisa Loeb, Ellis Paul, Martin Sexton, Tony Trischka, Suzanne Vega, Jerry Jeff Walker and Dar Williams.

For further information, visit www.columbia.edu/cu/postcrypt/coffeehouse.

RECOMMENDED READING
FOR SONGWRITERS

If you're interested in further developing your knowledge of songwriting, music and the music business, here's a list of relevant books on the topic. Within this industry, knowledge is power, and while these books can't in themselves guarantee you success as a songwriter, they might ease the passage on your journey towards fortune and fame.

ESSENTIAL BOOKS

CAMERON, JULIA: *The Artist's Way* (Jeremy P Tarcher/Putnam, ISBN 1-58542-146-4)
This is a truly inspirational book and thoroughly recommended to get your creative juices flowing. It's not just for songwriters but for all people involved in creativity, although its style might not appeal to everyone.

CARTER, WALTER: *Writing Together: The Songwriter's Guide To Collaboration* (Omnibus, ISBN 0-7119-1713-2)
An essential read for any collaboration, this book will help the reader to avoid most pitfalls when it comes to writing with another person and will hopefully encourage better results.

MITCHELL, KEVIN M: *Essential Songwriter's Rhyming Dictionary* (Alfred Publishing Co, ISBN 0-88284-729-5)
Don't leave home without it! A rhyming dictionary is an essential tool of the songwriter, and this one is worth its weight in royalty cheques, being very easy to use and coming complete with tips on lyric writing and rhyming.

NICKOL, PETER: *Learning To Read Music* (How To Books, ISBN 1-85703-390-6)
A really easy-to-understand, quick and comprehensive book on music theory. A few terms are a little dated, but this is otherwise a brilliant resource for the uninitiated.

HIRSCHHORN, JOEL: *The Complete Idiot's Guide To Songwriting* (Alpha Books, ISBN 0-02-864144-2)
This US-based book takes a lighthearted approach to songwriting and works very well by providing nuggets of information in a simple and entertaining format. Covers everything, albeit briefly.

KIMPEL, DAN: *Networking In The Music Business* (Writer's Digest, ISBN 0-89879-597-4)
A clear and uncomplicated exposition on the art of networking, this is a useful book if networking is a foreign or difficult concept to you.

ORMONT, RONDA: *Career Solutions For Creative People* (Allworth Press, ISBN 1-58118-091-1)
This is a fantastically practical book that will help all types of creative people to find their 'lifeline' career, demonstrating both the security and flexibility with which they can achieve their goals and dreams as artists, musicians, poets, actors and songwriters. Essential for anyone struggling to balance their artistic goals with career security.

DANN, ALLEN and UNDERWOOD, JOHN: *How To Succeed In The Music Business* (Omnibus, ISBN 0-7119-9433-1)
A thoroughly practical look at the UK music business, this book is presented in a direct question-and-answer format. It asks the questions that every songwriter/artist really wants to know and provides the answers in plain English.

MMF: *The Music Management Bible* (Sanctuary Publishing, ISBN 1-84492-025-9)
This is essential reading for anyone seriously intending to enter the music industry. Comprehensive and written by today's top managers, this book contains everything you need to know to survive as a writer or performer. Indispensable in everyday business.

DANNEN, FREDRIC: *Hit Men* (Vintage Books, 1991)
This is a brilliantly entertaining read about the American music business, its association with the Mafia, payola and scandal. Horrifying, shocking and hilarious by turns. Read it with the light on!

WHITE, PAUL: *Home Recording Made Easy* (Sanctuary Publishing [second edition], ISBN 1-86074-350-1)
Simply the best introduction to recording at home on a computer. Paul White is a legend in the field of music technology and home recording.

Music Week Directory (Miller Freeman Entertainment)
Includes names, addresses and other contact details of record companies, music publishers, retailers, manufacturers, management companies, radio, TV, studios, venues, etc. The essential contact manual for the music business.

PASSMAN, DONALD: *All You Need To Know About The Music Business* (Penguin, ISBN 0-14-024010-1)
This book lives up to its self-explanatory title. Written by a top US music-industry lawyer, it covers all areas of the industry, including record and publishing deals, touring and merchandising. This is one book not to be without if you take your business side seriously.

On Songwriting

ROOKSBY, RIKKY: *How To Write Songs On Guitar* (Balafon, ISBN 0-87930-611-4)

RANDOLFI, MICHAEL; READ, MIKE; and STARK, DAVID: *Inspirations: Original Lyrics And The Stories Behind The Greatest Songs Ever Written* (Sanctuary Publishing, ISBN 1-86074-300-5)

PERRICONE, JACK: *Melody In Songwriting* (International Music Publications, ISBN 063400638X)

SCOTT, RICHARD: *Money Chords: A Songwriters' Sourcebook Of Popular Chord Progression* (Faber Music Ltd, ISBN 0571511082)

ZOLLO, PAUL: *Songwriters On Songwriting* (Da Capo Press, ISBN 0-30680-777-7)

GILLETTE, STEVE: *Songwriting & The Creative Process* (Sing Out!, ISBN 1-881322-03-3)

CITRON, STEPHEN: *Songwriting: A Complete Guide To The Craft* (Hodder & Stoughton, ISBN 0-340-39155-3)

BRAHENY, JOHN: *The Craft & Business Of Songwriting* (Omnibus Press, ISBN 0-7119-1820-1)

JOSEFS, JAI: *Writing Music For Hit Songs: Including New Songs From The '90s* (Schirmer, ISBN 0825672457)

LUBOFF, PAT and PETE: *88 Songwriting Wrongs & How To Right Them*, (Writer's Digest Books, ISBN 0-89879-508-7)

ON LYRIC WRITING

DAVIS, SHEILA: *Successful Lyric Writing* (Omnibus, ISBN 0-7119-1720-5)

DAVIS, SHEILA: *The Craft Of Lyric Writing* (Omnibus, 1985)

ON TV AND FILM WRITING

DAVIS, RICHARD: *Complete Guide To Film Scoring* (Berklee Press, ISBN 0-634-00636-3)

BELL, DAVID: *Getting The Best Score For Your Film* (Silman-James Press, ISBN 1879505207)

ON MUSIC THEORY

BLACK, DAVE and LUSK, LINDA: *Essential Dictionary Of Musical Notation: The Most Practical And Concise Source For Music Notation* (Alfred Publishing Co, ISBN 0882847309)

BLACK, DAVE and GEROU, TOM: *Essential Dictionary Of Orchestration* (Alfred Publishing Co, ISBN 0739000535)

BURROWS, TERRY: *How To Read Music* (Carlton, ISBN 1-84222-308-9)

SHELDON, CAMILLA and SKINNER, TONY: *Popular Music Theory: Grade 2 And 3* (Registry Publications, ISBN 1-898466-41-6)

TAYLOR, ERIC: *The AB Guide To Music Theory Part 1* (Associated Board of the Royal Schools of Music, 1989)

ON ARRANGEMENT

BLATTER, ALFRED: *Instrumentation And Orchestration* (Longman, ISBN 0582281180)

PISTON, WALTER: *Orchestration* (Gollancz, ISBN 0575026022)

RUNSWICK, DARYL: *Rock, Jazz And Pop Arranging* (Faber Music Ltd, ISBN 0571511082)

MANCINI, HENRY: *Sounds and Scores* (Warner Brothers Publications, ISBN 1854724460)

ON THE HISTORY OF SONGWRITING

RICE/RICE/READ/GAMBACCINI: *Guinness Book Of British Hit Singles*

READ, MIKE: *Major To Minor: The Rise And Fall Of The Songwriter* (Sanctuary Publishing, ISBN 1-86074-316-1)

SULLIVAN, PAUL: *Sullivan's Music Trivia* (Sanctuary Publishing, ISBN 1-86074-511-3)

JASEN, DAVID: *Tin Pan Alley: The Composers, The Songs, The Performers & Their Times* (DI Fine, 1988)

ON THE MUSIC BUSINESS

COLBECK JULIAN, and MITCHELL, TONY: *How To Make A Hit Record* (Ananya, ISBN 1-85470-007-3)

BARROW, TONY and NEWBY, JULIAN: *Inside The Music Business* (Blueprint, ISBN 1-85713-012-X)

POE, RANDY: *Music Publishing: A Songwriter's Guide* (Writer's Digest, ISBN 0-89879-415-3)

Music Week Directory (Miller Freeman Entertainment)

KIMPEL, DAN: *Networking In The Music Business* (Writer's Digest, ISBN 0-89879-597-4)

BRAHENY, JOHN: *The Craft & Business Of Songwriting* (Writer's Digest, 1987)

The Music Business: An Insider's Guide To Breaking In (Inside Sessions [DVD], 2002)

ON MUSIC PRODUCTION

WHITE, PAUL: *basic Digital Recording* (SMT [Sanctuary Publishing], ISBN 1-86074-269-6)

WHITE, PAUL: *basic Effects & Processors* (SMT [Sanctuary Publishing], ISBN 1-86074-270-X)

WHITE, PAUL: *basic Mastering* (SMT [Sanctuary Publishing], ISBN 1-86074-289-0)

WHITE, PAUL: *basic MIDI* (SMT [Sanctuary Publishing], ISBN 1-86074-262-9)

WHITE, PAUL: *basic Mixing Techniques* (SMT [Sanctuary Publishing], ISBN 1-86074-283-1)

WHITE, PAUL: *basic Sampling* (SMT [Sanctuary Publishing], ISBN 1-86074-477-X)

WHITE, PAUL: *Crash Course Home Recording* (SMT [Sanctuary Publishing], ISBN 1-84492-017-8)

WHITE, PAUL: *Creative Recording Part 1*: Effects & Processors (SMT [Sanctuary Publishing], ISBN 1-86074-456-7)

WHITE, PAUL: *Creative Recording Part 2: Microphones, Acoustics, Soundproofing And Monitoring* (SMT [Sanctuary Publishing], ISBN 1-86074-229-7)

WHITE, PAUL: *EMERGENCY! First Aid For Home Recording* (SMT [Sanctuary Publishing], ISBN 1-84492-000-3)

WHITE, PAUL: *MIDI For The Technophobe* (SMT [Sanctuary Publishing], second edition, ISBN 1-86074-444-3)

WHITE, PAUL: *Recording & Production Techniques* (SMT [Sanctuary Publishing], second edition, ISBN 1-86074-443-5)

ROBERTS, MARK: *Rhythm Programming* (SMT [Sanctuary Publishing], ISBN 1-86074-412-5)

RECOMMENDED LISTENING
FOR SONGWRITERS

'Listen to great music of all kinds. Listen to great songs. Just listen to them. Listen hard. Every one thing feeds the other.'

– Will Jennings, songwriter

Great songs are a wonderful source of inspiration for a songwriter. The following albums all contain examples of great songs and are singled out here for their craft, technical prowess and sheer creative innovation.

IMPORTANT NOTE: The following list is not considered to be a definitive collection of the greatest songs ever written; rather it is a cross-section of the various directions in which a song can be taken with the overall aim of educating the aspiring songwriter musically.

The Beatles: *1* (2002)
Every one of the songs on this album is a justifiable classic. Simply studying and learning to play all of them is a songwriting masterclass in itself. Even the most simple-sounding of The Beatles' songs contains surprising songwriting twists and techniques.

Bob Dylan: *Blonde On Blonde* (1966)
After a thorough listen to this album, by a wordsmith of the highest order, you'll begin to understand why he's had the impact that he has. Dylan's songs have a strength and depth that should be the goal of any singer/songwriter.

Stevie Wonder: *The Definitive Collection* (2003)
A standard-bearer for every singer and songwriter, a natural genius for melody and a multi-instrumentalist to boot, Wonder is also the principal source of samples for today's rap artists. This is no surprise, considering his formidable talent in the art of creating a groove, ably demonstrated on tracks like 'Superstition', 'I Wish' and 'Living For The City'. Awe-inspiring.

Burt Bacharach: *The Look Of Love* (1996)
For a classy insight into melodic development and harmonic construction, Burt Bacharach is your writer. Each one of the tracks on this album is a

standard. There is much that an aspiring songwriter can learn here from this master of melody.

Diana Ross And The Supremes (Holland, Dozier And Holland): *The No 1s* (2004)
The fathers of Motown produced a string of hits that helped to define a whole musical culture, with the help of some very talented artists and musicians. This album is essential listening for anyone looking to get a handle on the arts of arrangement and chorus writing.

The Beach Boys: *Pet Sounds* (1966)
The album that inspired *Sgt Pepper's Lonely Hearts Club Band*! As songs go, 'God Only Knows' attains the kind of melodic and harmonic perfection that few others will ever reach.

Simon And Garfunkel: *The Essential* (2003)
This album features possibly the best music written for an acoustic guitar and two voices. Paul Simon's ear for melody, lyrical power and song construction mark him out as one of the best singer/songwriters ever. Essential study for the archetypal singer/songwriter.

Prince: *The Hits 1* and *2* (1993)
An eccentric genius he might be, but there's no denying Prince's talent for writing hook-laden songs. His ability to produce such diverse, quality songs as the heart-rending ballads 'Nothing Compares 2 U' and 'Purple Rain', the power-poppy 'Raspberry Beret' and '1999', and the brazenly funky 'Kiss' and 'Sexy MF' sets him apart from all other writers.

Led Zeppelin: *Untitled* (1971)
For any heavy-rock writer, this album is an object lesson in power riffs and disciplined ensemble playing. The much-celebrated 'Stairway To Heaven' is a perfect exercise in long structure, while for an example of effective repetition, check out 'When The Levee Breaks'.

Bob Marley: *Legends* (1984)
Bob spread his political and religious messages to a wide audience via the commercial vehicle of great songwriting, bringing reggae to the masses.

Joni Mitchell: *Hejira* (1976)
Study this album for classic singer/songwriter material with attention to fine lyrics and use of open-tuned acoustic guitar. Features bassist *par excellence* Jaco Pastorius.

Michael Jackson: *Thriller* (1982)

Created by one of the most formidable production and writing teams ever, comprising Michael Jackson, Quincy Jones and Rod Temperton, this album demonstrates the art of great songwriting and masterful production values. Just listen to the drive and irresistible groove and build of 'Billie Jean'.

Queen: *Queen II* (1974)

Devout practitioners of the art of multitrack overdubbing, Queen's attention to arrangement and songwriting craftsmanship on this album is staggering. Also listen to *News Of The World* for its sheer energy.

Faithless: *Sunday 8pm* (2001)

Rollo Armstrong, Dido's brother and musical backbone, made the difficult crossover from the club scene to enjoy mass appeal. This album of his is a perfect blend of blessed outbeats, strong choruses and the most mellifluous rapping ever.

Fleetwood Mac: *Rumours* (1977)

A definitive album for the Mac that exemplifies the effective use of vocal harmonies, melodic guitar work and compact song structures.

Red Hot Chilli Peppers: *BloodSugarSexMagik* (1990)

This album features funk rock at its melodic best, combining the tightest grooves, melodic guitar and rhythmic vocals. Standout tracks include 'Under The Bridge', 'Funky Monks' and 'Give It Away'.

ABBA: *Gold* (1992)

It's hard to fault these songs, laden as they are with so many hooks. If one of your songs had just one melodic hook of the quality featured here, you'd have a hit on your hands, and ABBA songwriters Benny and Björn tended to stuff four or more into each composition!

Kate Bush: *The Sensual World* (1989)

Here, the emotional depth of Bush's songs is matched only by the scale of the arrangements.

Madonna: *The Immaculate Collection* (1990)

This album shows how great a pop song can really be. Madonna's overt self-promotion shouldn't overshadow the quality of her and Patrick Leonard's songwriting talents.

Nirvana: *Nevermind* (1991)
'Smells Like Teen Spirit' was a wake-up call to a generation. Here, grunge's finest (and maybe only) hour demonstrates the art of contrast at its extremity, featuring singable melodies against a backdrop of quiet verses and monstrous choruses.

U2: *The Joshua Tree* (1987)
U2's joint songwriting results are what every band should aim for: strident, passionate, original and catchy. Never resting on their laurels, they continue to push and test their songwriting abilities. However, it is this album that defined their craft for simple, honest and emotional songs. A band at its best.

Jeff Buckley: *Grace* (1995)
A seminal release from a singer/songwriter who had just begun to explore the boundaries of popular songwriting before meeting a tragic end. Here, his ethereal voice combines with fine lyrics, highly inventive styles and unusual arrangements, along with a great example of his use of altered guitar tunings.

Norah Jones: *Come Away With Me* (2002)
This album could almost be said to have saved the art of real songwriting in a commercial world drowned in manufactured pop. Simple, sparse and devastatingly effective, Arif Mardin's production demonstrates how to let a song breathe without it ever sounding empty.

Radiohead: *OK Computer* (1996)
While *The Bends* is my preferred album for great acoustic rock songwriting, with 'High And Dry' and 'Fake Plastic Trees' showing intelligent lyrics combined with phenomenal melodies, it was this album that demonstrated Radiohead's ability to push the boundaries of traditional songwriting.

Rolling Stones: *40 Licks* (2004)
This album is rock 'n' roll at its strutting best. Generating a potent cocktail of killer guitar riffs and spat-out lyrics, here the Stones provided the template for many a rock band, few of which have matched the instantaneous recognition of such hooks as those of '(I Can't Get No) Satisfaction', 'Brown Sugar' or 'Jumping Jack Flash'.

David Bowie: *Best Of Bowie* (2002)
Possessing a gifted ability to mimic many a musical genre, Bowie's songs are insightful, highly original and eminently hook-laden, and a great source of inspiration for lyrical exploration and stylistic manipulation. It's hard not to marvel at the sheer breadth of his ability, particularly on cuts such as 'Space Oddity', 'Changes', 'Fame', 'Heroes' and 'Let's Dance'.

REM: *Automatic For The People* (1992)
Suffused with themes of suicide, death and sexual jealousy – hardly standard topics of successful songwriting – the sheer emotional depth and clarity here of such songs as 'Everybody Hurts' and 'Man On The Moon' defies convention.

The Smiths: *The Queen Is Dead* (1986)
The combination of Morrissey's unconventional introspective lyrics and melancholic melodies with Johnny Marr's chiming pop guitar created songs that were deeply affecting and personal, and never more so than on this album. Melancholy has never been packaged so sweetly.

Eminem: *The Marshall Mathers LP* (2000)
Ruthlessly self-aware and armed with a barbed sense of humour, Eminem leapfrogged over other rap artists by sticking to basic subjects that people can relate to: getting wasted, girl problems, family arguments. By so doing, he took hip-hop to a global level.

Sting: *The Very Best Of Sting & The Police* (2002)
Every track on this album is a masterclass in the art of songwriting. Sting's attention to melody, lyrical development and harmonic integrity have created some of the most affecting and memorable songs ever written, including 'Every Breath You Take', 'Message In A Bottle', 'Roxanne' and 'Fields Of Gold'. Most songwriters would be happy to have written just one of these tracks in their lives!

RECOMMENDED WEBSITES
FOR SONGWRITERS

Websites are prone to disappear, but below are a few of the more established ones that are worth checking out.

www.britishacademy.com
The website for the British Academy of Composers & Songwriters, the recognised trade association for the UK songwriting and composing community. Contains industry events diary, listings of members, music-industry news and useful links for songwriters.

www.songwritershalloffame.org
A fascinating website dedicated to recognising and honouring the accomplishments and lives of the men and women who have created the popular song.

www.taxi.com
The site of an independent A&R company specialising in giving artists, bands and songwriters access to the people in the music business. Contains industry advice, interviews from top songwriters, advice on the craft of songwriting, musician referrals and industry listings of artists looking for songs.

www.musesmuse.com
An extensive resource and information site featuring news, articles and interviews relating to the songwriting community. Possibly one of the best and most practical sites on songwriting.

www.songwritersresourcenetwork.com
A resource site for every songwriters' needs, featuring tips on songwriting, competition information, news, a quiz section, relevant links and a networking resource centre.

www.songlyricist.com
A free news and education resource for aspiring song lyricists, containing up-to-date information about the art and business of song and lyric writing; tips,

articles and advice to help song lyricists connect with the music industry; and opportunities to get feedback on your songs from music-industry pros.

www.songwritersdirectory.com
This site is a comprehensive database for songwriters and songwriter resources, containing detailed songwriter listings, an artists' page and a useful networking centre.

www.songwritersshowcase.co.uk
Songwriter Showcase is a UK-based online and live showcase service for anyone who writes or performs original music. It offers an extremely interactive service.

www.hitheads.com
An online A&R, management and labels directory with a drag-and-drop upload facility and professional consultation services available free to members.

www.songlink.com
Website of the newsletter and magazine that links songwriters and publishers with artists and companies who are looking for songs around the world. Contains success stories, artist listings, industry news and membership information.

www.bbc.co.uk/radio2/soldonsong
A magnificent website dedicated to the art and craft of songwriting, containing interviews, features, discussion forums and advice on songwriting from successful songwriters and artists.

THE LANGUAGE OF SONGWRITING:
A SONGWRITER'S GLOSSARY

This section contains descriptions of the key music terms and industry language that you'll need to be aware of as a songwriter. It's important to be able to understand *and* be understood in this industry, so take some time to read through these lists.

KEY MUSIC TERMS YOU SHOULD KNOW

Arrangement: A composition with different instruments or voices arranged (ie put together in a defined structure) for performance/recording.

Backing Track: The basic instrumentation of a song to which vocals and overdubs will be added.

Ballad: A song that tells a story. Especially prevalent in folk music. In most modern music genres (eg pop and jazz), the term refers to any song that's downbeat, slow and emotional (eg 'Yesterday', 'Lady In Red').

Bar: A measure of musical time, generally made up of two, three or four beats. Also know as a *measure* (US).

Beat: The basic unit of musical time, normally grouped together into regular sections called *bars* (see above). Different characteristic rhythms can be produced by accenting various beats in a bar.

Bridge: A part of a song usually placed after the second chorus to give a fresh perspective. A bridge might consist of only music, or of both lyrics and music. It is sometimes referred to as the *middle-eight* or the *release*.

Chord: Describes three or more notes played simultaneously. Chords are the building blocks of harmony.

Chorus: The most repeated and memorable part of a song, usually containing the hook.

Chromatic: Describes a scale built totally on half steps, or *semitones* (ie the chromatic scale on the piano uses all 12 black and white notes). The chromatic scale often lends an exotic or sinister feel to a songs.

Click Track: An audio track that contains a metronome beat at the tempo of the music, allowing musicians to synchronise accurately to parts recorded during a performance. The click track is removed just before mixing takes place.

Composition: An original piece of music, with or without lyrics, comprising harmony/chords and melody.

Harmony: The musical base layer of a song – usually in the form of a series of chords – upon which all other elements are built.

Hook: The most memorable fragment of a song. A hook might be melodic, rhythmic, lyrical or might even be the production of a recording.

Intro: The start of a piece of music or song.

Key: Refers to the scale and related harmonies from which a piece of music is derived.

Major: A type of key, chord or scale. Major keys or scales are generally considered to produce a happier sound than minor keys.

Melody: An arrangement of single notes in a musically expressive succession. *Melody* is a generic term that incorporates the principal tune of a piece of music.

Metre: Refers to how the regular rhythmic divisions in a bar of music are subdivided.

Middle-eight: A musical link between two different sections of a piece of music, traditionally eight bars long. Also known as a *bridge*.

Minor: A type of key, chord or scale. Minor keys or scales are generally thought to produce a sadder sound than major keys.

Mixing: The process of merging several tracks of music through a bank of volume and tone controls in order to get the right balance and sound quality.

Note: A unit of sound defined by pitch and duration. Melodies are made up of notes played or sung one after the other, while chords comprise different notes played simultaneously.

Outro: The end section of a piece of music

Pitch: Refers to how high or low a note is.

Range: Distance between the lowest and highest tones of a melody, an instrument or a voice.

Rhythm: A word with wide and general use in music but specifically referring to recognisable patterns of longer and shorter notes.

Riff: A short, repeated phrase of music.

Scale: An ascending or descending series of notes dividing the octave.

Tempo: The speed at which a piece of music is played, usually measured in beats per minute (bpm).

Time Signature: An indication of the number of beats per bar and the time value of each beat, such as 2/4, 4/4 and 6/8.

Verse: The section of a song in which a different sets of words is sung to the same repeated melody, as opposed to a chorus, in which the words and melody are both repeated.

KEY MUSIC-INDUSTRY TERMS YOU SHOULD KNOW

A&R: The Artists and Repertoire department of a record company, which selects acts and oversees the recording process.

Administration: Process whereby a publisher or recording company handles of all the financial, copyright and contractual work necessary in the production of a song or catalogue of songs.

Advance: Money paid up-front to writers and artists which is later deducted from their royalties.

Assignment: Transferral of a copyright from one publishing house to another.

Brief: A written or verbal guideline to how a track should ultimately sound.

Catalogue: The total collection of songs that a music publisher has under his or her control.

Clearance: Limited permission obtained by a radio or TV station to use copyright material.

Compressor: Device that limits sound and keeps it more consistent and even.

Commercial: Having mass appeal.

Co-publishing: Assignment of publishing rights to a song to two or more individuals.

Copyright: The exclusive legal right granted for a specified period to a songwriter to print, publish, perform or record their original material.

Cover Record: A recording by an artist other than the one who originally recorded the song. The term sometimes refers to the recording of a song performed by an artist who is not the writer.

Crossfade: The fading of one element or track out of a mix while another is faded in.

Crossover: Refers to a track that appeals to two or more markets.

Cut: A chosen selection on an album.

Digital Recording: Recording medium in which sound is transformed into a succession of binary numerical values.

Distributor: A company that handles the dissemination of a record company's product to retail outlets.

Dynamics: Variations in volume.

Fader: A control on a mixing desk, used to alter sound levels.

Gig: A live performance.

Hold: To keep a demo for further evaluation.

Incidental Music: Background music, usually found in film and TV scores, to give a particular scene added emotional or atmospheric flavour.

Jingle: A soundtrack to a (usually radio) commercial, with or without lyrics.

Label: The imprint of a recording company. Often refers to the company itself.

License: Permission to use a song.

Limiter: A device that minimises sound peaks in a recording.

Lip-synching: A technique used at outdoor events and on TV in which the artist simply mouths the words to a pre-recorded track.

Master: A completed song recording that is ready to be reproduced as a finished product.

Mechanical Copyright: The right of the creator(s) of a song to profit from its reproduction as a physical format.

Mechanical Royalties: Earnings from the sale of physical product (eg CDs, cassettes, vinyls).

MP3: Compressed file format used to store audio files on a computer.

Music Publisher: An individual or company that specialises in acquiring commercial songs and placing them with artists on film and television and then collects the royalties generated by this.

On Spec: Describes any work done by a writer or performer without pay.

Overdub: Extra recorded sound added to a song in order to heighten the total effect.

Performance Royalties: Money earned from the use of copyright material on radio, TV, at concerts, etc.

Piracy: Unauthorised copying and sale of recordings.

Plug: To promote an artist or song.

Producer: The person in charge of directing a recording artistically, technically and financially, from its inception to the final mix.

Rate: An agreed-upon royalty percentage.

Reverb: The electronic reproduction of echo on recordings.

Royalty: A sum paid to a writer in return for the right to use of a piece of his or her music in a performance or recording.

Sampler: A recording device able to record almost any sound digitally and make this recording accessible to – and controllable by – a synthesiser or computer.

Sequencer: A hardware unit or software program which, when connected to a synthesiser, is capable of memorising sequences of notes and other data.

Session: A meeting held to record or, sometimes, rehearse music.

Soundtrack: The audio section of a film that includes narration and music.

Standard: A song that has enjoyed a long life and continues to be popular.

Synch Fee: Payment for the use and placement of music to visual images, such as in a film.

Synchronisation: The addition of music to a film.

Take: An attempt at making a recording or section of recording.

GENERAL MUSIC GLOSSARY

Arpeggio: The notes of a chord played in succession instead of simultaneously.
A Cappella: Singing without instrumental accompaniment.

Acoustic: Describes an instrument that provides sound without using electronic amplification (eg an acoustic guitar or drum kit).

Acoustic Guitar: Guitar whose body acts as a sounding board and an amplification chamber for the sound that is produced by the strings.

Alliteration: Literary device whereby words that share an initial letter are grouped together.

Amplifier: Electronic device that is used to increase the volume of sound of particular instruments, such as guitars, vocals, keyboards and any instrument that can be hooked up to a microphone.

Augmented: Describes an interval (ie the distance between two notes) that has been increased by a half step (semitone).

Backbeat: A drum beat whereby beats two and four in a bar of 4/4 (ie the 'off beats') are accented. The backbeat is a constant feature of most 20th-century popular music, as the loud snare drum falls on these beats. Reggae, in particular, places emphasis on the backbeat.

Bass Drum: The largest and lowest-toned drum, which has a cylindrical body and two membrane heads.

Bass Guitar: A four- or five-string low-tuned electric guitar that evolved from the upright double bass in the 1950s. It generally plays the lowest musical pattern in a composition and provides the harmonic foundation.

Blues Notes: Flattened notes – usually thirds, fifths, sixths or sevenths – that produce a distinctive bluesy sound.

Bongos: A pair of small, conical or cylindrical Afro-Cuban drums that are permanently attached to one another. One of the drums is larger than the other and tuned at a lower pitch than its partner.

Bouncing: A process used in multitrack recording whereby several tracks of music are re-recorded onto one or two tracks in order to free up other tracks.

Brass: Refers to instruments made of brass or some other metal and which sound when air is blown through them. Brass instruments include the trumpet, trombone, tuba, French horn, cornet and bugle.

Clef: Signifier that appears at the beginning of each line on a stave of music to indicate the relative pitch of each note that appears on that line.

Contrast: Distinction between two or more pieces (or sections) of music by virtue of their differences in tone, instrumentation, melody, etc.

Cycle Of Fifths: A progression through all the 12 keys (major or minor) where each new key is a perfect fifth away from the previous key. The cycle of fifths can be imagined as a circle, starting from the key of C, with each progressive key – to G, D, etc – having an additional sharp, until the key of F♯/G♭, at which point the keys exhibit a regularly diminishing number of flats.

Distortion: An effect applied to the amplification signal of an instrument, generally a guitar. Distortion also occurs when a signal fed into an amplifier is too strong for the device to handle.

Effects: Devices or techniques that are used to make a sound more interesting, such as chorus, compression, delay, distortion, flanging, gating, phasing, pitch-changing and reverb.

Engineer: A person who operates the equipment in a recording studio and helps the producer to obtain the sound he or she wants. The engineer will also mix the song or album, under the producer's supervision.

Figure: A brief melodic or rhythmic pattern out of which longer passages are developed. Also know as a *motif* or *motive*.

Flanging: A swirling effect that occurs when a signal is mixed with a delayed copy of the same signal, while the delay time changes continually. You can hear this effect when a jet plane passes overhead, because the direct sound is being mixed with the delay reflection from the ground, and the relative delay time changes with the angle of the plane.

Flat: An accidental that reduces the pitch of a note by a semitone.

Glissando: A continuous slide on an instrument where the intermediate steps between pitches can be heard.

Grace Note: A quick ornamental note played immediately before the actual intended or written note.

Hi-hat: An arrangement whereby two cymbals are placed horizontally on a stand. The lower cymbal is stationary and attached to the stand while the upper cymbal is moveable and attached to a spindle that runs through the body of the stand. As a pedal at the foot of the stand is depressed, the top portion of the hi-hat comes together with the lower portion.

Imitation: The repetition of a phrase at a different pitch to the original in another part or voicing.

Interval: The distance between any two notes.

Jam Session: The period of time when any group of musicians informally play or sing together. Spontaneous improvisation is one of the key factors of a jam session and can often be used as part of a songwriting process.

Layering: A recording technique whereby each instrument is recorded separately and all are then mixed together.

Lead Sheet: A composer's self-written sheet of music that includes the tune, lyrics and chords.

Leger Lines: Small horizontal lines used to extend a musical stave upwards or downwards beyond its normal limits.

Legato: Musical direction meaning literally 'smoothly' (Italian).

Lick: A musical phrase, melody or passage that a lead guitarist can use in moments of spontaneity or planned progressions.

Metronome: A clock-like machine that ticks at any user-defined speed.

Mode: A set of scale-like notes from which melodies might be constructed. Modes are referred to either by their Greek names (Aeolean, Dorian, etc) or by the degree of the scale from which they are derived (first mode, second mode, etc).

Modulation: A shift in tonality from one key to another.

Natural: An accidental that cancels a sharp or flat.

Octave: The interval of an eighth, eg the gap between the note C to the next C, eight notes above or below.

Orchestration: An arrangement of a composition for the group of instruments in an orchestra, including strings, woodwinds, brass and percussion.

Ostinato: A persistent phrase or rhythm repeated through all or part of a piece of music.

Percussion: A group of instruments that are usually sounded by being struck with sticks. Includes timbales, wood blocks, triangle, xylophones, marimbas, vibraphones, shakers, maracas, bells, tambourines and drums.

Phasing: An electronic sound process that creates a sweeping effect by modulating a narrow notch signal filter. The resultant sound is similar to flanging.

Pizzicato: A musical direction – literally meaning 'pinched' (Italian) – to pluck the strings of an instrument, usually with the finger. Fingernails can be used to release the string to produce something known as 'fingernail pizzicato'.

Portamento: A continuous slide over an interval without sounding the discrete intermediate steps between.

Recapitulation: A part of a movement in a piece of music in which themes from the first section are restated

Repetition: The restating of a phrase or melody.

Rest: A period of silence in music.

Score: A written piece of music showing the notes to be played or sung by each instrument or voice.

Semitone: The smallest interval in Western music. Also known as a 'half step'.

Sequence: A series of notes in a set order. The term also refers to the repetition of a phrase or melody at a higher or lower pitch.

Sharp: An accidental that raises the pitch of a note by a semitone.

Sixth: The interval between two notes that are six notes apart on the scale.

Snare Drum: A cylindrical drum whose top is covered with a skin and with a set of wires or strings strung across the bottom. Snares are normally used to emphasise the second and fourth beats of the bar, or 'off beats'.

Solo: Any instrumental improvisation that takes place when the vocalist is silent.

Staccato: Musical direction, literally meaning 'detached' (Italian), instructing the performer to play the notes in a short, truncated manner.

Stave: The five horizontal lines on which Western music is written. Also known as a *staff*.

String Quartet: A group of four string instruments comprising two violins, a viola and a cello. Also refers to a piece of music written for such an ensemble.

Syncopation: Accenting system whereby any note that doesn't fall on one of the main beats (generally the first and third beat) in a bar is played louder than the others.

Synthesiser: An electronic instrument, usually in the form of a keyboard, that produces a wide variety of electronic sounds by reshaping an electronic signal through the use of waveform generators, modulators and oscillators.

Tenth: The interval between one note and the tenth note in the scale above it. Also known as a *compound third* (ie an octave plus a third).

Third: The interval between two notes which are three notes apart in the scale.

Tone: Interval comprising two semitones.

Tonic: The 'home' note, or chord, of a key or scale. Also know as the *key note*.

Tracking: A recording technique whereby the primary arrangement is recorded first and then improvised solos (vocal or instrumental) are recorded and inserted afterwards.

Transpose: To play a piece of music in a different key, but without changing anything else in the score.

Trilling: The repeated playing of two notes in rapid succession.

Triplet: Three notes played in the time of two.

Twelve-bar blues: A form of song construction that relies upon a fixed sequence of chords occurring over 12 bars. Its form comes from a three-line verse or chorus, each line of which consists of four bars.

Up Beat: The last beat of a bar, which has the feeling of leading into the first beat of the next bar.

Woodwind: A group of instruments that produce sound when air is blown through them via the vibration of air inside the instrument. Woodwind instruments include the flute, piccolo, clarinet, recorder, bassoon and oboe. NB: The saxophone is technically considered a woodwind instrument, even though it's made of brass, because its sound is generated by air passing over a reed rather than through a mouthpiece.

END SONG

AUTHOR'S NOTE

Writing this book has been a wonderful journey for me. It has taught me so much about the craft of songwriting, and I hope that you, the reader, have gained as much understanding, appreciation and admiration of this art as I have.

The business of songwriting is not an easy path to choose. As Ivor Novello Award-winner Rick Nowels observes, 'Only the obsessed need apply.' Lyricist Don Black, too, is adamant that any person who truly desires to be a professional songwriter 'must have fire in their belly'.

This is because songwriting is principally about passion. Whether you write for your own personal satisfaction, for friends and family or with the intention of forging a full-time career and making your millions, you have to write for the love of it.

'Be faithful to the music and the music will be faithful to you.' – Lamont Dozier

In other words, if you simply believe that you can write a great song, one day you will. A great song appeals to the deepest emotion in all of us. Perhaps no other art creates the intensity of personal connection that a song can generate between two people. It is a truly wonderful gift to be able to write a great song.

As I've emphasised throughout this book, however, the difference between a good song and a great song is an ingredient that remains completely indefinable yet is always tangible when heard. It appears to be the case that either a songwriter is born with the ability to write a great song or else greatness comes as a result of luck, the will of God or sheer bloody-minded persistence. Eighteenth-century poet and painter William Blake best summed it up when he wrote, 'To create a little flower is the labour of ages.'

However, having read this book, you should at least have the tools, thinking and mindset required to be able to write better songs. The writing of that great song will ultimately be down to you. It's a matter of constantly perfecting your craft, of each day striving to make the next song better than the last, of simply writing and enjoying the experience.

When I was talking with Don Black, he told me about an interview he had conducted with the wonderful French icon and multi-million-selling songwriter

Charles Aznavour, who, at 80 years old, is still in amazing health. Don said to his friend, 'How do you feel about being 80?'

'I'll give you a bit of advice,' Charles replied. 'A man who knows what he's doing tomorrow will never grow old.'

'So what are you doing tomorrow, Charles?' Don asked him.

'I am going to be writing,' said Charles.

ABOUT THE AUTHOR

Since picking up the harmonica 15 years ago, Chris Bradford has worked actively throughout a wide cross-section of the music industry. Primarily a singer/songwriter and performer, Chris has also experienced life as an artist manager, A&R scout, music-event manager and international sales and marketing manager for Sanctuary Publishing. With various bands, Chris has gigged and travelled extensively throughout Europe, America, Africa, Australasia and South America. Chris runs his own company, Burning Candle Music, which focuses on songwriting and music production, music-event management and music-project management. Chris is a member of the Executive Songwriters' Committee of the British Academy of Composers & Songwriters and is a degree lecturer in Composition and Arrangement at the Academy of Contemporary Music, Guildford. He lives in Marlow, Buckinghamshire, UK. For further information, visit www.burningcandlemusic.co.uk.

ABOUT THE ACADEMY

The British Academy of Composers & Songwriters is the largest composer/songwriter membership organisation in the world, representing the interests of over 2,500 UK writers and composers. The Academy's Fellows include Sir Paul McCartney, Sir Elton John, John Barry, David Arnold, John Adams, Sir Peter Maxwell Davies and Sir Malcolm Arnold.